SKYSCRAPERS
HIDE THE HEAVENS

A HISTORY OF NATIVE-NEWCOMER
RELATIONS IN CANADA

FOURTH EDITION

First published in 1989, *Skyscrapers Hide the Heavens* continues to earn acclaim for its comprehensive account of Native-newcomer relations throughout Canada's history. Author J.R. Miller charts the deterioration of the relationship from the initial, mutually beneficial contact in the fur trade to the displacement, marginalization, and assimilation of the Indigenous population, through to the current era of conflict and reconciliation.

The fourth edition has been revised and expanded to incorporate recent scholarship and discuss developments over the past twenty years in federal government policy and Aboriginal political organization. It includes analysis of the Idle No More movement, the Truth and Reconciliation Commission and the haunting legacy of residential schools in Canada, land claims in the courts, and public debates.

Widely used in Canadian university courses in history, Indigenous studies, sociology, education, and law, *Skyscrapers Hide the Heavens* is also critical reading for journalists, lawyers, others working with Indigenous issues, and anyone looking for a deeper understanding of the impact of the ongoing evolution of Native-newcomer relations in Canada.

J.R. MILLER is a professor emeritus of history at the University of Saskatchewan. He is the author of numerous works on issues related to Indigenous peoples including *Shingwauk's Vision* and *Residential Schools and Reconciliation: Canada Confronts Its History*, both published by University of Toronto Press.

Your buildings tall, alien,
Cover the land;
Unfeeling concrete smothers,
   windows glint
Like water to the sun.
No breezes blow
Through standing trees;
No scent of pine lightens my burden.

I see your buildings rising skyward,
   majestic,
Over the trails where once men walked,
Significant rulers of this land
Who still hold the aboriginal title
In their hearts
By traditions known
Through eons of time.

Relearning our culture is not difficult,
Because those trails I remember
And their meaning I understand.

While skyscrapers hide the heavens,
They can fall.

Rita Joe, *Poems of Rita Joe*
(Halifax: Abanaki Press, 1978)
Reprinted by permission of the author

SKYSCRAPERS
HIDE THE HEAVENS

A HISTORY OF NATIVE-NEWCOMER
RELATIONS IN CANADA

FOURTH EDITION

J.R. MILLER

UNIVERSITY OF TORONTO PRESS
Toronto Buffalo London

Maps

Preface to the Fourth Edition

This fourth edition has been necessitated by the passage of time and the growth of historiography in the Native-newcomer history field. Since the third edition was prepared during the winter of 1998–9, a large number of significant events have occurred in Native-newcomer relations in Canada. Similarly, in the nearly two decades since the work was revised, scholars have added greatly to our understanding of the relationship's evolution. This edition is intended to incorporate some of the recent writings and provide analysis of events in Native-newcomer relations that have taken place since the end of the 1990s.

As always, it is a pleasure to acknowledge and thank the institutions and individuals who were generous in their support of the research for and writing of this revision. My research was underwritten for many years by the Canada Research Chairs Program and several grants of the Social Sciences and Humanities Research Council of Canada. Colleagues Lesley Biggs, Keith Carlson, and Katie Labelle provided helpful suggestions and, sometimes, corrections. Donald B. Smith, Professor Emeritus of History at the University of Calgary, kindly provided a host of items relevant to the topic over the years. Ted Binnema, Cecilia Morgan, A.J. Ray, and Bill Waiser responded to queries and requests for assistance. David Garneau, an extraordinary artist on the faculty of the University of Regina, was generous in allowing me to use some of his works to illustrate a chapter. Dr. Christian Miller provided invaluable help in retrieving and migrating electronic files of the third revision of *Skyscrapers* to a more advanced word processor for this project, and Carolynn Schmidt did a wonderful job of eliminating the gremlins that crept into the manuscript in the process of updating the files. The editorial staff of the

University of Toronto Press were, as always, professional and thorough in their attention to the manuscript. I also wish to thank copy editor Barbara Kamienski of The Editing Company for her careful and creative work on the manuscript. My wife, Dr. Lesley Biggs, was a wonderful resource about structure, style, computer complications, and, sometimes, even questions about theory. It is to her that this work is, with love, dedicated.

Note on Terminology

In this edition, more varied terminology is used to describe Indigenous peoples than was the case in previous editions. This innovation also responds to changes over the past two decades. In this fourth edition, the term First Nation(s) is used exclusively for those peoples who were previously labelled Indians, or status Indians. Wherever appropriate, the more specific name of a group, such as Mi'kmaq or Plains Cree, is employed. The peoples of mixed ancestry are described as Métis. The circumpolar Indigenous peoples are referred to as Inuit, although some historical sources cited use the term Eskimo. The terms Indigenous, Aboriginal, and Native are used to refer collectively to the peoples whom the 1982 constitutional amendments described as "the Aboriginal peoples of Canada" and are used more or less interchangeably.

Preface to the Third Edition

This edition attempts to address the numerous significant developments in Native-newcomer relations since the appearance of the first edition in 1989. What needs to be addressed are both the historical and the historiographical developments that have transformed the field in the last decade. So far as actual events are concerned, Oka, the Royal Commission on Aboriginal Peoples, *Delgamuukw*, and Nunavut are only the most prominent of the many incidents and events that have kept Aboriginal issues in the news throughout the 1990s. More than the media have paid attention; academics and other researchers have turned to Native history and the history of Native-newcomer relations in greatly increased numbers and have produced a mountain of literature. This recent scholarship and the high-profile events that were in part its inspiration have prompted this revision.

This edition incorporates the new scholarship in varying degrees throughout the text. Some sections, most notably the early chapters, are relatively lightly sprinkled with additional references, but others, such as the chapter on military relations, have been heavily rewritten. A few topics, particularly relations in the North, are the subject of completely new material. The sections in the first edition that covered the period since 1970 have been drastically restructured and expanded to bring the treatment up to the end of the 1990s.

What have not been revised are the main contours and principal interpretations of *Skyscrapers Hide the Heavens*. This edition retains the focus on the motivations on both sides that brought the relationship into existence, the attempt to survey and explain the shifts in the relationship, and the effects for both parties of their relations with each other. In some instances, additional wording has been used to provide a more nuanced interpretation than was found in the first edition. For example, the quick survey of relations in New France attempts to bring out more explicitly that the relationship had deleterious consequences, and the sections that deal with the fur trade emphasize that relations were usually better in the early than the later phase of the exchange. Similarly, references to an "era of irrelevance" have been modified to make it clear that this irrelevance is largely to be understood in policy terms, and that Aboriginal peoples never ceased to have some sort of involvement with non-Native people in the nineteenth and twentieth centuries. This last point clearly reflects the influence of recent scholarship.

Even though this revision does not substantially alter the interpretation provided a decade ago, the reader should not conclude that the author assumes infallibility or omniscience. Quite the contrary. Particularly in a field such as the history of relations between Aboriginal peoples and newcomers in what is now Canada, most findings should be treated as contingent because the field continues rapidly to evolve and be enriched. The accelerating rate of research into topics on the Native-newcomer theme ensures that next year, or next decade, interpretations on this point or that will have to be modified, if not rejected. In particular, the growing attention to Aboriginal sources, especially oral accounts, which has been such a noticeable development in the 1990s, has revised, as it will continue to do, many of the opinions reached by Euro-American scholars relying solely on sources generated by Europeans and their colonial descendants. In this field, investigators find themselves in the position of the Cree man who went to Montreal in the 1970s to give testimony in a legal action about his traditional hunting territories. He had no problem responding positively to the invitation to talk about his home territory and way of life. However, the oath concerning telling the truth, the whole truth, and nothing but the truth gave him pause. He hesitated, "I am not sure I can tell the truth … I can only tell what I know."[1]

Academic historians are like the Cree hunter in at least two ways. We can tell readers only what our experience and research allow us to know, and we are also dependent on many other people to achieve our investigative objectives.

It is a pleasure once more to record my grateful appreciation for the help I have received from colleagues, students, and sometimes even strangers in the preparation of this new edition. A large number of people who provided citations, photocopies of material, and suggestions are thanked in the notes. I should particularly like to express my profound gratitude to my colleague Bill Waiser and a long-distance friend, Brisbane consultant Peter Jull, both of whom provided innumerable leads, answered multiple questions, and went the extra mile by reading the new chapters of this version. A research grant from the Social Sciences and

Humanities Research Council supported some of the research, and another from the Publications Fund of the University of Saskatchewan underwrote the illustrations. Again, Gerald Hallowell of the University of Toronto Press was generous with his time and wisdom in advising on a number of points, especially the selection of illustrations. His assistant, Jill McConkey, was indefatigable and efficient in looking after matters at the press in Toronto. It is a pleasure once more to acknowledge the skill, care, and imagination with which Rosemary Shipton edited the manuscript. Her many suggestions have improved the text and internal design.

My wife, Mary, was, as always, helpful and supportive as this revision was carried out, particularly during a three-month sojourn in Cambridge in the autumn of 1998.

The usual disclaimer applies: no one but the author is responsible for the defects that remain in spite of all the help and advice that these many kind people provided.

Preface to the First Edition

Two themes are meant to dominate the arguments that follow. The first is the simple proposition that the nature of a relationship between two peoples of different backgrounds is largely determined by the reasons they have for interacting. This notion is a variation on the theme popularized by Marshall McLuhan that "the medium is the message." But in my case I did not adopt this view directly from McLuhan. Rather, it was from the pioneering social scientist to whom McLuhan was himself indebted intellectually, Harold Adams Innis, that the idea came. The insights that Innis had about the first two Canadian industries of the historic period, the cod fishery and the fur trade, were the starting point for many of my own ideas about relations between Natives and European newcomers. In some respects, the arguments in the pages that follow are merely the application to Indian-European relations of some of Innis's interpretations.

The other theme that this work emphasizes was suggested by a generation of Canadian scholars much younger than Harold Innis. From people such as B.G. Trigger, C.J. Jaenen, A.J. Ray, S.F. Wise, S. Van Kirk, R.A. Fisher, J.L Tobias, T. Morantz, D. Francis, and G. Friesen I learned that Indian peoples were not the passive victims that were found in so many older accounts of Canadian history. In the works of these scholars I discovered that the indigenous peoples had in fact been active agents of commercial, diplomatic, and military relations with the European newcomers and their Euro-Canadian descendants. Indians, and later the mixed-blood people called Métis, largely determined the terms of trade, the nature of military alliances, and the outcomes of most martial engagements down to the nineteenth century. Even after Indians became numerically inferior to, and economically dependent upon, Euro-Canadians, they continued to assert themselves in their relations with governments, churches, and the ordinary population. Readers will not find in this account a portrait of the Indians of Canada as people to whom others did things. If these pages succeed in persuading some people that the Native peoples have always been active, assertive contributors to the unfolding of Canadian history, they will have achieved their primary objective.

In this work these themes are illustrated within the framework of a historical study of the evolution of relations between indigenous peoples and European newcomers to North America. What follows, then, is not a work of Indian history, but a study of the history of Indian-white relations in Canada.

In elaborating these two themes I have had to be selective. Any attempt to survey an evolving relationship over five centuries in five different geographical and economic zones is, besides being foolhardy perhaps, of necessity somewhat superficial. Specialists in Canadian history will not find all the topics that they would have liked dealt with here. To take only a couple of examples from a recent period, there is no attempt to portray the urban friendship centre movement and community development programs of the 1960s and 1970s. To keep this survey within manageable limits, the omission of some specific topics was necessary. It is hoped that those that are examined are both numerous and representative enough to give an accurate picture of the relations between indigenous peoples and other Canadians.

As has already been intimated, this study has been greatly stimulated by the work of others. It is also one that relies heavily on the research and publications of other students of the topic. Because the subject was so vast, it was impossible to do exhaustive primary research on all phases of it myself. Such a task would have taken a lifetime. On some topics, particularly where published studies are lacking, the evidence used is mainly from primary documents; in dealing with other issues that have been well studied I have relied on what I hope is an extensive and thoughtful reading of others' work. I am greatly indebted to all those whose works are cited in the notes.

I am also obligated to many people whose names do not always appear in the references. I should like to express my thanks to the Office of the Dean of Arts and Science and the Office of Research Services of the University of Saskatchewan, which provided assistance in meeting the costs of photocopying and illustrations. A generous Canadian Writing Award from the Association of Canadian Studies was of great help in completing the final stages of research, preparing illustrations and maps, and photocopying the final draft. Revisions to the manuscript could be carried out expeditiously, thanks to a Research Time Stipend granted by the Social Sciences and Humanities Council of Canada. The students in History at the

University of Saskatchewan during the winter term of 1987 also provided me with a number of useful suggestions for improvement of an early draft of this study. One of them, Christine Fowke, allowed me to use a map she had drafted, and cartographer George Duff prepared that and the other maps that accompany the text. Professor A.J. Ray kindly permitted the use of one of his maps in the generation of the map in this work that depicts the location of the western Indians around 1820. My colleague Bill Waiser gave generously of his time to read an earlier version of the manuscript and to make valuable suggestions for improvement. In addition to all the people mentioned so far I should like to acknowledge several who have given me helpful advice over the past few years: M. Davidson, J. Pollard, D.B. Smith, E.B. Titley, and J.D. Wilson. Gerald Hallowell, a friend of many years as well as an editor of great acuity, was efficient, helpful, and supportive in seeing the manuscript from first submission to publication. Anonymous readers for the University of Toronto Press and Social Science Federation of Canada provided a number of useful suggestions for correction and improvement. Rosemary Shipton edited the manuscript with sensitivity and insight.

Finally – and most important – my wife, Mary, patiently read several drafts and offered valuable suggestions on structure, argument, and style.

Of course, none of these long-suffering people is responsible for any errors of fact or interpretation that remain.

First Nations of Canada

ARCTIC

Inuit

Beothuk

ATLANTIC

Mi'kmaq
Mi'kmaq
Maliseet
Abenaki

Montagnais

NORTHERN
WOODLANDS

Naskapi

Mahican
Mohawk
Tuscarora
Oneida
Onandaga
Cayuga
Seneca

St. Lawrence Iroquois

Cree

Algonkin
Nipissing
Huron
Petun
Ottawa
Neutral
Erie

Cree

Northern Ojibwa

Ojibwa
Mississauga
Menominee
Potawatomi
Winnebago
Sauk
Fox
Kickapoo
Miami
Shawnee

Ojibwa

Métis

Chipewyan

SUBARCTIC

Yellowknife

Western Woods Cree

Woods Cree

Koyukuk Cree

Dogrib

Métis

Saulteaux

Hare

Slave

Beaver

Woods
Cree

Assiniboine
Sarcee
Stoney

Chipewyan
Métis

Assiniboine
Assiniboine

PLAINS CREE

NORTHERN
PLAINS

Crow

Mountain
Indians

Sekani

Métis

Blood
Piegan

N.
Piegan

Kootenay

Shuswap
Interior
Salish

Kaska

WESTERN

Tahltan
Tagish
Inland
Tlingit

Tsetsaut
Gitksan
Nisga'a
Tsimshian

Bella
Coola

Carrier
Chilcotin

Coast
Salish

Kwagiulth

Nuu chah
nulth

Cowichan

NORTHWEST
COAST

Haida
Coast
Tlingit

Koyukon

Kutchin

Tanana

Tanana

Kolchan

Ahtna

Holikachuk

Ingalik

Han

Tutchone

ARCTIC

Inuit

Inuit

Inuit

Inuit

0   500   1000
Kilometres

N

INTRODUCTION

CHAPTER ONE

Indigenous Peoples and Europeans
at the Time of Contact

On 24 July 1534, after more than a week of observing and bartering with the Native inhabitants, the newcomers set about erecting a landmark at the mouth of the harbour at Gaspé. Jacques Cartier's men

> had a cross made thirty feet high, which was put together in the presence of a number of the Indians on the point at the entrance to this harbour, under the cross-bar of which we fixed a shield with three *fleurs-de-lys* in relief, and above it a wooden board, engraved in large Gothic characters, where was written, LONG LIVE THE KING OF FRANCE. We erected this cross on the point in their presence and they watched it being put together and set up. When we had returned to our ships, the chief, dressed in an old black bear-skin, arrived in a canoe with three of his sons and his brother; but they did not come so close to the ships as they had usually done. And pointing to the cross he [the chief] made us a long harangue, making the sign of the cross with two of his fingers; and then he pointed to the land all around about, as if he wished to say that all this region belonged to him, and that we ought not to have set up this cross without his permission.[1]

The encounter contained many of the elements of early relations between Aboriginal peoples and intruders. The French explored, traded, and attempted to leave their permanent mark on the place. The Natives happily bartered, but rejected the white men's presumption at erecting a signpost. This epitome of early relations was all the more remarkable because it brought together two dramatically different

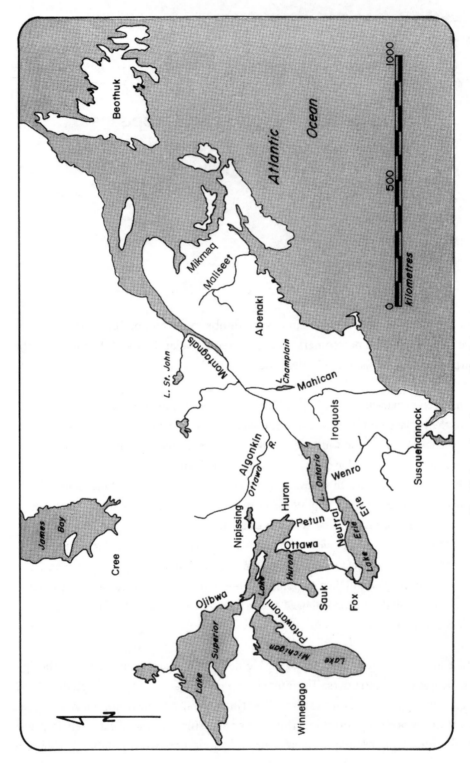

First Nations of northeastern North America at contact

peoples, two contrasting societies that would nonetheless cooperate successfully for centuries before relations deteriorated into conflict and confrontation.

The Aboriginal societies with whom Cartier and those who followed him came into contact were diverse and well established in their respective territories. According to social scientists, their ancestors had entered North America from Siberia by way of the Bering Strait in search of game perhaps as long as forty thousand years ago. Sometime in the subsequent millennia, they had made their way southward, in part following a path in the lee of the continental spine formed by the Rockies and Sierras, and diffused throughout the continent. Evidence unearthed in the Yukon of what were undoubtedly the original human occupiers of the continent indicates that they were there as long as twenty-seven thousand years ago.[2] According to Aboriginal accounts, on the other hand, each First Nation had been brought to life by the Creator in the lands it occupied. The Onondaga, one of the five nations of the Iroquois Confederacy, believed that they were descended from a chief's wife who fell from the sky into boundless water and was saved by the animals, who called the earth into being by bringing soil up from the depths by great exertion. In this Iroquois account, the earth rested on the back of the Great Turtle. Hence, the Iroquois referred to their world as Turtle Island.[3] The scientific account was invariably more prosaic than the creation stories of the First Nations.

Scientists explain that these peoples began to diffuse into the northeastern part of the continent approximately twelve thousand years ago. As the glaciers retreated northward at the end of the last ice age, humans migrated after them in search of fish, game, and arable land in which to cultivate a few crops that they had developed further south. Chief among these agricultural products was maize, or corn, which was being grown and harvested a thousand years ago in the territory that at present is southern Ontario and Quebec. Other groups of Aboriginal peoples who lived north of the arable land, in the Precambrian Shield or the colder regions to the north of that, were more dependent on hunting and fishing. And, naturally, those peoples who migrated to the eastern seaboard developed an extensive fishery, which they supplemented with hunting and with the gathering of berries and nuts. In short, long before the Europeans intruded in North America, the Indigenous peoples had entered and diffused into many parts of the continent, in the process showing an impressive ability to adapt to local climatic, topographical, and ecological conditions.

By the year 1000, the northeastern part of the continent was peopled by a myriad of bands, villages, and confederacies. Upon this complex and heterogeneous human community, later scholars have imposed a system of classification that permits a clearer understanding of their nature. Anthropologists divide the Indigenous peoples of northeastern North America into two principal linguistic groupings or language stocks: Algonkian and Iroquoian. Within each of these linguistic families, there were many distinct collectivities. Generally speaking, what distinguished these groups were their languages and economies.

Algonkians consisted of a large number of nations or tribes. In present-day Newfoundland were found the Beothuk, who were distinctive for their habit of decorating themselves with ochre, a reddish substance that led newcomers to describe all the Indigenous peoples of the continent as "red Indians." The Beothuk were primarily hunter-gatherers and fishing people. It was either Beothuk or Inuit who made contact with the first European immigrants who attempted settlement in northern Newfoundland and Labrador, the unfortunate Norse. Within three years the Norse had retreated to Greenland, repulsed by the Native people they called *skraelings*. Later contacts would be more successful for the Europeans and less happy for the Indigenous populations.

On the land mass of North America itself dwelt many other Algonkian nations. In what are today northern New Brunswick, Prince Edward Island, and Nova Scotia lived the Mi'kmaq, and to the southwest in central and southern New Brunswick, the Maliseet (Welustuk). Still further south, in what now is the state of Maine, was the Abenaki Confederacy, which contained such groups as the Passamaquoddy and Penobscot. All these nations were migratory peoples who relied on a combination of fishing, hunting, and the gathering of berries and nuts. Their migrations followed a seasonal pattern in search of sustenance: in winter they generally moved in small bands, though in summer they would gather in larger groupings at suitable places for fishing and berrying. The unity of these peoples was largely imposed retrospectively by anthropologists; aside from participation in a common language stock and similar economy, they were highly diverse.

The same could be said of other Algonkian peoples who inhabited the lands north of what they called "the river of Canada," the St. Lawrence. East of what is now the St. Maurice Valley were the Montagnais (Innu); along the Ottawa River were found Algonkin; and near Lake Nipissing the nation that gave the lake its name. The other major Algonkian nations were the Ottawa, found on the east side of Lake Huron; the Ojibwe, or Chippewa, near Lake Superior; and the Cree in the more northerly lands that were drained by rivers flowing into James Bay. Indeed, various groups of Cree were to be found throughout northerly regions stretching to the western prairies and the woodlands north of the plains. As with the Mi'kmaq and Maliseet of the Atlantic region, what all these Algonkians of the interior had in common was language and economy. They were all principally hunter-gatherers, although some who occupied fertile lands cultivated some crops. Reliance on the wild rice that was found in some lakes was also common.

The other major linguistic grouping of eastern and central Canada was the Iroquoian. It, too, consisted of a number of different people. In the St. Lawrence lowlands were people whose identity has baffled scholars. They occupied this region in the early sixteenth century when French explorers penetrated it, but vacated the district by the seventeenth, when the next wave of French exploration took place. (They are usually identified simply as the St. Lawrence Iroquoians.) In what is today New York State was found a larger, more permanent concentration of Iroquoians, usually known as the Five Nations Confederacy. The five peoples that constituted this extraordinary League of the Iroquois were stretched in a band extending from west of the Hudson River to the lands south of Lake Ontario. From east to west they were the Mohawk, Oneida, Onondaga, Cayuga, and Seneca. (In 1723 they would be joined by a sixth people, the Tuscarora, who were fleeing agricultural settlement in the Thirteen Colonies, to become the Six Nations.) To the west of the Iroquois Confederacy were smaller groupings of Iroquoian peoples known as the Wenro and the Erie. Farther south, in present-day Pennsylvania, lived the Susquehannock.

In the part of the Great Lakes–St. Lawrence drainage basin that lay north of the lakes and river were numerous other important Iroquoian groups. Immediately north of Lake Erie lived the Neutral, and north of them the Petun, or Tobacco, Nation. But the biggest Iroquoian grouping in what would later become Canada was the Huron Confederacy, which consisted of four nations who called themselves the Bear, Rock, Cord, and Deer. "Huron" was a term that would be applied to them by the French, who used the French word *hure* (literally "boar's head," but also "brute" or "ruffian") in reference to the hairstyle affected by Huron men.[4] These people called themselves Wendat, which literally meant "islanders" or "dwellers on a peninsula." It is not clear whether the term referred to the fact that Huronia, the territory they inhabited near Georgian Bay, was surrounded on three sides by water or if it was a reference to their belief that the world was an island that rested on a turtle. The term was later to crop up as the name of an American people, the Wyandot, which was formed in part by Huron fleeing Huronia in the seventeenth century. Indeed, some scholars refer to the peoples of Huronia as the Wyandot Confederacy.[5]

The Huron, like all the Iroquoians, had a number of features in addition to their language that distinguished them from Algonkians. Their economy relied on crops as well as game and fish. For most of them, the staple crop was corn, or maize, but the Petun – as their alternate name illustrates – also grew tobacco that they both consumed and traded with others. The Huron, like the Iroquoians, relied on a trio of food crops – corn, beans, and squash – known as the Three Sisters, which grew together. Because the Iroquoians relied on crops, they were of necessity much more sedentary than the migratory Algonkians. Their usual practice was to reside in one place for ten or twelve years, until soil exhaustion forced them to move on. When the time for relocation approached, the men of the village would prepare the new fields a year in advance of the time when the women would begin to plant, tend, and harvest the crops. Once the agricultural site was readied, the village would move. The Iroquoians' relatively secure food supply meant that theirs was a sedentary lifestyle and that their concentrations of population were much greater than those of migratory hunter-gatherers. Some of the towns in Iroquoia numbered as many as 1,500 people, and villages of several hundred were quite common for all the Iroquoians. This settlement pattern was responsible for one of the physical features that distinguished the Iroquoians: they lived in large multi-family dwellings called longhouses, and these distinctive buildings were found in fortified, palisaded villages. The members of the Iroquois Confederacy were sometimes called the Haudenosaunee, or "people of the longhouse."

Other consequences flowed from the economy and settlement pattern of the Iroquoians. For one thing, the important economic role of the women, who were responsible for agricultural operations (the men having to carry out what might be termed the capital side of farming), had led to a prominent social and political role for the females. Although there were differences of degree between Iroquoians and Algonkians, in all the First Nations of Canada the role and status of women were much more elevated than in European society.[6] Whereas the Algonkians were patrilineal and patrilocal, the Iroquoians were matrilineal and matrilocal. One scholar of Wendat history refers to them as "a matricentric society."[7] What these terms mean is that a person in Iroquoian society traced his or her family identity through the mother: one belonged to the family of one's mother. Furthermore, when a man married, he took up residence with the family of his bride. A household, which was the basic unit of society among Iroquoians, consisted of a woman, her female relations, their spouses, and dependants. (An Algonkian band's composition was a group of male kin who hunted together, their spouses, and their dependent families.) Among Iroquoians, chieftainship was hereditary among families of certain female lines, and the prominent women of the tribe had much to say about selecting the individual male who would become chief on the death of a leader.

The large concentrations in which Iroquoians lived had also led them to develop sophisticated instruments of social control and political decision-making. For example, each Iroquoian belonged to a clan (e.g., Turtle) as well as a nation (e.g.,

Rock). Villages consisted of representatives of each of the clans, meaning both that every Iroquoian had potential hosts in other villages and that there was a disincentive to war with other villages or nations of the confederacy. Paralleling such ingenious social institutions were political structures that enabled the relatively large Iroquoian nations – and the Huron and Iroquois Confederacies in particular – to reach and carry out agreements. A tribe or nation possessed its own territory and its own council of *sachems* (chiefs). A confederacy had a representative council; the grand council of the Five Nations consisted of fifty chiefs representing the different nations roughly according to their size. An insight into the values of Aboriginal society resided in one of the grand council's practices: all decisions had to be unanimous. This requirement was in part the product of Natives' avoidance of coercing others. The Jesuit missionary Le Jeune observed that Aboriginal people would "only obey their chief through good will toward him" and that they had "reproached me a hundred times because we fear our Captains, while they laugh at and make sport of theirs. All the authority of their chief is in his tongue's end; for he is powerful in so far as he is eloquent and, even if he kills himself talking and haranguing, he will not be believed unless he pleases them."[8] Still, the Huron Confederacy was politically well enough organized to forge an alliance with nearby Anishaabeg peoples that endured for centuries, even after a Huron defeat at the hands of the Iroquois.[9]

Algonkians and Iroquoians might have differed greatly in social and political structures, but what they had in common was commerce, warfare, and religion. Long before the European intruded in North America, the Indigenous inhabitants had developed systems of trade, patterns of commerce that were based on considerations of geography and economics. Particular nations such as the Huron found themselves well placed athwart or adjacent to water transportation routes to exact a toll from those who wished to travel through their territory and to initiate commercial transactions with either those traversing their region or people to whom they could travel themselves. Similarly, some Algonkians, such as the nation that controlled the Ottawa River, found that their locations near travel routes induced them into commerce. The other major factor was possession of goods of particular importance. One such was the copper that communities on the shore of Lake Superior had and traded with other First Nations to the east. This important metal – apparently the only metal that Indigenous peoples of eastern North America knew prior to contact – was used for both utilitarian and decorative purposes by tribes far from Superior. Other important trade items were tobacco and maize, both of which were the property of the agricultural Iroquoians. Surplus corn was the basis of Huron influence long before the European came; communities that wanted tobacco for both ritualistic and recreational purposes found themselves trading with the Tobacco nation or with intermediaries such as the Huron, who were located between the Tobacco and most of the Algonkian peoples.

For First Nations, trade had critically important social aspects. The right to trade with another tribe was a customary property right of certain families, usually prominent families who had initiated the commerce. Such commercial rights were an important factor in the affluence and prominence of these leading families, a reservoir of wealth that fed their prestige and influence. But in Aboriginal society this prestige was established and maintained not by piling up and hoarding wealth but by distributing it among one's followers. Generosity was a defining characteristic of these societies, as the Jesuit Father Ragueneau observed:

> No hospitals [shelters] are needed among them, because there are neither mendicants nor paupers as long as there are any rich people among them. Their kindness, humanity, and courtesy not only make them liberal with what they have, but cause them to possess hardly anything except in common. A whole village must be without corn, before any individual can be obliged to endure privation. They divide the produce of their fisheries equally with all who come.[10]

The sharing and redistribution of material goods were not just admired but required; acquisitiveness and selfishness were abhorred and shunned. Another important social aspect of Native commerce was the accompanying exchange of people. Those families of different nations that engaged in trade usually swapped sons to cement the commercial association. Having a fellow tribesman living with a family in another tribe was both a surety of continuing commercial intercourse and a deterrent to friction and conflict between the two groups.

But, in fact, commercial motives were frequently a cause – one of the two principal causes – of warfare in Aboriginal society. It was not uncommon for one group to attack another in order to acquire food or products, or to force acquiescence in the aggressor's use of hunting or fishing territories. It is possible that warfare based on such motives was responsible for the dispersal of the St. Lawrence Iroquoians in the sixteenth century. The other usual cause of warfare in pre-contact times was retribution. In societies without coercive authority or police functions, a major deterrent to violence against people was the requirement that those whose kin or tribesmen had been killed avenge the fallen. A family that had lost a member to another in the nation was theoretically obliged to kill a member of that other family, though in practice such obligations were transmuted into acceptance of a compensatory payment for the loss. No such transformation of the duty to seek vengeance occurred in the case of violence by a member of one nation against a different people. Most of the non-commercial warfare that existed prior to European incursions was attributed by Natives to retribution, vengeance, and replenishing population losses.[11] Warfare was not racially or ethnically motivated. One nation warred with another for revenge or for commercial reasons; it did not fight the other simply because the other was a different people. Belonging to the same linguistic family no more accounted for peaceful relationships between nations than differences between Algonkians and Iroquoians accounted for hostile relationships between them. An Iroquoian people was as likely to fight another Iroquoian group as an Algonkian one.

Although warfare was common before the coming of the Europeans, it was not usually very extensive or destructive in those times. Non-commercial war in particular tended to be focused narrowly on a particular family or village, and its objectives were satisfied with the death of relatively few people. Once members of another nation were killed or captured to be tortured to death later, the need to engage in violence was satisfied, although admittedly a new obligation to spill blood would have been created in the other group. The other important feature of this warfare was that the tactics and weapons employed were not especially destructive. Attacks from hiding, and lightning raids by small parties using arrows and clubs, were the norm. Both the style of attack and the weapons used meant that warfare did not lead to wholesale slaughter. No doubt such considerations were little solace to prisoners as they trudged back to their captors' village.

Among some Indigenous peoples, the death of captives taken in battle was not only expiation of the obligation to seek retribution but also a religious rite. Torture was commonly employed among both Algonkians and Iroquoians, and for the Iroquoians torture was a type of religious observation in honour of the sun. Captured prisoners – men of young or middle age were particularly important – were taken back to the village of the successful raiding party. Prisoners were adopted by a family in the victors' village, and in some cases the adoptees were taken into the family to replace someone who had died or been killed in battle.[12] Often, though, the male captive was subjected to lengthy and ingenious torture in which fire and knives were extensively employed. The prisoner was expected to bear pain without crying out or showing any sign of suffering. It was even better if he laughed at his torturers and told them that he was enjoying the treatment that he was receiving. Such stoic and defiant behaviour was greatly admired; those who manifested it would receive special attention later.

The usual practice was to torture the prisoner intermittently, reviving him from time to time, and ensuring that he survived the night. The Iroquoians followed the practice of putting the prisoner to death at the rising of the sun, final proof that the torture was in part religious ritual.[13] In the case of a prisoner who had been particularly brave, the captors would roast his heart and apportion it among the young men of the village. "The prisoner's body was then cut up in order to be cooked and eaten. Some ate the body with horror; others relished the taste of human flesh. We are again dealing with an act that was primarily of religious significance."[14]

Religious beliefs underlay this ritual cannibalism. All the Indigenous peoples of North America held metaphysical, theological, and ethical ideas that are categorized as animistic. Animistic religions place humans in the physical environment without drawing any distinction or barrier between them and the physical world. Creation myths could vary from one nation to another, but the underlying understanding of what constituted being was the same for all First Nations. All people, animals, fish, and physical aspects of nature were animate; all had souls or spirits. Even items of human manufacture had souls – and souls required respectful treatment at all times. At particular times they might require expiation and placating. There were rituals or prayers to show respect to animals or to dangerous passages in the river, invocations to ensure that the animal about to be taken and eaten would not avenge itself on its takers by warning away its brothers and sisters in the future. Similarly, there were numerous taboos that had to be observed to placate spirits: fish bones should not be thrown into the fire lest the fish be angered at this humiliation and prevent its kin from being caught in future. Such a belief system was based on the assumption that all the world was a continuum, that everything was animate, and that humans held no special place on the earth and in the cosmos.

Other religious rituals had more specific purposes than showing respect for the other souls of creation. The torture of prisoners was both a tribute to the sun and a part of the male cult of prestige through battle. Iroquoians believed that by eating a portion of the heart of a captive who had borne torture with great courage, they would gain a portion of his bravery. Some rituals, such as the Huron Feast of the Dead, had social purposes. Every ten or twelve years, probably when the village changed locations to get fertile land, the Huron disinterred the corpses of those who had been buried in the burial grounds of their village, cleaned the bones, wrapped them with gifts in fine beaver pelts, and reinterred them in a common ossuary. The ten days of preparation and ceremony were marked by feasting and the exchange of gifts, and the entire ritual had the effect of bonding together more closely the various Huron clans and families, and even nations.[15]

Other rituals aimed to ward off or cure disease, and in some nations curing societies had an important social and religious role. There was no distinction whatever between medicine and religion, for the simple reason that disease was believed to be caused by evil spirits, some of them implanted by witchcraft. All religious behaviour was closely associated with the giving of feasts and presents, an important redistributive and bonding process that was vitally important to Indigenous society. Selfishness was considered not just antisocial but also evidence of witchcraft. Witchcraft was one of the few charges in Native society that justified putting someone to death. Though religion permeated every aspect of life, there was no separate religious institution or priestly class. Shamans, who oversaw ritual and carried out curing rites in most First Nations, were "part-time specialists," employed as occasion required to deal with the spirit world.[16]

Indigenous communities, then, were highly diversified societies of people who – as people everywhere at all times have done – had adapted to their environment and worked out a code of behaviour for living compatibly with their world. There was no monolith called "Indian," but a wide variety of Indigenous peoples, whose differences depended upon the topography and fauna of the region in which they lived, and the resulting nature of their economy. The First Nations that occupied the northeastern part of North America six hundred years ago had evolved to accommodate themselves to their world and to one another. Their values and institutions were still experiencing slow change at the time of the first contact with Europeans. Though they had pronounced differences, they also shared some features. They participated in some activities, such as commerce and warfare, and thereby learned of each other's different ways. Their theology and ethics were roughly similar. But in spite of these significant similarities, it made little sense to regard them as one undifferentiated human community. To label all the Indigenous peoples simply "Indians" and treat them as though they were the same made about as much sense as naming all newcomers "Europeans" and pretending that there were not sharp differences among them. Any newcomers to North America would have to take the distinctive nature of Native societies into consideration; immigrants would have to adjust, too.

It was not "Europeans" who came to North America but Basque whalers, West Country English fishers, Dutch traders, and French missionaries. Though it would take the Native populations some time to understand, the differences among the intruders were pronounced, and their different natures and purposes had much to do with the type of relations they established with the inhabitants of the continent they began to reach in the late fifteenth century. And yet, like Aboriginal communities, the Europeans, too, had common features that united them and differentiated them from the First Nations. These included their social and economic structures, their political systems, and their beliefs.

European societies of the sixteenth century were highly stratified and their governments coercive in nature. In all the Western European states, there was a well-established hierarchy of nobles, gentry, burghers, and common people. Though those of higher rank could have obligations to the less fortunate, individualism was more deeply ingrained among them than it was among the peoples of North America. The ethic of sharing was not as important and all-pervasive among these European peoples as it was in North American societies. Their polities, though they varied in detail, all employed coercion to enforce decisions. Absolutism was firmly entrenched in some countries, while the beginnings of parliamentary government were stirring in others. But in all of them it was expected that policy, once arrived at by debate or fiat, would be enforced. The king's troops, the local militia, or the community's tiny police force would impose the decisions of court, parliament, or magistrates on people. From the standpoint of those who gave the orders for enforcement, the only problem was that military and police power did not reach nearly as far as the ambitions of the rulers. Often the freedom people enjoyed in these societies was a function of the inability of the powerful to coerce them effectively.

European countries were not only structured societies and authoritarian polities; they were also acquisitive economies. By the sixteenth century, the beginnings of a market mentality could be detected in some of them, particularly Holland and England. The significance of capitalism lay in its psychological character: capitalists both acted on and promoted a desire to acquire material goods, not simply for consumption and other social purposes, but for reinvestment for the purpose of acquiring still more property. This economic motive also encouraged the development of an individualistic spirit that, in economically advanced countries, was beginning to erode communal ties of village loyalty and clan solidarity. In time this impulse, strengthened by the individualistic intellectual traditions that were a product of the European Renaissance, would remake the social ethics of Europe. The same forces, abetted by economic motivation, were bringing about a new reliance on machine technology and novel forms of energy. This revolution, like the impact of the Renaissance and the expanding grip of capitalist ethics, was remaking Western Europe into an increasingly individualistic and acquisitive human community. At its best, this process would lead to considerable prosperity and a high degree of personal liberty; at its worst, to unbridled selfishness and yawning chasms between affluent and poor.

Though the Western European countries had economies that were diversified, and though the primary economic ambitions of these peoples differed widely, there were but a few economic reasons for the Europeans' approach to North America. After the era of abortive Norse exploration and settlement, the first contacts were made by fishing boats sometime in the fifteenth century. Although many European countries sought protein in the waters of North America, the Basques, Spanish, French, and English emerged as the most numerous and prominent of the fishers off Newfoundland and Nova Scotia. They were in search especially of whales and cod, which were found in incredible profusion on the Grand Banks.

Although the fishing boats of the various European countries all sought mainly the same thing, they would do different things with it. By an accident of geography and history, different fishers were forced to ply their trade in different ways in North America. Those from the more southerly regions had quantities of solar salt that they could use to preserve the fish on board their vessels before returning to Europe. Those from more northerly areas, particularly Normans, Bretons, and English, did not have access to a supply of salt from the Bay of Biscay. They could not use the "green fishery" of their southern competitors, so had to follow the dry method. The significance of this was that those Europeans from more northerly countries began the practice of landing for protracted periods, erecting stands on which they dried the cleaned cod before packing it on board ship for the return voyage. These stays ashore meant that they came into contact, and conflict, with the Indigenous inhabitants to a much greater extent than those who landed less frequently and for shorter periods in search of fresh water, food, and wood for repairs. Thus, the contact between Native peoples in the future Canada revolved around the interaction with northern French and British rather than Spaniards and Basques, and the explanation for this lies, to a great extent, in the simple question of whose home territory yielded salt evaporated from sea water and whose did not.

In time, and for reasons that will be explained later, this first contact led to an extensive commercial relationship between coastal Algonkians, such as the Mi'kmaq, and Europeans. Occasional visits of fishers produced meetings; meetings led to barter of tools and clothing for furs; and out of these encounters grew the second major Canadian economy of the European era, the fur trade. In the case of both fish and fur, there were two important aspects that helped to shape the ensuing relationship of Europeans and Native peoples: Europeans were motivated by the desire for gain, and the achievement of this economic goal required the cooperation of the peoples with whom they came into contact.

The other two principal motives for European expansion to North America in the fifteenth and sixteenth centuries were exploration and proselytization. From the accounts of Marco Polo's voyages to the lands of the Great Khan, and from other (even more fabulous) accounts, Europeans knew that regions with great riches in the form of spices and precious metals lay in the East. Thanks to the discoveries of science and the speculations of navigators, it was both thinkable and feasible to sail west in search of the riches of the East. Many of the early European explorers, in part at least, sailed to North America in search of Asia. Some of them thought that these western lands were the East, as the application of the term "Indians" to the people of what explorers thought at first were the Indies graphically illustrates. As Giovanni da Verrazzano noted of the Natives he encountered in the Carolinas in 1524, "They resemble the Orientals." In the same area the "trees emit a sweet fragrance over a large area," and, while he was not sure what the source of the fragrance was, "We think that they belong to the Orient by virtue of the surroundings, and that they are not without some kind of narcotic or aromatic liquor. There are other riches, like gold, which ground of such a color usually denotes."[17] Navigators and ship captains in both the fifteenth and sixteenth centuries probed westward – at first in search of the Orient and later, when they realized that North America was not Asia, in hopes of finding a waterway through this land mass to the lands of the Khan. They, too, like the fishing boat captains and the fur traders who followed, would discover that they needed the cooperation of the peoples whom they encountered on their voyages of exploration.

Finally, there was also a non-monetary reason that European countries began to send people to North America from the seventeenth century onward: religion. Europe was Christian, and from that simple social fact many important consequences followed. For one thing, Christians, like the Hebrews from whom they were both historically and theologically descended, held a world view that contrasted sharply with the animistic beliefs of the Indigenous peoples of North America. Amerindians believed that they were only one species among many. A Native's spirit was but one among a myriad of spirits of people, animals, fishes, flora, and minerals. In contrast, Christians believed that they held a special place in creation. At the irreducible core of Christianity was the dictum that God had created humans in the deity's image, and that the non-human world was available for humans' use and God's glorification. While Christianity recognized a duty of stewardship in the use and exploitation of the non-human things that God had put on earth for Christians' advantage, it also confirmed that humans were on a higher level of existence than animals, fish, and the rest of the natural world. This world view had fuelled Western society's development of science, and subjugation of nature by means of technology, ever since the Renaissance. By the sixteenth century, it had so shaped Christians' attitudes that they saw themselves as the more important part of a duality – humans and nature. It was an interpretation of reality and humans' place in creation that differed fundamentally from that of the populations of North America.

The significance of religion to the early contact between Europeans and Aborigines did not end with Christianity's influence on the European view of the world; Christianity also had a bearing on which European peoples would undertake the exploration and economic development of the northern part of what would later be known as North America. The Vatican had decreed that all new lands were to be divided by the Christian nations of Spain and Portugal. Francis I of France did not accept his exclusion from the potential riches of the western hemisphere. "Show me Adam's will!" he is supposed to have said of the papal edict.[18] In practice, France secured Rome's acquiescence in French efforts to find new lands to the north of those already being exploited by the Iberian states. It was politic and convenient to direct most of the voyages that the French Crown sponsored to the northerly latitudes. So, in part, it was that the French concentrated many of their attentions on the region that would later become Canada. Certainly that was true of state-sponsored evangelical efforts, which were themselves another manifestation of the Christian nature of Europe.

It was a historically important coincidence that much of the early period of European exploration and penetration of North America was an era of intense religious feeling. The Catholic Church had been wracked and divided by a drive for reform led by those who protested against the spiritual flabbiness and fleshly venality of an institution that had held a monopoly of religious services for centuries. The emergence of various forms of Protestantism would play a profoundly important role in the relations of North American peoples and European newcomers in many of the Anglo-American colonies that would develop. In the Roman Catholic Church in general, and in France in particular, the rise of a Protestant challenge provoked both a Counter-Reformation and the emergence of a newly militant spirit of Catholicism. Both Catholic renewal and Catholic militancy were to have profound effects on the Aboriginal peoples of North America.

The upheavals within the ranks of European Christianity stirred renewed desires to take Christ's message to all the world, and new vehicles for taking it at precisely the moment when France was poised to explore North America. The year of Jacques Cartier's first voyage, 1534, was also the year in which the Spaniard Ignatius Loyola established the Society of Jesus. Just as the Catholic revitalization motivated both clerics and rulers to follow the Biblical injunction to evangelize, coincidentally new missionary bodies emerged to fulfil this aim. The Récollets, a particularly strict branch of the Franciscans, and the Jesuits, an aggressive and militant order, were but two of the many organizations that were founded or renewed in the aftermath of the Protestant Reformation. The Jesuits in particular moved eagerly to spread the Christian Word, and by the seventeenth century they were ministering to the Chinese and other Asians. It was the presence of groups such as these missionary orders that would make the seventeenth century – a period of intensive and concerted efforts to explore and develop Canada – a century of faith. Without this recent evolution in Christianity in Western Europe, the early history of Canada, and the first stages of Indigenous-European relations, would have been vitally different.

It would have been difficult at any time and in any part of the globe to have found two more diverse human communities than the First Nation band and Cartier's men who came together at Gaspé in the summer of 1534. The Indigenous inhabitants consisted of a multitude of bands and nations of hunter-gatherers and agriculturalists who had adjusted to their environment and lived in harmony with it. They had, especially the agrarian Iroquoians among them, developed elaborate social and political institutions and practices to cope with their large concentrations of population. Their technology and value system made their pressure on the resources of their world light. Lacking iron and firearms, they were unable to inflict much damage on fellow humans and animals; their animistic religion restrained them from even developing the desire to do so. Their economic organization meant that they lived in smaller population concentrations than did Europeans, often faced more threats to their physical well-being, and were forced to coexist with one another and with nature. While they shared a rudimentary form of commerce, similar motives for engaging in warfare, and an essentially similar cosmology and ethics, they had had neither need nor occasion to combine for economic or political purposes.

The other of the two Canadian solitudes, the Europeans, were like the North American Natives in that they both differed from and resembled one another. While it would have made as little sense to lump a Basque whaler and an English navigator under one heading as it would have to label both Beothuk and Mohawk with one name, there were also underlying similarities. In Europe, population concentrations were large compared to those in North America; political systems had developed that were authoritarian and coercive rather than communitarian and consensual; and the various economies were increasingly driven by the capitalistic motive of acquisition and investment. European nations also shared a common Christian faith, and, while differences of theological and ecclesiological detail might in the fifteenth century cause them to war with one another, that common faith gave them a similar attitude towards the environment. Their outlook was that of scientifically inclined creatures of God, who were beginning to believe not only that the world was created for their enjoyment but also that the rules governing it were knowable and exploitable for economic purposes. Perhaps the different arrangement of the Europeans' mental furniture was the thing that distinguished them most from the Native peoples of America.

When Europeans began to undertake voyages to the New World, they were setting in train a process that would bring these two contrasting communities out of solitude and into contact. The wonder of it was that early interactions between two such different societies should have been so cooperative.

Part One

COOPERATION

CHAPTER TWO

Early Contacts in the Eastern Woodlands

The earliest European ventures in North America proved abortive. About the first millennium after the birth of Christ, Norse visitors attempted to colonize parts of Newfoundland and Labrador from Iceland and Greenland. In the latter place, the Norse had already encountered an Inuit population they called *skraelings*. They applied the same name to the Natives of Newfoundland, but the population they encountered was probably Beothuk or some other Algonkian people. Little is known of the relations between the would-be settlers and the Natives save that, in spite of friendly initial contact, there was conflict that led to the abandonment of European settlements at such places as the present-day l'Anse aux Meadows.[1] This first failed attempt at colonization set a pattern for Aboriginal-European relations in both the Atlantic and continental areas of Canada. Penetration of Newfoundland for agricultural settlement led to resistance and repulse by the Indigenous people.

After the unsuccessful Norse attempt, contacts apparently became intermittent and commercial, rather than systematic and agricultural, for almost five centuries. The Norse continued to visit the coast of North America in search of timber for use in Greenland and Iceland, and probably also in search of fish, walrus, and even the polar bear. North America was part of the vast northern European trade territory that the Norse maintained for several centuries. Although this trade declined in the fourteenth century and Norse control of commerce was replaced by that of the Hanseatic League of German states, the earlier voyages and meetings would be important later on. It was not so much that the Norse had come into frequent contact with the Native population as that they had established sailing routes that others

would follow, thereby encountering North Americans. These early European contacts were motivated by the search for the products of the sea. Fish was extremely
important in the European diet. The Catholic calendar's fifty-seven fast days and
numerous other days (including each Friday and Saturday) on which the faithful
abstained from meat meant that during the equivalent of five months of the year no
flesh was to be eaten.[2] The paucity of other inexpensive sources of protein ensured
that there would be a heavy demand for fish, such as cod, that was nutritious and
relatively inexpensive. There was also high demand for the great sea mammal, the
whale, whose meat, fat, and oil were all valuable. The importance of the prosaic cod
can be seen from the fact that Azorean fishers called Newfoundland the Land of
the Bacalhau (codfish).

Through the latter years of the fifteenth century, ships came from many European
countries in search of sea products. The Basques became noteworthy for whaling,
while the French and English were particularly interested in the cod and other fish
of the Grand Banks. The Basque also established a continuing pattern of European
borrowing: they adapted technology and technique from the Inuit to enhance the
yield of their whaling ventures.[3] The continuity between these increasingly frequent
voyages and the earlier Norse approaches lay in the fact that all followed a northerly
route across the Atlantic to the western hemisphere. Such a route not only took
advantage of already existing Norse knowledge of sea lanes but also kept ships as
close to land as long as possible. Equally important for the later history of North
America, these routes ensured that the European vessels would come into contact
with the Indigenous peoples of Canada.

Late in the fifteenth century, another motive began to incite the Europeans to
explore the western hemisphere. In the 1490s, merchants from Bristol began to underwrite the voyages of a Venetian navigator whom they called John Cabot, a man
who argued that one could reach the Orient by sailing to the northwest. Probably
in 1494, Cabot's ship poked about part of the Atlantic region and possibly also Cape
Breton, and in 1497 he made landfall on what he called New Found Land. Cabot
– like Christopher Columbus, who had reached the region he called the Indies by
a southern route in 1492 – was seeking the riches of the territories of the Great
Khan that Europe had learned of from Marco Polo. Even when Cabot and others
finally realized that Newfoundland was not Asia, their voyages in search of Eastern
riches would persist and be imitated. French explorers would also mistake North
America for Asia, and, once they realized their error, they regarded it as a land mass
barring the way to the fabled East. When European navigators gave up on Canada
as the Orient, they would continue for some time to search for a northwest passage
through it to Asia. Like those who had come on the fishing ships, they would come

principally by the northern route; and like them, they would encounter the Natives in the process.

As the sixteenth century rolled on, the approaches of the different European countries to North America began to fall into a pattern. To a great extent, the efforts of the English and the Basques remained focused on Newfoundland, Labrador, and the north-shore region of what the local inhabitants called the River of Canada. English and northern French fishing captains, who did not have large supplies of cheap salt to practise the green fishery, were forced to land and erect stages (or flakes) on which to dry their catch. What inclinations they might have had to turn these brief landings into the beginnings of settlement were discouraged, first, by the Natives' resistance, and, later, by an English policy forbidding settlement. More southerly Europeans, who did have large quantities of salt, made less use of the shore and, consequently, had little land-based contact with the Algonkians of the Atlantic region. When the French began to direct serious attention to North America in the sixteenth century, they focused on the mainland and became involved in extensive contacts with the Natives. As events would soon demonstrate, all these fishing and exploration voyages had, in the meantime, been encouraging the growth of yet a third form of contact, one that pushed the French in particular to undertake unprecedented efforts to sail to Canada.

This new form of contact was a commerce that had grown up spontaneously between the Europeans and the Indigenous peoples. When the French navigator Jacques Cartier was cruising the coast in 1534, he met some First Nations canoes in the area of the Bay of Chaleur. The encounter was instructive. The Mi'kmaq "set up a great clamour and made frequent signs to us to come on shore, holding up to us some furs on sticks."[4] It was clear from the fact that the First Nations people initiated both contact and commerce, as well as from the fact that the females among the group remained hidden in the woods during the approach to the Europeans, that there had already been considerable interaction between newcomers and themselves sometime previously. How eager the inhabitants were for the trade was illustrated by the fact that they "showed a marvellously great pleasure in possessing and obtaining these iron wares and other commodities, dancing and going through many ceremonies and throwing salt water over their heads with their hands." They "bartered all they had to such an extent that all went back naked without anything on them; and they made signs to us that they would return on the morrow with more furs."[5]

Cartier had learned, as had no doubt other voyagers before him, that a commerce was emerging out of this occasional contact in the fishery. This trade was an attractive and mutually beneficial sideline for both sides. To the Indigenous people,

European depictions of Aboriginal response to the arrival of Jacques Cartier
exaggerated its positive nature.

the trade represented an opportunity to barter their used skin clothing for orna-
mental and utilitarian European products; for the newcomers, it was a chance to
develop a lucrative ancillary activity in the midst of fishing and exploring. Other
European activities apparently were less welcome and beneficial to the inhabitants
of the Atlantic region with whom Cartier and others made contact. The fact that
the Mi'kmaq women hid when they spied Cartier's ship hints at one problem that
had ensued from contact. Another European activity that would have mixed results
was presaged in Cartier's conclusion after a few days' observation that the Natives
"would be easy to convert to our holy faith."[6] A further problem was the Europeans'
presumptuous behaviour in ignoring the Indigenous people's control of the territory, as exemplified in their erecting a cross.[7] Indubitably, the Natives rejected
European attempts to proclaim their control by right of discovery of these lands.

    Further problems arose when Cartier kidnapped Dom Agaya and Taigoagny,
sons of the Iroquoian chief Donnacona, to take them back to France. Donnacona
was a leader of some of the St. Lawrence Iroquoians, who in the sixteenth century
dominated the River of Canada from present-day Lake Ontario to the Gaspé. As
later Indigenous leaders were to observe bitterly, the newcomer "began by stealing

the people from their land, and were to end up by stealing the continent from the people."[8] In this particular case, the boys returned the following year, on Cartier's second voyage. But other navigators and explorers also kidnapped or persuaded Natives to return to Europe as living proof of what they had found in the West, and often the North Americans did not survive. As ethnohistorian James Axtell has observed, "The first extractive industry in colonial North America was kidnapping."[9]

Cartier's subsequent voyages also began the process of European penetration of the northern part of the continent by means of that massive waterway, the River of Canada. In 1535, Cartier travelled farther upstream to Stadacona, or Quebec City, and then onward over the protests of the Aboriginal peoples of that region to the upriver village they called Hochelaga, the future site of Montreal. The Stadaconans tried unsuccessfully to deter the Frenchmen from sailing past their village, because they wanted to prevent the Hochelagans from getting direct access to European technology. Already the Indigenous population was trying to monopolize trade in the interests of maximizing profits, a tendency that would develop at regular intervals on both the European and First Nation sides of the commercial frontier. Cartier's westward voyage in the interior was undertaken in search of the region that the Natives called the Kingdom of the Saguenay; it ended at the rapids in the river that became known by the ironic title of La Chine (China).

During the French visitors' overwintering at Stadacona, new patterns were established within the developing relationship. The initial good relations between Cartier's men and Donnacona's people gave way to suspicion, to the point that the French fortified their winter quarters against the Iroquoians. Moreover, the winter brought dreadful suffering to the Europeans in the form of scurvy, which killed almost one-quarter of them and left most of the remainder gravely debilitated. Then, although extermination of the sojourners would have been child's play, the Natives instead saved them from certain suffering and possible death by showing them how to make a tonic containing ascorbic acid from bark, cedar needles, and water. Without this assistance, Cartier's party well might have perished.

By the end of Cartier's third voyage to the new world in 1541–2, the relationship had been established and attitudes formed. The Europeans had settled on the motives that would drive their contacts till the eighteenth century: fish, furs, exploration, and evangelization. The Native people had tolerated the first, eagerly embraced the second, cooperated in the third when doing so did not threaten their interests, and still remained blissfully ignorant of the fourth motive. Attitudes had begun to form, too. At first, Cartier thought that "this people may well be called savage, for they are the sorriest folk there can be in the world, and the whole lot of them had not anything above the value of five sous, their canoes and fishing-nets excepted."[10]

The Europeans usually formed a poor first impression of North Americans, though on longer and closer contact they would moderate the severity of their judgment. The negative nature of the French view has been exaggerated by translators, who have not always fully understood the words that people like Cartier used. Usually, the French referred to the Indigenous people as *sauvages*, a term which could have the English translation "savages." But *sauvages* could also have a more neutral meaning, such as "forest dwellers" or people residing in natural surroundings. Or it could mean something not domesticated, something occurring naturally in nature, such as *riz sauvage*, wild rice.[11]

What *sauvage* meant depended completely on the context. Cartier in 1534 probably meant that the people he encountered were in a rude and impoverished state. Later missionaries would refer to a convert as "un bon sauvage vraiment chrétien" (a good, truly Christian person), a use of the term *sauvage* that could not translate as "savage" and still make sense. In such a case, it was obviously the term for the Native inhabitants of the woodlands. At other times French observers who referred to Indigenous people as *sauvages* meant only that they were primitive and barbarous by French standards. Which meaning was intended could be understood only from the context, a subtlety that was too often missed in the direct and blunt translations into English that rendered all Native people "savages," whether they were "truly Christian" converts or warriors torturing prisoners. Later generations, both First Nation and Euro-Canadian, would pay dearly for this use of language as a blunt instrument.

Such concerns lay far in the future in the aftermath of the French explorations of the early sixteenth century. For reasons largely having to do with political and religious affairs in Western Europe, the French Crown was distracted from the 1540s onward from further explorations. The fact that Cartier had brought back only people, fool's gold, and worthless quartz rather than spices, gold, and diamonds meant that there was little incentive to continue the voyages. In the latter half of the sixteenth century the contacts that persisted were the now familiar ones of fishing and whaling vessels, which presumably continued the ancillary enterprise of trading in furs as opportunity in America and markets in Europe were available.

When French voyages of exploration resumed early in the seventeenth century, they focused primarily on the Maritime and St. Lawrence regions. They were different from the tentative probings of the previous century. In the first place, when Samuel de Champlain and his ships felt their way up the River of Canada, they discovered that the St. Lawrence Iroquoians had disappeared, most likely dispersed by the incursions of other nations. The First Nations with whom Champlain most

The Maliseet, like the Mi'kmaq, were among the first to encounter European
newcomers in the Atlantic area.

frequently came into contact were Algonkians, whether Mi'kmaq of the Maritimes
or Naskapi and Montagnais (Innu) along the north shore of the river. The second
major change was found in the Europeans who came, rather than the people who
met them. French efforts in the seventeenth century differed from those of the previous century in that they placed a greater emphasis on evangelism.

If the sixteenth century had been the century of religious wars in Europe, and
if the eighteenth would be the century of the Enlightenment, then the seventeenth
was the century of faith. In the case of France's Most Christian Majesty, there was a
greater emphasis on spreading the Christian Word, and the Crown's support of exploratory voyages to North America was now conditional on the willingness of the
ships' captains to carry missionaries. Since France was still an absolute monarchy,
the Church was in no way exalted above the station and prestige of the monarch.
On the contrary, in any battles with the Crown's representatives, the agents of the
Church would invariably lose. But France and its royal head nonetheless supported
and promoted missionary efforts as part of the outreach program France was beginning to North America.

The addition of faith to the other motives – fish, fur, and exploration – did not
change the nature of the relationship between Europeans and Indigenous peoples.

This Jesuit map of Huronia and its surrounding lands was partially
based on knowledge provided by Native informants.

Nor did it alter the pattern of contact to any great extent. If the French in the seventeenth century had begun to concentrate their efforts on the Maritime area they called Acadia and on the St. Lawrence region, for which they would adopt the First Nation name Canada, other nations maintained the kinds of contact they had earlier. The English sailed each year to the Grand Banks off Newfoundland and Acadia, and their government's prohibition on settlement in this part of the New World meant that they encountered the local population only intermittently as they sought supplies or a place to dry their fish. The Spaniards and the Basques similarly continued their practice of regular, brief voyages to the Strait of Belle Isle, the Gulf of St. Lawrence, and portions of the river estuary, such as the Saguenay near Tadoussac, where the whales gathered. In other words, the seventeenth-century pattern of European contact ensured that it would be the French who most regularly and most persistently encountered the Indigenous populations.

The reasons the French had for coming ensured that their attitude towards the First Nations would not change fundamentally in the seventeenth century, whether they were exploring and settling in the Bay of Fundy area or pushing their way up the St. Lawrence. The French who came for fish, fur, faith, or more knowledge of the geography and topography of this strange new land soon discovered that they needed the people they met there. Even in the fisheries off the east coast, and even for those fishing boats that practised the green fishery, a minimal level of tolerance towards them by the Native population was an essential precondition of their success. Should the newcomers irritate and offend the much more numerous First Nations, they would soon encounter both maritime and land-based assaults that would make catching and processing the cod impossible. Since the Indigenous peoples possessed canoes, they were capable of depredations on isolated vessels. And for those, such as the English, who had to land to pursue the dry fishery, the threat of Native hostility was very serious. Even as conditions were in the seventeenth century, the occasional landings caused some annoyance and much curiosity among the local population. From the point of view of visiting fishing crews, the light-fingered Beothuk who helped themselves to some of the things that the visitors left behind were a nuisance. But these irritations only underscored the degree of dependence on First Nation tolerance under which the Europeans laboured.

The same was true of the relationship between the Indigenous peoples and those French, such as Samuel de Champlain, who coasted the Maritimes and sailed up the St. Lawrence in search of a passage through this landmass to Asia. They were dependent on Native informants for knowledge of what lay beyond the next hill or lake, and the fact that the Natives – polite people – tended to respond to their questions with the sort of answers they thought these newcomers wanted to hear meant that much confusion occurred. French explorers and cartographers heard a great deal about a western sea and a Kingdom of the Saguenay, both of which owed more to their own desires and Indigenous politesse than fact. In addition to being dependent on the First Nations for knowledge, the explorers relied on them for safe conduct and for the means to travel in the interior. As was the case with fishing captains, if European navigators alienated the locals they would find themselves completely frustrated in their efforts to do their job. Moreover, explorers soon learned that they required Native canoes – especially the birchbark canoe that could carry a heavy load but was still light enough to portage – to get beyond the rapids at the place they called Lachine. Champlain and those who came after him would also soon learn that they needed other Indigenous tools, such as the contraption they called a toboggan and the gear they put on their feet to travel over snow during the long winters. Those who came to explore and map found themselves even more dependent on the goodwill and assistance of the local populations than did the crews of fishing boats.

But the most dependent of all were those who came for fur and faith. First Nations would not have allowed European fur traders to come in large numbers to take the furs and process them themselves. In any event, conducting the fur trade principally with European labour would have proved so prohibitively expensive that the commerce would quickly have been abandoned. It made much more sense, to both the Native harvesters of fur and the foreign purchasers of pelts, to practise a division of labour in the fur trade. The First Nations collected the furs in large quantities and brought them to the Europeans. The Europeans, for the most part, purchased furs gathered by others and transported them to overseas markets. This division of labour made the commerce in fur symbiotic: each party to the exchange of pelts needed the other.

This mutual dependence particularly characterized the branch of the fur trade that was to dominate in the seventeenth and eighteenth centuries: the trade in beaver fur. The fickle winds of fashion and the physiology of the *castor canadensis* combined to ensure that First Nations and Europeans were bound by ties of self-interest. In Europe in the seventeenth century, the broad-brimmed, shiny hat made of felted fur was all the rage. Since the Baltic supplies of suitable fur had been largely exhausted, it made perfect sense to seek a replacement in North America. Certain characteristics of the fur of the beaver ensured that it would become the fur of choice for felters and hatters. Beaver fur consisted of two types of hairs or filaments. One was a soft, downy hair that had tiny hooks or barbs at the tips. This construction meant that the soft, shorter hair of the beaver's pelt made an ideal felt – smooth, shiny, flat – for hatters. Barbed filaments linked and locked, producing a

The artist's ignorance of the beaver and its behaviour demonstrated
why Europeans needed Native cooperation in the fur trade.

felt that stayed flat and thin. The other type of hair in the beaver's pelt were longer, coarse guard hairs. They ensured that there was an essential role for the Native North Americans to play not only in catching the beaver and taking its pelt but also in giving it its preliminary processing. The best beaver pelt for felting purposes was one from which the guard hairs had been removed, leaving the soft, lustrous down. Fortunately, the First Nations removed the guard hairs before trading the pelt. They "processed" the beaver fur simply by wearing it next to their skin in garments consisting of several pelts sewn together with leather thongs. After a year's wear as a garment, it ceased be a simple beaver pelt; it became *castor gras*, or greasy beaver. The skin was soft and supple, and the guard hairs had been removed by abrasion, sweat, smoke, and heat.

But the French fur traders did not refer to the most highly prized beaver fur simply as *castor gras*; the fur that they wanted above all others was what they called *castor gras d'hiver* (greasy *winter* beaver). The best pelt was the one taken in the winter, when the down, the beaver's natural insulation against the cold, was thickest. But the fur traders hoped to be safely and profitably back home by winter, and they would have had an extremely difficult time taking the prime winter beaver even if they had – lamentably, from their point of view – still been in North America. The beaver spent the winter in remote lakes and streams, under the protection of a lodge it built of branches and mud. The surface of these lodges was extremely hard, and their underwater entrances difficult to detect. The Natives, who for centuries had been catching the beaver for fur and meat, knew how to reach the ponds where lodges were to be found, how to locate the entrances, and how to destroy the structures so as to get at the inhabitants. Consequently, the First Nations were essential to taking the *castor gras d'hiver* in its prime, just as they were to its proper processing. A trade in the beaver pelts that seventeenth-century European furriers craved was simply impossible without the cooperation of the North Americans. Europeans who came in search of prime furs needed the Native population's knowledge, skills, and cooperation.

Obviously, the French who came to harvest souls rather than skins were also dependent upon the people whom they sought to proselytize. In the earliest years of French contact in the seventeenth century, until the late 1620s, it was particularly a branch of the Franciscans known as the Récollets who carried the evangelical burden to Algonkians in Acadia and to both Iroquoians and Algonkians along the St. Lawrence and in the interior. From the 1620s onward, however, they were replaced by the Society of Jesus or Jesuits, one of the most formidable teaching and missionary orders of the Roman Catholic Church. (The Récollets would return to share the mission field in 1670, concentrating on Acadia. Sulpicians moved into the Montreal area in 1657.) Equally important were organizations of female religious: the Ursulines and Hospitallers, both of whom arrived from France in 1639; and the Sisters of the Congregation, a secular association created by Marguerite Bourgeoys in Montreal in 1653. New France was officially closed to Protestants, and although many individual Huguenots came as fur traders and merchants, Protestantism had no official presence in France's colony. Certainly, no Protestant missionaries were allowed in.

Récollets differed from Jesuits in that they believed that Aboriginal people had to be remade into French persons before they could be turned into Christians. These Franciscan priests believed that "none could ever succeed in converting them, unless they made them men before they made them Christians."[12] Consequently,

Mother Marie de l'Incarnation exemplified the evangelical motive
for interaction with the Aboriginal peoples of New France.

the Récollets tried to assimilate the First Nations in order to Christianize them. The Jesuits, who had had considerable cross-cultural experience in Asia, took a less assimilationist approach. It was not that the followers of Loyola considered Aboriginal ways laudable; rather, they thought that these manners were defects capable of correction. Jesuits believed that it was unnecessary for First Nations to adopt European ways in order to come to accept Christ; moreover, there were some Native beliefs that could be incorporated into Christianity, thereby making the new dispensation both more intelligible and attractive to the intended pros- elytes. Prolonged experience in New France persuaded the Jesuits that contact with Europeans often debased the Natives they wished to convert. Eventually, they con- cluded, as a Jesuit historian put it in the 1740s, that "there was no longer any doubt that the best mode of Christianizing them, was to avoid Frenchifying them."[13] Jesuits wanted to convert First Nations; they did not usually consider it necessary to assimilate them as well.

Whatever the missionary order and whatever its approach to proselytizing the North Americans, the evangelists needed cooperation. They were as dependent on the Natives as they were on the French Crown that encouraged their work and the ship captains and fur traders who carried them, often reluctantly, to North America and into areas where Indigenous peoples were to be found. If First Nations refused to tolerate the presence in their canoes of black robes, as they called the Jesuits, the priests would never gain access to the regions where Aboriginal peoples were found in large numbers. And if these declined to trade for food and shelter, then the missionaries could not stay among them even after they reached their villages. If the Indigenous population was hostile, missionaries could quickly find them- selves achieving not their primary objective, conversion, but the second of their priorities, personal martyrdom. And, as the Jesuits quickly discovered, unless First Nation converts cooperated by becoming lay missionaries or catechists, the spread of Christianity throughout their nations would be slow.

The missionaries soon discovered that they could no more realize their North American objectives by themselves than could their fur-trading, exploring, or fishing compatriots. European presence in North America was dependent on Indigenous goodwill and cooperation because the Native was vital to the realiza- tion of all the purposes the Europeans had in coming to the continent. Whether the Europeans came for fish, fur, to seek a passage to Asia, or to find a place in the people's heart for their God, the newcomers were dependent on the Native. It was not merely that First Nations greatly outnumbered the Europeans – though that was also important; it was that the interloper could accomplish nothing without the help of the host society.

But why did First Nations cooperate with the fisher, the fur trader, the explorer, or the black robe? Native motives were many and varied. The fishing boats rarely threatened them or their resources. There was a bountiful supply of fish, and, besides, sharing was an ethical imperative. Moreover, in the Atlantic region the presence of European fishing boats soon led to the development of a trade in furs from which the Indigenous peoples derived benefit. From the First Nation side of this commercial nexus, the advantage in the fur trade was access to European technology. It must have been, as the behaviour of the people whom Cartier encountered in the 1530s illustrated, a strange and wonderful thing to discover that these hairy strangers were eager to get their hands on old furs that the Natives had worn. That these fools would take worthless hides in exchange for wondrous things such as mirrors, glass beads, and items made of iron was amazing.

The only metal that Indigenous North Americans had previously known was copper from the shores of Lake Superior that had been diffused throughout eastern North America by well-established trade routes. But copper, though useful for some decorative and utilitarian purposes, was too soft to be used for those things that mattered most to local people. The other elements that Natives used were bone for pointed items, wood for clubs and clumsy kettles in which liquids were heated by the immersion of a series of heated rocks, and stone as an edge for clubs and some scraping tools. Iron was an ideal substitute for weapons such as arrow heads and spear tips, for tools such as knives for skinning and cutting, and, perhaps above all, for containers. The difference in routine between being able to carry pots with them on trips – rather than adjusting the band's itinerary to reach the large, fixed wooden vessels in which food preparation was often carried out – on must have been monumental.

The Aboriginal reaction to kettles amused the French, who took such vessels as much for granted as Natives did greasy beaver pelts. The Huron thought that among these *gens du fer* ("iron people"), as they took to calling the French, "the greatest captains in France were endowed with the greatest mind, and possessing so great a mind they alone make the most complicated things, such as axes, knives, kettles, etc." Accordingly, they "concluded therefore that the King, being the greatest captain and chief of them all made the largest kettles."[14] An Acadian visitor to Paris was certain that the street "where there were then many coppersmiths" must contain the establishments of "relatives of the King." He asked "if this was not the trade of the grandest Seigniors of the Kingdom."[15] But it was hardly strange that Natives seemed overwhelmed by the iron kettle; little wonder that the proud possessors of them would use and patch these wondrous vessels nearly to the point of destroying them – and then trade them to members of some less fortunate band that did not

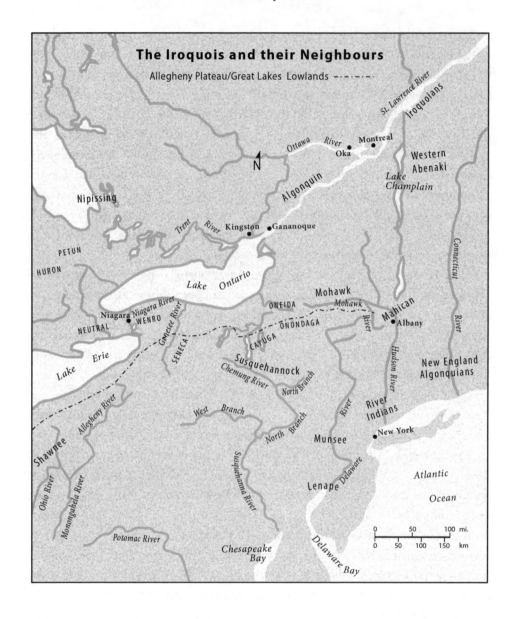

Map of Iroquoia, showing the height of land that separates river drainage system

have direct access to such goods. The chance to obtain iron, brandy, and decorative items constituted an important reason for Aboriginal cooperation in the fur trade.

For some First Nations, the early fur trade offered enormous commercial potential. Iroquoian nations, especially, found that their geographical locations put them into advantageous positions for trading, both with other nations and with the French. Moreover, their possession of such important goods as a portable supply of protein and tobacco made it possible for them to journey far afield to trade, and to have important commodities to exchange once they got there. The greatest profits on the Aboriginal side of the trade were realized not by those who caught and processed the furs, but by those who gathered the pelts from other Natives by commerce or war and then traded them to the newcomers. Whether the pre-contact commerce in food, copper, and other goods had conditioned the Huron and others, or whether they responded rapidly to the creation of market conditions, there is no doubt that the First Nations reacted quickly and shrewdly to the opportunities that the fur trade created. The development of middleman or intermediary strategies by such groups as the Huron, and the emergence of the practice of refusing to trade with the first vessels of the season, were immediate adjustments to the economic opportunities created by the European presence. First Nations of the lower St. Lawrence and Acadia understood that two or more ships full of traders at anchor meant higher prices for furs than one shipload of would-be purchasers. Indigenous people were as swift to exploit their advantages as any European.

And there could be no doubt about who was the dominant partner in this early phase of the commercial relationship. The Native peoples dictated that the trade should follow forms that had existed among them for centuries. For example, trade did not begin immediately after an encounter; exchange was preceded by speech-making and gift-giving. As early as 1603, Champlain was initiated into this practice when Anadabijou, the local Montagnais leader near Tadousssac, provided food, smoked the pipe with the strangers, and made a speech that culminated in his observation to his colleagues that "in truth they ought to be very glad to have His Majesty for their great friend." His fellow Montagnais exclaimed "*Ho, ho, ho,* which is to say, yes, yes."[16] It would take newcomers some time to appreciate that participating in such ceremonies was the First Nations' way of making them kin with whom they could associate and trade safely. Newcomers joining in Native ceremonies and becoming fictive or ascribed kinfolk of their hosts was but one feature of the new relationship that indicated that First Nations were the dominant partners.

In some cases, trade ostensibly took the form of an exchange of presents, a fiction that conformed to First Nation usages and ethical imperatives much more than European proclivities towards market behaviour. Particularly well-situated groups, such as the Algonkin of Allumette Island in the Ottawa River, used their position and power to exact tolls from canoe brigades, including those of traders, who passed through their territory. The mastery they exercised was demonstrated graphically by their leader Le Borgne in 1650. Offended by the efforts of a group of Huron under Jesuit leadership to evade his toll collection, Le Borgne had the priest "suspended from a tree by the arm-pits." He told "him that the French were not the masters of his country; and that in it he alone was acknowledged as chief."[17] The clearest evidence of where the power truly resided in the early commercial relationship was found in the communications between Europeans and Indigenous people, especially French fur traders and the Wendat. The affluent and proud Huron refused to lower themselves to learn the newcomers' language. If the French wanted to trade, they could speak the First Nation language. They did.

The Indigenous peoples also used the valuable trade goods they derived from the fur trade in a network of exchanges among themselves. Though their ethical systems emphasized sharing, such values did not extend to giving away valuable goods to people from other nations. Iroquois or Montagnais traders were perfectly capable of exploiting their monopoly of European goods by exacting high prices for kettles or knives when they passed them on to less favoured nations in the interior. It was common to use kettles until they were almost worn through before trading them. In these transactions, as in the various techniques they used to monopolize the trade and exact the best terms for themselves, the Natives demonstrated shrewd commercial instincts as well as the fact that they controlled the trade. If they participated in commerce, it was because they benefited substantially from it.

To a considerable extent, the Indigenous peoples' desire to maintain the commercial link to the French explains both their cooperation with explorers and their toleration of missionaries. First Nations recognized quickly that the former posed a threat to their commercial well-being, but they had to accommodate the cartographers to maintain friendship with their compatriots. The missionaries posed a less obvious, longer-term threat to their spiritual health and their cultural identity; the First Nations were less successful in developing strategies to counter this menace. From the earliest times, Natives had to balance their wish to retain access to European goods against their desire not to allow the Europeans contact with their trading partners. The St. Lawrence Iroquoians had tried to discourage Cartier's penetration of the upper St. Lawrence, first to Hochelaga and later beyond present-day Montreal. Similarly, in the seventeenth century, Champlain and others frequently found their desire to be escorted into the interior, so that they could explore and map the water routes, frustrated by Natives' unwillingness to take the white men into these regions. But even those local people who were reluctant to jeopardize their control of the interior trade by allowing Europeans direct access usually had to give in. Accordingly, Champlain was accompanied into Huronia in 1616, and many after him were guided to the northern interior as well. The First Nations' concern not to undermine the trading partnership usually persuaded them to accommodate the Europeans.

But the commercial nexus did not operate only to the advantage of the Europeans; the desire for good relations with First Nations could lead the explorers to accommodate Indigenous wishes as well. A clear, early example of the way in which the desire to maintain good relations with the Natives induced the newcomers to take actions they might otherwise have avoided was Champlain's participation in 1609 in an Algonkian raiding party into the territories of the Iroquois, in which firearms were employed deliberately for the first time against surprised Native forces. As Cartier's penetration of the River of Canada and Champlain's use of muskets on the shores of the lake that was to bear his name showed, the cooperation of Europeans and Indigenous peoples in a commercial relationship facilitated other activities.

If it is obvious why First Nations helped the Europeans to fish, trade in furs, and explore, why did they tolerate the fourth of the newcomers' activities? Why did the Huron in the 1630s and 1640s allow Jesuits to reside in Huronia and to proselytize? The key to understanding the reluctant agreement to play host to missionaries, whether in Huronia or among the migratory Algonkian bands, was the First Nation conception of the commercial alliance. In trade between peoples of different villages and nations, there were well-established ground rules. One was that the family or band that initiated exchange with an outside group enjoyed a monopoly of access to that group. Such behaviour was continued in trade with the French: families who traded first with the Europeans controlled the right to trade with them.

A second feature of Indigenous commerce was an exchange of personnel.[18] When different bands or nations traded regularly, they often exchanged members of their communities. These hostages to commerce, usually sons of families active in the trade, resided in the village of the trading partner. So, too, it would appear, did the Huron regard the young French fur traders, such as Etienne Brulé, and the missionaries. It was logical enough for the Natives to assume that Europeans practised this form of exchange, too. Did the intruders not persuade them to allow a few of their young men, and occasionally even a chief, to return with them across the water, promising that their people would come back with the big ships the following year? Missionaries were simply another form of hostage to the trade. The French, under

Champlain's encounter with the Iroquois in 1609 represented the integration
of the European and his firearms into North American rivalries.

pressure from the government in France, wanted the Huron to accept missionaries
among them. To maintain the commercial alliance, and assuming that the arrival of
missionaries represented a continuation of the tradition of exchanging personnel,
the First Nations accepted the strange black robes among them.

For their part, the missionaries but dimly perceived how the First Nations regarded them. The Jesuits knew they were dependent on the fur trade in the sense
that without the trade and without commercial voyages from the interior to the
St. Lawrence, the means for them to minister to the inland nations would not exist.
But the priests rarely comprehended that they were dependent on the trade in an
even more fundamental sense: without commerce, their hosts would have spurned
their presence.

In short, when contact resumed in the seventeenth century, it was principally the
French who came to northern North America, and they came for four reasons.
From the time of Champlain's voyages till the dawn of the eighteenth century, the
French came for fish, for fur, for exploration, and for evangelization. The First
Nations were indispensable partners – frequently a dominant as well as neces-
sary partner – in all these activities. For the newcomers to preserve fish, to gather
fur, to probe and map the land, and to spread the Christian message, Aboriginal

cooperation was essential. For their part, the Indigenous peoples found it acceptable, and occasionally desirable, to humour the newcomers. To a minor degree,
the explanation could be found in Native traditions of sharing and avoiding the
coercion of others. Also significant from their point of view was the fact that the
Europeans accommodated them concerning language, ceremonies, and kinship
practices. A more important reason for their toleration of and cooperation with the
French was that the newcomers' activities were compatible with the continuation of
local ways. Fishing boats were no threat, given the rich stocks of fish and the brief
landfalls by fishers. Fur traders were a source of valued goods, and their activities did not require much change in Indigenous economic activities. Explorers and
cartographers were less obviously useful, and might have posed a long-term threat
if they expanded the French acquaintance with First Nations that were dependent
on intermediaries such as the Montagnais or Huron. But cooperation with them
was necessary to maintain the commercial relationship. The same consideration
explained the grudging acceptance of missionaries in Native villages.

In the seventeenth century, the Europeans came to North America in pursuit
of goals that could not be reached without First Nation cooperation. The North
Americans found good, practical reasons for cooperating with the newcomers. In
short, the relationship in these early decades was one of mutual benefit. Certainly it
posed no threat to the Indigenous peoples, who were more numerous, more at home
in the North American environment, and capable at any moment of repelling the
few thousand French who initially came to their shores. Accordingly, First Nation–
European relations in this initial period were not only mutually beneficial but also
harmonious. European motives and Native interests were largely compatible.

CHAPTER THREE

Commercial Partnership and Mutual Benefit

Harmonious relations did not mean that there were no problems, much less change. For both First Nations and Europeans, constant interaction in the fur trade and in missionary settings brought rewards and problems, advantages and setbacks. For Europeans, there were more of the former than the latter: they prospered, acquired new tools and techniques, and were influenced positively by Indigenous customs. But for First Nations, association with the European was a mixed blessing. Undoubtedly the new technology based on iron greatly improved everyday life and hunting, but it also made warfare more destructive. French brandy also was a popular means of recreation, but it wreaked a fearful havoc at times. More serious still were the scourges of disease and religion. One killed the bodies of thousands of Indigenous peoples; the other eroded the belief systems that were both a reflection and a support of their relationship with the cosmos and each other. If the seventeenth-century relationship was initially mutually beneficial, it was also influential. Moreover, the advantages of commercial interaction probably lessened for Native traders as time wore on.

On the European side, the most obvious consequences of their contact with the Indigenous population were profit and expansion. Down to the late decades of the seventeenth century, the fur trade was sufficiently profitable to bring a succession of French companies to New France. Another manifestation of the success of the trade was the competition that it brought. If the French formed trading links with Algonkians such as the Montagnais and with Iroquoians such as the Huron, rivals from Holland and later England set up offsetting partnerships with the Five

Nations of the Iroquois. Each European power developed a trading network based both on the geography of the continent and the First Nations with whom geography brought them most readily into contact. For the French, this meant a close association with the Mi'kmaq of the Maritime region, with the Algonkian along the St. Lawrence, and with the agricultural Huron of the interior who were accessible by way of the St. Lawrence drainage system. The topography of North America drew the French in by the St. Lawrence, up the Ottawa River, across Lake Nipissing, and through the French River to Lake Huron and, finally, Georgian Bay. This natural line of water approach largely determined the groups with whom the French would cooperate.

Similarly, for the Dutch and English traders who entered North America by way of the river that Henry Hudson named, a different path of approach and a different set of alliances and partnerships were developed. For fur traders and explorers in these more southerly areas, penetration of the continent was achieved by ascent of the Hudson River, and then either transfer into the Mohawk River, which would take travellers eventually to the lower Great Lakes, or overland travel to Lake Champlain and to the Richelieu River, which emptied into the St. Lawrence above Donnacona's village. Fairly quickly, a rival fur-trade network of Iroquois and Dutch or English developed, with strategic centres at Fort Orange (Albany) and New Amsterdam (New York). The Iroquois, especially the Mohawk whose easternmost position drew them into earliest and most frequent contact with the newcomers, were as essential to the European traders south of New France as the Montagnais and Huron were to the French. Between the rival networks that developed along their respective drainage systems, a fierce and unremitting competition for mastery of the trade grew.

This competition had both benign and malignant consequences. Among the positive effects of the struggle for furs was the compulsion to push ever farther inland in search of newer sources of pelts, better furs, and unspoiled trading partners. It was the goad of the fur trade and the profit motive that drove French traders and military officers to probe the lower Great Lakes, the Ohio and Mississippi Rivers, and the network of rivers in present-day northern Quebec and Ontario. In the process of pursuing furs, they also induced the Maritime First Nations to exhaust the fur resources of their region. Before the seventeenth century was over, the Mi'kmaq found their role as fur traders destroyed by the efficiency with which they and other nations had trapped the beaver. By the end of the century, the fur resources of the interior were by no means exhausted, but much of the European's ignorance of the interior lands had dissipated. Thanks to fur-trade exploration, most of the principal arteries of the eastern half of North America had been tested and the results recorded; and the restless European was beginning to cast wondering eyes westward in search of the vast body of water the Natives had described and they, with hope, had named *la mer de l'Ouest* (the western sea). Without the fur trade there would have been no stimulus of competition to search out new fur lands, and without the profits to underwrite the voyages there would have been no means to carry out the search. Most important of all, without the Indigenous peoples, the canoe, maize, and other products of Native society, none of the great exploratory trips would have got much farther than Lachine. What Iroquois scholar Arthur Parker observed of the Thirteen Colonies' debt to North American corn is applicable to Canada as well: the "Maize plant ... was the bridge over which English civilization crept, tremblingly and uncertainly, at first, then boldly and surely to a foothold and a permanent occupation of America."[1]

Other effects of the seventeenth-century relationship on the Europeans were harder to measure than the length of a trip to the mouth of the Mississippi. The need to support the fur trade and the missionary effort induced the French Crown to end the administration of New France by a succession of commercial monopolies and to establish it as a Crown colony in 1663.[2] The desire to promote the missionary drive contributed to the decision to found the religious settlement of Ville Marie near the confluence of the Ottawa and St. Lawrence Rivers in 1642. As Montreal, it was to develop as a thoroughly secular fur-trade centre, largely supplanting Trois-Rivières in that role. And the need to overawe, if not conquer, the Iroquois who were doing so much damage to Montreal and the fur trade in the 1640s and 1650s induced France to send several regiments of troops. But none of these initiatives fundamentally changed the nature of the French presence in Acadia and Canada or greatly swelled the population. And what areas of French settlement there were occurred in regions that the First Nations used only in transit.[3] There were but a few thousand permanent residents in the French settlements in the St. Lawrence Valley when royal rule and the Carignan-Salières Regiment arrived in the 1660s, and agriculture and manufacturing were still minor adjuncts to commerce. Throughout the seventeenth century, New France remained in essence a commercial colony rather than an expanding agricultural settlement. As such, it was not a major threat to the Native population with which it traded, for fur traders did not cut down trees or drive off game. The European presence, and hence the impact of Europeans on North America and its Indigenous population, remained small-scale, commercial, and compatible with the customs and economic activities of the continent.

Even harder to gauge than expansion through exploration and the establishment of small commercial and administrative centres were the effects that contact with the local population had on the Europeans' manners, customs, attitudes, and mores. Some physical signs of the transfer of Indigenous values and practices to the Europeans were unmistakable. The French women's adoption of the short skirt that Native women wore was one that scandalized many a clerical visitor from France. Similarly, the use of the canoe in summer and the toboggan and snow shoes in winter demonstrated that the European was as capable of adopting usable technology as the Native woman who now cooked in an iron kettle. Colonial French began to borrow words from First Nations' languages. To *Canadiens*, a black bass was *achigan*, one of many "creative borrowings" from local languages, and a cranberry *atoca* rather than the French *canneberge*.[4] Food was another area of transfer from the Indigenous to the outsider. Corn was merely the most prominent item in a list that included beans and squash as well. Also among the crops that the French bartered for with the Native was one plant that was to have a devastating effect on the European. Tobacco from the area north of Lake Erie was traded throughout eastern North America by the Petun (Tobacco), Huron (Wendat), and other commercial nations. Ontario tobacco made its way to France as Virginia tobacco did to England, in both cases with deadly long-term consequences

But it was perhaps in the area of values and attitudes that the First Nations had their greatest, though least measurable, effect on the Europeans. Particularly among the young men who voyaged into the interior in search of new routes or furs, there was a tendency to emulate Indigenous ways. The Europeans greatly admired the First Nations for their hardihood, their dignity, their skills in coping with the environment, and their sophisticated ways of dealing with one another. A perverse manifestation of this respect, as well as a product of the motive of conspicuous consumption, was the development of a Native slave trade. First Nations people were especially coveted as slaves by French merchants and administrators in the towns, precisely because slaves had almost no economic value in New France. The fact that the colony was not an agricultural settlement that grew large surplus crops for export on plantations requiring a great quantity of labour, as well as the independence and pride of the Indigenous people, ensured that there would be neither need for unfree labour nor available, tractable slaves. The Natives who were enslaved by the tribes with whom the French traded in battles with more distant nations were useful only to demonstrate their owner's affluence and status. These *panis* (apparently a corruption of the name for the Pawnee) were a bizarre product of Indigenous independence and French snobbery, a decorative slave caste with no economic purpose.

It was the independence and other positive characteristics that most affected the European youths who worked in close proximity to First Nations. The young voyageurs struggled to copy the Natives' stoicism in the face of adversity and endurance when confronted with hardship, deprivation, and pain. They also copied,

Sarrazin receives a Pitcher Plant

This depiction of surgeon Michel Sarrazin receiving a pitcher plant from
a Native symbolizes how Europeans benefited from Indigenous knowledge.

to the extent that their employers and governors could not prevent, the autonomy
that North American society inculcated in its young. French males found the liber-
ated sexual attitudes of young Aboriginal women before matrimony as attractive as
the missionaries found them repugnant. Many of the French formed liaisons with
First Nation women, but, since most of the intermarriage and interbreeding took
place in the interior, the results of this miscegenation were largely concentrated in
the interior villages. Over time, the mixed ancestry population was reabsorbed into
Native society. But what was definitely brought back to Montreal and Quebec were
the local people's independent attitudes.

It would not be accurate to attribute all the independence or insolence that French visitors increasingly noticed in the *Canadien* population to the influence of First Nations. Other contributing factors were the scarcity of labour and the abundance of arable land in New France: the demand for workers made ordinary Canadian labourers and artisans affluent, and the availability of land gave what would in Europe have been an impoverished peasantry the opportunity to reach the same heights. Also, the fact that the young Canadian male always had the alternative of escaping to the *pays d'en haut* (the fur-trading country in the interior) gave him an option his more constricted European counterpart did not enjoy. If a *Canadien* exercised the frontier option, he would come under the influence and example of the Natives. It is not surprising, then, that by the end of the seventeenth century Canadians were developing their own ways, not always to the satisfaction of French authorities, who persisted in thinking of themselves as the betters of these colonials. Land, affluence, the open fur-trade frontier, and the First Nation role model all contributed to the emergence of a distinctive Canadian. Neither French peasants nor North American braves, they were a bit of both. They called themselves *habitants*, and many of their habits were those of the Natives they admired. Over the decades, these people were becoming, thanks in part to the First Nations, *Canadiens*.

First Nations did not reciprocate French admiration. On the whole, though the Natives respected European technology and were prepared to associate themselves with those who produced it, they were unimpressed by Europeans. The ambivalence of many First Nations people towards the newcomers was expressed by the grandmother of convert Pierre Pastedechouan, who described Natives' reaction to the appearance of a French ship: "They thought it was a moving Island," and "their astonishment was redoubled in seeing a number of men on deck." But when the Frenchmen in their armour gave them ship's biscuit and introduced them to wine, they were appalled. They dismissed the intruders as people who "drank blood and ate wood, thus naming the wine and the biscuits."[5] Aboriginal appreciation of the French did not necessarily improve over the decades. They considered many white men ugly, and their impression of Europeans' physiological features was not at all aided by the fact that many of them considered facial hair a sign of stupidity.[6] After all, if things were as wonderful in France as these visitors claimed, why did they subject themselves to the hardships of a journey to North America? As a Mi'kmaq put it, "For if France, as thou sayest, is a little terrestrial paradise, art thou sensible to leave it? And why abandon wives, children, relatives, and friends? Why risk thy life and thy property every year, and why venture thyself with such risk, in any season whatsoever, to the storms and tempests of the sea in order to come to a strange and barbarous country which thou considerest the poorest and least fortunate of the world?"[7] The newcomers had big canoes and weapons, but they could not mend their own kettles, let alone survive in the North American environment unaided. They did not know even elementary things about how to greet people and parley before engaging in commerce. And these strangers had a distressing and repugnant tendency to behave selfishly. In First Nation societies, people who carried on as the hairy interlopers did would be labelled witches and put to death.

To some degree, the increasing reliance of Indigenous people on the trade goods they gained through the fur trade could have led to dependence and ensuing problems. There is scattered evidence that some bands relied on European goods so thoroughly and for so long that they lost the ability to make similar items of bone, wood, or stone that they had used before the Europeans came. The Jesuits and some other observers claimed that Natives who traded intensively with the French became dependent on the flow of European goods and experienced hardship when the supply was temporarily interrupted or permanently choked off. But too much should not be made of these kinds of comments. For one thing, Europeans often mistook the passing hardship caused by a temporary pause in supply for real suffering that resulted from a permanent loss of skills.

It is even more important to remember that European observers often failed to distinguish between Indigenous use of trade goods that undermined traditional ways and usages that merely reinforced their old beliefs and values. Europeans often noted the Natives' eagerness to accumulate iron goods and other products of European technology; what they failed to notice was the traditional uses to which these items were put. In European society, accumulation was motivated primarily by the desire to consume and to reinvest; in Aboriginal society, accumulation was but the prelude to consumption and redistribution. So it was with a vast quantity of trade goods that ended up not being used by the Natives who traded for them, or passed on at a profit to other Natives, but interred in elaborate funerary rites such as the periodic Feast of the Dead. As well, many prominent First Nations people desired goods only to give them to their followers, an act that was both their duty and an opportunity to reinforce their status. Such uses of European goods, far from undermining Indigenous values and carrying capitalist notions with them, reinforced traditional values.[8] What mattered about the Natives' participation in commerce and their acquisition of European goods was not that they traded or even that they made profits. What counted was the fact that they did so for traditional reasons. As long as these motivations remained dominant, trade and European goods did not fundamentally remake Indigenous societies.

What did alter North American society were some other things that came along with commerce: disease, alcohol, and Christianity. Although Indigenous people were hardy and knew how to cope with their world, by using clothing adequate to the weather and religious rituals equal to the task of placating the spirits, they had no immunity to many of the diseases that the Europeans unwittingly brought with them. Centuries of exposure to such contagious diseases as measles and small-pox had produced a high degree of immunity in Europeans, but Natives soon fell victims to such diseases in large numbers. Estimates vary widely and precision is impossible, but it seems reasonably clear that those First Nations who came into frequent contact with the newcomers suffered dreadful losses. The Huron who har-boured Jesuit missionaries and French traders probably lost half of their popula-tion to measles between 1634 and 1640.[9] Since the new diseases tended to strike disproportionately at the old and the very young, these sudden losses meant that the Huron were deprived in great numbers of both the preservers of their tradi-tions and their future soldiers. And it is quite likely that half or more of the 200,000 to 300,000 Aboriginal inhabitants of Canada in the early decades of contact were removed by disease over the ensuing three hundred years.[10] Canadian history lacks the instances of germ warfare that disfigure the history of the Thirteen Colonies and the United States, but disease nonetheless wreaked havoc among the First Nations of the future Canada.

Though one might expect that the disease of alcoholism was a major threat, such was not the case, even though alcohol was a social problem. There can be no doubt, given the horrified accounts of officials and missionaries, that alcohol often had devastating effects upon Aboriginal people. The descriptions of the scenes that un-folded at the Montreal fur fair each year when the canoe brigades arrived leave little doubt that consumption of brandy led to acts of violence against their own families and others, particularly those from other nations. There was a note of desperation in the response of a Native leader to "some worthy Frenchmen" who criticized his people's drinking: "It is you who have taught us to drink this liquor; and now we cannot do without it."[11]

But several aspects of these oft-observed problems need to be taken into account so as not to gain a distorted appreciation of the alcohol problems among the vast majority of Aboriginal people. In the first place, those Natives who drank to excess after trading their furs in Montreal might not have touched brandy since their last visit to the fur-trade emporium. Alcohol was a bulky, heavy product to transport by canoe and over portages the 1,000 kilometres to Huronia, not to mention the great-er distances to the more northerly fur-bearing areas south of James Bay. The French Crown and Catholic missionaries discouraged the use of brandy as a trade item, although competition from the English in the south and the Englishmen's apparent willingness to use the vast supplies of cheap rum they possessed for trade often meant that gubernatorial and clerical prohibitions were ignored. Still, the quantity of brandy reaching the more distant nations could not have been very great during most of the seventeenth century. Finally, in interpreting the significance of the use of alcohol, it is important to consider the motives the First Nations had in using it and the manner in which they employed it. To many, the intoxication that could be derived from ardent spirits was merely an aid in the vision quest, a religious obligation. And Native people tended not to drink, whether in moderate or excessive amounts, regularly and persistently; they inclined more to the "binge" style of consumption. While such habits were conducive neither to the imbibers' health nor the tranquillity of their neighbours, these ways of handling alcohol did not of themselves lead to alcoholism.

In fact, the role of alcohol in the erosion of Aboriginal societies in this early period of contact is one fraught with confusion and contradiction. Some observers argue that alcohol brought on social disintegration and psychological collapse. Others contend that alcohol was the symptom rather than the cause of these social and personal debilities. Their argument is that the abuse of alcohol was motivated by a desire to escape the frustrations of a society already experiencing collapse, an implosion of values and social glues.[12] In some accounts, the excessive use of alcohol is a subconscious act of rebellion: the "Indian" is an adolescent; the bottle is rock music; consumption is protest.[13] Whether First Nations became demoralized because they drank too much, or whether they drank too much because they had been demoralized by other influences can never be known for sure. What is beyond doubt is that alcohol, whether cause or effect, was associated with demoralization.

Almost as imponderable is the therapeutic use that Aboriginal people may have made of alcohol. Indigenous societies were, perforce, close-knit and intense. Peoples living and working together found themselves in steady, intimate, and perhaps stressful relations. The need for occasional release from these pressures would have been great. There is some evidence to suggest that Native people sometimes used alcohol for such purposes, or, if they did so and transgressed, excused themselves by blaming their misbehaviour on the alcohol. The Jesuit Le Jeune reported that a Montagnais rebuffed an accusation from a French official that he was responsible for killing an Iroquois prisoner and thereby spoiling chances of making peace by saying, "It is thou ... and thine, who killed him; for, if thou hadst not given us brandy or wine, we would not have done it."[14] Alcohol served as a licence to permit, and an excuse to expiate, actions against people that in a normal, sober state would be unacceptable. Its consumption also permitted blunt talk, as in the case of the leader who responded to the criticisms of "worthy Frenchmen" with a plea of dependence. This man added, "If you refuse to give it to us we will apply to the English," turning an apparent whine into a threat.[15] In other words, alcohol could serve as a social lubricant in close-knit Indigenous communities.

The impact of the introduction of European firearms was equally difficult to determine. Again, as with alcohol, the French made greater efforts than did the English to restrict the distribution of muskets, trying as far as possible not to trade them with any but converted Natives. But even if this policy was ever effectively and consistently followed, it had to be abandoned as competition from the English, who traded weapons freely, drove the French to make muskets, powder, and ball available to their commercial partners, too. These weapons had an important impact on Aboriginal warfare and on the Natives' ability to kill animals and fowl. Prior to the intervention of the European there certainly had been war, but it had been small-scale, localized, and not very destructive. The introduction of firearms changed this pattern by making warfare more devastating. Now an opponent or rival could be killed more easily than would have been the case had it been necessary to stalk him and strike with arrow, club, or bone-tipped spear. However, given the unreliability and inaccuracy of the musket of this era, care must be taken not to overestimate how much damage could be done with the new weapon. According to one authority, "Excepting possible psychological or ceremonial utility, it is unlikely that European firearms conferred any advantage whatsoever on Aboriginal people. In fact, the bow was a superior weapon. Until the development of breech-loading, and later, repeating rifles, during the nineteenth century, the gun offered no practical advantage over Native weapons."[16]

Similarly, the musket made depredations on the animals more effective, just as extensive commerce created new incentives to kill more animals in search of furs to trade. What is obvious about this change is that Natives with muskets had greater capability to kill much larger numbers of birds and animals more easily. What seems almost as obvious is that they employed the new technology to harvest more furs, a response to the incentive of the new commerce. What is not as clear is the effect of these changes on First Nations' relationship to the natural world. Did the introduction of commercial motivations and large-scale harvesting dilute or destroy the Indigenous peoples' perceptions of the animals they killed as fellow sojourners on earth? Did the fact that they were now, apparently, taking many more animals, and taking them for commercial reasons rather than subsistence, destroy the place of mammals, rodents, and fowl in First Nations' mental map of the cosmos? The evidence on the point is neither clear nor unequivocal, but it is difficult to imagine how such large changes in Aboriginal treatment of the creatures of the

natural world could not have led to alterations of their interpretation of animals'
role in the universe.

As the interpretive puzzles surrounding alcohol and First Nations' relations to animals hint, one of the areas of greatest potential influence was religion. The First
Nations of North America were not religious ignoramuses, not spiritual blank
sheets of paper on which missionaries wrote their Word. Theirs was an animistic
religion: they believed that creation was inhabited by spirits that had to be treated
according to rituals passed from generation to generation. Human beings had no
distinctive or elevated role in the world. The relationship of Aboriginal people to
the spirits and to the Great Spirit was no different from that of the beaver or the
stream or the trees. Closely associated with such beliefs was a system of ethics that
espoused communalism, consensual practices, and a high degree of tolerance. All
such tenets of Indigenous religion would come under systematic attack.

Missionaries differed among themselves, as did French people in general. There
were those in both the mercantile and clerical communities in New France who
regarded First Nations as *ni foi, ni roi, ni loi* – as people without religion, without a
political system, and without the restraint of a code of law.[17] There were others who
appreciated, especially after prolonged exposure to Aboriginal communities, that
the Indigenous population had religious beliefs and their own codes of conduct and
political decision-making. The problem was, so far as these observers were concerned, that their beliefs were those of the devil and their legal and political codes
wrong-headed. Whether First Nations held wrong beliefs or no beliefs, they should
be exposed to correct beliefs and converted.

The impact of the missionary thrust in New France was significant. In both
Acadia and in the interior of the continent, Catholic missionaries worked as-
siduously under trying circumstances to spread their message. Their first success
came in 1610 when the Mi'kmaq chief Membertou and twenty of his family were
converted. This was the beginning of the extensive, enduring conversion of the
Mi'kmaq. Throughout New France, missionaries faced a language barrier that could
be surmounted only if they learned the First Nation language. In the case of the
migratory Algonkian, this was very difficult, as was ministering to them generally.
Missionaries who wanted to preach the gospel to them had to travel and live with
them. Those who did so in Acadia or far north of the River of Canada found their
desire for martyrdom largely met by the living hell they experienced. The hardships
of travel, the privations of hunger, and the inconveniences of living in close proximity with people whose customs differed greatly from those of the European were
all trials for the missionaries.

Things were little better for those Jesuits who resided with sedentary Iroquoians such as the Huron to learn the language and propagate Christianity. While living in a Huron longhouse was not as difficult as living with a small band of migratory Algonkian, it was not easy either. Even after the Jesuits secured permission to establish separate dwellings in Huron villages, the black robes found their life a trial. Hostile Natives ridiculed them and embarrassed them by teaching the priests obscenities while supposedly introducing them to the Huron vocabulary. Youngsters frequently bothered them, and the sociable Natives thought nothing of entering their dwellings at any hour of the day. The fact that they indulged their children much more than Europeans did simply made the pestering of the children all the more difficult to end. For their part, the First Nations were aghast at the firm discipline Europeans exercised on their children, to the point that they called French mothers "porcupines" because of their apparent lack of tenderness.[18] Many would-be converts drew back when they learned that conversion meant that they would spend the afterlife apart from their kin. Converts could not participate in rituals such as the Feast of the Dead; they became outcasts in their own villages.

The chief obstacle to the black robes, however, was not hardship or boisterous children; it was their professional rival, the shaman. Priest and shaman quickly sized each other up for the competitors that they were. These tribal curers and invokers of the spirit world sought at every turn to undermine the authority of the European preachers. The latter quickly learned to turn their knowledge against the shaman in the battle for followers. What medical training they had came in handy in curing the sick, effecting cures where shamanistic rituals and prayers had proven unavailing. When the priest succeeded in curing someone who had not been helped by the shaman's incantations against the evil spirit causing the malady, the efficacy of the missionary's spirit or *manito* rose in the estimation of the Natives. If the missionary could predict accurately an eclipse of the sun, as the Jesuits in Huronia did on one occasion, the Aboriginal people would be impressed. And if the black robes prayed for rain for the crops before a shower, again their prestige rose and the power of the spirits they invoked became more obvious to the First Nations people.

The effects of the religious relations, as well as several other dimensions of the seventeenth-century relationship between Indigenous peoples and French newcomers, can be seen in microcosm in the history of the Jesuit missions in Huronia in the 1630s and 1640s.[19] This formidable effort was by no means the only evangelical project the Europeans undertook. Priests worked steadily in Acadia and in the north of the interior, and both priests and female religious also carried out educational and medical efforts in Quebec. The Jesuits even experimented with a boarding school for youths, but gave it up when they saw the boys' unhappiness.

The creation of hospitals and the provision of medical care, however, were successful and permanent missionary efforts carried on by both priests and nuns in the settlements. But the experiment in Huronia was instructive about the First Nation–European relationship.

In Huronia, the Jesuits had to combat hostility, indifference, and hardship. They were tolerated at first only because they were essential to the fur trade. Their peculiar habits, such as an apparent aversion to women and their obsession with privacy, made them suspect in the eyes of many Huron. When disease began to ravage the Huron villages, the Jesuits responded by baptizing as many as possible in the hope of ensuring their place in heaven. Native people quickly noted that those on whom the Jesuits sprinkled water and over whom they said incantations all too frequently died. The Jesuits were widely suspected of practising witchcraft against the Huron, and they might well have been murdered had their Huron hosts not feared that violence against them would destroy the commercial connection.

In the 1640s, the fortunes of the Huron declined while those of the evangelists were in the ascendant. The ravages of disease were now exacerbated by a series of raids on Huronia by the Iroquois from south of Lake Ontario, who sought, apparently, to disperse the Huron as they had the Mahican earlier in order to gain unchallenged access to hunting and fur-bearing territories. (The word "apparently" is used advisedly, because the most recent research on Iroquois external policy rejects a long-standing interpretation of Iroquois motivation as commercial, arguing that in the seventeenth century the Five Nations were stimulated to engage in extensive campaigns by honour, desire for revenge, and the necessity to replace population lost to disease.)[20] The fact that the Iroquois were armed with muskets from Albany made their attacks all the more destructive. Within Huronia there were two quite different responses to the twin scourges. Many Huron accepted conversion to Christianity, or at least apparent conversion. How far these conversions were motivated, subconsciously perhaps, by the fact that converts enjoyed a privileged trading relationship with the French and could barter with the newcomers for firearms is impossible to know. The wave of baptisms divided the Huron Confederacy, just as disease and Iroquois attacks seriously threatened it. Among Huron traditionalists – the unconverted whom the Jesuits termed pagans – it became a moot point whether succumbing to the Iroquois quickly was worse than eventual collapse, as disease and conversion proceeded apace. The presence of convert and traditionalist factions within the villages loosened the cohesive bonds among the Huron. Converts could not join in rituals, would not travel or work on their sabbath, and frequently refused to participate in the sharing practices that were essential to Huron life.

The death of Jesuit Isaac Jogues at the hands of the Iroquois
was an incident in the destruction of Huronia in 1649.

As events transpired, baffled traditionalists found that the question of whether joining the Iroquois was preferable to erosion by disease and Christianity was settled for them by the Iroquois. In 1648 and 1649, the Five Nations conducted extensive campaigns that destroyed the villages of Huronia. Hundreds were killed, several Jesuit priests were martyred, and the advanced and sophisticated civilization that was Huronia was dispersed. Some Huron were absorbed voluntarily or as captives into the Iroquois villages to replace lost soldiers, others fled southwestward to link up with other First Nations, and some eventually located in the French towns in the St. Lawrence Valley for refuge. One Huron refugee described his people's fate poignantly to a Jesuit: "What you seest is only the skeleton of a great people, from which the Iroquois has gnawed off all the flesh, and which he is striving to suck out to the very marrow."[21]

The settlement of the refugee Huron at Ancienne Lorette near Quebec constituted the second Aboriginal reserve in New France. Earlier a group of Algonkians had unsuccessfully tried to develop an agricultural settlement under Jesuit leadership at Sillery. The Sillery settlement was the site of some titanic struggles between Christian missionaries and Native traditionalists, especially over the status and autonomy of the women in the reserve.[22] Later, refugee Abenaki from the Maritime region and Mohawk converts from Iroquoia would form the basis of two more reserves, those on the Chaudière River and Sault St. Louis, or Kahnawake (Caughnawaga), southwest of Montreal. The various reserves were under both the spiritual and material direction of missionaries, and, while the purpose of the priests was to convert the inhabitants to Christianity and agriculture, other aspects of Native culture, such as language, were not attacked. Reserve settlements at Akwesasne (St. Regis), west of Kahnawake on the south shore of the St. Lawrence, and Kanesatake (Oka), on the confluence of the Ottawa and St. Lawrence Rivers that was known as Lake of Two Mountains, rounded out these groupings of what became known as the *les domiciliés*, the *sept feux* (literally, seven fires), or the "praying Indians" or Seven Nations of New France.[23]

The unhappy experiences of such groups as the Huron and Abenaki at newcomers' hands were instructive about the relationships of Europeans and First Nations in seventeenth-century Canada, but care should be taken not to draw too drastic conclusions from the fact that the Huron fate was death or dispersal. Commercial wars were not new; they had not arrived with the Europeans and their trade goods. There was considerable evidence of both trade networks and commercial warfare from the period before European contact. Just as it is essential to avoid concluding that the contact was utterly negative for the Indigenous peoples, it is important to appreciate that the changes that the Europeans brought with them were merely another in a long series of evolutionary phases that First Nations societies – like all human societies – experienced. Pre-contact Indigenous societies were not static but dynamic; they continued to evolve after the white people came. Europeans did not introduce change into Indigenous society; they were merely the latest form of change.[24]

And what sorts of modifications, on both sides of the relationship, did the meeting of Natives and French newcomers in North America produce in the seventeenth century? As has been noted, most of the changes that the Europeans experienced were positive. As a result of interaction, profits from fishing were possible. Thanks to the cooperation of the Aboriginal peoples, there emerged a thriving fur trade that underwrote most of the settlement and development that occurred in New France. Yet it is important not to exaggerate the size of this French presence. As historian William Eccles observed, fur traders were like mariners rather than farmers: they ranged over the territories from which they extracted riches without changing those regions to any great extent.[25] Moreover, the commercial frontier was dependent for its continued success and profitability on not allowing agricultural settlement – which threatened the ecology on which traditional Indigenous economies and ways of life depended – to flourish. A commercial New France was a colony with low population, a colony that bore lightly on the land and its Native inhabitants.

First Nation participation in the vital commerce in fur also extended the French presence and influenced its reshaping into something discernibly Canadian. It was thanks to the fur trade and its Aboriginal participants that French exploration of the interior's networks of waterways was possible. If at the end of the seventeenth century the French commercial empire stretched from the Gaspé to Louisiana and from Tadoussac to the regions south of Lake Superior, it was because First Nations made that expansion possible. They permitted it: they helped by serving as guides, and their distinctive means of transportation and food supplies enabled the French to traverse their commercial hinterland. None of this would have been possible without Aboriginal cooperation. And the close and constant proximity to Native society that this cooperation brought about caused the French, or *Canadiens* as they preferred to be called, to change in attitudes and practices. The European newcomers adopted many elements of Indigenous dress and language, as well as their spirit of independence and aversion to coercion. A large part of the emerging Canadian identity that French officials decried in the eighteenth century had its roots in contact with Native society.

First Nations people changed, too, as a result of contact with the *gens du fer*. They now had access to weapons, household goods, decorative items, and alcohol, all of which they embraced with enthusiasm. In some cases they may have developed a dependence on these goods and allowed their customary techniques and equipment to fall into desuetude. The strengthening of the commercial motive for hunting may have begun to reshape their attitudes towards the creatures of the natural world. Certainly firearms and iron tools made it possible to harvest larger numbers more quickly. And the First Nations were dramatically affected by the diseases that the Europeans unwittingly introduced. In some cases, as in Huronia in the 1630s, the impact of disease was horrendous.

But while the European presence undoubtedly worked changes on Indigenous society as early as the seventeenth century, it did not fundamentally remake it. Even the use of iron goods did not mean the adoption of European attitudes towards those items and their accumulation. The devotion of the new articles to such old practices as funerary rituals is a strong argument against exaggerating the degree of change. Even the notorious alcohol in some cases was used as an aid to conventional Aboriginal religious practices. In the language of the anthropologists, European technology brought about "non-directed change": it was change that affected surface appearances but did not alter underlying attitudes.[26] The most important thing about non-directed cultural change was that it did not disrupt the bases of society or alter its internal relationships.

Why the modifications that took place in this early period were the relatively benign non-directed change is easily explained. The Europeans were too few to force much change, and most of them had no reason to want change in Indigenous society. French cartographers lacked a reason to try to transform Natives into French people. Explorers needed knowledgeable and skilled intermediaries to guide them; they had no reason to get them to alter the very ways that made them successful navigators and guides in the wilderness. Similarly, fur traders wanted to exploit, not alter, existing hunting methods and dress. Finally, the French military presence was one that also lived in "creative symbiosis" with the First Nations,[27] who were valuable allies precisely because of their ability to survive in and fight effectively from the woods. The frontiers of commerce and navigation created no impetus to remodel the Natives, and the newcomers were too few to effect change in any event.

But what of the missionaries? Did they not want to bring about a transformation of Indigenous society? Some, such as the Récollets in the early years, undoubtedly did. Others, such as the much more numerous Jesuits, did not believe that assimilation was a necessary precondition to conversion. But did missionaries not want to change Aboriginal belief systems, and did they not succeed in the many cases of conversion that they recorded with prayerful thanks? Certainly, missionaries hoped to implant Christian beliefs in First Nation minds or souls. And certainly many Natives said that they accepted those beliefs. But what is impossible to determine is how deep conversion went.

The test of shamans' claims to authenticity was whether their dreams were proved valid, whether their cures were effective, and whether their placating of the spirits was efficacious. When subsequent events showed the black robes had predicted or prayed effectively, their credibility as shamans rose along with the stock of their God. When they failed, they often found their new converts lapsing. Many so-called converts simply incorporated the Christian god into their religion alongside the many other spirits. Some were thoroughly converted, no doubt, but many were probably only partial or temporary converts.[28] And, since the missionaries were few in number, they could not have much effect on Aboriginal societies in general. It is important not to exaggerate the long-term impact of the evangelical efforts, just as it is essential to keep perspective on the limited changes that the fishers, traders, administrators, and soldiers wrought. Always, it is important to bear in mind what the Mi'kmaq said: "*Aoti Chabaya* … That is the Indian way of doing it. You can have your way and we will have ours …"

During the seventeenth century, then, French and First Nations interacted along commercial, evangelical, and navigational frontiers. The encounters were mainly beneficial, because the Europeans were few and interactions took place over the astrolabe, across the trading counter, and within the rustic chapel. Some early French leaders, such as Samuel de Champlain, were optimistic about future relations between newcomers and Natives. Speaking to members of a First Nation in 1633, he said that "the French had always loved and defended" the Natives with whom they traded, and promised "our young men will marry your daughters, and we shall be one people."[29] Relations never became that rosy, but in the first, commercial era they were surprisingly good. In the eighteenth century, military cooperation, which had been a minor aspect of the relationship in the seventeenth century, would become much more important. The consequent emergence of the First Nations as ally would profoundly alter Aboriginal-European relations in North America.

CHAPTER FOUR

Military Allies through a Century of Warfare

Of the many aspects of First Nations–European relations, none is more misunderstood than the military. Europeans often claimed that Natives' destructive style of warfare proved that they were inherently barbarous and savage. These condemnations reached a crescendo during the American Revolution, when both American propagandists and British opposition politicians accused the English military of "loosing" First Nations on innocent farmers in the Thirteen Colonies. Aboriginal warriors were said to be gorily addicted to scalping and torturing prisoners. These charges were unfounded. Indigenous warfare was different from European warfare not because it was Native but because it was North American. First Nations had not had the long periods of familiarity with explosives that led to the development of strategies employing artillery, infantry, and naval vessels in complicated schemes of attack, siege, and defence. Nor did Native societies have complex dynastic relationships among them that were, as in the European case, based on both blood and marriage. Finally, First Nations did not have a rigid hierarchical organization and coercive system of decision-making and enforcement that allowed rulers and generals to throw thousands of common people into bloody confrontations. Natives simply did not fight as the Europeans did, with large formations of infantry backed up by artillery in structured clashes that resulted in enormous loss of life.

The North American environment and the nature of First Nations' social and political structures ensured that their approach to warfare would be small-scale, relatively bloodless, and usually of short duration. North American geography led the Natives to concentrate their efforts on what the French called *la petite guerre*, or guerilla warfare. The difficulties of travel and of maintaining supply lines ensured

This Iroquois warrior on the warpath embodied the threat to New France posed by the Iroquois Confederacy before 1701.

that war parties were usually small. They travelled quickly to the target, fell on the enemy, and retired swiftly with their trophies and prisoners. In many cases, warriors were motivated by a desire to prove their manliness as much as anything else, and in these cases, too, small-scale raids satisfied them. Indigenous warfare consisted of ambushes from forest cover, raids on unsuspecting encampments or travelling parties, and brief clashes. To European military officers, such warfare was cowardly and treacherous; to First Nations, it was sensible, suited to their world, and appropriate to their military objectives.

Much of the misunderstanding over Native warfare stemmed not just from First Nations' style of battle but also from the way they treated their captives. (See chapter 1.) Europeans accused Natives of barbarity for their torture and scalping of victims. People from the patriarchal Old World were particularly aghast at the prominent role that women played in torture: "You should have seen these furious women," they said, "howling, yelling, applying fire to the most sensitive and private parts of the body, pricking them with awls, biting them with savage glee, laying open their flesh with knives; in short, doing everything that madness can suggest to a woman. They threw fire upon them, burning coals, hot sand; and when the sufferers cried out, all the others cried still louder, in order that the groans should not be heard, and that no one might be touched with pity."[1] Such practices shocked French and British alike.

The Europeans' revulsion arose from an ethnocentrically inspired misunderstanding.[2] In the first place, many of the captives whom Native parties took in battle were not tortured or killed, but adopted by families of the victorious nation to replace fallen kin.[3] Other captives were enslaved, either used as drudges in the victors' camp or bartered to the French.[4] Those who were tortured were part of a religious ritual that honoured the sun, the patron of war. The purpose of torture was in large part to break the enemy's spirit and reassure the victors that they were braver and hardier than their foes. In the treatment of female prisoners, Natives were much more humane than Europeans. For example, First Nations despised rape of women.[5] When a female Iroquois prisoner who had been handed over to the French was asked if she feared mistreatment, "She replied that she was now of their Nation; that she did not fear they would do her any harm."[6] Her reaction reflected attitudes that had been built up in response to Native treatment of female prisoners. There was none of the brutal rape and collective violence common to victorious European armies.

Europeans who were aghast at Native habits of cannibalism and scalping failed to understand the significance of what was taking place. Eating the flesh of the captive – especially the heart of an enemy who had endured torture with particular stoicism – was a means of absorbing the spirits that accounted for the victim's more laudable qualities. And, as has been pointed out, it was a bit obtuse of Europeans "who believed in transubstantiation and literally eating their Lord in their communion service" to miss the spiritual significance of Native cannibalism.[7] Scalping, like ritual cannibalism, was misunderstood by the Europeans. The taking of trophies had, after all, been a common enough practice among all armies at least since records were kept. First Nations took heads, scalps, individual limbs, or even a quarter of the body as evidence of their victory. Scalps were particularly useful to record the triumph and, later, taunt the comrades of the fallen enemy. Few things were better to wave in front of a captive who was being tortured. Scalps were also conveniently portable and could be carried on future raids, both to reassure the attackers and, if opportunity arose, to rile the attacked. Surely the people of countries who guillotined, hanged, drew and quartered those guilty of hundreds of offences, and put heads on pikes as a warning should have been able to understand the symbolic, cheer-leading, and deterrent purposes of the native North American practices.

In any event, as is well known, it was the Europeans who encouraged and promoted the increased incidence of scalping by offering bounties for enemy scalps. Moreover, the existence of iron knives made scalping – never an easy physical feat – less difficult than it had been. There is even some evidence that European bounties encouraged the adoption of scalping where it was previously unknown. The Mi'kmaq of the Maritimes, for example, apparently did not scalp captives until their French friends taught them to do it.[8] Where scalping had previously existed, it spread thanks in large part to bounties that the English and the French began to pay in the late seventeenth century. Killing and scalping captives became the procedure of choice; taking them back alive to be ransomed by the Europeans was now uneconomic as well as dangerous.

Contrary to much European and Euro-American propaganda, from the earliest clashes between First Nations warriors and newcomers, the Indigenous people fought for their own interests, not those of strangers. In other words, notions that one Aboriginal nation or another took up arms to advance a commercial or strategic aim of the French or British were erroneous. As the Onondaga orator Otreouti (known to the newcomers as La Grande Gueule or Garangula) explained to Onontio (as the Iroquois called the governor of New France) in 1684, "We carried the English into our Lakes, to trade there with the Utawawas and Quatoghies, as the Adirondacks brought the French to our Castles, to carry on a Trade which the English say is theirs. We are born free. We neither depend upon Yonnondio nor Corlaer [governor of New York]." And, lest Onontio miss the point, Otreouti added, "We may go where we please, and carry with us whom we please, and buy and sell what we please."[9] As these forceful words make clear, First Nations pursued their own, not foreign, interests in both trade and war.

First Nations also insisted on using their own traditions and values in conducting diplomacy and war. One example was the use of ceremonies – the pipe, speeches, and gift-giving – to establish and renew the ascribed kinship that underlay their political and commercial partnerships.[10] In the case of the northeastern First Nations, another custom they insisted on was the use of wampum to shape negotiations and embody agreements. Wampum, often in the form of belts, was made of the seashells collected in the Atlantic in particular, strung together into patterns and colours that conveyed important messages. White symbolized peace, dark purple, war. No message was regarded as credible unless it was accompanied by the presentation of a belt of wampum. No record of a peace agreement was more compelling than one embodied in the same type of artefact.[11] One of the striking things about the use of wampum in the Northeast was that both French and British had to learn quickly to employ the belts in order to conduct business with the Indigenous peoples.

Above all, First Nations did not engage in warfare because it was endemic to them; they had no more blood-lust than any other human community. Indigenous warfare was motivated by desires for revenge, for commercial advantage, and to replenish populations lost to disease and battle. From the first French martial encounter, Champlain's participation with Algonkians against Iroquoians, to the protracted wars between French and Iroquois in the late seventeenth century, the underlying motive on the Indigenous side was commerce. The French and the Huron and most northern Algonkians were commercial rivals of the southern Iroquoians and their Dutch and English trading partners at Albany; raids and battles, in part at least, were merely commercial "policy by other means" for the Iroquois. The Five Nations warred systematically against the neighbouring Mahican in the 1620s and 1630s, against the Huron and other northerly Iroquoians in the 1630s and 1640s, and against the other trading partners of the French intermittently from the 1650s until a treaty of peace and neutrality was concluded in 1701. The principal purpose of these campaigns might have been to eliminate rivals, as well as to gain access to their hunting territories and transportation routes. The French sometimes considered the Iroquois especially barbarous, but the Five Nations were simply acting as did Algonkian allies of the French, often with French support and encouragement. It was the French Crown that in the 1660s had determined "to exterminate completely" the Five Nations.[12] Native warfare had limited objectives; it was not the manifestation of some insatiable blood-lust.

Indigenous warfare and European attitudes towards it became more important in the eighteenth century than they had been earlier. Ironically, the Age of Reason turned out to be a hundred-year battle for control of North America. During the first six decades of the century, a struggle between France and England for supremacy embroiled a number of First Nations in the toils of European dynastic ambitions. During the next fifty years, from the Peace of Paris in 1763 to the end of the War of 1812, the victorious British and Anglo-Americans decided, and then reconfirmed, a subdivision of the continent they had wrested from the French earlier. In all these phases of the struggle for America, from the War of the Spanish Succession to the War of 1812, First Nations played a vital role because of their numbers and because most of the struggles took place in Native-controlled territory. During this century of continental war the three principal arenas of struggle were Acadia, the interior region south and southwest of the lower Great Lakes, and the valley of the St. Lawrence.

The shift of emphasis from the North American as navigator, trader, and proselyte to the Native as warrior and ally began in 1700 because of French strategic considerations. Rivalries over succession to the Spanish throne led France to prepare for war with other European powers. To guard against the eventuality of war with England, French officials began to strengthen their strategic position throughout the world, including North America. Orders were issued to build a string of military forts along the interior track of fur-trading posts through the Ohio and Illinois Country, linking up with France's southern colony of Louisiana to create a military chain-link fence that would pen the Thirteen Colonies in east of the Allegheny Mountains.

Such an ambitious plan, the North American facet of a global strategy, could work only if France neutralized England's principal Native ally and turned its own commercial links with a variety of tribes into a military alliance. The first of these policy aims, neutralizing the Iroquois, was accomplished temporarily by the Great Peace of Montreal of 1701, a critically important treaty with the Five Nations that was negotiated in 1700 and ratified in 1701.[13] The Iroquois were worn down by their battles with the French-Algonquian alliance by the end of the seventeenth century.[14] They also entered the Great Peace because their position between Canada and New England made them potential targets of both European powers. Since they stood to gain little from the victory of either state, they sought neutrality. By the Great Peace, the Iroquois promised to remain neutral in any conflict that might break out between England and France. This was important not only because it ended the wars with the Iroquois that had been going on since the 1640s, but also because it deprived England of its most formidable ally in North America. In the past, the French had regarded the Iroquois as both the greatest enemy and the essential protection of their commercial empire in New France. The Iroquois raids so overwhelmed both the French settlements and their fur-trade network that at their height, as an Iroquois chief boasted, "They were not able to goe over a door to pisse."[15] But as threatening as the Iroquois were, they were essential to the French fur trade: if they had not blocked the path to Albany, nations in the interior would have been able to go to the English traders there. The 1701 treaty removed the Iroquois as a military threat, though they still acted as a barrier to commerce between First Nations of the interior and the English merchants. For the Iroquois, this treaty marked a shift to a strategy of neutrality in the struggles of the Europeans. The Five Nations cleverly solidified their position by negotiating an agreement with the English at Albany in 1701 as well.[16]

The tactic of neutralizing the Iroquois by treaty did not have a lasting effect. The Five Nations once again became, at least nominally, allies of the British by the Treaty of Utrecht (1713), by which France recognized British suzerainty over the Iroquois Confederacy. (The Iroquois Confederacy would soon consist of Six Nations in 1723 when the Tuscarora would be incorporated into it.) To a great extent this setback was offset by two factors: France blithely ignored its commitment to treat the Iroquois as subjects of the British whenever it suited French military interests to do so, and the Iroquois' behaviour was predicated on the assumption, as the Onondaga orator Otreouti (Garangula) had explained, that they owed obedience to no other power. The Six Nations continued to pursue their own interests, as they always had done.

During the remainder of the struggle between France and Britain for control of North America, Native alliances were vital in all areas of the contest. In the north, where France occasionally captured Hudson's Bay Company posts such as Fort Prince of Wales, the assistance of their Native allies was important both to journey overland to the edge of James Bay and to hold the fort once they had taken it. In the Maritime region, France officially conceded "Acadia with its ancient limits" to Britain by the Treaty of Utrecht, but fortunately no one knew where those limits lay, and the Mi'kmaq and other First Nations of the region did not regard themselves as bound by any agreement European powers made. From 1713 to the fall of Acadia in 1758, French strategy in the Maritime theatre relied on the Mi'kmaq and on Louisbourg, their naval base on Cape Breton. As its repeated capture by American colonial and British forces illustrated, Louisbourg possessed more the illusion of strength than the reality, but the Mi'kmaq alliance was a real source of military advantage to France in its confrontation with the British in Acadia. And, finally, the

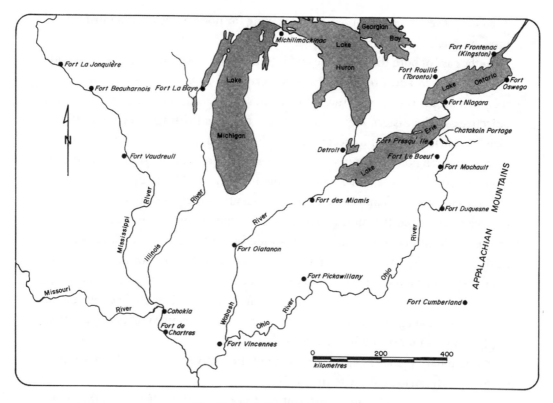

The Ohio and Illinois Country, 1754

French were able to use their commercial links with First Nations as the basis of military alliance in the southwest interior, the Ohio-Illinois Country south of the lower Great Lakes.

But why did the First Nations respond to the European struggle by siding largely with the French? In the first place, it is important to note that there was no uniform Native reaction, no single pattern of military behaviour. The Mi'kmaq were solidly pro-French, the Iroquois sought to play French and English off against each other to their own advantage, and the nations of the southwest interior were usually pro-French. The Iroquois strategy was easily understood: given their vulnerable location, and given their exhaustion from the protracted struggle with the French in the seventeenth century, it made perfect sense for them to try to sit out the wars and to profit as much as they could from the European rivalries that lay behind them. To both British and French, this often made the Iroquois look treacherous and unreliable. In the case of the British in particular, such censure was strange, given their own unreliability as allies with some northeastern First Nations. In any event, such judgments misunderstood Iroquois motives and underestimated their strategic sense: the Six Nations were jockeying for position, just as the British and French were.

In the case of both the Maritime and interior Natives who tended usually to side with the French and *Canadiens* in these territorial struggles, the explanation of their behaviour was similar. They acted from self-interest; they pursued their own objectives. In the eastern region that is today mainland Nova Scotia and northern New Brunswick, two factors accounted for the solid support of the French: The first of these was religion; the long-standing presence of Catholic missionaries in the region had led to the development of close ties between the Mi'kmaq and the French. The descendants of Membertou, in the seventeenth and eighteenth centuries seem to have experienced the most extensive and thorough conversion to Christianity. In the eighteenth century, Catholicism would be both a continuing link between Native and European, and the First Nations' badge of defiance against the British who after 1713 claimed their territory and tried to force them to acknowledge the suzerainty of the Protestant power. Maintaining the Catholic faith, like refusing to take an oath of allegiance to the British Crown, was an effective manner of expressing Mi'kmaq support of and identification with the French. The French, in turn, used missionary priests as agents to maintain the Native alliance in Acadia and to encourage Mi'kmaq hostility to the British.

Underlying the Mi'kmaq predisposition towards Catholic France rather than Protestant Britain was another factor that had nothing to do with denominational loyalties. First Nations in general perceived the two European powers in North America differently because they were different economically. "In the seventeenth century, the Amerindians seem to have stereotyped the Englishman as a farmer or town-dweller whose activities gradually drove the original agriculturalists deeper into the hinterland, whereas the stereotype of the Frenchman was a trader or soldier laden with baubles and brandy who asked only for furs and hospitality."[17] An Oneida village told a Protestant minister that "the English have an insatiable thirst for land, especially for new settlements."[18] Or as Iroquois converts to Catholicism put it in 1754, "Brethren, are you ignorant of the difference between our Father [the French] and the English? Go see the forts our Father has erected, and you will see that the land beneath his walls is still hunting ground, having fixed himself in those places we frequent, only to supply our wants; whilst the English, on the contrary, no sooner get possession of a country than the game is forced to leave it; the trees fall down before them, the earth becomes bare, and we find among them hardly wherewithal to shelter us when the night falls."[19] First Nations perceived the two European peoples differently.

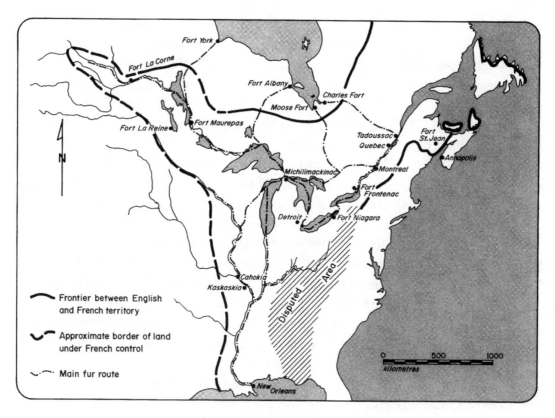

French possessions in North America, 1750

To many nations, the French were merchants and soldiers who did not want to take possession of their lands but merely to trade for the fruits of the forest; the British, though some of them were merchants, were also largely agricultural settlers who inexorably dispossessed the original inhabitants with their expanding farming settlements. Even in the Maritime region, where the Acadians were also farmers, the distinction held, because the settlers of French descent had farmed principally on diked and reclaimed land, not seriously infringing on traditional Mi'kmaq territories. In contrast, the British, who moved into the peninsula in the eighteenth century, established their farms on Mi'kmaq land and across Native transportation and hunting routes.[20] The French followed up on their religious links and on Mi'kmaq opposition to British possessiveness about the land by making generous presents to the First Nations in order to maintain their support. Even so, the French sometimes complained that they were "trahis par nos plus affidés Sauvages," a complaint that

testified to Mi'kmaq "determination to make their own decisions despite the ex-
hortations of French officials and missionaries."[21] The Mi'kmaq pursued their own
objectives, but, given the differences in the forms that British and French presence
took, and aided by the religious ties to the Catholic French, they tended to favour
the French in Acadia. A series of treaties that Britain made with various Mi'kmaq
bands between 1726 and 1760–1 proved transitory and ineffective in neutralizing
the dominant First Nation of the region.[22]

In the interior, the issue was clearer: the French were less of a threat and more
of a benefit than the English to the nations south of the lower Great Lakes and
down the Illinois and Mississippi Valleys. French settlement in the valley of the
St. Lawrence was small-scale, and the region itself was uninhabited at the time
when French villages began to develop. Further inland, in the Ohio and Illinois
Country, the French presence was military and commercial, not agricultural. But
in some of these regions, the Anglo-American agricultural expansion that was
trying to poke its way through the mountains threatened the lands that belonged
to hunter-gatherers. Particularly from New York and Pennsylvania southward, the
heavy emphasis on agriculture in the economy meant that the local Euro-American
population was unwelcome in Indian Country.

The French, in contrast, were in the region primarily for strategic reasons. Their
continuation of a fur trade when it was no longer profitable – an economic emphasis
that also meant they were much less numerous than the Anglo-Americans[23] – was a
consequence of their desire to maintain alliances with the interior First Nations so
as to deny the area to the British. France built military posts and made lavish gifts
of trade goods, weapons, and ammunition to the nations of the region not because
French merchants had a lucrative market in Europe for the inferior furs that could
still be gathered in this region, but because the French military encouraged and underwrote commerce for purposes of alliance. Trade was but a means to a strategic
end for the French. To the First Nations of the region it little mattered what French
motives were so long as they were compatible with their interests. The military and
commercial French were no threat.

But the Pennsylvanians and Virginians who wanted to invade Native territories to plant crops had to be repelled. In 1748–9 the stage was set for a decisive
clash of the agricultural and military-commercial frontiers. In September 1748, the
new governor of New France recommended a policy of retaining interior posts
and maintaining First Nation allies in spite of the fact that the fur trade of the
Illinois Country was no longer economically desirable. A few months later, a group
of leading Anglo-American entrepreneurs and plantation owners formed the Ohio
Company to purchase half a million acres in the Ohio Valley and to sell it in turn to

would-be agricultural colonists from the seaboard. "The military fur trade frontier was about to clash, head on, with the Anglo-American land settlement frontier."[24]

This clash occurred in the 1750s in what the French called the Seven Years' War and the Americans, significantly, termed the French and Indian War. This campaign was merely another phase of the struggle that had begun with the War of the Spanish Succession (1702–13) and continued with the War of the Austrian Succession (1744–8). It was a struggle that saw most of the First Nations of the southwest interior aligning themselves with the French against the British and land-hungry Anglo-Americans. The fact that the French gave lavish presents and seemed to hold the winning hand for much of the 1750s also induced many tribes to support them.[25] The French victories were attributable to their superior colonial military organization and to the Native alliances. The Canadians might number only about one-tenth of the half million or so Thirteen Colonists, but every *Canadien* male was a trained militiaman and, together with Native allies, was a formidable foe. As a frustrated British officer observed, "You might as well send a cow in pursuit of a hare as one of our soldiers loaded as they are against naked Indians or Canadians in their shirts."[26] Repeatedly the First Nations and French in the interior thrashed both British and American colonial troops that were sent into the region: Washington and his ragtag militiamen were sent packing from the Ohio Valley in 1754, and Braddock's forces were almost wiped out the next year by a combined Native, Canadian, and French force that attacked his neat formations of redcoats from forest cover.

What turned the tide against France and ensured the triumph of the agricultural frontier in Nova Scotia and the American interior was a shift not in the western hemisphere, but in Europe. When Britain chose a "blue-water strategy" that sought to take advantage of its superior naval power, it set in motion a series of events that starved the French and Canadian campaigns by interrupting the transoceanic flow of supplies from France. Victories of the British fleet off European coasts were more important than the tardy and dilatory taking of Louisbourg for the last time in 1758. Canada, with its support from France throttled by British dominance of the sea lanes, had to draw back from the interior. The line of forts was shortened, as French and Canadians fell back on their St. Lawrence Valley bastion. In Acadia, the British expelled the Acadians in 1755, took Louisbourg three years later, and established effective control of the region before the decade was over. Finally, in 1759, Quebec fell, and the following year British control of the seas ensured that France would not retake its colonial capital. When Montreal capitulated in 1760, the Seven Years' War ended in North America. The fortieth article of the Capitulation of Montreal laid a

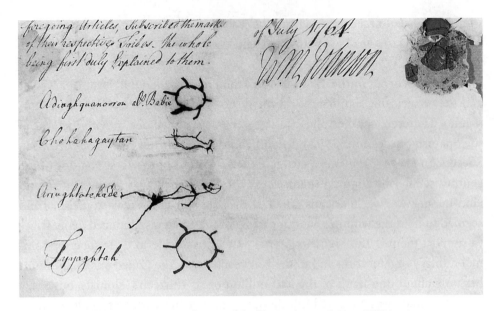

The totems, or personal signs, of the Huron signatories to a 1764 treaty
with Britain were the counterpart of William Johnson's seal and signature.

basis for First Nations religious and land rights when it conceded that the "Indian
allies of his most Christian Majesty, shall be maintained in the Lands they inhabit;
if they choose to remain there; they shall not be molested on any pretence whatsoever, for having carried arms, and served his most Christian Majesty; they shall
have, as well as the French, liberty of religion, and shall keep their missionaries."[27]

The arrangements that ended the struggle – the Peace of Paris of 1763 and the
Royal Proclamation of the same year – fundamentally altered relations between
First Nations and Europeans. In the first place, by the Peace of Paris France ceded
her title and claims to all territory in the northern part of North America save
for a portion of the Newfoundland shore that her fishers were accustomed to use.
Second, the Royal Proclamation that the new rulers issued in 1763 laid down a
number of limits and guidelines for all inhabitants of what had previously been
France's interior colony, but had special interest for the First Nations of the re-
gion south of the lower Great Lakes. The definition of the boundaries of the new
British province called Quebec was a narrow one: the height of land north of the
St. Lawrence constituted the northern bound, and the southern was a line drawn
arbitrarily and roughly parallel to the River of Canada that included the Gaspé
Peninsula but little else. The western boundary was another line drawn south from
Lake Nipissing across the St. Lawrence to the forty-fifth degree of latitude. Both the
controversial "Acadia with its ancient limits" and the southwestern hinterland were

severed from their traditional commercial metropolis in the St. Lawrence Valley.[28] If France had abandoned Canada to the British by the Peace of Paris, then Britain had greatly trimmed the extent of its new possession.

But the section of the proclamation that had the greatest impact on First Nations, both immediately and throughout the remainder of Canadian history, was not the boundary definition but the provisions concerning Indigenous lands: "And whereas it is just and reasonable, and essential to our Interest, and the Security of our Colonies, that the several Nations or Tribes of Indians with whom We are connected, and who live under our Protection, should not be molested or disturbed in the Possession of such Parts of Our Dominions and Territories as ... are reserved to them, or any of them, as their Hunting Grounds," therefore, any lands that had "not been ceded to or purchased by Us as aforesaid, are reserved to the said Indians." Furthermore, "We do hereby strictly forbid, on Pain of our Displeasure, all our loving Subjects from making any Purchases or Settlements whatever, or taking Possession of any of the Lands above reserved, without our especial leave and Licence for that Purpose first obtained." By the proclamation "no private Person" was allowed "to make any purchase from the said Indians of any Lands reserved to the said Indians." If First Nations wanted to sell lands reserved to them, "the same shall be Purchased only for Us, in our Name, at some public Meeting or assembly of the said Indians, to be held for the Purpose by the Governor or Commander in Chief of our Colony." And, finally, the proclamation permitted trade with the Natives only to those who "do take out a Licence for carrying on such Trade from the Governor or Commander in Chief of any of our Colonies."[29] Some of these provisions continued a line of policy development found in earlier Nova Scotia treaties, such as Mascarene's Treaty (1726) and the Treaty of Halifax (1752), the latter of which explicitly recognized Aboriginal peoples' continuing right to hunt and fish.

These clauses of the Royal Proclamation that sought to regulate lands in the interior were intended to avoid conflict between the Indigenous population and land-hungry immigrants. The boundary definition, in combination with the restrictions on trade, meant that the interior hinterland was closed to agricultural expansion and subject only to limited commercial penetration. The provisions governing acquisition of First Nation lands only by and through the Crown were designed to prevent a species of semi-official fraud – what historian Francis Jennings labelled "the deed game"[30] – that had begun to develop in the Thirteen Colonies. The proclamation aimed to put a stop to schemes in which colonial land developers purported to purchase lands from dependent and/or unrepresentative Natives and then called on the colonial legislatures to make good their claim and protect the agricultural settlers who wanted to take up the newly acquired lands. In 1764, Britain's

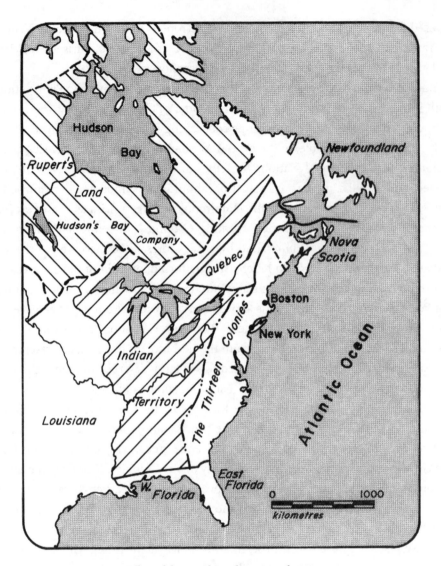

Effect of the Royal Proclamation of 1763

representative in the region, William Johnson, followed the proclamation up with a conference attended by some 2,000 chiefs at Niagara, at which the Superintendent of the Northern Indians explained the proclamation, made commitments of non-interference to the leaders, and secured First Nations agreement, which was recorded in a belt of wampum.[31]

In the longer term, the Royal Proclamation would have even more profound implications. First Nation organizations would later base part of their arguments for recognition of Aboriginal title to unceded lands on the proclamation, which could

Wampum was often used to record important events, which could be
referred to in speeches at subsequent diplomatic exchanges.

reasonably be read to imply royal recognition that Natives had rights to lands that
pre-existed the assertion of British title. In the 1990s an Aboriginal legal scholar
made a convincing argument that the proclamation, when read together with the
solemn agreement the following year at Niagara, constituted "a treaty between First
Nations and the Crown which stands as a positive guarantee of First Nations self-
government."[32] While the clauses of the Royal Proclamation of 1763 would by no
means be the only legal basis of the twentieth-century arguments for Aboriginal

title or self-government, they would prove an important part of the modern case for First Nation control of lands that had not been ceded to the Crown.[33]

In 1763 and 1764, the interior nations reacted defiantly to the French loss and the termination of their presents. Minavavana and sixty Ojibwe warriors, "each with his tomahawk in one hand, and scalping-knife in the other," trooped into Fort Michilimackinac to set British fur trader Alexander Henry straight: "Englishman, although you have conquered the French, you have not yet conquered us! We are not your slaves. These lakes, these woods and mountains, were left to us by our ancestors. They are our inheritance; and we will part with them to none."[34] Pontiac, an Ottawa chief, responded by organizing an armed resistance, in the process refashioning the anti-white message of a Delaware prophet, Neolin, into a specifically anti-British cause.[35] The immediate reason for Pontiac's rising was a British decision to cut off the supply of presents that the French had employed to win and hold the allegiance of the First Nations in the Illinois Country. Minavavana had warned Alexander Henry that "your king has never sent us any presents, nor entered into any treaty with us, wherefore he and we are still at war."[36] General Amherst, a policy-maker "with the moral vision of a shopkeeper and the arrogance of a victorious soldier," spurned the advice of more experienced Indian Department officials who recommended continuation of the French practice of gift-giving.[37] The failure to give presents, in effect, broke the kinship ties between Europeans and First Nations, and terminated their relationship. The fact that interior Natives had not been defeated in the Seven Years' War also spurred them. But underlying the conflict was the old antagonism between a frontier of commerce and an expanding margin of agricultural settlement. Pontiac's appeal to arms captured the conflict graphically: "And as for these English, – these dogs dressed in red, who have come to rob you of your hunting grounds, and drive away the game, – you must lift the hatchet against them. Wipe them from the face of the earth, and thus you will win my favour back again, and once more be happy and prosperous. The children of your great father, the King of France, are not like the English."[38]

Before Pontiac and his warriors were cowed by British troops, they had taken several of the western posts and killed over 2,000 settlers who menaced their lands. For his part, a frustrated Amherst retaliated by urging the use of germ warfare against the warriors. Could it "not be contrived to send the Small Pox among those disaffected tribes of Indians?" he asked a subordinate. Whether the proposal to distribute infected blankets from a hospital was ever implemented is not clear, but even the contemplation of such a practice is appalling.[39] Such tactics, if used, had no impact on the First Nations' conviction that they were fighting for their own lands. Even while making peace, Pontiac maintained that the First Nations held title to the lands of the interior.[40] Although American historians would refer to the bloody and unsuccessful uprising as the "Conspiracy of Pontiac," it was in fact only another angry response by hunter-gatherers to the encroachments of farmers.

The British military officials who now governed Quebec were not blind to either the restiveness of the Thirteen Colonies or the dangers of a full-scale Native war in the interior. In part, the proclamation that closed the Ohio Country to settlement and outlawed entrepreneurial purchases of First Nation lands was designed to prevent a clash between the Anglo-Americans and the Natives. Ironically, the British on the St. Lawrence found themselves drawn into the same economic and military postures as the French and the *Canadiens* they had ousted from power. To keep the interior nations reasonably tranquil, the government of Quebec encouraged the resumption of the fur trade out of Montreal and cleared the way for continued Canadian commercial activities in the southwest interior. This British policy was confirmed in the Quebec Act of 1774, which restored the interior hinterland to the jurisdiction of Quebec. The adoption of this policy towards the Natives was instructive: it proved that the French had enjoyed better relations with the First Nations than the British and the Anglo-Americans, not because they were French, but because they were merchants and soldiers who did not threaten Native lands as the Americans did. If there were any doubt about that, it was removed by the American Revolutionary War.

The rebellion of the Thirteen Colonies was partially incited by British policy towards the interior First Nations. Britain's approach was embodied in the Quebec Act, which the American rebels described as one of the "Intolerable Acts" that justified their rising. Besides wanting to avoid an all-out Native war in the interior, the British wished to retain the loyalty of the *Canadiens* and their traditional allies in the event of an American rebellion. The restoration of the fur trade and the traditional pursuit of good relations with the First Nations were components of this strategic plan. During the fighting after 1775, the British strategy of maximizing the advantages its northern position gave it, along with its continued reliance on commerce in the St. Lawrence colony paid off. In the War of Independence, the alignment of the various First Nations was extremely important. Thanks to the influence of geography and commerce, the British were supported by more of the Native groups than were the land-hungry Americans.

There was no single pattern to the alliances between Indigenous people and Europeans during the Revolutionary War, and there was no truth to the charge that First Nations made barbarous allies. The one consistent theme was that Natives chose their fighting partners, or in some cases chose not to fight at all, according to their own definition of where their interests lay. The erroneous notion that the British "used" First Nations in the war against the colonists was articulated in the Declaration of Independence and reiterated by generations of American propagandists and historians. The Declaration of Independence charged that the British king "has excited domestic insurrections among us, and has endeavoured to bring on the inhabitants of our frontiers, the merciless Indian Savages, whose known rule of warfare, is an undistinguished destruction of all ages, sexes, and conditions."[41] And colonial propagandists put in the mouths of British officers such charming sentiments as:

> I will let loose the dogs of hell,
> Ten thousand Indians who shall yell,
> And foam and tear, and grin and roar,
> And drench their moccasins in gore.
>
> They'll scalp your heads, and kick your shins,
> And rip your guts, and flay your skins,
> And of your ears be nimble croppers
> And make your thumbs be tobacco-stoppers.[42]

Assumptions that Natives were "used" and that their methods were barbaric were nonsense.

As the case of the various nations of the Iroquois League shows, the Indigenous response was based on a complex of factors, including the varied perceptions of Americans to the east and British and *Canadiens* to the north. The Iroquois minority who were most sympathetic to the rebels and who advocated neutrality, the Oneida, were relatively well disposed to the Americans principally because they had been ministered to for many years by Puritan missionaries from New England. And even the Oneida implied that First Nations should consult their own self-interest when they pleaded with the New England colonies not to be asked for military assistance: "Let us Indians be all of one mind and live in peace with one another, and you white people settle your own Disputes betwixt yourselves."[43]

Those Iroquois who supported the British were motivated by a combination of personal ties and calculations that their lands would be better defended by the British, whose proclamation policy had kept back the land-hungry farmers, than by the colonies from which those American settlers came. In addition, the Mohawk were greatly influenced by their ties to the family of William, now Sir William, Johnson, Britain's "superintendent of Indian affairs for the Northern Department" after 1755, who from his base in the Mohawk Valley of New York had distributed presents to the Natives and protected their lands from white encroachment.[44] Molly Brant, the sister of the Mohawk leader Joseph, was married to Johnson, and that connubial link serves as a reminder of the importance of personal ties, as well as the political role of women in Iroquoian society.[45] Also important was the Iroquois perception that American power threatened them, a view that became embodied in their name for the commander-in-chief of American forces, the president. The Iroquois term for the president was, and is, Town-Destroyer. This dubious title originated in the name they accorded George Washington, the future first president, after he marched through Iroquoia burning their palisaded villages.[46]

Finally, nations such as the Mohawk and others to the south were motivated to support the British and Canadians by a desire to protect their lands. It was still the Americans who were trying to expand their agricultural frontier into what the proclamation had termed Indian "hunting grounds," and it was still the British who resisted that expansion. As some of the tribes in the Ohio Country put it to a representative of the rebel Continental Congress, "You have feloniously taken possession of part of our country on the branches of the Ohio, as well as the Susquehanna, to the latter we have some time since sent you word to quit our Lands as we now do to you, as we don't know we ever gave you liberty, nor can we be easy in our minds while there is an arm'd Force at our very doors." They added, "We now tell you in a peaceful manner to quit our lands wherever you have possessed yourselves of them immediately, or blame yourselves for whatever may happen."[47] Those nations, such as the Mohawk and some Cherokee further south, who allied themselves with the British, were doing as Pontiac had a decade earlier. They threw their support behind commerce and against agricultural expansion. "They were neither beasts howling for blood for its own sake, nor merely paid pawns of the whites. For them, the Revolution was another bitter episode in a struggle as old as European settlement in North America."[48]

Much of the bitterness that First Nations experienced in this latest phase of alliance with the Europeans in the north stemmed less from the destruction of wartime than the dispossession wrought in the peace. The nation that had thrown its support to the victors fared worst of all. Although the Oneida were supposed to be conceded lands in their traditional territories, it was not long until the surging agricultural frontier overtook and dispossessed them. The Mohawk were at first chagrined to discover that their territorial claims had been abandoned in the talks that produced the 1783 Treaty of Versailles. British negotiators recklessly surrendered all claims to the lands south of the Great Lakes that they, the Canadians, or the First Nations had held. This betrayal prompted a group of Six Nations leaders to

Joseph Brant, an important Mohawk ally of the British in the Revolutionary War,
had a lengthy and influential career in Canada.

reprimand a British official: "They never could believe that our King could pretend to cede to America What was not his to give, or that the Americains [sic] would accept from Him What he had no right to grant." The Six Nations "were the faithful allies of the King of England, but not his subjects ... they would not submit to it." If George III had done so, "it was an act of Cruelty and injustice that only Christians *only* were capable of doing."[49] The anger of betrayed Indigenous allies was, unsurprisingly, intense. Historian Elizabeth Elbourne has described the expulsion of a "significant portion of the Six Nations" from the United States as "the ethnic cleansing of the American Revolution."[50]

Britain's response to First Nations' anger over the expulsion of its allies from the new republic was to make provision to resettle the principal of her Native allies north of the Great Lakes. Land was obtained from the Mississauga and other branches of the Ojibwe through treaties made according to the requirements of the Royal Proclamation, and comrades-in-arms from the Six Nations were invited to share parts of the territory that soon would become Upper Canada with white-skinned Loyalists. Led by Mohawk Captain Joseph Brant, a group of Iroquois numbering over 1,500 settled a large tract along both sides of the Grand River in the vicinity of present-day Brantford, while a smaller number under the leadership of Captain John Deseronto established themselves on the Bay of Quinte. Britain was motivated to establish refuges for Iroquoian allies out of both a sense of obligation to them and a desire to retain their loyalty and military alliance.

For a decade after 1783, the British continued to shape their policy according to their desire to maintain peace while retaining the support of the First Nations both south and north of the lower Great Lakes. Fear of a Native uprising that might embroil the British and Americans in another war accounted for the fact that from 1783 to 1794 Britain violated the terms of the Treaty of Versailles by maintaining control of the posts in First Nation territory. The proclaimed, but in reality minor, reason for this retention of the western posts was the refusal of the American Congress to honour Loyalist claims for damages in their old home territories; the real motive was fear of an uprising along the lines of Pontiac's campaign of 1763–4. At times British representatives even harboured unrealistic hopes of encouraging the formation of a Native buffer state between the United States and their own new settlements to the north of the Great Lakes. For their part, the western nations expressed symbolically their opposition to American land hunger when they stuffed the mouths of the soldiers they slaughtered in a battle in 1791 with earth.[51] In any event, any chance of such a grand strategy's success collapsed thanks to events in Europe.

When Britain went to war with France in 1793, her planners felt compelled to normalize relations with the United States. One of the major outstanding issues was the illegal retention of the posts. Furthermore, the Americans had indicated by a series of First Nation wars that they had fought since the 1780s, and which had culminated in the rout of the Natives in the Battle of Fallen Timbers in 1794, that the new republic was determined to take effective control of the lands that the Treaty of Versailles had, rightly or wrongly, given it. Britain, in search of peace with her former colonies, pulled back from her commitment to the First Nations in the disputed region south of the Great Lakes in 1794, concluding the Jay Treaty with the Americans in Europe and slamming shut the gates of Fort Miami in the face of warriors fleeing from the battle of Fallen Timbers. The British perfidy at Fort Miami in 1794 caused an embittered Joseph Brant to upbraid a British official by saying, "This is the second time the poor Indians have been left in the lurch."[52] However, the Jay Treaty would have an interesting legacy for some North American First Nations. Once again, Britain made some provision for its former allies whose interests it was abandoning, this time by negotiating for land following the Royal Proclamation for up to 3,000 of them from the Ojibwe along the Thames River in southwestern Ontario. The Jay Treaty had other, long-standing consequences. Ever since 1794, some of the First Nations affected by it, such as the Akwesasne (St. Regis) band, have claimed the status of an independent nation. They insist that they are neither American nor Canadian and claim that they have the right of free passage across the international border in such localities as Cornwall, Ontario.[53]

Relations between First Nations and Europeans in the eighteenth century revolved around military alliance. The fact that the European powers were engaged in a protracted struggle to determine the political affiliation of the northern part of North America meant that First Nations were increasingly important to the non-Natives as military allies. Indigenous peoples did not cease entirely to play their customary roles as guides and navigators, commercial partners, and objects of proselytization. But, while the commercial, navigational, and evangelical contacts continued to be important, the relationship of allies largely predominated. In the military relationship the Native continued to play a major, perhaps even dominant, role. Particularly down to the end of the Seven Years' War, the desire to maintain First Nation military support largely determined European actions. As the heavy flow of presents to the Natives clearly indicated, the Europeans badly needed the Natives. But if the military relationship of the eighteenth century continued to be one in which the Indigenous person was the dominant partner, it was a break with the seventeenth-century pattern of relations in that the results of the interaction were mainly negative for the First Nations. Obviously, a century of on-and-off warfare meant major losses of life for the First Nations. These were costs that the Natives reckoned before entering into military association. In the final analysis, however, the relationship was disastrous because the power that represented the agricultural frontier – first Britain and the Anglo-Americans, then the Americans – triumphed over the more northerly commercial frontier. Britain and the Anglo-Americans defeated the French and *Canadiens*; then the Americans defeated the combined forces of the British and Quebec. First Nation allies suffered substantial territorial losses when the final reckoning came.

Part Two

COERCION

CHAPTER FIVE

From Alliance to "Irrelevance"

Between the 1790s and the 1830s Native-settler relations in the eastern third of the continent changed profoundly. In both the Maritime and central regions, peace was followed by substantial immigration, first of Loyalists and later of British settlers. The bulk of this influx deposited itself in Nova Scotia and the region west of the Ottawa River, although some migrants entered Quebec and marginally affected relations there. As important as the influx of settlers destined to clear the forest and establish farms were two other factors: the end of the Montreal-based fur trade and the normalization of relations between the new republic to the south and Great Britain. The amalgamation of Montreal's North West Company with the Hudson's Bay Company in 1821 stopped fur-trade operations from Montreal. At a single stroke, commercial cooperation between eastern First Nations and the Europeans was drastically diminished. At about the same time, a smoothing of relations between the United States and Great Britain occurred first in the Maritime region and somewhat later in the central colonies of Lower Canada and Upper Canada. This reconciliation removed the threat from the south and diminished the military significance of Aboriginal people in the eyes of British planners.

The lessening of the American menace, the presence of greatly increased numbers of Anglo-American and British colonists, and the termination of the Montreal-based fur trade changed the European's approach to the relationship with the Indigenous population. The association was no longer one that emphasized military alliance, but rather one in which the dominant partner sought the removal of the Native from the path of agricultural settlement. To both the British official and the frontier farmer, First Nations became less desirable as comrades-in-arms;

increasingly the Indigenous population was an impediment to the objectives that the immigrant population had in an era of peace and settlement. In short, the Indigenous peoples in eastern British North America declined in military importance. As an early historian of the relationship put it, from "the point of view of the European, the Indian had become irrelevant."[1] While this irrelevance was largely in terms of policy-making and large-scale economic trends, at the day-to-day level of relations, many Natives and newcomers continued to interact for largely economic reasons.

The most immediate problem after the close of the Revolutionary War had been the angry reaction of Britain's erstwhile allies south of the lower Great Lakes. Provision had to be made for the allies, especially the Mohawk, who had been dispossessed. An obvious place to look for lands to replace the lost portions of Iroquoia was the vast tract north of the lower Great Lakes and the upper St. Lawrence River. Britain initiated a policy of acquiring lands by treaty from the Mississauga where there were established patterns of occupation and usage. The Mississauga, a branch of the Anicinabe who were found in several parts of northern Ontario and around the west end of Lake Ontario, readily parted with land to enable the relocation of former allies. One of these, an 1787 treaty west of the Bay of Quinte, became known as the "Gunshot Treaty," because the depth of the land involved back of the lake was the distance at which a shot could be heard on a still day.[2] In the eastern part of the future Ontario, where there was little utilization of the lands, the British simply put the wheels in motion to locate the Native Loyalists, such as the bands associated with Captain John Deseronto, near the site of the town that bears his name.

By agreement with the First Nations, Europeans were settled in this region, too. When it became clear that non-Native Loyalists were also attracted to the fertile lands west of the Ottawa River, Britain approached the resident First Nations for permission to settle the new land frontier with disbanded Loyalist troops and their families. Accordingly, the settlements along the north shore of the St. Lawrence and at the west end of Lake Ontario that began in 1784 were made up of a mixture of European Loyalists, such as Johnson's Mohawk Valley tenants who located in what would become Glengarry County, and Indigenous Loyalists, such as the Iroquois who established themselves on the Grand River, near Brantford. This early establishment of the foundations of Ontario involved two practices that were to prove incompatible with and inimical to the interests of the Indigenous peoples: obtaining land, in accordance with the Royal Proclamation of 1763, by negotiation; and attempting to settle non-Native farmers and First Nations in close proximity.

British policy-makers had to worry about the Americans who stayed south as well as the Loyalists who came north. British Indian Department policy towards her Indigenous allies south of the Great Lakes, a policy that included the continuation of giving presents at posts in British territory, was intended to maintain their friendly neutrality, while ensuring as far as possible that the First Nations would side with Britain in the event of another war with the American republic.[3] The citizens of the United States remained suspicious and resentful of what they took to be British meddling with the Native peoples in their country. This phase of uneasy relations in the old Northwest culminated in the War of 1812, the final chapter of the long struggle for control of the continent that had begun a century earlier.[4]

In Upper Canada (the future Ontario), the main prize coveted by the War Hawks from land-hungry states who were largely responsible for the Congressional decision to go to war against Britain, the First Nations would once again play a vital military role. Upper Canada, which stretched west from the Ottawa River along the north shore of the St. Lawrence and the lower Great Lakes, was the most vulnerable of the British North American colonies. Over-confident American expansionists predicted that taking it would be a "mere matter of marching," thanks to the inadequacies of British defences, the fragility of its long supply line from Quebec, and the nature of the Upper Canadian population.[5] Since the 1790s there had been such an influx of American agricultural immigrants that the populace was as much or more American as British, both in its sentiments and in its leanings. The British worried about the ability of Upper Canada to withstand the anticipated American invasion, and would have despaired altogether were it not for the fact that many First Nations were prepared to side once again with the British.[6]

The principal nations to whom Britain looked were the Loyalist Mohawk and the western tribes in American territory who were led by Tecumseh (Tecumthé, Shooting Star)[7] of the Shawnee and his brother The Prophet, or Tenskwatawa (The Open Door). Reminiscent of Neolin, the Delaware prophet who had prepared the ground for Pontiac in the 1760s, Tenskwatawa urged followers to heed the message the Master of Life had given him in a revelation: "I am the Father of the English, of the French, of the Spaniards and of the Indians ... But the Americans I did not make. They are not my children but the children of the Evil Spirit. They grew from the scum of the great water when it was troubled by the Evil Spirit and the froth was driven into the woods by a strong east wind. They are unjust – they have taken away your lands which were not made for them."[8] As The Prophet's words signified once again, First Nations fought not as instruments of Europeans' policy but as agents in pursuit of their own interests. The fundamental reason for Indigenous

The cooperation of Tecumseh with Brock and the British forces, romantically
depicted here, was vital to the survival of Upper Canada in the War of 1812.

support of the British cause in the War of 1812 was simply explained: "Tecumseh
and his followers had not yet given up hope that an Indian state could be created
in the Ohio Valley and that the continuous stream of white settlers from across the
mountains could be checked. Alliance with the British in the War of 1812 offered
the opportunity that alliance with France had offered some of the same people in
the time of Pontiac."[9] For First Nations groups who fought with the British, the War
of 1812 was merely a continuation of earlier hostilities.

The British enjoyed their greatest successes in the land war in Upper Canada
as long as the First Nations fought in large numbers alongside them. At the outbreak of war, a small British force seized Michilimackinac, an early indicator that
caused the Natives to flock to the British colours. In the words of an American
general, the "surrender of Michilimackinac opened the northern hive of Indians
and they were swarming down in every direction." Almost "every tribe and nation
of Indians, excepting a part of the Miamis and Delawares, north from beyond Lake
Superior, west from beyond the Mississippi, south from the Ohio and Wabash, and

The death of Tecumseh at the Battle of the Thames signalled the collapse
of the Aboriginal-British alliance in the War of 1812.

east from every part of Upper Canada and from all the intermediate country, joined
in open hostility, under the British standard against the Army I commanded."[10]
Soon after the fall of Michilimackinac, Detroit surrendered without a shot because
its American commander believed the rumours that the British forces facing him
included 5,000 Native warriors and because his line of communications to the east
had been cut by Tecumseh and his warriors. Britain's Native allies fought bravely
and effectively in the southwest portion of Upper Canada until growing disgust
with the incompetence of British military leadership and Tecumseh's death at the
Battle of Moraviantown in the autumn of 1813 disheartened them and caused
the force slowly to melt away. While First Nations were active warriors in Upper
Canada they ensured that their views were considered and respected. British leaders consulted their chiefs, Britain assured them it still adhered to the creation of "a
Native state," and on occasion First Nations leaders such as Tecumseh effectively
determined strategy.[11]

The First Nations in the southwest interior were not the only ones to flock to the
British colours. The Six Nations also fought effectively in the Niagara Peninsula, as
did some detachments of the "praying Indians" from such Lower Canadian settlements as Kanesatake (Oka), Kahnawake, and Akwesasne (St. Regis). So too did

a contingent of Ottawa under another famous war chief, Blackbird. The battle of Beaver Dam in the Niagara region, like the battle of Moraviantown in the south-west in which Tecumseh fell, was an Indigenous, not a British or Canadian, victory. Without the contributions and sacrifices of these First Nations, Upper Canada might well have proved "a mere matter of marching" before reinforcements of British regulars could arrive and the will of the Upper Canadian population to resist their invading cousins could establish itself. When Indigenous support dissipated late in 1813 and in 1814 as a consequence of Tecumseh's death and British naval losses on the Great Lakes, the British cause suffered a serious setback.

After the death of Tecumseh, First Nations leaders feared British resolve to resist and to honour its commitment to them would fade. At a meeting with the Governor, Sir George Prevost, in Quebec City in November 1813, Metoss, a Sauk chief, articulated their concerns:

> Father, we have often heard of you from our young men, but we never saw you before.
>
> Father, we are come now a long distance to smoke the Pipe of Peace with you.
>
> Father, the Long Knives are our enemies as well as yours; but, Father, when you made peace with them [in 1794] we buried the tomahawk in the ground.
>
> Father, you have sent to us to say that you are now fighting with the Long Knives and want us to fight beside you.
>
> Father, we wished for peace, we love our hunting; but, Father, we love you and our great Father across the Salt Lake. We will tear the tomahawk from the bowels of the earth, to bury it in the bosoms of the Long Knives – our enemies and yours.
>
> …
>
> Father, we will not bury the tomahawk again until our great Father desires us. But, Father, you must never make peace with the Long Knives until we have conquered back our hunting grounds, from which the Long Knives have now driven us.

Prevost assured them that he would ask the king not to make peace with the Americans until Native hunting grounds had been restored.[12]

The end of the War of 1812 meant the defeat of the First Nation strategy of resistance and the onset of a long period of peace in the interior of the North American continent. In talks that led to the Treaty of Ghent (1814), the British tried to obtain terms that would protect their allies, but their efforts to secure a territory south of the lower Great Lakes exclusively for the First Nations, a sort of Native buffer state, failed in the face of American determination not to consider any such arrangement. The peace treaty restored the boundaries that had existed before the outbreak of hostilities, and the text also created a moral obligation – unenforceable and unenforced – to restore to the First Nations those lands and rights they had possessed in 1812.[13] The war and the Treaty of Ghent meant that the strategies of those nations that had supported first the French and then the British from the north against the Americans were now rendered inoperable. The region south of the Great Lakes had become decidedly American and agricultural, and after the War of 1812 the region north of Lakes Ontario and Erie began to undergo the same sort of development. The Treaty of Ghent was reinforced in 1817 by the Rush-Bagot Convention, which furthered continental peace by severely restricting naval forces on the Great Lakes and Lake Champlain. The War of 1812, then, marked the end of an important phase of relations in the interior, an epoch in which the Native and the European were allies in a common cause.

The pattern of relations after 1783 was different in the Maritime colony of Nova Scotia because immigration and peace came to that region sooner than they did to Upper Canada. The dominant factors in the Maritimes were the arrival of thousands of Loyalists, most of them white-skinned, and the non-arrival of the War of 1812. Even prior to the American Revolution, British authorities had signalled their disinclination to pay any heed to First Nations in Atlantic Canada when they carved up the island the Mi'kmaq called Abegweit (Prince Edward Island) into a series of large estates and distributed them to absentee Protestant landlords. The migration of the Loyalists into the vast tract called Nova Scotia meant the creation of a new province, New Brunswick, in 1784, and consequent pressure on First Nations such as the Maliseet, Penobscot, and, of course, the Mi'kmaq, as agricultural use of the land expanded. Agrarian development was greater in Nova Scotia than in New Brunswick, which had relatively little land suitable for agriculture, but even in the latter the arrival of the Euro-Americans meant pressure on the Indigenous peoples because of the rapid development of an export trade in timber. British officialdom made little effort to protect the customary land-use rights of the First Nations in the region.[14] Later, the fact that the New England states were opposed to the War of 1812 meant that the final phase of the struggle among the Europeans for the continent bypassed the Atlantic region. The Maritime colonies sat out the War of 1812; the Indigenous inhabitants did not have this last chance to play their role as allies.

What occurred instead in the Maritime region, especially in Nova Scotia and New Brunswick, was a discouraging pattern of First Nations–European relations that was to become all too familiar elsewhere during the nineteenth century. As the immigrants moved in, they dispossessed the original inhabitants, in spite of pledges to respect the relatively small areas of land set aside for Natives. Colonial governments in the three Maritime colonies never found it convenient to use the limited forces at their disposal for the protection of First Nation lands, though it was easy enough to persuade them to have British troops or militia sent in when hard-pressed Native people resisted.[15] Squatters simply encroached on Native encampments, improved their property with buildings and agricultural development of the land, and then defied efforts to make them move. Colonial judges and legislators had neither the will nor the means to protect First Nations. The consequence of these developments was that as agricultural and forestry development proceeded in the Maritimes in the early nineteenth century, the Indigenous peoples were dispossessed and reduced to scratching out an existence with hunting and handicrafts.

The Maritime region, and Nova Scotia and New Brunswick in particular, was the site of the earliest examples of a common nineteenth-century occurrence: futile efforts by overseas organizations to protect and assist North American First Nations. In the nineteenth century, as a sort of obverse of British imperial expansion, there developed bodies that sought first the emancipation of non-white colonial populations and later the protection of them from whites in their own homelands. The humanitarians came to the Maritimes initially in the form of the non-denominational Protestant missionary New England Company, which between the 1780s and early nineteenth century sought to provide assistance and education to the First Nations of the region.[16] Efforts to provide education were diverted by colonial administrators of missionary funds to support of schools for the white children. Programs of apprenticing young Native children to Euro-Canadians to assimilate and train them often became a means for colonists to acquire cheap labour and hard cash.

The New England Company's abortive effort in New Brunswick was as revealing as it was unavailing. A program intended for humanitarian purposes was distorted, in the hands of a colonial population unsympathetic to First Nations, into a source of British funds and a means to exploit the Natives. It was in part thanks to the ineffectiveness of such missionary initiatives in the face of colonial hostility and cupidity that the Indigenous population of the Maritimes went through the debilitating evolution that it did in the last decades of the eighteenth century and first half of the nineteenth century. A population that had ceased to have commercial and military utility to the Europeans became, at best, irrelevant and, at worst, an obstacle to the settlers, who now outnumbered them.

In Newfoundland, humanitarian efforts to mitigate European depredations were more belated and even less successful than in the mainland Maritime colonies. It was only in the second and third decades of the nineteenth century that government and colonials became alarmed at the rapid decline in the numbers of Indigenous people and made efforts both to protect them and to learn from them. The Beothuk had probably numbered approximately 1,000 when Europeans began

The New England Company, a Protestant missionary organization
in Britain, shifted its efforts to British North America
after the American Revolution.

to make contact with them in the fishery in the fifteenth and sixteenth centuries.[17] Initial interactions had produced some conflict, as the Natives pilfered equipment from shacks which the fishers left behind after using the shore to dry their fish. But the opportunities for extended conflict had been limited by two factors: In the first place, the policy of the British, who were the Europeans who made most use of the shore in the dry fishery, had forbidden permanent settlement in what they called the New Found Land. Second, after initial clashes, the Beothuk, who did not possess firearms, had adopted a strategy of withdrawal from contact with the Europeans, retreating to the interior and northern peninsula of the island. But such a strategy proved no more successful in protecting them than the cooperation of the Huron or the policy of resistance of the First Nations in the Ohio and Illinois Country did.

Although there was no record of conflict between Beothuk and Europeans between the sixteenth century and the eighteenth century, the Beothuk nonetheless suffered. European diseases had probably already reduced their numbers to five or six hundred before contact and conflict between the First Nation and New-foundlanders resumed in the eighteenth century. The occasion of this renewed contact was the increasing use of the island by settled Newfoundlanders, and in particular their fishing and pursuit of birds, game, and fur-bearing animals. Their hunting and trapping activities brought them into occasional and bloody contact with the Beothuk. Again, since they had firearms and the Natives did not, the results were devastating to the Beothuk. A final factor was the increased use of the southern part of Newfoundland by the Mi'kmaq after 1713. The effects of tuberculosis and other diseases caused the Beothuk population to continue to dwindle throughout the eighteenth century. While their population in 1768 was probably about 350, by 1811 there were only seventy-two Beothuk left in two camps; by 1819 the number had declined to thirty-one, even though efforts were now being made to befriend and protect remnants of the Beothuk people. But it was all too little, too late. By 1823 disease and attacks had reduced the Beothuk population to thirteen, and in 1829 Shawnadithit, the last survivor, succumbed to tuberculosis.[18] The original "red Indians" were no more.

The fate of the Beothuk has been the subject of much controversy and misinformation. Older notions that the Europeans somehow "used" the Mi'kmaq against the Beothuk are invalid, as is the controversial charge that Europeans hunted Beothuk for "sport." While the Beothuk were the victims of repeated murderous attacks by individuals and small parties, they were not systematically hunted down, nor were they objects of a campaign of genocide. Since their fate was extinction whatever the intent of the Euro-Canadians who deliberately or unwittingly were the cause of that end, such a distinction might seem irrelevant. But such is not the case. It is no fairer or historically valid to accuse Newfoundlanders of eliminating the Beothuk deliberately than it is to allege that "using" Natives in forest warfare was defensible because their "blood-lust" was such that they would have fought in any event. This suggestion, now discredited by military historians, demeans First Nations who pursued their own objectives. Accusations of genocide in Newfoundland similarly diminish Europeans' humanity by accusing them of actions they did not perform. The fate of the Beothuk was a tragedy, not proof of European malevolence.

By the time Shawnadithit succumbed to disease in Newfoundland, relations between First Nations and Europeans in central Canada were about to enter a new and significantly different phase. In Lower Canada the impact of the changing order on the Aboriginal population was relatively slight. Immigration to the francophone colony after the Revolutionary War was small in comparison to that of Upper Canada, and the European portions of it settled mainly in areas where they did not come into contact and competition with Indigenous populations. The arrival of some Loyalist First Nations did increase the numbers of Natives in the enclaves at Kahnawake and Kanesatake (Oka or Lake of Two Mountains), and Akwesasne (St Regis) got its real start as a consequence of the arrival of Mohawk moving out of the way of the victorious Americans. Non-Native Loyalists and later British immigration, however, tended to focus on Montreal and the Eastern Townships, where land was held in familiar freehold tenure rather than the *seigneurial* system that *Canadiens* used in most of the settled parts of the province. As a consequence, their arrival hardly disturbed the largest numbers of Lower Canadian First Nations, who were scattered in small hunting bands in the Shield country north of the arable region as well as in the even more northerly areas.

An important exception to this generalization was the community of Kanesatake on the Lake of Two Mountains. This settlement had begun early in the eighteenth century when a mixed community of Mohawk, Nipissing, and Algonkin were relocated from the north side of Montreal Island with the Sulpician priests who ministered to them. Theirs was one of the refugee mission communities that the French called *domiciliés* and Americans referred to as "praying Indians" or "the Seven Nations of Canada." Gradually during the latter part of the century, friction developed between the Natives and the priests, the former claiming that the land at Kanesatake belonged to them, and the Sulpicians pointing to the seigneurial grant from the French king that had made them seigneurs as well as spiritual shepherds. In the first half of the nineteenth century, this friction was exacerbated by the pressure of incoming settlers. The hunting-oriented Algonkin and Nipissing suffered especially from this pressure on resources, as they also did from the closure of the Hudson's Bay Company post at Oka following the 1821 amalgamation of the fur companies. During the nineteenth century the Algonkin and Nipissing voluntarily relocated with governmental help to more remote locations, leaving the Mohawk alone to face their priest-landlords in what was becoming an increasingly bitter confrontation over land ownership and access to resources such as wood.[19] In contrast to the situation at Oka, in Lower Canada in the early nineteenth century most First Nations continued to live in a traditional way based on a wilderness economy in the northern, unsettled regions of the colony.

The post-1783 influences were felt in the part of the old province of Quebec that lay west of the Ottawa River, the area that became the colony of Upper Canada in 1791. In Upper Canada the Europeans' impact was considerable; within a short period of time, vast numbers of them invaded an Indigenous-controlled area that had previously had few non-Natives in it. As already noted, the relocation of Loyalist Indians had required the British authorities, following the policy of the

Oka, on the Lake of Two Mountains, was both a Roman Catholic
mission settlement and an Aboriginal community.

Royal Proclamation of 1763, to secure First Nation agreement to any access to lands
through negotiation and treaty. The fact that Loyalists were followed in the 1790s
and 1800s by many so-called Late Loyalists – really just land-hungry American
farmers – meant that this policy had to be continued.

After the conclusion of the War of 1812, the only change in this pattern involved
the country of origin from which the immigrants came: from the 1820s onward
most new Upper Canadian settlers hailed from the British Isles rather than the
United States. Regardless of their point of origin, these farmers and townspeople
soon swamped the Indigenous population. Upper Canada's population increased
by a factor of ten – from 95,000 to 952,000 – between the end of the War of 1812
and the census of 1851. (The total population of British North America went
from approximately 750,000 in 1821 to 2.3 million by 1851.) Whereas in 1812 the
Indigenous population in Upper Canada had already been reduced to about one-
tenth of the total population of the colony, the inundations of the 1820s and 1840s
reduced it to demographic insignificance.[20]

Attempts to remove First Nations from the land and the initiation of a policy
designed to change them from Indigenous to modified Europeans were the consequences of the Upper Canadian population shift. The policy of acquiring title to

Native lands by treaty was continued after 1815, with one important modification. In the past, land surrender treaties had involved the exchange of title and claims to tracts of land for lump-sum payments. But in postwar Upper Canada, continuation of such a policy seemed prohibitively expensive to British administrators. And now that the Rush-Bagot Convention had brought real peace to North America and made the First Nations less important for military purposes, British authorities were increasingly preoccupied with the cost of Aboriginal affairs.

From 1818 onward a new land-acquisition policy was followed. Instead of using one-time payments, a system of acquiring the land in return for smaller, annual payments, or annuities, was pursued. The theory behind the scheme was that the lands would be sold to settlers who would make a down payment of 10 per cent and mortgage the remainder. In reality, mortgagors were expected to pay only the annual interest, not the principal. The revenue derived from the settlers' annual payments was used in turn to pay the annuities to the Natives from whom the tract had been purchased in the first place. From the British viewpoint, the policy had two attractions: it eliminated most of the large expenditures on land surrenders, and the First Nations indirectly funded a large part of the acquisition cost of their land through instalment payments made from revenues derived from the land.[21] To the Natives, such payments probably seemed familiar and welcome, resembling as they did the annual presents that many of them had been accustomed to receive from the British in the days when military alliance had been important, and that some of them continued to receive in the decades after the War of 1812. In this way, during the fifteen years after the war, vast areas of Native lands in Upper Canada were transferred to agricultural settlers in seven land treaties. While there certainly were instances in Upper Canada of the Maritime pattern of Euro-Canadian encroachment on lands under First Nation control and subsequent dispossession of the Indigenous occupants, most of the land settlement in the new colony took place in accordance with the Royal Proclamation, but with little profit to the account of the Mississauga.

Closely associated with the evolution of land policy in Upper Canada was a shift of responsibility for Native matters from the British military to the civil authorities. Once a lasting peace was established in North America, it was merely a matter of time until Britain recognized that its erstwhile Indigenous allies were now an expensive encumbrance and an obstacle to agricultural expansion. Not only were they irrelevant militarily, but they were a social responsibility. In 1830 Great Britain transferred jurisdiction over Aboriginal affairs in Lower and Upper Canada from military officers to civilian administrators in each colony. Significantly, the Americans at the same time shifted responsibility for Native peoples in the republic to the War Department.[22]

This reassignment of jurisdiction in 1830 reflected the past changes in First Nations' relationship with British Americans and presaged still more novelties in the way in which the two associated. The transfer of jurisdiction over Native matters from military to civil administration, like the policy of removing Indigenous people from the land through treaties and annuities, led to attempts to refashion the Natives. After all, if they were no longer useful militarily and could pose an obstacle to settlers' development of an agricultural economy, why not simply eliminate them completely? But how could such a thing be done? The obvious choices were extermination or assimilation: eradicating the Natives through violence and disease, or coercively remaking them into ersatz Europeans who lived and behaved as Euro-Canadians did. The former option, extermination, was not really open to either British officials or colonial settlers. In the first place, such an approach involved endless warfare and horrific expense, not to mention loss of life. Such a policy would provoke the increasingly numerous humanitarian organizations in Britain to create enormous political problems for any imperial government that followed such a bloody approach.

Furthermore, there was little in the Canadian tradition that would have created a desire to exterminate Natives. Colonial societies in British North America did not have a history of bloody conflict with the First Nations in what they regarded as their part of North America. The fact that the relationship had previously been a cooperative one that had taken place along frontiers of exploration, commerce, and alliance meant that, on the whole, First Nations had been perceived positively. Without an entrenched attitude of hostility and fear of Native people in British North America, there was no colonial predisposition in favour of coercion or elimination of the Indigenous population in Canada.

The political culture that was already well developed in Canada was one in which government played an active role in economic development and social policy. Government authority had preceded settlement and economic expansion from the days of the French intendants to the era of agricultural settlement, when public funds were paying for development projects such as the canals around Niagara Falls and on the St. Lawrence. Since it was the British-Canadian state, not individual settlers or local groups, that took the initiative in dealing with Indigenous people, the likelihood of conflict was reduced. The state acted in a more restrained manner in dealing with Native populations than did mobs of frontier settlers or rude local assemblies. The prominent role of the state and the tradition of cooperative relations between First Nations and newcomers explain why Indigenous people were not subjected to a strategy of extermination when they ceased to be militarily and economically useful in the early nineteenth century.

Not extermination, then, but assimilation became the method that the British and British-Canadians employed. The approach was implied in the words that the British secretary of state for war and the colonies used when explaining the shift of jurisdiction to the civil authorities in 1830: "It appears to me that the course which has hitherto been taken in dealing with these people, has had reference to the advantages which might be derived from their friendship in times of war, rather than to any settled purpose of gradually reclaiming them from a state of barbarism, and of introducing amongst them the industrious and peaceful habits of civilized life."[23] The words "gradually reclaiming them from a state of barbarism" and "introducing amongst them the industrious and peaceful habits of civilized life" constituted the key element in policy as it was developed and implemented under civilian control. "Thus British policy changed at this time from a utilitarian plan of using Indians as allies to a paternal programme of gradually incorporating the First Nations into non-Native society."[24] There was a shift from non-directed cultural change to coercion, in the form of directed cultural change.

Social scientists distinguish carefully between non-directed and directed cultural change. The former was the sort of changes – borrowings and adaptations – that had occurred on both sides of the relationship in the seventeenth and eighteenth centuries. First Nations might adopt European goods, but frequently used them to strengthen traditional practices. The Europeans might borrow the Natives' dress or style of forest warfare, but employed both costume and *la petite guerre* within a framework that remained recognizably European. Adoption of the abbreviated skirt was not accompanied by acquisition of the Iroquoians' distinctive views on the role of women by the *Canadiens*. And employment of Indigenous fighting tactics was undertaken within a grand strategy that was based on European perceptions and interests. On the whole, the adoption of European goods had not meant profound changes in the values, rituals, and beliefs of the Natives before the nineteenth century. This non-directed cultural change remained the pattern as long as First Nations outnumbered the newcomers, and as long as the First Nations could maintain their traditional economies.

Directed cultural change, which usually set in when the immigrants outnumbered the Indigenous population, meant a very different type of adaptation. The ideas and values of the more dominant party in the relationship were asserted over the dependent one; there were deliberate and systematic attempts by the dominant group to change the culture of the weaker; and the more vulnerable of the two parties was subjected not just to the rules and sanctions of its own society but also the taboos and requirements of the more powerful group. It was, in short, coercion. The consequence of such a pattern of change was usually the undermining of the weaker party's beliefs, social and political structures, and psychic well-being. The will to resist directed change often collapsed under the onslaught of increased numbers of newcomers, disruption of the traditional economy, and the ministrations of humanitarian groups that sought to inculcate their religion and secular beliefs in the minds of the Indigenous population. It was not the fur traders or even the soldiers who worked the worst damage on Canada's First Nations; it was the missionaries, the schoolteachers, and the bureaucrats who thought they knew better than the Native peoples what was good for them.

If changed demographic and military conditions made the shift from non-directed to directed cultural change possible, the introduction of new European ideas provided the momentum to carry the transition on. These novel ideas included, but did not end with, the Christianity and associated beliefs of the humanitarian organizations that were springing up in Britain. An important adjunct to the growth of British humanitarianism was the development of scientific racism. The belief that various races had distinct qualities, particular virtues, and different vices was hardly new in nineteenth-century Britain or British North America. The British had long tended to regard non-white populations that they encountered throughout the world as beneath them. Indigenous populations were, after the initial phase when they outnumbered and overawed the British, usually looked down upon as economically, socially, and politically inferior. What was different in the nineteenth century was that the development of a series of schools of scientific and pseudo-scientific thought meant that such prejudices acquired a veneer of scientific legitimacy. Now the crude habit of judging other societies by one's own had the gloss of respectability.

Phrenology and the early stages of cultural anthropology, to mention but two types of this scientific racism, emerged within just such an ethnocentric framework. When Europeans began reading people's heads for clues to their nature or cataloguing their physical features and behaviour so as to understand them better, they simply assumed that Europeans were the norm against which everything else human in the world was to be measured. The appropriately named Charles White put the point well when, in defining the highest physical type, he asked where but among Caucasian societies in Europe one could find "that nobly arched head, containing such a quantity of brain ...? Where that variety of features, and fulness of expression; those long, flowing, graceful ring-lets; that majestic beard, those rosy cheeks and coral lips? Where that ... noble gait? In what other quarter of the globe shall we find the blush that overspreads the soft features of the beautiful women of Europe, that emblem of modesty, of delicate feelings ...? Where, except on the bosom of the European woman, two such plump and snowy white hemispheres, tipt with vermilion?"[25] Where, indeed! Given such ethnocentric nineteenth-century attitudes, it was hardly surprising that those whose skulls differed from the Caucasian or whose social rituals were unrecognizable were regarded not just as different, but as inferior.[26]

The tendency to rank all other peoples below Caucasians was strengthened by the development and perversion of the evolutionary ideas of Charles Darwin and certain of his intellectual predecessors. The theories of natural selection, competition, and survival of the fittest were improperly transferred from the non-human to the human world by enthusiasts who also usually managed to change "fittest" to "best" in the process. This was a gross distortion of what evolutionary theorists had in fact argued. This social Darwinism, as it became known, was used to legitimize the tendency of Caucasians in Europe and North America to regard other peoples as inferior. Familiar, ugly racism was refurbished with scientific cosmetics; prejudice became scientific truth. In Britain these ideologies were used to justify expansion and domination in Africa and Asia; in the United States they were employed to defend first the institution of slavery and later the "Jim Crow laws" that succeeded it; and in British North America and Canada they served as handy rationalizations to justify attempts to coerce and change First Nations.

Between the American Revolutionary War and the aftermath of the War of 1812, the relations between First Nations and Europeans in the eastern portion of Canada underwent a profound change. Warfare ceased to figure prominently in government planning after the Rush-Bagot Convention of 1817 demilitarized the Great Lakes, and the commerce in animal furs collapsed after the amalgamation of fur-trade companies in 1821. The First Nations' utility as allies and trading partners was destroyed from Upper Canada to the Atlantic. Into the vacuum created by these changes moved, first, large numbers of immigrants who dispossessed First Nations of their lands in one fashion or another. As the Indigenous peoples ceased to be allies and economic partners, they increasingly assumed the roles of obstacle to development and consumer of public funds. Chief Golden Eagle of the Lake Simcoe Ojibwe in Upper Canada complained as early as 1805 that the authorities had "told us the Farmers would help us, but instead of doing so when we encamp on the shore they drive us off & shoot our Dogs and never give us any assistance as was promised to our old Chiefs."[27]

The response by Euro-Canadians to this changing relationship was to begin to develop Aboriginal policy as part of the work of civil government and to mount numerous and extensive programs to assimilate the Native. As First Nations moved from alliance to "irrelevance," the European responded with a change of attitude from eager gratitude to pity and contempt. Shinguakonce (Little Pine), the influential chief of the Garden River Ojibwe near Sault Ste. Marie, poignantly noted in an 1849 letter to the governor:

> When your white children first came into this country they did not come shouting the war cry and seeking to wrest this land from us. They told us they came as friends to smoke the pipe of peace; they sought our friendship, we became brothers. Their enemies were ours, at the time we were strong and powerful, while they were few and weak. But did we oppress them or wrong them? No! And they did not attempt to do what is now done, nor did they tell us that at some future day you would.
>
> Father, time wore on and you have become a great people, whilst we have melted away like snow beneath an April sun; our strength is wasted, our countless warriors dead, our forests laid low, you have hunted us from every place as with a wand, you have swept away all our pleasant land, and like some giant foe you tell us "willing or unwilling, you must now go from amid these rocks and wastes, I want them now! I want them to make rich my white children, whilst you may shrink away to holes and caves like starving dogs to die."[28]

Equally eloquent were the words of a disgruntled young Mississauga chieftain:

> You came as a wind blown across the Great Lake. The wind wafted you to our shores. We rcd. you – we planted you – we nursed you. We protected you till you became a mighty tree that spread thro our Hunting Land. With its branches you now lash us.[29]

Cooperation was giving way to coercion. Unfortunately, for the Garden River Ojibwe, the Mississauga, and other First Nations, there was worse to come.

CHAPTER SIX

Reserves, Residential Schools, and the Threat of Assimilation

The shift of responsibility for Aboriginal affairs from military to civilian officials foreshadowed a major change in the relationship. Before 1830, the men who dealt with First Nations had acted diplomatically, treating Indigenous peoples as powerful nations with whom they had to parley to achieve agreement on a course of action. This diplomatic mode had been a natural outgrowth of the underlying character of the relationship, military alliance. The new approach was based on an official view that

> the most effectual means of ameliorating the condition of the Indians, of promoting their religious improvement and education, and of eventually relieving His Majesty's Government from the expense of the Indian department, are,
>
> 1st. To collect the Indians in considerable numbers, and to settle them in villages, with due portion of land for their cultivation and support.
>
> 2d. To make such provision for their religious improvement, education and instruction in husbandry, as circumstances may from time to time require.
>
> 3d. To afford them such assistance in building their houses, rations, and in procuring such seed and agricultural implements as may be necessary, commuting where practicable, a portion of their presents for the latter.[1]

The intention of civil government, now that First Nations no longer were militarily useful, was to concentrate them in settled areas, or reserves; to subject them to as much proselytization, schooling, and instruction in agriculture as "circumstances" made necessary; and to do these things at least in part with the Natives' own funds.

The Chapel of the Mohawk, in Brantford, Ontario, symbolized an enduring link between the Six Nations and the Anglican Church.

The strategy was based on an assumption that complete assimilation was "the only possible euthanasia of savage communities."[2]

Existing Christian missionary endeavours provided the foundation for such a policy in Upper Canada. Since the 1790s the Moravian Brethren had been working among Natives whom one of their brethren had brought from the United States. The Church of England's Society for the Propagation of the Gospel in Foreign Parts, by virtue of the Anglicans' lengthy ministry to the Mohawk, was well established on the Grand River. Anglican ministrations to the Bay of Quinte Iroquois were more modest and intermittent. However, the most extensive and effective evangelical efforts among the First Nations of Upper Canada were those of the Methodists. Especially after a mixed-ancestry Mississauga named Peter Jones converted to Christianity in 1823, the Methodists enjoyed considerable success at a number of centres. Jones was but one of several Native clerics and missionary workers – others included John Sunday, Peter Jacobs, and George Copway – who accounted for many of the advances that the Methodists made in places such as the Credit Mission near Toronto, Grape Island, Rice Lake, and Lake Simcoe. As well as securing the adoption of Christianity, the Methodists were particularly successful in promoting abstinence from alcohol and the adoption of sedentary agriculture and literacy among their followers. Finally, the Catholic Church's Society of Jesus began a long and moderately successful ministry to the Natives of Manitoulin Island at Wikwemikong.[3] These religious agencies stood ready to assist officialdom with its new policy in the 1830s.

Government intended to participate directly in carrying out the policy of peaceful "euthanasia" in Upper Canada as well as employing missionaries. The administration's desire to reduce its expenditure for annual presents by encouraging First Nations to become economically self-sufficient through agriculture was one motive for government experiments of the 1830s. Another reason was found in the new generation of officials who supervised Aboriginal policy after 1830: these men, who had not been reared in the Johnson tradition of treating Natives as military allies, tended to regard them as social and economic problems who would benefit from Christianization and the adoption of sedentary agriculture. Moreover, officials in Upper Canada wanted to settle First Nations on reserves with schools and farming to counter the Americans' provision of schools and missions in regions where some of the "wandering tribes" affiliated with the British resided.[4]

Finally, many of the Upper Canadian Indigenous peoples recognized that they needed new skills and economic pursuits in an era of increasing Euro-Canadian settlement and agricultural development.

In 1827 a northern Ojibwe, Ashagashe, told officials at Drummond Island, in the Michilimackinac area,

> Father, we have observed with some degree of jealousy the establishment of a place at Michilimackinac, at which the children of our great father are taught the means of living in the same way the whites do, where they also learn to *mark their thoughts* on paper, and to think the *news from books* [to read and write] as you do ...
>
> Father, tell our father that we squeeze him hard by the hand, and trust that he will assist us; tell him that we want some hoes and spades to dig with; don't leave our father until you get him to say yes.[5]

And Yellowhead, head chief of the Lake Simcoe Ojibwe, also reported that:

> Our native brothers are desirous of forming a settlement, and we avail ourselves of this opportunity to address our great father on a subject of such deep interest to our tribe.
>
> Father, should our great father agree, we are desirous of being settled together, we shall then be enabled to pursue a regular system of agriculture, and greater facilities will be afforded us in following the precepts of our religious teachers. Those that have embraced christianity [sic] already feel its happy effects.[6]

In short, the rising cost of distributing presents, the pro-assimilation attitudes of a new generation of Indian Department officers, American missionary enterprise, and the desires of some of the First Nations combined to push government into an experiment in reserves and agriculture in the 1830s.

Reserves were established at Coldwater, near Lake Simcoe, and at Sarnia, and efforts were made to provide both education and practical instruction in farming methods. In sharp contrast to such church-directed efforts as the Methodist enterprise on the Credit River, however, the Coldwater-Narrows experiment at settling First Nations proved unsuccessful. Clearing for settlements began in 1830, but by 1837 the enterprise had collapsed. In part, the explanation for the failure lay in the fact the Indian Department officials expected too much too quickly of the Natives. The Ojibwe were reluctant to give up a mixed economy of hunting, fishing, and gathering for sedentary agriculture exclusively. Moreover, in contrast to the Methodists, who at settlements such as the Credit Mission worked through Indigenous missionaries such as Peter Jones, bureaucrats attempted first to direct and then to dominate the Natives and their traditional leaders. The experiment was troubled by denominational conflict between Methodists and Catholics, and by the encroachments of non-Native settlers who coveted the lands set aside for Native peoples.[7]

A key component of the experiments at Coldwater and the Narrows, one whose results satisfied neither First Nations nor Europeans, was schooling under the control of missionaries. Three partners with different, though partially compatible, objectives participated. From the government standpoint, education was a desirable adjunct to both the attempts to assimilate the Natives culturally and to teach them alternative skills such as agriculture. From the viewpoint of the churches – principally Catholic, Anglican, and Methodist – reading and writing in a European language were also essential to conversion and living as practising Christians. In the optimum case, education was an essential means of obtaining Native missionaries and catechists.

So far as the First Nations were concerned, the motive for participating in schooling was to acquire the knowledge that they recognized as essential to their continued survival and success at a time when the literate Europeans were becoming dominant. In 1830 Shinguakonce (Little Pine), leader of the Garden River Ojibwe, travelled the long way to York with his son, Augustine Shingwauk, to seek missionaries and schooling that, in the 1870s, would evolve into an early residential school. Shinguakonce was motivated by a strategy of schooling the young to help his people adjust to the alien ways of the numerous newcomers.[8] In the same year, Chief Keketoonce of the Saugeen people told Methodist-Mississauga Peter Jones, "I will be a Christian. It may be while I stretch out my hands to the Great Spirit for the blessings which my Christian brethren enjoy, I may receive a handful of the same before I die."[9] Others, such as Chief Shawahnahness of St. Clair River, were more ambivalent about the newcomers' ways, rejecting some parts while embracing others. In 1833 Shawahnahness told Peter Jones that his people "had already agreed amongst themselves *never* to abandon the religion of their fore-fathers," but also informed the missionary, "We agree to send our children to school that they may learn to read, put words on paper, and count, so that the white traders might not cheat them."[10] For sacred and/or secular reasons, some First Nations in Upper Canada were prepared to adopt British education. Hence, all three groups could agree on the desirability of providing schooling for Indigenous people, the government and missionaries for reasons that were compatible if not exactly identical. Natives often wanted the services of teachers, too, but for their own purposes: they wanted learning, but not the accompanying assimilationist efforts that were central to the purposes of officials and preachers.

In the 1830s in Upper Canada there was a considerable effort to provide day schools in or near First Nation settlements where First Nations indicated a desire for them or a willingness to accept them. Efforts were already in place in such centres as the Credit River settlement of Mississauga, and schools were established in reserve locations. The Methodists in particular were noteworthy for their efforts to teach trades, crafts, and agriculture along with basic formal education by means both of teachers, usually non-Natives, and "native exhorters and class-leaders."[11] Government initiatives tended to segregate the formal schooling and the efforts to inculcate agriculture, and in neither were they especially successful. Whatever advances the government and churches claimed in Native education in the 1830s tended to be in the superficial manifestations of assimilation, such as the Native peoples' adoption of the clothing and domestic arrangements of Euro-Canadian society.

The efforts to use schools as instruments of assimilation and for teaching alternative economic skills were disrupted in the mid-1830s by two important events. First, there was the growing realization among Methodist missionaries that the day schools were not as successful as they had hoped. The event that prompted this discovery was the second disruptive force, the efforts of a new lieutenant-governor to alter the policy of "civilization" that had been in place since 1830. The arrival of Sir Francis Bond Head as lieutenant-governor of Upper Canada in 1836 unsettled many groups in the colony, not least First Nations. Bond Head, who had worked as a mine manager in South America and had served as a commissioner under the new Poor Law of 1832 in England, thought that he was a thoroughly qualified expert on Indigenous peoples in the New World and on social engineering. He believed "that an attempt to make farmers of the red men has been, generally speaking, a complete failure," and "that congregating them for the purpose of civilization has implanted many more vices than it has eradicated." Therefore, "the greatest kindness we can perform towards these intelligent, simple-minded people, is to remove and fortify them as much as possible from all communication with the whites."[12] To that end, he proposed – and, more important, acted on his own proposal – that the First Nations not be converted to Christianity and a European way of life, but that they be left alone to live out their days in isolation and peace. Bond Head had a different approach to the "euthanasia" of the Indigenous population in Upper Canada. He was convinced, he said, that the Natives were dwindling in numbers and were destined to die out completely. On this assumption he began to implement a policy of taking land surrenders from as many First Nations as possible and relocating them on Manitoulin Island, where they would live out their remaining days.

The response to Bond Head's initiative was a clear indication of how much conditions had changed in Aboriginal affairs. Although the British Colonial Office initially evinced cautious enthusiasm at the lieutenant-governor's course, it was forced to back down swiftly and completely in the face of an angry protest from religious and humanitarian groups in both British North America and the United Kingdom. The Wesleyan Methodists claimed that the First Nations were greatly disquieted at this threat to their lands, and they objected to the proposed policy as an abandonment of the Indigenous population. They secured the cooperation of English groups such as the recently founded Aborigines Protection Society (1836) and the Society of Friends in lobbying the imperial government against Bond Head's proposals. The combination of outraged public opinion and strategic concerns in 1837–8 about armed risings in both Canadas, and about the danger of incursions by American brigands, reminded British officials that abandoning and removing the Natives of Upper Canada was both militarily foolish and politically dangerous. Britain countermanded Bond Head's suspension of the policy of settling First Nations and encouraging the adoption of agriculture, although the land surrenders that Bond Head had arranged with bands stood. Officialdom began again to look anxiously for a policy to replace that of the early 1830s.

The new policy consisted of a commission of inquiry and a revision of the assimilationist educational program. The inquiry, known as the Bagot Commission for the governor who established it in 1842, laid down many of the key elements of colonial policy that would govern Aboriginal affairs up to and beyond Confederation.[13] It reaffirmed the Crown's obligations to First Nations, in particular in relation to the important question of land and land tenure, and acknowledged the Natives' "right of occupancy" and "claim to compensation for its surrender" that had been embodied in the Royal Proclamation. Still, it proposed changes that would move in the direction of eliminating the distinctive Native use of land and reduce the government's obligations, financial and otherwise. First Nations would be provided with the means to become successful farmers and artisans, and they would be encouraged to adopt individual ownership of plots of land in the British freehold system, rather than the communal reserve ownership that had been used to that point. Efforts would be made to reduce financial obligations by taking a census of First Nations and restricting recipients of annual presents to those on it, and by stipulating that those who acquired sufficient education would no longer be eligible to receive presents. At the same time, administration of the payment of annuities would be tightened up, both to protect the government and to provide Native leaders with a proper accounting of their funds.

The government's decision to implement the Bagot Commission's recommendations led to the reorganization of the Indian department, a new thrust in First Nation education, and significant Native resistance. The offices were moved from

"Numbering the Indians, Wikwemikong, 15 August 1856." Taking a census was part of
the government's program of managing and assimilating First Nations in the future Ontario.

Kingston to Montreal, and several somnolent officials were replaced with a set of
new, presumably more energetic, "Indian visitors." But the recommendation to curtail the giving of annual presents remained a dead letter for a time because First
Nations strongly opposed any step in the direction of terminating the symbol of
their relationship with the Crown. Similarly, the plan to grant individual Natives
deeds to separate plots of reserve land encountered strenuous opposition from
their leaders, who regarded the scheme as antithetical to their own traditions of
communal ownership. Significantly, the Indigenous response to the other principal
recommendations, those dealing with education, was initially much more positive.

The reorientation of schooling for First Nations from day schools to residential institutions in the 1840s was an important change.[14] In 1828 a Methodist missionary on Grape Island had begun to provide instruction to four Native girls
who boarded with him and his family. Another school had been set up on the Six
Nations reserve near Brantford in 1829 by the New England Company, an English
non-denominational missionary organization. Though at first called a "Mechanics'
Institution" in recognition of its attempt to emulate metropolitan efforts at educating
the lower orders of an industrializing society, it soon became known as the Mohawk

Institute, and in 1833 it took its first boarders, ten boys and ten girls from the Six Nations reserve. The cost of lodging, feeding, clothing, and teaching the children was borne by the English missionary body.[15] It would be Canada's longest surviving residential school. In the short term, when Bond Head denounced the lack of progress on First Nation reserves and forced missionaries and teachers to reassess their methods, a model on which to base a new approach to schooling was available.

The Bagot Commission concluded that the failure of the day schools was rooted not in inadequate funding or assimilationist pressures on Indigenous people, but on the influence that parents exerted when the young scholars returned home from class. It recommended the establishment of boarding schools with farms, where the children could be taught agriculture or a trade, assimilated in the absence of parental influence, equipped to forgo annual presents, and readied to take up individual plots of land in freehold tenure. These "manual labour schools" should be funded by government and operated by all Christian religious groups willing and able to play a role in this important work. That groups such as the Methodists who had been active in education agreed with such notions was perhaps not surprising. In 1838 they had opened a small boarding school for girls at Alderville that grew to an enrolment of thirty by 1845.

What seemed more surprising was the initial Indigenous cooperation with and support for these boarding schools, which were designed for the thorough assimilation and education of their children. Natives in the Alderville area supported the Methodist establishment there with £100 from their annuities.[16] In these same years Ojibwe were encouraging one of their own, Methodist minister Peter Jones, to raise funds in the United Kingdom for another residential establishment at Munceytown.[17] Hence it was not surprising that, when the government decided to implement the Bagot Commission's recommendations on residential schooling, it got support from some of the First Nations.

At a conference at Orillia in 1846, an event that represented the last occasion on which the Indian Department would negotiate change with First Nations in eastern Canada, most of the chiefs in attendance approved the plan of creating residential schools and promised the Indian Department one-quarter of their annuities for twenty-five years for support of the institutions. But their reasons for wanting these schools were different from the government's: they wished to acquire the Euro-Canadians' learning in order to survive, but they had no wish to assimilate. That they did not accept the whole assimilationist policy of the government was made clear by at least two developments. After the Orillia conference, some bands refused to send their children to the residential schools at Alderville, Munceytown, and the Six Nations reserve. And at the Orillia conference, the chiefs' stout resistance to the idea that they give up their lands and congregate in the three sites that were proposed for such schools made it clear that they wanted only schooling, not a fundamental change in their way of life.[18]

This departure in education was to prove important for more Native people than only those of Upper Canada, and for a longer period of time than the chiefs at Orillia in 1846 could have foreseen. During the 1850s and 1860s the system of boarding establishments in the future Ontario was extended, as government and churches cooperated in the program. Moreover, the theory and practice of these residential schools were elaborated in an important statement by Chief Superintendent of Common Schools Egerton Ryerson. His recommendations laid out the complete assimilationist theory and methods that had lain implicit in the experiments at Coldwater and elsewhere in the 1830s as well as in the Bagot Commission report of 1842–4. The purpose of the schools, said Ryerson, was "to give a plain English education adapted to the working farmer and mechanic," it being understood of the Native that "with him nothing can be done to improve and elevate his character and condition without the aid of religious feeling." The "animating and controlling spirit of each industrial school establishment should ... be a religious one." The system of removing the children from the home and village, and subjecting them to constant indoctrination in Christianity and the three R's became well established. Combining a half-day of classroom work with a half-day in the shops or fields, an approach that was borrowed in part from similar institutions in the United States, would teach useful trades by practical experience while simultaneously supplying many of the basic needs of the school. "I think," concluded Ryerson optimistically, "with judicious management, these establishments will be able in the course of a few years very nearly to support themselves."[19]

This system of residential schooling would persist in Upper Canada up to and beyond Confederation, and after the acquisition of the Hudson's Bay Company lands in the Northwest it would be transferred there. What the missionaries and administrators responsible for this extension of residential schooling sometimes forgot was that First Nation resistance to the assimilationist purpose of these schools appeared almost immediately in the 1840s and 1850s. By 1856 colonial bureaucrats were coming to a doleful conclusion about the 1846 agreement to establish manual labour schools: "It is with great reluctance that we are forced to the conclusion that this benevolent experiment has been to a great extent a failure."[20] As the chiefs at Orillia had tried to make clear, they wanted schooling not refashioning.

There were other important developments in Upper Canada besides the creation of a reserve and educational program in the years between the transfer of policy to civil government in 1830 and the 1860s. Chief among these changes were modifications in the treaty-making process and in legislation dealing with First Nations. In 1845 the government of the united Province of Canada, which consisted of the former colonies of Lower and Upper Canada, granted permission to mining companies to explore along the northern and eastern shores of Lake Superior for minerals. Not for the first – nor, for that matter, for the last – time, Natives of the region complained to the man who represented the Crown, the lieutenant-governor, that the men employed by these companies were actually "trespassing on their property." As Chief Shingwaukonce of Garden River pointedly asked Governor Elgin, "Can you lay claim to our land? If so, by what right? Have you conquered it from us? You have not, for when you first came among us your children were few and weak, and the war cry of the Ojibway struck terror to the hearts of the pale face."[21] In a petition to the Crown Shinguakonce added, "I want always to live and plant at Garden River and as my people are poor to derive a share of what is found on my lands," signalling a desire to participate in the revenues to be generated from mining.[22] Before an investigation into the complaints could be fully carried out, the Natives began to threaten to attack one of the mines on the eastern shore of Lake Superior. A worried governor sent troops to the site to end the conflict, with gratifying results. As Lord Elgin was driven to observe, "I cannot but think that it is much to be regretted that steps were not taken to investigate thoroughly and extinguish all Indian claims before licences of exploration or grants of land were conceded by the Government in this Territory."[23]

The readiness of some of the Native people in the territory to assert their rights in the face of non-Native encroachment led to the negotiation of the Robinson Treaties in 1850. The Robinson-Huron and Robinson-Superior Treaties with the Ojibwe of northern Ontario were unusual in that they secured First Nations agreement to Euro-Canadian penetration of a much larger region than was immediately needed for the economic purposes of the non-Native entrepreneurs. In addition, the Indigenous people showed a lively concern about securing recognition of their title to tracts that would be reserved for their exclusive use in the pursuit of traditional economic activities. As Robinson reported to his superiors, "In allowing the Indians to retain reservations of land for their own use I was governed by the fact that they in most cases asked for such tracts as they had heretofore been in the habit of using for purposes of residence and cultivation, and by securing these to them and the right of hunting and fishing over the ceded territory, they cannot say that the Government takes from their usual means of subsistence and therefore have no claims for support, which they no doubt would have preferred, had this not been done."[24] In their retention of annuities as the means of payment, the 1850 treaties were a continuation of the traditions of the Upper Canadian era; in the First Nations' desire to hold on to large tracts that would permit them to maintain a traditional way of life, they were a harbinger of developments in the 1870s.

In the same year that the Robinson Treaties were negotiated, the legislature of the Province of Canada undertook important initiatives in dealing with Natives. In 1850 Canada passed "An Act for the better protection of the Lands and Property of Indians in Lower Canada" and "An Act for the protection of the Indians in Upper Canada from imposition, and the property occupied or enjoyed by them from trespassing and injury." As the titles of the measures indicated, the legislation was intended to protect First Nations' established right in both sections of the Province of Canada to the lands that had been set aside for them.

But the long-term significance of the measures lay in one particular feature of the legislation. The Act that applied to Lower Canada, or Canada East as it was now known, purported to define "Indians" as "persons of Indian blood, reputed to belong to the particular Body or Tribe of Indians interested in such lands and their descendents [sic] ... persons intermarried with any such Indians and residing amongst them, and the descendents [sic] of all such persons ... persons residing among such Indians, whose parents on either side were or are Indians of such Body or Tribe, or entitled to be considered as such: And ... persons adopted in infancy by any such Indians, and residing in the village or upon the lands of such Tribe or Body of Indians and their Descendents [sic]."[25]

In comparison with later "Indian Acts" this 1850 definition was fairly broad. Anyone in Canada East who was reputed to have Indian blood and to be living with a band, anyone married to such a person, anyone residing with First Nations either of whose parents was Indian, and anyone adopted as a child by Indians and still living with them was considered to be "Indian." The truly significant feature of this statute was that civil government, a body in which First Nations were not even eligible to have a representative, arrogated to itself the authority to define who was or was not Indian. This was a development that could have occurred only in a period when the original peoples had become marginal to the needs and aspirations of the immigrant population that dominated the territory. Earlier it had been neither possible nor desirable to treat commercial partners and military allies in such a high-handed fashion. In an 1851 amendment of the Lower Canadian statute, the government made changes to accommodate the wishes of First Nations,[26] but the innovation of the state defining status remained. Later, the government would expand this intervention by defining and distinguishing between "status" and "non-status" Indians.

The Province of Canada now found itself on the slippery slope that led from the moral heights of protection to the depths of coercion. As the titles of the 1850 acts so plainly illustrated, the legislation was designed to protect First Nations in Canada from the cycle of squatting-resistance-conflict-dispossession that had already begun in the arable portions of the Maritimes. This protective impulse was laid over top of the objectives of the Bagot Commission and missionaries to assimilate the Natives through education and the adoption of agriculture. Given this background, it was only natural that the next step in the process was to provide for the legal emergence of the Indigenous person who had been tutored and moulded from Indian status to full British colonial citizenship. In the process of making this transition, however, legislators ignored First Nation opinion and introduced ominous provisions that threatened to undermine the base of their identity and survival – their land. The Indian Department in this period also adopted a policy of denying presents to any First Nations woman who "married out" and giving any educated, self-supporting Indigenous person fee simple title to a portion of reserve land – thus reducing the size of the reserve over time. Such an educated Native would henceforth not receive annuities or have rights to band property.[27]

The Act for the Gradual Civilization of the Indian Tribes in the Canadas (Gradual Civilization Act) that was passed by the legislature of Canada in 1857 combined past assumptions and future objectives. It recognized implicitly that after a quarter-century of assimilative programs, colonial policy was at a crossroads. Governor Elgin made that point in 1854: "If the civilizing process to which the Indians have been subject for so many years has been accompanied by success, they have surely by this time arrived at a sufficiently enlightened condition to be emancipated from this state of pupilage in which they have been maintained; if on the other hand, the process has been inadequate to achieve the desired end, it has been long enough in unsuccessful operation to warrant the adoption of some other method of procuring this result."[28] The Gradual Civilization Act of 1857 proposed to move to the next stage: citizenship. The measure's preamble indicated that the legislation was built on the aspirations of the missionaries and the conclusions of the Bagot Commission: "Whereas it is desirable to encourage the progress of Civilization among the Indian Tribes in this Province, and the gradual removal of all legal distinctions between them and her Majesty's other Canadian Subjects, and to facilitate the acquisition of property and of the rights accompanying it, by such individual Members of the said Tribes as shall be found to desire such encouragement and to have deserved it," to that end the statute established ways in which First Nations males might become enfranchised.[29] The 1857 Act spelled out how they might become full citizens and drop their Indian status.[30]

The road to enfranchisement was not easy; the way of travelling it could be iron-ic. When Natives could meet the test of a special board and prove that they had been educated, were debt-free, and of good moral character, they would be enfran-chised and given twenty hectares of land. It was expected that such progress would be the result of the work of missionaries and teachers in residential schools, with their Christian environment and model farms. The 1857 measure thus established a paradox that marked policy for a century: though the measure was designed to permit Indians to drop their status in favour of full British North American citizen-ship, it began by defining them as non-citizens. In other words, legislation whose purpose was "to remove all legal distinctions between Indians and Euro-Canadians actually established them" in law. Furthermore, before Natives could overcome their status and realize the blissful integration that the preamble of the legislation contemplated, they had to meet a test that many – perhaps most – Euro-Canadians in the 1850s could not have satisfied.[31] That was plainly silly; but it was nonsense that would persist for more than a century.

Worse than the silly portions of the legislation were the serious ones that dealt with land. By providing that an enfranchised man would gain the right to freehold tenure of twenty hectares from reserve lands, this colonial measure presumed to deviate from the spirit of the Royal Proclamation policy. That earlier pronounce-ment had decreed that colonists, in their legislatures or otherwise, could not deal directly with First Nations for land. Only the Crown could alienate Native land. But the 1857 statute breached that defence of Indigenous control of their lands by cre-ating at least a presumption that a colonial legislature could interfere with reserve lands to the extent of parcelling out small plots to newly enfranchised band mem-bers. Ominously, in 1860 Britain transferred responsibility for Aboriginal matters to the legislatures of her British North American colonies. In accordance with the canons of responsible government, which meant colonial self-government, the mother country was transferring control of an important subject to Canada. But that meant that jurisdiction over First Nation matters was transferred to the leg-islative representatives of a settler society that had even less sympathy for Native people than did imperial Britain.

The measure of 1857 also ran counter to the clearly expressed wishes of First Nations. Though they had said on many occasions – and frequently backed up their assertions with their money – that they wanted education, they rejected the total assimilation that missionaries and officials intended to be the final outcome of schooling and evangelization. Similarly, the chiefs of Canada West had made it clear in the meeting at Orillia in 1846 that they wanted no part of provisions that would allow the conversion of lands that bands held in common to individual plots held in freehold tenure. The Gradual Civilization Act deliberately ran counter to those clearly expressed wishes by making provision for the conversion of reserve lands into alienated plots in the hands of men who would cease to be Indians upon enfranchisement. The reaction of the bands to both these provisions of the Gradual Civilization Act and to the intent to devolve administration of Aboriginal affairs to the colonial level was swift and blunt. At a council of the Six Nations and chiefs from fifteen other communities they summarized their complaints:

> 1st they pray for a repeal [of the section] of the Civilization Act which would admit the Enfranchisement.
>   2nd They do not wish to surrender any more land.
>   3rd They do not wish to be given over from the Imperial Government to the care of the Provincial one ...
>   4th If their Great Mother the Queen objects paying the Expenses of maintaining the Department they will consent to do so provided they are not transferred from the Great Mother's care to the Provincial authorities.[32]

As the chief of Kahnawake put it, "Relative to this Act for the Civilization of the Indians there is nothing in it to be for their benefit, only to break them to pieces."[33] Equally revealing was the response of the Indian Department: it replied brusquely that "the Civilization Act is no grievance to you," soon ceased the giving of annual presents, and proceeded with the transfer of jurisdiction over Indian affairs from London to the colony.[34]

What the 1857 Gradual Civilization Act and its aftermath illustrated very clearly was that First Nation–government relations were changing dramatically in the era of extensive European settlement in central Canada. After responsibility for Aboriginal relations was transferred from military to civil authorities in 1830, government officials began to plan for the removal of Natives from the path of settlement. To a great extent that had been done in the land surrender treaties that preceded immigration to parts of Upper Canada, and it was continued in more northerly regions by means of the Robinson Treaties. At the same time, a new alliance of church and humanitarian organizations, with government encouragement, promoted fundamental changes in those First Nations who remained within or close to areas of the colony where agricultural and commercial development was going on apace. They tried to convert Natives in religious terms and to remake them culturally by the twin instruments of church and school. The effort began with a network of day schools, but shifted in the 1840s to reliance on residential schools. In these new institutions, children were insulated from the influences of their own people and subjected to a program designed to lead them to forget who they were and adopt the ways and values of their teachers. The culmination of this process was expected to be their jettisoning of their Indian legal status in favour of enfranchisement. They would, once they had lost their Aboriginal identity, become citizens, and they would remove both themselves and their land from the Indigenous world.

In the process of making this transition in policy, both churches and governments edged steadily from protection to compulsion and from cooperation towards coercion. The shift from day schools to boarding schools was one symptom of that transition: residential schools were designed to enable missionaries to interfere with character formation and identity of the young, even though Native leaders had said repeatedly that they wanted not assimilation but schooling. Similarly, the pregnant provisions of the 1850–1 Act governing Lower Canadian Natives and the 1857 Gradual Civilization Act that applied to all First Nations in the Province of Canada were an assertion of legislative authority over and control of First Nations in Canada. The legislature now was saying that it would define who was an Indian as a preliminary to making it possible for the Indian to cease being Indian. Government had moved from negotiating in 1846 to dictating to Native leaders in 1857. And the 1857 legislation also violated the tradition of the Royal Proclamation of 1763 and contradicted First Nations' desires to hold their land communally. The Gradual Civilization Act simply brushed aside wishes in the first of many coercive actions directed against Indigenous peoples. When the Indian Department stated that "the Civilization Act is no grievance to you," it was giving an answer that only a government embarked on legislated coercion of First Nations would have thought appropriate. That reply showed how far relations between Natives and governments had travelled in the few decades since the Rush-Bagot Convention had ended the military threat from the south.

Other unsettling markers of the evolution were found in the Indian Department personnel and colonial legislation. From the 1830s onward in Upper Canada, the old generation of officials trained in the William Johnson school of forest diplomacy, who viewed First Nations as allies and treated them respectfully, was supplanted by representatives of the settlers. Two of the Province of Canada's representatives in the Robinson Treaties negotiations were examples: Alexander Vidal was a surveyor, and William Robinson was a son of the Upper Canadian Family Compact.[35] In the case of the fisheries, which were vital to the survival of First Nations, the state became less protective over time. A proclamation by the chief officer of Upper Canada in 1797 was forthright in protection of Native fisheries; an 1857 statute, which became law the same day as the Gradual Civilization Act did, permitted the taking of fish only by rod, effectively prohibiting fishing by Native people, who used mainly spears and nets.[36] For their part, the First Nation communities of Upper Canada had also begun to establish a pattern of resistance to these novel, threatening policies. They used passive resistance to combat the oppressive manual labour schools, withholding their children from the missionaries, to the point that by 1856 government officials considered the residential schools to have failed. So far as legislation such as the Gradual Civilization Act was concerned, First Nations communities similarly declined to cooperate with state plans for their voluntary enfranchisement. Between 1857 and the codification of the Indian Act in 1876 precisely one male, Elias Hill, a Six Nations man who had attended the Mohawk Institute, applied for and received citizenship. However, the provision of the Gradual Civilization Act by which the state intended Hill to take his share of reserve land with him as a freehold tenure was frustrated by the Council of the Six Nations, who simply refused to agree to the removal of the tract from reserve status. In this manner, at least part of the Gradual Civilization Act's program was thwarted in the case of the first status Indian to avail himself of it.[37]

In the decade after the Gradual Civilization Act a pattern that was to become all too depressingly familiar was established. First Nations in Canada West responded with protest to the new assimilative program. Their cooperation in establishing and supporting manual labour schools that had begun to develop in the late 1840s and early 1850s had been replaced with resistance. In many instances, bands were coming to regard missionaries and their schools as adversaries. It was significant that the Reverend Peter Jones, the convert who had been an early Native advocate of boarding schools and who had served briefly as the superintendent of the Methodists' institution at Munceyville, did not send his sons to boarding school.[38] After his death, his widow did send one son, Peter Edmund Jones, to Mount Elgin briefly.[39] Natives also protested against the 1857 legislation and demanded its repeal. They said that they would not sell any more of their land, and made plans to lay their grievances before the throne when the Prince of Wales visited Canada in 1861. They continued to support the objectives of using education and agricultural instruction to enable them to cope economically with the changes about them, but they emphatically rejected the Euro-Canadians' assimilationist strategy of which schooling and agricultural instruction were a part. For example, in 1871 Augustine Shingwauk, who had succeeded his father, Shinguakonce as chief, travelled to Toronto to ask missionary authorities to send a teacher to his community because before he died he hoped to see "a big teaching wigwam built at Garden River, where children from the Great Chippeway Lake [Lake Superior] would be received and clothed, and fed, and taught how to read and how to write; and also

Shingwauk Home in Sault Ste. Marie, Ontario, was established in the 1870s
in response to Ojibwe requests for "a teaching wigwam."

how to farm and build houses, and make clothing; so that by and bye they might go
back and teach their own people."[40] However, in the highly symbolic area of enfranchisement, First Nations simply refused to cooperate. They resisted by refusing to
cooperate with programs designed to obliterate their culture.

The government's response, in turn, was to slide further from protection towards
compulsion. By 1863 it was clear to the Canadian government that its policy of
enfranchisement was a failure. Similarly, increasing Native non-cooperation in the
educational sphere was noted and led to demands for compulsory schooling legislation that would eliminate parents' ability to withhold or withdraw their children
from the clutches of the preachers and teachers.

In 1869 the new Dominion of Canada moved the rest of the way towards coercion in another Enfranchisement Act. (At Confederation, jurisdiction for "Indians
and lands reserved for the Indians" had been assigned to the federal level of government.) Under the guise of providing First Nations with institutions of local
self-government, the Dominion established a mechanism that allowed Ottawa bureaucrats to interfere with the traditional leaders who had so often blocked their
initiatives. They could be set aside for "dishonesty, intemperance or immorality" by
the Governor General in Council and replaced with elected officials. The 1869 Act
also continued the assault on communal land-holding by re-enacting provisions of

an 1868 statute that had encouraged individuals to get "location tickets" for their share of reserve lands. And, finally, the post-Confederation statute meddled still more in the definition of who was an Indian by stipulating that an Indian woman who married a non-Indian would lose her Indian status. Both she and her offspring would cease to be Indians and to qualify for annuities or band membership if she married a non-Indian. This provision, like the whole of the statute, was a gross interference in First Nations' management of their internal affairs and a major escalation of the coercion that had been implied in assimilationist policies and the Gradual Civilization Act of 1857.

The downward slide of Native policy between 1830 and Confederation was both a reflection of the changing relationship and a portent of things to come. The move towards interference and compulsion was intelligible only against a shifting background in which First Nations became increasingly marginal to the material desires of the newcomers, but in which Indigenous people refused to concede their defeat. First Nation resistance, however, merely served to provoke more coercive policies by missionaries and officials. The do-gooders concluded that Native recalcitrance was the principal obstacle to the success of their policies. This evolution occurred because of two other factors as well, the rising influence of church and humanitarian groups in British North America and in the United Kingdom, and growing colonial control of relations with the First Nations. The influence of the humanitarian groups discouraged the use of the worst forms of force, but the alternative was merely the piecemeal adoption of paternalistic and coercive measures that led towards the extermination of Natives by peaceful rather than military means. These factors were reinforced, in turn, by the increasing influence of scientific and pseudo-scientific theories that appeared to explain the slow rate at which the First Nations were adopting Euro-Canadian ways while legitimizing the application of increasing degrees of compulsion.

Unfortunately, this pattern would be replicated in all its ugly detail in the West when Canada asserted its control of Hudson's Bay Company lands. The year 1869 was not just the year of another, yet more coercive, Indian Enfranchisement Act; it was also when the Dominion was to assume title to Rupert's Land. Canada's new written constitution, the British North America Act, said that "Indians and lands reserved for the Indians" were the responsibility of the federal government and parliament. Indigenous people in the Province of Canada knew by now what could be expected from that quarter. How would the First Nation and Métis populations of the lands west and north of Lake Superior respond when they came face to face with this new authority?

CHAPTER SEVEN

The Commercial Frontier on the Western Plains

West of the Province of Canada a belated version of the same pattern that had been established in eastern British North America was developing. In the East, First Nations and Europeans had cooperated for separate, though complementary, reasons from the sixteenth to the late eighteenth centuries in mutually beneficial relationships. The frontier on which Indigenous people and newcomers had met was one of navigation, commerce, faith, and military alliance. Until these sorts of arenas for interaction were supplanted in the early nineteenth century by an expanding agricultural frontier, relations between the two peoples had been fairly harmonious and without traumatic effect on either party. Though there had been borrowings in each direction, little directed cultural change had occurred before the Victorian era. In the western interior, much of this pattern was replicated. Europeans and western nations met and interacted for most of the same reasons, though the military aspect here was minor, with much the same results. But in western Canada, relations began later and passed through the various phases of cooperation to the age of the Native's perceived "irrelevance" in a much shorter space of time.

Contact began in the West because of the familiar commercial motive that led seventeenth-century Englishmen to emulate the French in their search for furs. In fact, it was renegade French traders, Pierre-Esprit Radisson and Médard Chouart, sieur des Groseilliers, who defected to the English in the 1660s, taking their knowledge of North American fur trade routes with them. Their familiarity with the waterways and Native peoples of New France combined with a growing interest among commercial elements in England to produce the Company of Adventurers

Harvesting buffalo by running the herd over a precipice was an Indigenous hunting method
that required great organization and discipline.

of England trading into Hudson Bay in 1670. The Hudson's Bay Company (HBC), as the firm was usually known, received a charter from the English Crown that purported to bestow on it a monopoly of commerce in all lands drained by the rivers flowing into Hudson and James Bays. By an audacious stroke of the pen, in other words, Charles II of England presumed to grant trading rights to a vast region encompassing parts of present-day northern Quebec and Ontario, Manitoba, Saskatchewan, Alberta, and portions of the Northwest Territories. And, though the significance of the act seemed not to cross the minds of king or traders, the formal wording of the Charter suggested that they were pretending to dictate to the many First Nations in that huge empire with whom they would trade. In fact, however, the governors of the HBC instructed their earliest representatives in western Canada to negotiate agreements with local nations to permit the Company to establish posts and operate in the country.[1]

The lands that King Charles assigned to the Hudson's Bay Company embraced a large number of First Nations of Algonkian, Athapaskan, and Siouan language stocks. In the East there were the Cree of northern Quebec and Ontario, as well as the Ojibwe in the region between Lake Superior and Lake Winnipeg, a people who would later generally be known as Saulteaux in western Canada.[2] There were also

Cree north and west of the Ojibwe, as well as the Siouan Assiniboine to the south. Like the Blackfoot Confederacy to the west of them, the Assiniboine relied on a plains culture that centred around the magnificent bison, a larder and clothier on the hoof. In the North the principal First Nation was the Chipewyan, a Dene or Athapaskan people for whom the caribou was nearly as important as the buffalo was to southerly nations. The Ojibwe depended on a mixed economy of hunting, fishing, and horticulture, in particular the gathering of the wild rice that grew in many of their region's lakes. The Cree were principally hunter-gatherers who relied on hunting, fishing, and the collecting of naturally occurring food products such as berries and nuts. As Gerald Friesen has aptly observed, the "cultures of the western interior of Canada were successful adaptations to the environment."[3] The rugged terrain and harsh climate of the western interior probably supported between 15,000 and 50,000 Native people in the middle of the seventeenth century.

Although there were wide variations among the western and northern Indigenous peoples, there were also some important similarities. It would be as foolish to generalize about the social structures and everyday life of such dispersed and different nations as it would be to suggest that a seventeenth-century Muscovite and a contemporary Londoner followed the same social routines. But, as among the First Nations of eastern Canada, there were some shared characteristics, just as there were among the different nationalities of Western Europe. Western Natives, like those to the east, had developed various forms of animistic religion that emphasized the presence of spirits in objects both animate and inanimate. They felt a sense of kinship with flora and fauna, and they had developed elaborate rituals and taboos to ward off evil and placate offended spirits. Not surprisingly in a region of dry climate and much sunshine, more especially on the southern plains, the spirit of the sun occupied a special place in Indigenous religion.

Western First Nations also shared with their eastern counterparts the fact that they had developed trade among themselves long before Europeans appeared bearing trade goods. Northerly Natives exchanged hides for corn from agricultural peoples far to the south, in the present-day United States. For example, the Assiniboine might trade hides and crafts, perhaps including beadwork they had acquired in commerce with the Cree to their north, for corn from the Mandan to the south. And some of that corn might, in turn, be traded northward to the Cree. And commerce in wild rice, furs, and various handicrafts was fairly common. Intertribal trade was highly ritualized and surrounded by ceremonialism, and the commercial relationships were frequently cemented by diplomatic ties between nations and kin-like links among individuals. Western nations also had well-developed traditions of warfare, which was usually motivated by vengeance, commercial calculations,

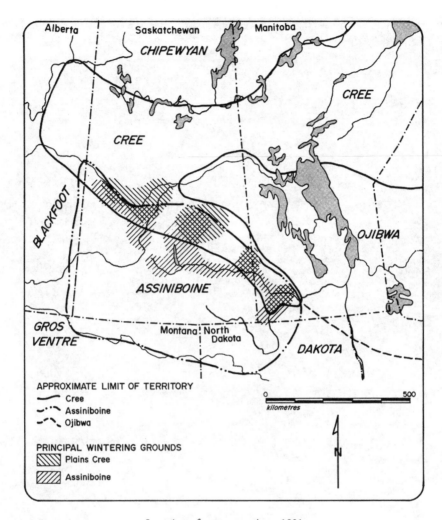

Location of western nations, 1821

or the need to perform rites of passage. Among western males the need to prove bravery in raids and battles was an especially strong stimulus to embark on war. A young man simply could not establish himself in his community without proving his manhood by martial acts against another tribe. But, again, as in the East, pre-contact warfare tended not to be very destructive. Until firearms were used, Indigenous warfare did not result in extensive loss of life.

In western Canada, then, the onset of fur trading brought together two different ways of life, the European and the Indigenous North American. And, as in the East, the fact that contact led to cooperation rather than repulse was explicable largely in terms of the mutual advantage that could be derived from interaction.

Preparing to participate in the Sun Dance, as Stoney John Hunter does here, was a solemn matter.

For the English, who began to undertake their regular voyages to the edge of James Bay and Hudson Bay in the 1670s, the benefit obviously lay in the furs that they obtained in these northerly latitudes, furs that were lush because of the climate and plentiful because of the limited demand that previously had existed in the region. For First Nations of the West, the motive for trading with the foreigners who came was access to products of European technology. In particular, cloth and blankets, tools and implements, weapons, and rum were prized items of the western commerce that began slowly after 1670 and continued fitfully for a century. As had happened in eastern Canada, the personnel of the HBC found themselves drawn into First Nations ceremonies involving the pipe and gift giving, as the Natives made "kin" of them prior to trading with them.[4] Important in the West was the fact the English were much readier to trade firearms and rum than the French were until competitive pressure from the English on both the Hudson River and Hudson Bay impelled them to follow suit in the eighteenth century. And, again, what needs to be stressed about contact in the fur-trade era of western Canadian history is that without Native tolerance of and cooperation with the English, these traders could not have maintained their initial presence at the edge, and later penetrated the interior.

Part of the explanation of the HBC's greater willingness to employ alcohol in the western trade lies in the fact that the English commercial penetration was not accompanied by a missionary presence. The French fur traders had not wanted to transport and support Jesuits in eastern Canada either, but they had been compelled to do so by the French Crown, which was responding with Counter-Reformation zeal to convert the world to Catholicism. French traders had also recognized that the presence of Jesuit missionaries in Huronia or among the migratory bands of Algonkians served to cement the commercial link, making missionaries a necessary evil in the trade. Such influences did not come into play in the West in the first century and a half of the HBC's activities. The English king and parliament saw no reason to insist on commercial support of evangelical efforts among the Aboriginal peoples of North America. Furthermore, the manner in which the Bay men conducted their trade for the better part of a century largely removed the necessity to station Europeans – even clergy – among the tribes with whom they traded. The HBC encouraged the Natives to bring their furs to their posts at the mouths of the rivers, such as the Nelson and the Churchill, that emptied into the northern waters. And while it is not true that for a century the English traders "slept by the frozen sea," as used to be said of them, their largely sedentary manner of conducting the fur trade removed the compulsion to probe the interior and to station Europeans among the nations there. Lacking a need to exchange personnel to hold the commercial alliance, English traders had one less reason to tolerate the presence of missionaries in their vast patrimony.

Although the HBC men did over the decades undertake some exploration of the western interior with the aid of local guides, by and large they relied on the First Nations to come to them to trade.[5] This manner of conducting the trade meant that, in western Canada particularly, well-situated groups of Natives emerged as intermediaries in the commerce. The Ojibwe had experience in this role: they had long transported furs to the French and the Canadians, and had returned European products both for consumption and for further trade with tribes such as the Cree and Assiniboine, which were more remote from the zone of commercial transactions. After the English established themselves on the Bay, some Ojibwe moved northwest to take advantage of the commercial opportunities that presented themselves. Gradually, however, it was the Cree and Assiniboine who became dominant as intermediaries in the western trade. The Cree moved westward around the turn of the eighteenth century and joined with the Assiniboine in playing the middleman role. Large numbers of Indigenous people, in other words, responded to the economic opportunities created by the emergence of a commercial frontier by migrating and modifying pre-contact trading networks so as to maximize the benefits of trade for themselves. In so doing, they spread the effects of European presence broadly throughout the western interior.

The coming of the fur trade meant diffusion of European technology, but not, at first, any dramatic alterations in Native societies. Perhaps the most visible change was the shift in territories of the various First Nations. Similarly, the volume of commerce among the nations themselves increased dramatically, as the intermediary ones developed a broad and lucrative trade. In some instances the go-betweens used goods they obtained from the French for one or two seasons and then sold them to the Blackfoot for triple the price they had paid for them at York Factory.[6] But such behaviour does not mean that First Nations had adopted a capitalistic ethos as a result of trading. Much as the Huron had used their new-found wealth in traditional ways, so First Nations in the West generally used the European items in ways compatible with established values in the early decades of the commerce.

One manifestation of this traditionalism was what Bay men regarded as the Natives' perverse response to market incentives. In the emerging capitalist society that was England, it was believed that a rise in the price of a good stimulated an increase in supply. If the price of furs rose substantially, according to the market theory that Adam Smith would codify in the eighteenth century, Natives should bring more furs to trade, and should keep doing so until the increased supply caused a decline in price. Even though western nations in the eighteenth century were demanding and discriminating consumers,[7] they did not respond as "eco-nomic men" to HBC manipulations of the price that were intended to lead them to produce more furs. The Indigenous peoples' demand for European goods was "inelastic"; once a fixed level of individual needs and desires had been satisfied, exchange ceased.[8] One estimate was that an individual required a total of 100 Made Beaver (MB), the unit of exchange in the fur trade, consisting of 70 MB for sub-sistence items and 30 for luxuries and amusements. If fur prices rose, the Native traders simply needed fewer furs to acquire the goods they desired. They did not respond to higher prices by increasing supply. (Another, more typical, market re-sponse might be that more individual First Nation traders would be drawn into the fur-trade commercial nexus, producing a larger volume of furs.) This non-market behaviour demonstrates that First Nations remained traditional, or pre-capitalist, in attitude and ethos while participating in the trade. Commerce reinforced and enriched traditional practices in the West; it did not supplant them. The contact of European traders with western Canadian Natives at first resulted only in non-directed cultural change.

The manifestations of that non-disruptive change were many and obvious. The persistence of kinship-based trading relations was one. The expansion and multi-plying of commercial patterns was another, as the Cree and Assiniboine replaced the Ojibwe as intermediaries and expanded their networks. The emergence of a group of Natives, known as the Home Guard Cree, who moved in close to the posts and came at some seasons to look to the traders rather than the resources of the country as their provisioner, was another. Over the entire year the relationship be-tween Home Guards and post was symbiotic: they were mutually dependent, the traders sometimes depending on "country provisions" for survival, and the Home Guards at other seasons needing European food obtainable at the post. On occa-sion these groups, some Assiniboine or the Home Guard Cree, could be reduced to hardship and deprivation if the supply of European goods was disrupted by war-fare between the French and the English in either Europe or North America. It is probable that the dependence of groups farther from the posts was much less, although sooner or later all western nations would be affected by the Europeans' introduction of firearms. In the first century of the trade from Hudson Bay, it was principally the Assiniboine and Woodland Cree (especially the Home Guard) who incorporated the muskets, but other groups were also affected, if only as victims of these more destructive implements of war. Early in the eighteenth century, firearms coming from the north met the horse coming from the south on the Canadian Prairies.[9] This meeting on the Canadian plains helped substantially in fashioning the unique Plains Indian culture that distinguished western Canada. Nations such

These Stoney horsemen were typical of the equestrian culture of the Plains.

as the Plains Cree and the Blackfoot were to create a complete way of life based on Spanish horses, English muskets, and the North American bison.

The introduction of European goods, whether firearms or horses, did bring about adaptations in First Nation society. Obviously, the muskets made warfare more destructive. Raiding parties would continue to swoop down for revenge or to prove virility by stealing horses, but, if resisted, they could now often do greater damage to each other. However, western First Nations did not immediately suffer large-scale losses as a result of alliance. Although there were attempts by rival fur-trading groups to draw Natives into alliance, on the whole western nations were exempted from the territorial strategies of the European powers. Early in the eighteenth century, French traders in the West enjoyed some success in getting the Sioux to worry the flanks of English traders. One consequence of this commercial-military strategy was a shift of the Assiniboine northwest away from danger.[10]

But western First Nations were spared the larger European territorial quarrels that had so marked the military history of the eastern half of North America in the eighteenth century. What rivalry and conflict occurred in the western interior was between rival British and French, or *Canadien*, traders, rather than European armies and their colonial and forest allies. The French strategy of encirclement that was employed from 1700 to the 1750s applied only to the area east of the Mississippi; there was no point in attempting such tactics in the West. Moreover, since French rule ended everywhere but Louisiana and the French Shore of Newfoundland in the 1760s, there was no reason for the extension of European quarrels and military alignments into western Canada in the second century of the HBC's existence. What warfare the Europeans encouraged in the West was largely commercial in nature. In this, of course, western Natives fought in their own interest, or abstained for the same reason.

More devastating was a consequence of contact that western First Nations shared with other Aboriginal peoples: disease. Here the Indigenous populations' lack of exposure and resistance to European ailments such as smallpox and tuberculosis proved as destructive as it had in the East. In particular, two massive smallpox epidemics of 1780–1 and 1837–8 decimated the lodges.[11] In some cases the HBC's employees were able to employ a crude form of vaccination in the second visitation, ensuring that the consequences in that case would be uneven. The Assiniboine were drastically reduced, but the Cree, whose proximity to traders made them candidates for a preventive program, were largely unscathed.[12] The Assiniboine might have been reduced to approximately a thousand souls by this second, devastating epidemic.

Other consequences of the contact that took place in the trade were happier. Certainly this was the case for the Europeans. From the First Nations they acquired geographical knowledge and guidance on trips of exploration and mapping. They also became acquainted with country food sources such as caribou and waterfowl, gaining knowledge that in some situations was invaluable for survival. They also adopted some of the clothing styles and the guerilla tactics of Indigenous warfare. It is probable that the influence of western Natives on English attitudes was less intense than that on the *Canadiens* of the St. Lawrence, because prolonged contact between Natives and English was minimized by the way in which they conducted their trade for the first century after 1670. But informal interaction there was.

The mingling of First Nations and Europeans in the western fur trade had an extremely important social result. Miscegenation produced a new Indigenous people who emerged as a distinctive group. Sexual contact between the races had also occurred earlier in other parts of Canada, of course, but in western Canada the resulting mixed-descent community was more extensive and had longer-lasting social and political results. Officially, the employees of the Hudson's Bay Company were not supposed to have close relations with the female Native population. Company policy forbade such behaviour. But given the isolation of HBC posts and the loneliness that inevitably troubled the miserable males stationed at them, it was hardly surprising that such prohibitions were more often honoured in the breach than in the observance. There were cases in which senior officers of the company, while flouting the rules themselves, attempted to enforce the regulations among subordinates, usually with unhappy results for the officers. Gradually the rules were conveniently forgotten, at least in North America, and liaisons between European traders and Native women became frequent.

The presence of *Canadien* traders in the West from the 1770s onward considerably hastened the process of *Métissage*. These traders from Montreal, sometimes also from the Michigan-Wisconsin territory, became more common in the West after the Quebec Act reopened the hinterland in 1774 and Jay's Treaty of 1794 forced them out of the American northwest. To prosecute the distant western trade, the Montreal men formed a succession of partnerships between 1779 and 1804 that were known as the North West Company. Nor'Westers faced no prohibitions on associating with Indigenous women, and they clearly understood the commercial value of entering unions with them. One Nor'Wester who reluctantly formed a relationship with a First Nations woman observed resignedly, "There is no end to relationships among the indians."[13] As a result of what Montrealers called *mariage à la façon du pays* (marriage according to the custom of the country), commercial links could be established and maintained with the First Nations. A Native wife's family would have a special relationship to their new, Euro-Canadian family member. Unlike European and Euro-Canadian societies, First Nation societies did not draw a distinction between public and private spheres; neither did they treat women according to an idealized stereotype of weak and helpless femininity. Marriage entailed obligations between the parties, and women were expected to do considerable work alongside their husbands.[14] A First Nation wife knew the transportation routes and was expert at taking or trading for skins. Although such marriages were often dissolved when the newcomer left the country, the wife usually returning to her own people without any fuss or difficulty, many relationships were stable and enduring. What was involved was marriage and economic partnership, not casual sexual gratification and exploitation.

The development of the unique institution of *mariage à la façon du pays* itself indicates that First Nations adapted to, rather than being fundamentally altered by, their fur-trade contacts with Europeans. It was the few and amorous Europeans who had to conform to local usages, not the much more numerous Natives who adjusted to the newcomers, as the Indigenous people expected the newcomers to woo, win, and wed their daughters in Indigenous fashion. First Nations insisted that the traders pay the customary bride price or gift to the girl's family before the marriage could take place. And the union was often accompanied by traditional First Nation rituals such as feasting and gift giving, the smoking of a symbolic pipe, and other familiar practices that varied from nation to nation. Such marriages further demonstrated that the fur trade was a relationship in which the Natives dominated and from which they benefited.

Although the *Canadiens* may have entered into relationships with western women with fewer difficulties than the Hudson's Bay Company employees, both took First Nation wives and produced many children. In many cases, the offspring of these unions were themselves incorporated into the fur trade as employees of the commercial companies. In the early nineteenth century, growing numbers of these mixed-ancestry people began to locate in the valleys of the Red and Assiniboine Rivers in what is now Manitoba. Their numbers were augmented by other mixed-descent families from the Michigan-Wisconsin regions, because, as one historian has noted of the establishment of the settlements in the vicinity of the junction of the rivers, there were "many roads to Red River."[15] During the first half of the century, these groups would develop as two distinguishable, though in many ways similar, peoples. The Métis were the offspring of the French Canadians in the North West Company and First Nation wives; the country born were the descendants of English or Scottish and Native marriages. (Both groups were and are sometimes referred to as Métis, a blending of terms that somewhat confuses historical references to the two groups.) Both engaged in casual employment for the Hudson's Bay Company, dabbled in what the company regarded as illegal trading with men not connected to it, and occupied a provisioning role in the trade that grew very important as the HBC extended its network inland in response to competition from the Nor'Westers between the 1780s and early nineteenth century. The Métis were also particularly noteworthy for the way in which they took to the buffalo hunt and made it part of their annual cycle. A distinctive way of life was developing in the narrow, river-front strip farms that stretched back from the Red River in the neighbourhood of the HBC's Fort Garry.

One of the factors encouraging the emergence of a distinctive mixed-ancestry community, and of that community's sense of its own identity and purpose, was the competition between rival fur trade companies in the late eighteenth and early nineteenth centuries. After the abandonment of the posts in the American northwest in the 1790s, the Montreal-based fur traders swung their attentions increasingly to Rupert's Land. Ultimately they extended their trading networks well into

The Red River cart of the Métis was a vital cog in the fur-trade
transportation system of the nineteenth century.

the Canadian northwest, reaching the watershed formed by the Mackenzie River as
it flowed into the Arctic Ocean. The response of the fur trade to competition and
the expense of operating over vast distances had always been concentration and
monopoly. So, after the Revolutionary War, the Montrealers fashioned the North
West Company, an amalgamation that combined the leadership and capital of a
group of Scottish Canadians with the brawn and daring of largely *Canadien* voyageurs and trip men. The North West Company simply ignored the HBC's claims to
monopoly rights in the Hudson Bay watershed, and even resorted on occasion to
violence. This conflict encouraged the growth of a sense of Métis nationhood.

Although the emergence of this cultural identity among the Métis was probably
only a matter of time, a decision by a Scottish noble accelerated it. Lord Selkirk's
determination to establish an agricultural colony in the Red River area posed an
immediate threat to the North West Company and a longer-term danger to those,
such as the First Nations and the mixed-ancestry community, who relied on the
resources of the country. Colonists meant farms; agriculture meant conflict with
commerce. The proposed Selkirk settlement lay athwart the routes used by the
Nor'westers in particular, and the prospect of such a colony meant an economic
challenge to both First Nations and Métis, who controlled the provisioning trade.

The Montreal men began to point out to the Métis that they were a special people, the New Nation, and that Red River was their territory. The Selkirk settlers were interlopers who had no right to invade their lands and ruin their way of life.

Métis unrest reached a crisis point in 1816. Encouraged by the Nor'westers and led by the able young country-born Cuthbert Grant, the Métis attacked and pillaged HBC posts. As they tried to make their way to meet up with a North West Company brigade, they instead encountered Governor Semple, the leader of the Selkirk settlement, and a band of farmers at Seven Oaks. When the clash was over, twenty-one settlers and one of Grant's band lay dead. For the Métis, the event was the symbolic establishment of nationhood. Seven Oaks was critical to the development of their sense of identity and common purpose. It also led Selkirk belatedly to negotiate with local Saulteaux and Cree for a treaty in 1817.[16]

Seven Oaks was but one of the signs of the change in the western fur trade, an evolution that would have great significance for the First Nations. Between the beginning of the trade in earnest in the 1670s and the 1820s, a large and mutually beneficial trade in furs had emerged. The competition had intensified – driving the commerce further to the north and west, while encouraging amalgamation of at least one of the fur-trade companies – about a century after the Charter of the Company of Adventurers. The arrival of the Nor'westers increased competition, stimulated the use of alcohol in the trade, and created incentives to use force to drive the other trader out. Temporarily, the First Nations were even better positioned to benefit materially from commercial competition. The fur trade was, as already seen, a mutually beneficial trading relationship in which both parties adapted, but neither party changed the other fundamentally. Certainly Natives in the fur trade in western Canada during its first century and one-half experienced only non-directed cultural change. But the beginning of agricultural settlement at the behest of Selkirk was only the prelude to other important developments. Five years after Seven Oaks, the Montreal-based traders succumbed to competition and distance. Competition with the HBC over such enormous distances was proving too great an economic strain; not even concentration into one company had relieved the pressure for long. In 1821 the Montrealers capitulated to the inner dynamic of the fur-trade frontier: the North West Company and Hudson's Bay Company amalgamated under the title of the latter. The fur trade from the Montreal base ceased. The Bay had defeated the River.

In the half-century between the termination of the Montreal-based fur trade and the entrance of Rupert's Land into Confederation, major changes occurred in the relationship between Europeans and First Nations in what was emerging as the

Canadian West. After the amalgamation of 1821, shifts in Hudson's Bay Company policy and in the patterns of the western trade depressed the economic condition of the Natives and provoked militant reactions. The fur-trade frontier began to be challenged by new forms of the European economic presence. In the Red River district, the early stirrings of the agriculturalists' coming, in combination with the arrival of missionaries and the religious institutions of which they were a part, helped to usher in an era of greater prejudice and discrimination by Caucasians against Native peoples. By the time the West was integrated politically into the new Dominion, its Indigenous populations were being marginalized by economic change and vanishing resources. They were being ushered into their very own age of "irrelevance" to the needs of the small Euro-Canadian population. At times the changing relations provoked armed resistance, but in most other ways the Native inhabitants were unwilling or unable to do much to hold back the changes that were destroying their way of life.

After 1821 the most important factor in the relations between western First Nations and the traders was the absence of competition in the fur trade. Having eliminated the North West Company's demand for furs, which had driven up prices and encouraged violence and alcohol abuse, the HBC moved to trim its expenses. Many casual employees, particularly Métis and country born in Red River, found themselves without work; and most First Nations found the prices that they could get for their pelts dropping. The economies that Governor George Simpson effected had their greatest impact in the northern departments of the company's vast territory, but to one degree or another these changes reached almost all the Natives in the lands in which the HBC traded. At the same time, the company's increasing concentration on operations in more remote, northerly districts created enormous demand for provisions, especially pemmican – a mixture of buffalo meat and berries held together with bison fat and pounded into a dense mass of protein. This need provided economic opportunities for both Métis and First Nations such as the Saulteaux and Plains Cree. A provisioning trade was born.[17]

Not all of Governor Simpson's changes were intended to benefit the company at the expense of westerners. Simpson's "reforms" included attempts to curb the widespread use of alcohol, a measure that no doubt was beneficial to First Nations. Unfortunately, whatever good effects flowed from this change were more than offset by the continuing problem of disease, in particular the massive 1837–8 epidemics in the western interior. Although the terms of the commercial relationship had turned somewhat against the First Nation and mixed-descent populations throughout the West, the essence of the link continued to be that each party harboured a benign attitude towards the other. A minuscule fly in the fur-trade ointment, however, was the increasingly shrill criticism flung by church and humanitarian groups against the Hudson's Bay Company for doing nothing to "raise their level of civilization."[18]

The philanthropists were going to make it their business in western Canada, as they had already done in Maritime and central Canada, to interest themselves on behalf of the Native populations. Their concerns and ministrations were the humanitarian side of the juggernaut of British imperialism and trade. In 1820 John West of the British Church Missionary Society (CMS) arrived in Red River to minister to the anglophone and non-Catholic part of the mixed-ancestry community.[19] After the arrival of Father J.-N. Provencher in Red River in 1818, the Roman Catholics continued their efforts in the Prairie region, the one continuing link between Quebec and the West in the years between 1821 and the 1870s, particularly through the male missionary order the Oblates of Mary Immaculate, or Oblates.

This form of missionary presence was different from that of the early Jesuits and the commercial and military Europeans who had hitherto dominated the relationship. These missionaries, especially the Anglicans of the Church Missionary Society, had a program for the assimilation of Aboriginal peoples. Unlike the Jesuits in New France, whose sophistication and worldwide experience had led them to reject the notion that it was necessary to turn First Nations into Europeans before they could be made into Christians, the nineteenth-century evangelists were convinced that assimilation had to precede, or at least accompany, religious conversion if the latter was to be thorough and lasting. This was so, paradoxically, even though both the missionary society and the Oblates placed heavy emphasis on learning Aboriginal languages, and the Anglicans sought to "indigenize" their presence by training Native clerics and turning their institutions over to them. In part, this difference between seventeenth- and nineteenth-century evangelical attitudes to Indigenous culture was attributable to the lesser degree of familiarity with cross-cultural relationships that the missionaries of the nineteenth century had. But in part it was also based on an increasingly racist attitude towards Indigenous peoples in the British Empire that was infecting and affecting British attitudes towards Native peoples in Canada. British humanitarianism was the soft core of a drive to bring about directed cultural change whose hard outer shell was racism. That "science" was increasingly "proving" that attitudes of superiority towards Native peoples were justified merely made that shell all the tougher.

In western Canada, after the 1820s, an attempt to bring about directed change was visible in and around the small outposts of European settlement, as at the forks of the Red and Assiniboine Rivers in Rupert's Land. John West was typical. Unwilling or unable to master the local languages, his approach was to teach English so as to impart the Word in his own language to his country-born students, who often spoke Cree. Schools made their appearance in Red River, not as agencies of social control so much as institutions of culture change. Both day schools and a residential school were used. When the desire to educate was frustrated by the migratory habits of the pupils' families, the decision was made to teach agricultural methods as well as basic academic subjects so as to lead the people from a peripatetic way of life to sedentary agriculture. Thus, in the tiny Anglican experiment at Red River in the 1820s were found the principal elements of the later drive to assimilate First Nations throughout many parts of Canada: schooling, religion, and agriculture. With the missionaries came the "policy of 'the Bible and the plough.'"[20]

European women were the other unsettling presence in the West. There had always been women in close relationship to the Europeans, of course, because the fur trade encouraged unions between male traders and First Nation women. Over time, observers noted that fur traders began to turn more and more towards the mixed-ancestry daughters of these earlier marriages between First Nations women and European traders. Apparently, Métis and country-born women had all the skills and advantages of their mothers, but found it easier to adapt to life with Europeans. The final stage of this process was commented on by a Hudson's Bay trader in 1840: "There is a strange revolution in the manners of the country; Aboriginal wives were at one time the vogue, the half-breed supplanted these, and now we have the lovely tender exotic torn from its parent bed to pine and languish in the desert."[21] The fur trader expressed poetically an ugly social reality. White men preferred white women when Caucasian females were available and the economic usefulness of Indigenous women had declined. This racial preference was encouraged by both the attitudes and practices of senior HBC men such as George Simpson. In the 1820s in Red River, Simpson began to shun and socially ostracize the First Nation and mixed-descent wives of Company men, and he soon replaced the succession of Native companions he himself had had with a British wife. The racist tendency to look down on Indigenous women – and, by extension, on Natives in general – was greatly strengthened by the presence of an increasing number of European women. Such attitudes were generally encouraged by the missionaries, who regarded *marriage à la façon du pays* as no marriage at all.

These attitudes began to drive a wedge between the previously close-knit Europeans and mixed-descent people in the western interior. There is also some evidence that these developments encouraged a rift between the Métis and the country born, though this is not absolutely proven.[22] However, it is certainly true that in some cases, members of the country-born community associated themselves with the British Caucasians and with the small trickle of "Canadians" who began to arrive at mid-century because of the economic and social advancement that they believed such associations would bring.[23] The growth of a white female population and a clique of white missionaries in Red River in the decades after 1821 began to jeopardize the racial harmony of the community. Here was a gloomy local example of what was happening to Native-newcomer relations generally in British North America.

But in other, practical ways the mixed-ancestry community in Rupert's Land was growing in confidence and comfort at the time. If it was true that the serpent of racism had entered the garden, it was still a pretty lush and comfortable arbour in which to reside. If Simpson's economies had reduced employment and lowered prices for furs and pemmican, and if the Métis and country born had now to compete with the First Nations for the revenues of the provisioning trade, there were also compensations. In particular the growth in demand for buffalo robes in the United States in the first half of the century was creating an economic alternative for both First Nations and mixed-ancestry groups, especially after 1844, when the opening of a trading post at Pembina, on American territory, provided relatively easy access to the southern market. The annual bison hunt of the Métis, with its quasi-political organization and socially integrating rituals, became a force for strengthening the Métis sense of collective identity that had emerged at the battle at Seven Oaks. Unfortunately, the increasing demand for buffalo hides to which the Métis responded with the elaborate annual hunt encouraged a great expansion of the hunting of these animals.

The development of an alternative commercial market, in this case for buffalo robes, also raised the old question of the Métis community's relations with the Hudson's Bay Company. The HBC, after all, claimed to have a licence to all the trade of the region, and it resisted efforts to exploit the advantages of trade in the south. The Métis, with Seven Oaks still a memory and with their growing sense of unity, were not likely to acquiesce easily to company attempts to curb their commercial ambitions. The clash, in some ways a non-violent version of Seven Oaks, came in 1849 in the *Sayer* case. Guillaume Sayer was a Métis trader whom the company prosecuted for trading with the Americans in breach of their monopoly. Sayer's countrymen, with Louis Riel among their leaders, organized a local version of the buffalo hunt they used on the plains and overawed the court. Court and company found a sensible way out: the jury convicted but recommended mercy; the HBC's chief factor claimed to be satisfied and dropped charges against other Métis freebooters. The armed men who surrounded the courthouse understood the significance of what had happened. They discharged their weapons in celebration and shouted, "Vive la liberté! La commerce est libre!"[24]

For First Nations in the western interior, there was less reason to celebrate in these years of transition away from commercial relations with the Europeans. One

sign of impending change was the initiation of treaty-making in the West, a sure indication that more newcomers wanted to come – and to come not just to trade but
to remake the region. In 1817, even before the amalgamation of the fur trade, Lord
Selkirk had arranged for a treaty with the First Nations of the Red and Assiniboine
Rivers area in preparation for the agricultural settlement he planned to sponsor
and direct. With representatives of Saulteaux and Cree, Selkirk's agent had bargained an annual payment of "one hundred pounds weight of good and merchant-
able tobacco" to each nation in return for a "tract of land adjacent to Red River and
Assiniboine River" that extended "in breadth to the distance of two English statute
miles back from the banks of the river." When the Natives asked what constituted
two statute miles, they were informed "that it was the greatest distance, at which a
horse on the level prairie could be seen, or daylight seen under his belly between
his legs."[25] The agreement was an interesting blend of tradition and innovation.
It paralleled what was happening in Upper Canada by using modest annual payments rather than a large one-time financial settlement, and it adopted a distinc-
tively western Canadian definition of the extent of the ceded lands. The closest
approximation in previous treaties had been the "gunshot treaty" in Upper Canada.

Other aspects of the new era after 1821 were more problematic for the First
Nations than the treaty of 1817. After the amalgamation of 1821, the dramatic increase in demand for the products of the bison affected some of them seriously. In
central Manitoba, for example, the Saulteaux found themselves increasingly dependent on the Hudson's Bay Company for foodstuffs by the 1860s, as the land's
ability to provide adequate supplies of game and fish declined. The western Ojibwe
became virtual employees of the company, but without the security of real employment. If the HBC's needs changed, the Ojibwe would find themselves abandoned.

The effects of shifting trade patterns had more immediate and more negative
effects on the nations of the southern plains in the 1850s and 1860s. The leading
groups were the Dakota, a Siouan people, many of whom were based in the United
States; the Blackfoot Confederacy of present-day southern Alberta; and the Cree
and Assiniboine who began to gravitate to the southwest in pursuit of the bison
herds that yielded such profitable products. These groups resented the expanding
Métis buffalo hunt. In 1857 the Cree announced that they would try to prevent
the mixed-descent bands from hunting in their territories or traversing them for
any commercial purposes. The First Nation-Métis confrontations over access to
the bison resource produced many conflicts. One of the major encounters, part
of Métis legend, took place between them and the Dakota at the Grand Coteau,
the escarpment that separates the Missouri and Assiniboine River systems in the
northern United States and southern Canadian plains, in June 1851. A youthful

Gabriel Dumont was a member of the party that fought off the Dakota from inside a circle of carts reinforced with sacks of food and other materials. These encounters became all too frequent in the middle decades of the century, as the resources of the plains came under increasing pressure from First Nations, Métis, and non-Natives.

The decade of the 1860s was one of increasing warfare between the Cree and the Blackfoot as a consequence of the former's invasion of the latter's traditional hunting territories. Such conflicts between Blackfoot and Cree and their Assiniboine neighbours were not new; there was a well-established tradition of raiding and small-scale skirmishing.[26] In the past these incidents had usually been the consequence of a desire on one side or the other to steal horses. Such exploits were demonstrations of manliness, rites of passage into adult society among the Plains First Nations. Horse-stealing, like counting *coup* (usually a non-violent exploit such as sneaking into a foe's camp and touching one of the sleeping enemies, but occasionally also the taking of the scalp of a fallen rival), was a means of winning full acceptance into adult society. In the 1860s, however, the conflicts became increasingly serious and destructive, for they were motivated by a desire to restrict access to a diminishing resource by the various First Nations. Towards the end of the 1860s, Native diplomats tried repeatedly but futilely to restore peace, but the general rule remained enmity and bloodshed between the Cree-Assiniboine and Blackfoot forces. In 1875, the Blackfoot frustration led them to send a message to the Canadian government's representative in Red River: "We pray for an Indian Commissioner to visit us at the Hand Hills, Red Deer River, this year and let us know the time that he will visit us, so that we could hold a Council with him, for putting a stop to the invasion of our Country, till our Treaty be made with the Government."[27]

These developments among both Métis and western First Nations reflected the increasing pressure that the innovations brought by Europeans were applying to traditional ways. Although the years from the 1820s to the 1860s would later be regarded by the Métis as a golden age in which they prospered and refined their cultural practices and institutions, the period was in fact part of a transition towards a new, less glittering age. The First Nations, who were first affected by the changes and who attempted to resist the negative effects by protecting their hunting territory and principal resource, would be even more seriously disrupted by these alterations. They knew, as the Métis appeared not to, that the coming of Euro-Canadians meant, directly or indirectly, trouble for the Indigenous populations. For those among the Métis and First Nation communities in the western interior who did not appreciate the threat, rumours that the Province of Canada wanted to acquire the entire region from the Hudson's Bay Company began to bring the danger into focus.

CHAPTER EIGHT

Contact, Commerce, and Christianity on the Pacific

Between approximately 1770 and 1870, the First Nations north and west of the plains area went through a similar experience to that of their Prairie neighbours. The subarctic, Cordillera, and Northwest Coast regions contained a bewildering array of Indigenous peoples, but almost all of them found that history subjected them to the common experience of contact and commercial intercourse with European newcomers. The effects of this interaction were uneven. The northern Athapaskans, isolated as they were by distance and climate, probably experienced the least disruption of their traditional ways. The peoples of the British Columbian interior felt the impact of European commerce later than most other Native people in Canada, but they went through the same phases in a compressed period of time. The coastal nations of the Pacific province actually profited immensely, in both material and cultural terms, from the fur trade in their region. But all three groups – northern Athapaskans, First Nations of the Cordillera and British Columbian interior, and Natives of the Northwest Coast – became familiar with the impact of European commerce after the 1770s and later European evangelization.

The Athapaskan-speaking groups of the area north and west of the plains comprised a number of separate peoples. From north to south, from Alaska to the Prairie provinces, they numbered the Kutchin, Nahani, Hare, Dogrib, Yellowknife, Slave, Chipewyan, Beaver, and Sekani. (The Sekani, Beaver, and Slave actually resided in the northern part of present-day British Columbia, but are usually classified with the other Athapaskans as part of the subarctic cultural area.)[1] In many ways they resembled the Algonkians, though the Chipewyan were inveterate enemies of the

Algonkian Cree. Theirs was principally a migratory hunting, fishing, and gathering economy, and their social structure was based on the small hunting groups
that were also found among many Algonkians. During the brief summers, larger
concentrations of up to one hundred people would assemble at commonly known
sites that were good for fishing and hunting. Given the harsh land in which they
lived and their mobile way of life, Athapaskans' population concentration and political organization were at a rudimentary level. One of the distinguishing features
of their culture, however, was its rich artistic accomplishments. Decorated clothing, adorned carrying bags for infants, and other colourful items of everyday use
displayed an astonishing richness.[2] With hide, quills, hair, and sinew, Athapaskans
produced parkas and footwear that were as attractive as they were useful. It was almost as if the small Athapaskan bands, unable to accumulate many material goods,
poured their creativity and pride into artistic expression.

Before the twentieth century, most of the Athapaskans had only restricted contact with Euro-Canadian society. From about the 1770s onwards, the commerce in
furs began to impinge on their homeland, introducing the varied influences and
adaptations that have been noticed elsewhere. On the whole it was the more southerly groups such as the Chipewyan, Slave, and Beaver who were most in contact and
most influenced. However, since the fur trade, especially after the amalgamation of
1821, was a fairly restricted presence, its impact was less among Athapaskans than
it was on the Cree, Saulteaux, and Assiniboine to the south. The greatest negative effect of contact was disease, the most positive, the acquisition of tools and weapons.

The First Nations of the British Columbian interior came into contact with
European strangers later than the Athapaskans and felt a greater impact. These
groups included, from north to south, the Carrier, Chilcotin, Interior Salish, and
Kootenay, and each of these groupings in turn contained a number of smaller sub-
groups.[3] The Interior Salish, for example, numbered the Thompson, Lillooet, and
Shuswap among their nation. The Carrier broke down into Upper Carrier, Lower
Carrier, and Babine. The classification of these various peoples was based upon
their languages, and each major linguistic group contained within it several dialects. In general, the Cordillerans of British Columbia depended on hunting, fishing, and gathering of natural foods for their survival. Their degree of nomadism
and population concentration depended greatly on the topography, climate, and
resources of the region in which they dwelt. All the First Nations were engaged
in trade, sometimes over long distances, well before Europeans arrived.[4] As will
be seen, the interior nations briefly became part of the fur trade in the nineteenth
century, but prior to their involvement there was an important maritime phase of
the fur trade on the Pacific.

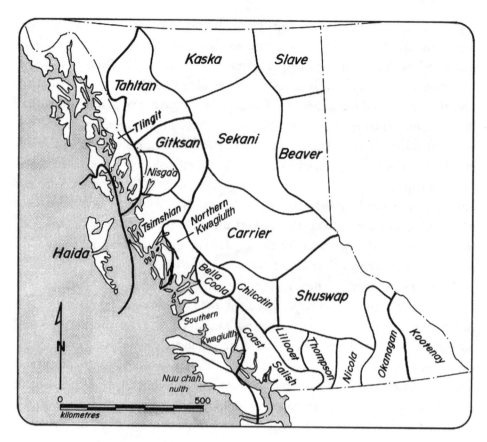

First Nations of British Columbia, ca. 1770

In a cultural sense, the northwest Pacific coast, where the maritime fur trade began late in the eighteenth century, was one of the wonders of the world. In the many fiords of the mainland and of the large island to which Captain George Vancouver would give his name dwelt a bewildering array of First Nations. In the future British Columbia, no fewer than thirty-four languages were spoken before contact, with the greatest variety found in the coastal region.[5] Although they had many similarities, especially in their dependence on the sea and lush vegetation of the region, these peoples are classified into a large number of ethnic divisions by anthropologists, their separate existences in the isolated portions of the coastal areas having produced sufficient distinctiveness to justify such treatment. Running from north to south down the coast were found the Tlingit, Tsimshian, Bella Coola, Kwakwaka'wakw (Kwagiulth), and Coast Salish; the Haida were concentrated in Haida Gwaii (the Queen Charlotte Islands), while the Nuu chah nulth (formerly

Nootka) resided on the west coast of Vancouver Island. Within an ethnic division
(such as the Tsimshian) there might be language subdivisions (Tsetsaut, Tsimshian),
not to mention several major dialects (Gitksan, Nisga'a, and Tsimshian). There were
also other groupings based on social and political organization, which were more
meaningful than dialect, language, or ethnicity. The Pacific First Nations were a
diverse, distinctive human community.

The Haida, Nuu chah nulth, Kwakwaka'wakw, Tsimshian, Bella Coola, and Coast
Salish were characterized by three features. The first was their Maritime orienta-
tion, which in pre-contact times gave them a level of affluence and comfort largely
unknown to other First Nations in the future Canada. No fewer than five species
of Pacific salmon sent millions of their kind to the rivers to spawn each season,
and herring and smelt were there, too, in great profusion. The eulachon, or candle-
fish, which provided coastal peoples with a valuable oil also spawned in the rivers,
while clams and crabs were easily available in many centres. Sea mammals such
as whales, seals, porpoises, and the sea otter added to the rich supply, and on the
mainland many freshwater fish, such as trout, could be taken easily. The maritime
resources of the area permitted a rich and secure life for the Indigenous peoples of
the northwest Pacific coast. These vast resources had also stimulated an extensive
pre-contact trade among the nations. For example, Coast Salish peoples produced
dog-hair blankets and slaves captured in raids, for exchange with Nuu chah nulth
for dugout canoes, shark's teeth, and dentalia shells used for decoration and art-
work.[6] In fact, Maquinna, a Nuu chah nulth chief, was a dominant intermediary
trading figure before any Spanish turned up.

The second feature was affluence, which, combined with a prolonged rainy
winter season, encouraged the development of a spectacular art culture. The vast
moisture-laden clouds that were generated by the warm Japan Current emptied
their water on the land and produced immense forests of fir, spruce, hemlock, and
cedar. Affluence, precipitation, and easily available timber created both a need for
substantial houses and the means to build them. Many of the coastal peoples dwelt
in relatively large population concentrations in massive wooden houses. Affluence
and a sedentary existence also made it possible for these coastal nations to develop
their art to heights unreached by other peoples in North America. The Haida in
particular were noted for their elaborate art, including baskets and the tall poles
and cabin fronts that graphically recorded their history and identity. The same
factors also produced complex and sophisticated social and political structures.
One measure of the impact of affluence on the Northwest Coast First Nations was
the hierarchical nature of their social structure: their villages consisted of nobles,
commoners, and slaves, the latter usually the unfortunate victims of war.

Captain James Cook's sojourn at Nootka Sound on Vancouver Island
in 1778 spurred the growth of the Pacific fur trade.

A third distinguishing characteristic among some of these peoples, a feature that
was also an offshoot of their material wealth and leisure, was an extensive and time-
consuming ceremonial life that passed the long, rainy winters while filling certain
social needs at the same time. The most famous of these practices, one that was
most pronounced among the Kwakwaka'wakw, though some others practised it as
well, was the potlatch. This important feasting ritual served several social purposes.
It was employed as a rite of passage, as in marking the coming of age and taking
of a name of a young person. It was used to reinforce a person's status or to challenge the higher status of another. And the potlatch could even be used to overawe
neighbouring villages. These potlatch purposes were summed up in the phrase "to
make my name good."[7] The means in each case was the same: distribution of vast
quantities of food and gifts at monumental feasts. It was for use at these potlatches
that many of the beautiful coastal works of art and utility – such as bent-corner
boxes, copper escutcheons, and highly decorated eating utensils – were created.
The potlatch was deservedly called a form of "fighting with property," but it also
was an ingenious method for registering important events, reordering status relationships within a group, and redistributing material wealth.[8] The potlatch and the
totem pole were just two of many distinctive features of Pacific societies that had
emerged prior to the coming of the European.

Although it was Spaniards who came first to the Pacific coast, they were quickly
followed and then supplanted by Englishmen and Americans.[9] The Spaniard Perez
encountered the Haida in July 1774, in the first meeting whose record has survived,
and traded for furs with them. Four years later, the British captain James Cook

These potlatch goods at Alert Bay, BC, were an example of the material
wealth that was redistributed at the sharing ceremony.

spent weeks in Nootka Sound and discovered the availability of sea otter furs. By the
1790s the maritime fur trade was well established, American vessels having joined
the British and Spanish. This form of the commerce dominated until the second
decade of the nineteenth century, when a land-based trade that involved coastal
and interior groups such as the Interior Salish, Kootenay, and others developed. The
pattern of relations that emerged between the Europeans and Natives bore striking
resemblances to the commercial encounters that had begun earlier in the Hudson
Bay watershed, the Shield region of New France, and the Atlantic littoral.

The commercial relations on the Pacific "were part of a mutually beneficial trading relationship."[10] Bloody incidents between traders and Natives, especially in the
maritime phase, did occur. But generally relations were harmonious, as newcomers
and First Nations participated in a commerce for furs, especially that of the sea otter, that rewarded both parties. Indigenous people traded because commerce meant
access to European goods, and the coastal nations were both demanding and selective. The Nuu chah nulth spurned glass beads that were so obviously inferior for
decorative purposes to their own metalwork and wood products; the chief prizes
that Aboriginal peoples of the Pacific sought were iron products. The Haida called
the Europeans "Yets-Haida," which meant "iron men."[11] So quickly did Natives on the
Pacific learn to barter skilfully in order to exact the highest prices that as early as
the 1780s one Spaniard lamented that the truly profitable days of the trade were

over. Exactly as the French on the St. Lawrence had discovered, the First Nations on the Pacific also quickly learned to await the arrival of numerous vessels before trading. During the land-based phase of the commerce, the additional demand for furs from Russians and Americans as well as the "King George men," as Pacific traders called the English, enabled them to profit substantially. The other principal trade item in both the maritime and land-based exchange was the blanket, which served not just as clothing for the first peoples who obtained them from the Europeans, but also as a form of currency that they could use in the potlatch and in trade with more remote nations. As the interest in blankets partly indicated, coastal First Nations also soon made use of their access to the Europeans to forge for themselves a role as commercial intermediaries. Nuu chah nulth leader Maquinna, for example, became a go-between for British and American traders who sought furs from coastal groups, much as he had been between First Nations before contact with the Spanish and those who followed them.

The early trade in British Columbia, especially its maritime phase, brought about harmonious relations and non-directed cultural change. Certainly traders on occasional visits by means of vessels had neither reason nor opportunity to interfere with the First Nations' way of doing things. There was no incentive to attack the more numerous and well-organized Natives. The dominance of the Indigenous partner in the commerce was signalled on the West Coast by the language of business. A dialect called "trade Chinook," based on Indigenous languages, developed as the common tongue of business people in the fur trade. But the familiar patterns of losses to disease and the adverse effects of alcohol abuse could also be seen on the Pacific in the first few decades of both the maritime and land-based fur trade there. Although the maritime trade did not, for obvious reasons, encourage marriage between Europeans and Natives, some liaisons did occur, and during the land-based period of commerce more enduring relationships developed alongside the temporary unions that had typified the maritime phase. The emergence of Home Guards near some of the forts was also observable in the land-based phase, though what proportion of them were First Nation and what fraction of mixed ancestry is unclear.

Finally, the Pacific fur trade enriched the material life of the Aboriginal peoples. But here, too, European goods meant principally cultural efflorescence rather than substantial change: European tools made producing the art easier, and affluence allowed for more elaborate ceremonial.[12] "There is little doubt that the fur trade produced an increase in the number and size of potlatches among the coastal Indians."[13] Greater wealth also allowed the Kwakwaka'wakw to use potlatching, rather than traditional warfare, to humble enemies and rivals. An elderly Kwakwaka'wakw man said in 1895, "The white men came and stopped up that stream of blood with wealth. Now we fight with our wealth."[14] In general, as the case of the Songhees near the future Victoria illustrated, trade between the Natives and Europeans enriched the potlatch.[15]

The Pacific fur trade relationship between the 1770s and 1820s, in other words, was a "mutually beneficial economic symbiosis" that brought about non-directed cultural change.[16] The essence of the relationship was identified by a trader who pointed out that his kind "are desirous of gain" and asked, "Is it not self-evident we will manage our business with more economy by being on good terms with the Indians than if at variance"?[17] Mutually beneficial interaction and non-directed change added up to harmony and profit for both sides in the early decades of the relationship in British Columbia. In this respect the Pacific coast was like Rupert's Land before the amalgamation of the rival companies, or the eastern woodlands before farmers began to encroach on the forest in the early nineteenth century.

Between the amalgamation of the fur trade companies in 1821 and the union of British Columbia with Canada in 1871, a pattern that was similar to that on the plains, though less traumatic, emerged on the Pacific. The period from 1821 until the 1850s was one in which a land-based fur trade supplanted the old maritime commerce. But, although the locus of trade shifted from the decks of ships to posts beside rivers, the nature of the commercial relationship between First Nations and Europeans did not. The economies instituted by Governor Simpson of the Hudson's Bay Company might have meant serious loss of income for the Natives had not continuing competition from both Russians in the north and Americans to the south forced the company to keep its cost-cutting there to a minimum. Even so, one authority estimates that the reduction in prices for furs reached 40 per cent.[18] Although the HBC would eliminate most of this Russian and American competition over the decades, by the time this dominance was accomplished the fur trade was already declining in importance on the Pacific anyway.

Many features of the commercial relationship of Native and non-Native populations on the Pacific were reminiscent of developments that had occurred earlier on the plains, in the eastern woodlands, and by the Atlantic. Bands that were providentially well situated exploited their position by preventing other peoples from gaining access to the traders, thus carving out a lucrative role for themselves as intermediaries in the trade. In most cases the commerce between these middlemen and less fortunately situated groups was built on a network of trading relationships that had existed before the Europeans arrived with their iron goods and alcohol. In some cases a Home Guard emerged in close proximity to the fur-trade posts, and

The totem pole, identified with Northwest Coast peoples,
has emerged as a symbol of Indigenous people generally.

sometimes these groups became dependent on the posts for subsistence. A particularly noteworthy example of this development were the Songhees who moved from the Cadboro Bay area in the 1840s to be close to Fort Victoria. First Nations women played an important role in the land-based fur trade in British Columbia, as they had in the western interior, because of their skills and knowledge, their role in cementing commercial alliance, and because of the mutual attractions that developed in many cases between the Native women and the strangers. And, finally, First Nations to a great extent continued to determine how, or even if, trade would be conducted. In this respect, the case of the interior Chilcotin was particularly instructive. They rebuffed all company blandishments and steadfastly refused to be drawn into commerce.[19]

Throughout the land-based era, the fur trade in the Pacific region nurtured mutually beneficial relations between Indigenous peoples and Europeans. Although exposure to alcohol and to prostitution around the posts was demoralizing to some First Nations, most other aspects of the trade were advantageous. As had been noticeable with the Huron in the seventeenth century, the coastal nations in particular benefited from the trade by accumulating great amounts of material wealth that were used to enrich their existing ceremonial practices. The Hudson's Bay blanket emerged as a sort of unit of currency on the coast, as local leaders accumulated numbers of them to use in the potlatch. The infusion of European goods enriched this process of redistribution and contention for status without disrupting it during the fur-trade period. Similarly, coastal art experienced its most significant growth. The totem pole, in particular, enjoyed great popularity in this affluent era.

The 1850s and 1860s were a transitional period in the Pacific region, as they were in the western interior. The dates 1849 and 1857–8 marked key points in the evolution that was under way: in 1849 Britain created the colony of Vancouver Island under company jurisdiction; in 1857, William Duncan, one of the most famous missionaries in Canadian history, came to the coast; and between 1850 and 1858 a horde of gold-seeking adventurers descended, briefly on Haida Gwaii (1850–3) and then more destructively on the mainland (1858). With the arrival of the prospectors, the frontier of settlement was born. Although the gold-mining phase seemed painful while it was going on, it would turn out to be trifling compared to the disruptive impact of government administrators, missionaries, and settlers on the First Nations of the Pacific.

If all the administrators had been like the second governor of Vancouver Island, these changes might not have been so negative for the First Nations. James Douglas, the governor of Vancouver Island from 1851 to 1864, and then of both the island

and the mainland colony of British Columbia, brought long experience in the fur trade to his dealings with the local population.[20] Douglas followed a policy of treating complaints against Indigenous people by the small but growing number of non-Natives in the colony scrupulously: individual malefactors were pursued and punished, but bands were not held accountable for the misdemeanours of individuals. This policy did not always satisfy settlers who claimed that Natives had engaged in unprovoked incursions on their lands or property, but it did preserve the peace.

Douglas also negotiated some fourteen treaties with First Nations in Victoria, Nanaimo, and Fort Rupert, securing access to the region for settlers in exchange for modest lump-sum payments from company stores.[21] (He was both governor and the HBC's chief factor of Vancouver Island.) Interestingly, as Europeans began to encroach on Aboriginal lands in British Columbia and Governor Douglas asked the Colonial Office for advice and models on which to base treaties, London referred him, not to the Royal Proclamation of 1763, but to New Zealand's land agreements. Because the governor's sole purpose was to secure title in order to permit settlement, the areas for which he bargained were few and limited in extent. For example, when the Cowichan on Vancouver Island indicated that they would like to negotiate a treaty as the Songhees in the Fort Victoria area had done, they were turned down because there was no interest in settling that far north on the island. What the Vancouver Island First Nations understood the treaties to mean, and what their motives for negotiating were, are less clear. It seems unlikely that they understood that they were agreeing to total and exclusive ownership – alienation, to use the English legal term – of land by the European power. In any event, the pattern of treaty-making came to a halt as Douglas's access to company supplies from which to make payment was terminated in the 1860s, when the governor had to share power with an elected assembly. The emerging settler society did not agree with Douglas that the best policy was to satisfy Native interests in advance of settlement.

As the incursions of miners and settlers increased in the 1850s and 1860s, Douglas also followed a policy of laying out tracts reserved for First Nations, regardless of whether or not there was treaty with them. The governor's instructions to commissioners were to give Natives what they wanted, in terms of both location and extent of the reserves. Near Kamloops, for example, the reserve that was set aside stretched some six miles along the North Thompson River, twelve miles on the South Thompson, and ran back to the mountains. If First Nations subsequently decided that they needed more land, Douglas wanted his officials to oblige them. And in marked contrast to what had occurred in the Maritimes and in central British North America, squatters on Indigenous lands in the Pacific were informed that they had to decamp. While Douglas was not without his prejudices and desires to "improve" Natives by education and other means, his administration stands out as singularly intelligent in comparison with others elsewhere on the continent and with those who came after him. The fact that Douglas was a former fur trader and had a mixed-ancestry wife explained much of his sensible approach to dealing with the First Nations;[22] the same fact went far to explain settlers' increasing hostility towards him in the 1860s.

Among the greatest problems that Douglas and the Natives had to face was the gold rush, which brought as many as 28,000 gold-seekers to the Fraser Valley in 1858. The sort of men who came up the Fraser in search of gold were not likely to worry much about Indigenous people or their rights. They were largely single adventurers without roots or commitment to the country, and those among them who came to British territory from the rush in California unfortunately brought with them American attitudes towards Indigenous people. But too much should not be made of national differences; underlying the conflicts between Natives and prospectors or miners were irreconcilable desires for territory and resources. First Nations often tried to stop the ingress of prospectors, either to monopolize control of the gold resource or to secure compensation for use of lands they considered theirs. Once the miners became established, there were the usual incidents about missing equipment, or attacks on First Nations men or their spouses. During the Fraser River rush there were also instances of gangs of miners engaging in armed vigilantism against Natives.[23] It was only with the greatest of difficulty that order was kept in the gold-mining districts during what was a brief but intense encounter. The Fraser rush was largely confined to 1858; the craze in the Cariboo occurred mainly in the early 1860s; and more remote valleys were the sites of strikes and rushes a decade later. What came after the prospectors and miners would be much worse.

What came after were large numbers of settlers and missionaries. Again, it is important to keep the proportions of the change in some perspective. What would become the province of British Columbia in 1871 remained predominantly First Nations in population until the 1880s. As usual, epidemics, especially smallpox in 1862, were devastating.[24] According to one authority, the Aboriginal population of the region declined from approximately 70,000 in 1835 to about 28,000 in 1885, mainly as a result of disease.[25] Not until the arrival of the railway and significant immigration in the 1880s would the non-Aboriginal population surpass the Native. But even a minority of settlers proved troublesome in the 1860s. The fundamental reason was that settlers on Vancouver Island and in the valleys of the interior wanted exclusive access to lands that First Nations regarded as theirs. The Natives, as they had with the gold seekers, sometimes tried to resist the invasion. As early as 1846 at Fort Rupert, at the northern tip of Vancouver Island, the local people, who

The mining frontier in British Columbia usually displaced the Indigenous people,
although these Natives on the Thompson River in the 1880s were trying to extract gold
from the river with the pan located on the right of the picture.

had been mining coal prior to the arrival of Scots miners, warned the newcomers
with a variety of threats, including "more than a dozen pikes planted along the
beach, each supporting a severed head."[26] In 1860 at Alberni on the island, First
Nations informed a large party that arrived on armed vessels that they wanted no
part of their proposed purchase of lands on which to erect a sawmill. Their spokes-
man pointedly told the intruders, "We do not want the white man. He steals what
we have. We wish to live as we are."[27] But the Natives were as realistic about the
white man's power as they were about the white man; they understood the threat of
the ships' cannon and reluctantly removed themselves from the spot after concluding terms for the land in the area. Other forms of resistance could be more forceful
if the size of the parties was different from those at Alberni in 1860. In 1864, for
instance, thirteen of the workers in a party of road builders were killed by Natives
in the Homathco Valley in the northern interior, in an incident known revealingly

as the "Homathco Massacre" or the "Chilcotin War."[28] How many bands responded to incursions by tactics of withdrawal is unknown.

The Indigenous peoples' problems were compounded by a change in the attitude of government administrators and the arrival of missionaries. After 1864 Douglas was no longer in charge of relations with the First Nations, and his successor, Joseph Trutch, lacked his sympathy with and understanding of First Nations and their practices. (In some ways the shift in British Columbia from supervision by fur trader to oversight by settler was reminiscent of what had occurred in Upper Canada from 1830 onward, when the administration of Aboriginal matters fell into the hands of representatives of recent immigrants rather than the older military group.) Trutch not only refused to apportion lands to Natives in reserves; he and his agents worked steadily to despoil those First Nations who had taken reserves of much of their land in response to settler demands that they be allowed access to property they regarded as standing unused. Government and settlers undertook these actions with a combination of legalistic justification and economic ambition to persuade themselves of the legitimacy of their actions. Tiresomely familiar doctrines about ownership of land being acquired only by the addition of labour in horticulture and husbandry were borrowed and articulated by the squeamish. Notions of the importance of rapid development and racist stereotypes of Indigenous shiftlessness and improvidence were bandied about by those who, like Trutch, were less concerned with moralizing than with economic growth.[29]

Whatever the rationalization used, the First Nations paid the price. They were in many cases forced off parts or all of lands they had been guaranteed. The most infamous instance was the Songhees reserve in what was now the growing settlement of Victoria. Natives there were moved in response to the demands of people who had their eye on real estate; the dislocation was justified with preachings about removing them from the degradation brought by alcohol and commercial sex. The fact that Victoria was becoming a summer haunt for northern bands in search of trade and recreation simply made the settlers all the more uneasy. The coerced removal of the Songhees from the settlement to an area across the harbour was a metaphor for the dispossession of thousands of British Columbian First Nations in the era of settlement and under Trutch's ministrations. During the epidemic of 1862, settler alarm persuaded authorities to move the Songhees to the San Juan Islands temporarily.[30] Pressure to eject them from Victoria continued, and in 1911 a negotiated removal for which they were financially compensated finally got them out.[31]

The era of transition was also marked by the arrival of more concerted missionary action. The Oblates began their work in the lower mainland of the future British Columbia in the 1840s, and over the next five decades spread their missions up the

The flag that Oblate missionaries gave to converted chiefs in British Columbia
contained symbols for the scriptures, the papacy, and European technology,
along with the words "Religion," "Temperance," and "Civilization."

Fraser, into the Cariboo district, and even into the remote country of the Carrier in
the northern interior. Their most notable contribution to the history of missions to
the Natives was the "Durieu System," which was developed by the Oblate bishop for
whom it was named. The system, an adaptation of Jesuit practice in South America,
had two phases: one of repression of faults and another of character formation.
Wherever possible, as at Mission City on the Fraser, the Oblates gathered their new
followers in settlements of their own, the better to protect them from contact with
the Europeans' vices. For purposes of detecting and repressing faults, Durieu and
his Oblate followers appointed chiefs, captains, and watchmen, who also meted
out punishments. Especially controversial were the whippings that were part of
the public penance in which these missionaries believed. A more positive aspect
of the system was an emphasis on symbolism and religious spectacle. The Oblates
gave chiefs in whom they had confidence flags with the order's motto – "Religion,
temperance, civilization" – emblazoned on them, and they promoted and produced

elaborate passion plays, which for the Natives became important spectacles and feasts.[32] Later, ill-disposed local newspapers derisively referred to these Christian ceremonies as "potlatches."[33]

The other major evangelical presence on the Pacific was the Anglicans' Church Missionary Society. The Anglicans had ministered there in the 1840s, but from the later 1850s on their work became more extensive and better organized. In particular, the arrival of William Duncan of the Church Missionary Society at Port Simpson in 1857 inaugurated an important new phase in Native-newcomer relations along the frontier of faith. Duncan's efforts among the Tsimshian were merely a local example of an extensive missionary effort by British Christians in such places as Africa, New Zealand, and Australia.[34] The Church Missionary Society, as was also the case in the Prairie region, advocated a program that would lead to the indigenization of the Christian church by training Natives to become not just parishioners but also clergy of their own communities of worship. In British Columbia, Duncan's experiment would deviate from this pattern. European leadership would degenerate into control; and, partly in consequence, Natives would not assume leadership of the new institution.

In 1862 Duncan and a band of Tsimshian moved from Port Simpson to Metlakatla to get away from the corrupting influence of non-Natives and Native unbelievers. There, they established a type of commune that not only practised Christianity but also transferred education, industrial training, and Europeanized amusements. The First Nations were encouraged or coerced to become European in everything but their colour: their clothing, their houses, their decorum, and even their adoption of that quintessentially English of amusements, the brass band, testified to the complete change that Duncan was trying to effect. But Duncan found that even among adherents and supporters, compulsion remained a necessity. Not only was he preacher and teacher, but as magistrate he also directed the Native constables who enforced the community's laws.

Duncan's experiment was but a tiny island in the sea of relations at this time, and too much should not be made of it or its significance. Only part of one major ethnic group, the Tsimshian, was affected, and even among those in Metlakatla there were disruptions when a nativistic movement challenged the dominance of Christian beliefs.[35] Duncan subsequently had to remove from Metlakatla to New Metlakatla in Alaska because of conflict with his supervisors in England. Moreover, there were signs at Metlakatla and other missionary establishments that First Nations in the Far West tended, if left to their own devices, merely to appropriate the Christian god and incorporate it in their pantheon of spirits and ghosts. But what is significant is the way that Duncan and his experiment, like Bishop Durieu and his

These schoolboys at an Anglican boarding school at Metlakatla exemplified
the order and conformity that residential schooling sought to instil.

"System," were lionized in both Britain and the Dominion of Canada. Clearly, many
so-called humanitarians thought that attempting to impose the totalitarian control
and directed cultural change that Mission City and Metlakatla represented were
what was best for, and worked most effectively with, the Aboriginal inhabitants in
an era of settlement and missions.

From the mid-nineteenth century onward, Duncan and the Anglicans would
labour among the First Nations of the Pacific in the company of other Christian
groups. The Catholics, represented by the Sisters of Saint Ann and the Oblates,
competed with them both in coastal and interior locations. Anglicans and Oblates
were joined in the latter part of the Victorian era by Methodist missionaries, the best
known of whom were Thomas Crosby and his wife, Emma.[36] Crosby was actually

recruited by Tsimshian converts who sought his help in dealing with colonial authorities concerning their lands. His evangelistic efforts among his flock succeeded or languished according to the degree that his secular representations to Victoria were effective or unavailing.[37] All such efforts were manifestations of the increasing interest in evangelism in both Britain and British North America, a growing interest that would lead in the last decades of the century to massive overseas efforts as well as extensive endeavours within Canada to convert the people whom missionaries termed "the heathen." However well-intentioned their efforts were – and there can be no doubt that their motives, judged by their assumptions, were benign – the results would often be harmful to First Nations, who were already suffering the corrosive effects of the immigration of European and Euro-Canadian agricultural settlers.

Thus, in the Pacific region, the era that stretched from the fur trade to the entry of this vast territory into the Dominion of Canada in 1871 was one of dramatic shifts. In the North, in the lands of the Athapaskan peoples, the mutually beneficial fur trade had become well established after the 1770s, and changes in the organizational structure of the fur trade in 1821 did not have a profound effect. Indeed, it would not be until almost the twentieth century that the Euro-Canadian presence would have a heavy impact on the northern peoples. On the Pacific coast and in the Cordillera, the same pattern that had established itself in the plains region emerged after 1774. The fur trade, which had begun its maritime phase in that year, moved inland early in the nineteenth century and pretty well ran its course save in the northern interior in the half century after 1821. The land-based fur trade gave way to the mining and settlement frontiers in the 1850s and 1860s, much as the maritime fur trade had been supplanted earlier in the century by the commerce centred on the posts. Experiments in treaty-making, reserve allocation, and the directed cultural change of the missionaries all took place on both Vancouver Island and the mainland. At the time of British Columbia's union with Canada, First Nations were still numerically dominant in the new province, but those of them who had come into contact with settlers or missionaries, or Joseph Trutch's employees, understood all too well that their future was far from bright. British Columbia's terms of union with Canada in 1871 assigned jurisdiction over Aboriginal matters to the federal level, as Ottawa undertook that "a policy as liberal as that hitherto pursued by the British Columbia Government shall be continued by the Dominion Government after the Union."[38] The unintended irony of the latter clause spoke volumes about the ignorance and indifference towards Indigenous peoples that prevailed on both sides of the mountain ranges.

CHAPTER NINE

Resistance in Red River and the Numbered Treaties: "Bounty and Benevolence"

Canada's acquisition of Rupert's Land would create the need for a new policy for First Nations. Since the later 1850s, agrarian and business expansionists in the future province of Ontario had futilely been demanding the acquisition of the Hudson's Bay Company lands and their annexation to the Province of Canada. After the union of the Province of Canada was dissolved and its constituent elements merged into a general union of British North American colonies in 1867, Canada intended to acquire and absorb the Hudson's Bay Company lands to appease the commercial ambitions of Toronto and the land hunger of farmers in Ontario's southwestern peninsula. The acquisition of the Northwest, which would be attempted in 1869, was fraught with problems and challenges. And it would make clear the need for a new Native policy in western Canada.

The old Province of Canada and the new Dominion of Canada between them took several steps that largely shaped the policies that would be applied to western First Nations in the 1870s and 1880s. The first event of this critical phase, Canada's Gradual Civilization Act of 1857, defined who had Indian status, provided for the acquisition of full citizenship by educated Natives, and promised such enfranchised individuals a land grant from reserve lands. In 1867 the British North America Act assigned jurisdiction for "Indians and lands reserved for the Indians" to the federal government and parliament of the Dominion of Canada. The new Dominion's 1869 Gradual Enfranchisement Act repeated the provisions of 1857 for enfranchisement and conversion of parcels of reserve land into freehold tenure, but it added several novel and sinister elements. One was an additional criterion for Indian status:

a "blood quantum," or minimum percentage of twenty-five. Although the blood quantum remained part of the Indian Act until the 1920s, it appears to have been rarely, if ever, enforced. Second, the 1869 legislation introduced explicit gender discrimination by providing that any Indian female who married a non-Indian would lose her status. Finally, the Gradual Enfranchisement Act of 1869 levelled an attack on First Nation self-government. Recognizing that the obstacle to enfranchisement was Indigenous resistance that expressed itself through political organizations, the new act empowered Indian Affairs officials to remove elected leaders "for dishonesty, intemperance or immorality." The interpretation and application of these vague terms were conveniently left to bureaucrats in Ottawa. The 1869 act also restricted the jurisdiction of band councils to matters of municipal government. And, finally, the same measure established a governmental veto of Indian legislation by making all band measures "subject to confirmation by the Governor in Council."[1]

Although the Gradual Enfranchisement Act of 1869 was designed specifically for central Canadian First Nations who had long been in close contact with a Euro-Canadian population, its tactics of interference and coercion would later be carried over to western Canada when policy was developed for those regions. The young Dominion put the best face possible on this policy when, in 1871, it described its purpose as being "to lead the Indian people by degrees to mingle with the white race in the ordinary avocations of life."[2]

In the same formative period, important preparatory events took place in western Canada as well. One development that proved to be crucial to the future of both the First Nations and mixed-descent populations was the continued overhunting of the bison in response to high demand for buffalo robes and the decline of alternative economic activities for both the Indians and Métis. The emergence of the repeating rifle and the coming of the American transcontinental railroad in the late 1860s also made hunters' depredations on the herds all the more severe. Other people came, too, and their coming was noticed with disapproval by some of the Native population in the West. In the late 1850s and 1860s a trickle of Ontario settlers, mainly homesteaders but also some townspeople, began to make its way to the valleys of the Red and Assiniboine Rivers. They were the human manifestation of an Ontarian sense of manifest destiny, but unfortunately they brought with them the assumptions that the acquisition of the West was a foregone conclusion and that it would be for the best of all, both westerners and Ontarians. Potentially more dangerous was their view, articulated as early as 1857 by politicians of Canada West, that the acquisition and proper development of the West would determine "whether this country shall ultimately become a Petty State, or one of the Great Powers of the earth."[3] Such attitudes, as well as the assumptions of racial superiority that some of these newcomers displayed in their dealings with the Métis and country born, caused irritation. Unbeknownst to Canadians, an antipathy to their acquisition of the West developed.

The actions taken to unite the Hudson's Bay Company lands and the Dominion greatly aggravated these fears and suspicions. Canada's acquisition of the lands was carried out like a gargantuan real-estate transaction. Canada, with Britain's help and pressure, succeeded in obtaining the lands for the trifling sum of £300,000 and one-twentieth of the land. The HBC, which would take its 5 per cent of the land in many cases adjacent to its posts, was disgruntled by Canadian parsimony and British pressure. That dissatisfaction was nothing, however, in comparison to that of the population of some twelve thousand mixed-ancestry people in the region when they learned what had transpired. Their homeland was being sold for a song, and they were not being consulted about it.

The high-handedness and insensitivity of London and Ottawa, though explicable, were to prove disastrous. The inhabitants of Rupert's Land were not consulted partly because of Canada's anxiety to annex the lands before the Americans to the south could interfere and arrange events so that the territory would fall to them, as had Oregon, California, Texas, Florida, and other regions the Americans had coveted in the past. The administration of President Ulysses S. Grant did not, in fact, intend any overt action, because the top officials assumed that the Dominion would collapse and its constituent pieces would apply to join the United States.[4] But Prime Minister Macdonald still greatly feared American intentions. In any event, the failure to consult was also partly attributable to a belief that there was no one in the region to consult; First Nations and people of mixed First Nation and European ancestry simply did not figure in any political equation that Victorian politicians and bureaucrats attempted to solve. The Dominion was so unconcerned about local feelings that even before transfer from the Hudson's Bay Company was arranged, it took two other measures that were to offend the inhabitants. In 1869 Canada sent a party into the region to begin surveying the lands in preparation for immigration. And in the same year it appointed a governor for the region, William McDougall, and equipped him with an act for the temporary government of Rupert's Land. Both initiatives were added to the list of complaints that the people in Red River were compiling.

These grievances were both specific and general. The inhabitants of Red River objected to the lack of consultation, and they feared McDougall's appointment presaged a form of rule that would continue Canadian insensitivity and high-¿handedness. McDougall was a former Clear Grit, and as such was identified as an enemy of Catholicism and the francophone community. The fact that he was to govern the new territory with a council appointed by Ottawa simply made his selection all the more ominous. Under an apparently unsympathetic governor, the Métis and country born were not to be given any form of representative government with which to make their views known or to resist unfriendly acts by Ottawa and its appointee.

The Métis regarded the dispatch of a survey team to the district as an even greater threat. Both mixed-ancestry communities had developed a distinctive land-holding system, but it was one that might be jeopardized by the coming of Canadian rule. In the French parishes that stretched up the Red River from Upper Fort Garry (Winnipeg) and also in the English parishes along the Assiniboine, the farms ran back from the water in narrow strips. The occupants' title to their holdings was customary rather than formal. In the past the only authority in the region had been the Council of Assiniboia, a creation of the Hudson's Bay Company that had never seen the need to establish a land registry. Though there were rudimentary judicial and legislative institutions under HBC rule, there were no surveys, no land titles office, and no paper deeds. Such instruments were unnecessary in a region where settled population was sparse, where agriculture was an incidental economic activity, and where everyone knew one another and one another's rights and property.

The Métis recognized that the coming of Canadian authority and Canadian homesteaders could be threats to the security of their land title. The Canadian provinces in the East had formal systems of land tenure and land registry. If Canada chose to disregard customary title and treat the lands as being legally unoccupied, where would that leave the mixed-descent population and their river lots? The fact that a Canadian survey party in 1869 laid out their surveying lines in such a way as to cut across and disregard existing lot boundaries excited a fear that Canadian authority meant spoliation of the resident population. And for the Métis, in particular, there were related fears. Would the coming of Canadian authority, especially in the form of a Grit governor and his appointed council, mean an attack on their traditional institutions of culture – the schools and the Church? It was concerns such as these that impelled the Métis and the young Louis Riel to interfere with the surveyors and challenge the new governor in the summer and autumn of 1869.

Louis Riel, junior, emerged naturally as the leader of what would become known as the Red River Resistance. His family was prominent in the Métis community: his father, also known as Louis, had been one of the leaders of the challenge to the Hudson's Bay Company commercial monopoly in the Sayer case of 1849. Louis, junior, had gone east in 1858 as one of a party of young Métis who had been selected by the Catholic priests for education in Quebec. In Montreal, Riel had experienced both the currents that surged through French-Canadian society and a series of personal traumas. Nationalistic opposition among some francophones to the terms of Confederation and the intensely Catholic and nationalistic Ultramontane faction within the Catholic Church in Quebec were two intellectual fashions that influenced Riel. At the same time he suffered a series of personal blows: his father back in Red River died in 1864, and Louis felt powerless to do anything for the family left behind; he abandoned what he had thought was a priestly vocation and unsuccessfully sought alternative employment; and, finally, he fell in love with a young French-Canadian girl, but was rejected by her family at least in part because of racial prejudice. Riel was only one-eighth Native, but this was considered reason enough to reject him. By the time he returned to Red River in 1868, he was a troubled, if prominent and well-educated, young man.

On 11 October 1869, several Métis challenged the Canadian survey party headed by J.S. Dennis at André Nault's farm near St. Vital. When the locals informed the surveyors that they were trespassing, the Dennis party sensibly withdrew. This assertion of the local community's rights proved to be the prologue of a major drama. Within a fortnight the Métis had organized themselves into a National Committee and barred the road south in an effort to prevent the would-be governor from entering and asserting Canadian authority. After McDougall had been turned back, Riel and the others increased the pressure on Canada to negotiate the terms for the transfer of the territory: on the same day, another party seized control of Upper Fort Garry, the centre of authority in Red River. And, finally, Riel attempted to unite the people of the region so as to present Canada with a solid front. He and his Métis guards called on the parishes of the region to send delegates to a convention on 16 November that was to establish a provisional government. Riel and his followers defended their actions on the grounds that there was no legitimate authority in the region and that they, under the law of nations, had the right to establish their own government. Their Declaration of the People of Rupert's Land and the North-West argued that "it is generally admitted that a people is at liberty to establish any form of government it may consider suited to its wants, as soon as the power to which it was subject abandons it, or attempts to subjugate it, without its consent to a foreign power."[5] This assertion was a latter-day demonstration of the Métis sense of themselves as "the New Nation" that had grown out of the conflicts with the Selkirk settlers, the annual buffalo hunt, and the Sayer case.

Whether as a result of shrewd planning or luck, the timing of Riel's defiance of Canada was superb. In late autumn Red River's population was swollen by a number of seasonal employees of the Hudson's Bay Company, ill-paid boatmen, many of them Métis, who had both the daring and the inclination to follow a Métis-led resistance. Riel and the leadership solidified that support soon afterwards by taking over the Bay post at the upper fort, guaranteeing the resistors access to HBC stores with which to feed their poor followers. (In general, the Métis appear to have been more enthusiastic about the Resistance than were the country born, although by late winter the latter would be prepared to join with their francophone kin in belatedly endorsing the December creation of a provisional government.) Provoking the confrontation with the Dominion as winter closed in also made it extremely difficult for Canada to respond quickly and forcefully because of the difficulties of transporting troops in winter time.

Canada eventually did negotiate with the resistors in Red River, but not before tragic events intervened. The Dominion appointed individual emissaries to go west to discuss the situation with the inhabitants, and later it negotiated in Ottawa with three representatives that Riel's provisional government and a convention of inhabitants dispatched to treat with Canada. However, Canadian representatives and champions closer to the scene of resistance took steps that were to cause serious problems. Although Ottawa had served notice on the Hudson's Bay Company that the transfer would not take place as scheduled on 1 December because peaceful title could not be assured, McDougall acted in ignorance of this prudent move. He entered British territory and proclaimed his authority on 1 December. He also authorized a rising against the Métis forces by the Canadian party in the colony. Riel's troops captured the Canadians' supplies and took a number of the Canadians into custody. The following day, 8 December, Riel declared his provisional government. One of the Canadian prisoners, a young Ontario Orangeman named Thomas Scott who clashed with his keepers, was executed by the Métis in March for being insubordinate and abusing the guards. Riel's motivation was revealed by something he said at the time: "We must make Canada respect us."[6]

By the time negotiations occurred in Ottawa in the spring of 1870, then, drastic events in Red River had overtaken the diplomatic efforts of the Métis. In February an attempt by the Canadian party in Red River to rescue their fellow countrymen who were in custody was defeated by the Métis. J.C. Schultz, one of the Canadian party, escaped to Toronto, where he fanned the glowing embers of Ontarian resentment at the resistance into a conflagration. The death of Scott intensified Ontario feeling. Somewhat surprisingly, given this background, negotiations between Riel's representatives and the Dominion government produced agreement largely on the basis of demands that the convention in Red River had formulated, and that Riel and his clerical advisers had revised.

Under the Manitoba Act that came into effect in the summer of 1870, Manitoba entered the Dominion as a province, as Riel wanted, rather than a territory ruled from Ottawa, as Macdonald had desired. However, the extent of the new province was so small that provincial status was rendered almost meaningless. Similarly, the fact that the Dominion retained jurisdiction over Crown lands and natural resources in Manitoba, whereas control of these matters was provincial in the original four provinces, also reduced the significance of Manitoba's creation as a province. The legislature of the new province was to have two houses, like Quebec's, rather than being unicameral, as Ontario's legislature was. Either the French or English language could be used officially in the legislature and courts of Manitoba. And the denominational schools, Catholic and Protestant, were protected by section 22 of the Manitoba Act, which limited provincial jurisdiction over education by guaranteeing the educational rights that religious groups enjoyed "by law or practice" in the region at the time of union. In these respects, too, Manitoba was established on the model of Quebec rather than Ontario. Quebec had dual, confessional schools; and Quebec had official protection of both languages in its courts and legislature. This was unacceptable to many Ontarians, who were already incensed by Métis resistance and what they thought the priests' and politicians' connivance in it.

Ontario's wrath drove Ottawa to take actions that were to cause lingering resentments not just in central Canada but also in Manitoba. First, Macdonald and his cabinet decided that it was necessary to dispatch an expeditionary force to Red River, more for political and strategic reasons than out of military necessity. Ottawa was worried about American intentions towards the unsettled West, and it thought that sending British troops to Fort Garry would make it clear that the Dominion was asserting its control over the region. Second, sending a force to deal with the "rebels" would assuage Ontario's anger somewhat. The fact that all was now tranquil in Red River was overlooked in the interests of pursuing broad strategic and narrow partisan objectives. In addition, the federal politicians now reneged on a pact they had secretly made with the Roman Catholic prelate of St. Boniface, Bishop Taché, to grant an amnesty to Riel and his followers. Once Tom Scott's death began to inflame Ontario opinion, the politicians refused to carry out their promise to grant amnesty to the leaders of the resistance.

The final, critical element of the terms of the Manitoba Act was the provision concerning land. Security of title to individual holdings along the waterways was granted to those in possession of them when union occurred. And, by the act, 1.4 million acres were set aside so that the lieutenant-governor could make land grants of 240 acres to "the children of the half-breed heads of families residing in the Province at the time of the said transfer to Canada."[7] These provisions satisfied the most immediate and specific concerns about land rights, but they did not provide a secure, long-term land base for the mixed-ancestry population. Riel and his clerical advisers had wanted to get a large tract of land set aside as a resource for the community and as a barrier against the direct effects of immigration and settlement, but Ottawa was unwilling to make such a provision. A program to provide land grants to future generations by the federal government from Crown lands was the best that the Provisional Government could negotiate. But if the land grant itself was not very satisfactory, the language in which it was described was to prove extremely important to the Métis later on. The Manitoba Act explained that the grant was made "towards the extinguishment of the Indian Title to the lands in the Province," and Prime Minister Macdonald defended the provision in the Commons as necessary "for the purpose of extinguishing the Indian title and all claims upon the lands within the limits of the province ... It is, perhaps, not known to a majority of this House that the old Indian titles are not extinguished over any portion of this country, except for two miles on each side of the Red River and the Assiniboine."[8] The "half-breeds had a strong claim to the lands, in consequence of their extraction, as well as from being settlers."[9]

The aftermath of the Resistance and the Manitoba Act was largely damaging to the Native population. In the first place, the expeditionary force that arrived in Red River in August 1870, contained elements of the Ontario militia that were intent on wreaking vengeance. Forewarned, Riel escaped across the border to the United States before the troops arrived, but the Métis community suffered violence at the hands of the undisciplined forces. At least one innocent Métis died before the military administration gave way to a civil government. In the longer term, many of the mixed-descent community discovered that the land-grant provisions in the Manitoba Act for their young remained a nullity. Ottawa improperly altered the terms of the land grant to the disadvantage of the Métis; surveys proceeded slowly; government land offices proved unable to redeem the land scrip (or promissory paper) that the Métis were issued for real estate; and land was diverted to non-Native speculators.[10] Many of the Natives, abused by the triumphant Canadians and exploited by a bureaucracy apparently unable to honour the promises of the Manitoba Act, gave up and removed to the Saskatchewan country.[11] They hoped to re-establish their traditional way of life in new settlements such as St. Laurent and Batoche along the South Saskatchewan River, but relocation merely postponed a confrontation with the edge of Euro-Canadian immigration and settlement.

The First Nations' fear of, as well as the government's hope for, the arrival of that agricultural host in the former Hudson's Bay Company lands led to a series of initiatives by Ottawa in the 1870s. The North-West Territories Acts of 1875 and 1877 established rudimentary institutions of civil government, while the creation of the North West Mounted Police (NWMP) in 1873 both prepared for agricultural settlement and protected the Indigenous population in the meantime. Originally,

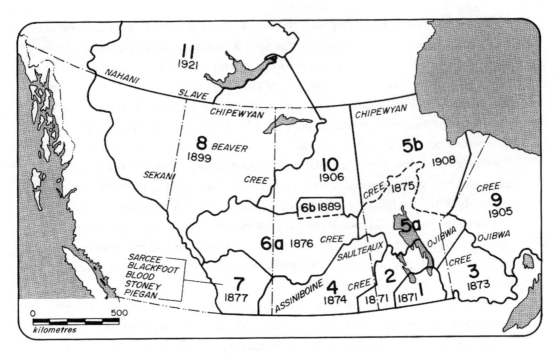

The numbered treaties, 1871–1921

before the troubles in 1869, Ottawa had intended that one-half the force would consist of Métis, whose knowledge and experience had seemed to make them ideal for the purpose. However, when the law marched west in 1874, the force consisted of eastern Canadian and British men, many of them with impeccably Tory political credentials. The creation of the mounted force was a response to the need, described picturesquely by lieutenant-governor Alexander Morris of Manitoba as the necessity facing Canada "to stable her elephant," to put peace-keepers into the field to "prevent the possibility of such a frightful disaster as befell Minnesota," referring to U.S. wars with the Dakota.[12] American officials knew that the more pressing problem was not the First Nations but the white-skinned interlopers who were usually responsible for inciting trouble. After a meeting with the president and U.S. secretary of the interior and secretary of war in 1877, the Canadian minister of the interior reported that "the true origin of the Indian difficulties in the United States was indicated by a question put to me by the Secretary of the Interior. 'How do you keep your whites in order?'"[13]

How perceptive both the Canadian official's comment about stabling its elephant and the American politician's question about keeping "your whites in order" were soon emerged in relation to the Canadian Prairies. The government was anxious to get the police into the West, in large part because of menaces from the south. The presence of a Canadian police force would strengthen the Canadian claim to the West, and the constabulary would expel the American whiskey traders who were debauching some of the First Nations of the southern plains from a series of "whiskey forts." The depths to which relations could descend in these settings were plumbed in the winter of 1872–3 in the Cypress Hills Massacre. A group of American wolf hunters tangled with a party of Assiniboine who were camped in the area to rest and consume alcohol. The upshot of the encounter was the death of a score of Aboriginal men and the capture and rape of five Aboriginal women. Such events, though neither frequent nor typical, occurred often enough in the troubled years of the 1870s to convince authorities in Ottawa that the police should be sent west quickly. The Plains nations recognized the beneficial aspects of the police presence. "If the police had not come to the country, where would we all be now?" asked Crowfoot, a Blackfoot chief, in 1877. "Bad men and whiskey were killing us so fast that very few, indeed, of us would have been left today. The police have protected us as the feathers of the bird protect it from the frosts of the winter."[14]

Negotiating a series of treaties with the First Nations of the western interior between 1871 and 1877 was part of the process of preparing for western development and protecting the Natives, too.[15] However, it is also important to note that initiation of the treaty-making process was at least as much the work of Indigenous people resisting Euro-Canadian incursions as it was the prescient preparations of the government. Because the Ojibwe near the Lake of the Woods objected to the progress of surveyors and troops through their territory, warning officials "do not bring Settlers and Surveyors amongst us to measure and occupy our lands until a clear understanding has been arrived at as to what our relations are to be in the time to come,"[16] the government began talks with them as soon as the Red River Resistance had been dealt with. Similarly, it was the fact that the Saulteaux in Manitoba "warned" settlers near Portage la Prairie "not to cut wood or otherwise take possession of the lands upon which they were squatting," and that some Plains Cree interfered with the work of the Geological Survey and construction of the telegraph line in 1875 that maintained the pressure on the government to negotiate.[17] Finally, also in the mid-1870s, the Blackfoot Confederacy sent a message of protest to Canada against the incursions on the bison of their territory by Métis and Plains Cree, as well as the unauthorized use of their land and its firewood by traders and settlers. They would interpret the coming of a treaty commissioner to Blackfoot Crossing in 1877 as a response to that remonstrance.[18]

At the same time, it is also important to recognize that Ottawa's decision to precede immigration and settlement of the western plains with the negotiation of treaties with the First Nations was merely a continuation of a century-old policy. The Royal Proclamation of 1763 had assigned the right to treat for access and title to Indigenous lands exclusively to the Crown, now operating through the machinery of the Dominion of Canada. This was the approach that had been followed when it was deemed necessary to make provision for Indian Loyalists who had fought alongside Britain in the American Revolutionary War and for Native allies who had joined the British and Upper Canadians in resisting the American invaders in the War of 1812. The practice had been continued after the War of 1812 in Upper Canada, where land cessions were negotiated. The final precedent – although it did not start off as a proclamation-inspired action – had been the Robinson Treaties of 1850 that secured from the First Nations north of Lakes Huron and Superior a large tract of land and permission for British Americans to occupy and to use it. When Ottawa instructed its officials to begin negotiations with the western tribes, it was following a tradition that had begun with the Royal Proclamation, however imperfect adherence to that tradition might have been.

But there was more to the motivations of the Canadian government than fidelity to a British-Canadian tradition. Negotiation in advance of settlement was also cheap. The alternative, American way was very costly. The republic followed a *laissez-faire* approach that allowed small bands of settlers to invade Indigenous territory, often leading to bloody repulses that precipitated the dispatch of militia by indignant assemblies. Besides being destructive of life and deterring development, such a policy was beyond Canada's financial means. In the 1870s, when the United States was spending $20 million a year on western wars, Ottawa's entire budget was only $19 million.[19] How would the Dominion bankroll a transcontinental railway across the Prairies if all its money was being spent on battling the Natives of the region? The Mackenzie government's defence of its expenditures on treaty-making in 1877 was revealing:

> My Commissioners have made further treaty arrangements with certain of the Indian tribes of the North-West Territories, by which their title is extinguished to a very large portion of the territories west of Treaty No. 4; and, although some of the provisions of this treaty are of a somewhat onerous and exceptional character, I have thought it nonetheless advisable on the whole to ratify it ... The expenditure incurred by the Indian Treaties is undoubtedly large, but the Canadian policy is nevertheless the cheapest, ultimately, if we compare the results with those of other countries; and it is above all a humane, just and Christian policy. Notwithstanding the deplorable war waged between the Indian tribes in the United States territories, and the Government

of that country, during the last year, no difficulty has arisen with the Canadian tribes living in the immediate vicinity of the scene of hostilities.[20]

The speech nicely captured both the frugality of the Mackenzie government and Canadians' smugness about their Native policy.

Besides being financially wasteful, the application of force meant political problems and a departure from well-established Canadian tradition. Any government that imitated the Americans would immediately find itself under attack from church and other humanitarian groups that took a lively, if condescending, interest in Aboriginal peoples. Moreover, in the Canadian experience it was unthinkable to say what an American general had in 1869: "The only good Indian is a dead Indian."[21] Until at least the second third of the nineteenth century, the Indigenous population had been partners with, not opponents of, the newcomers and their various activities. In Canada, historically, First Nations had been prerequisites to the success of the European traders and generals, not opponents of their efforts. At the same time, because of the problems of vast distances and sparse population, in Canada the state had played a much more active role in economic development than was the case in the United States. When Canadians began sorting out how to develop the resources of the western interior, they turned naturally to the federal state to ease the way, knowing that Indigenous people were not ferocious and implacable enemies, but cooperative people with whom it was possible to do business.

If the necessity to make peaceful preparations and a long tradition of negotiation rather than killing explain why the Dominion wished to negotiate with the western nations for access to the land, what accounts for Indigenous peoples' cooperation in the endeavour during the 1870s? First, it is essential to note that not all First Nation leaders favoured making treaty. For example, the Cree chief Big Bear was extremely suspicious of government negotiators and reluctant to sign a pact.[22] Second, some groups were influenced towards making treaty by missionaries whom they had come to trust. Men such as the Methodist George McDougall and the Oblate Father Scollen favoured the Natives' entering treaty because they believed an agricultural life was essential both for the First Nations' survival and for their successful conversion. Nonetheless, it also is important to bear in mind that the treaty-making process was one in which two active parties, government representatives and Aboriginal leaders, played roles; it was not a procedure in which one side consisting of bureaucrat and cleric dictated terms to the other. The Natives were as much agents as the government, though not actors with as much bargaining power as the federal commissioners.

The fur trade was the foundation of Indigenous-European relations in the West until the late
nineteenth century. Big Bear was trading furs at Fort Pitt in 1884.

Indigenous peoples' awareness of events in the United States and of the dwindling of the bison and other resources meant that they approached the negotiations
anxiously. They could say, as Sweet Grass wrote to Lieutenant-Governor Adams
Archibald in 1871, "We heard our lands were sold and we did not like it, we don't
want to sell our lands; it is our property, and no one has a right to sell them." But
they also knew that they needed "cattle, tools, agricultural implements, and assistance in everything when we come to settle – our country is no longer able to
support us."[23] The rapid depletion and impending disappearance of the bison was a
force that the Plains peoples recognized and feared. George McDougall explained
to an eastern friend in 1875 what the collapse of the buffalo economy meant to the
Plains First Nations:

> Just suppose that all supplies were cut off from Montreal: all factories closed because
> there was nothing to manufacture; the markets forsaken because there was nothing
> to sell; in addition to this neither building material nor fuel to be obtained; how sad
> would be the condition of the tens of thousands of your great city! Now, the situation
> of these prairie tribes is exactly analogous to this state. For ages they have lived upon
> the buffalo; with its pelt they make their wigwams; wrapped in the robe of the buffalo

Fort Carlton, on the North Saskatchewan River, was a site of negotiations for Treaty 6 in 1876.

they feared not the cold; from the flesh of this wild ox they made their pemmican and dried meat; while they possessed his sinews they needed no stronger thread; from its ribs they manufactured sleighs ... The manure of the buffalo is all the fuel they had – in a word they were totally dependent on the buffalo.[24]

Behind the eagerness of some leaders to negotiate lay a recognition that their way of life was collapsing, owing to rapid depletion of resources. For groups, such as the Ojibwe in northwestern Ontario, who were not directly affected by depletion of the bison, other economic changes, specifically loss of casual employment by the Hudson's Bay Company as the fur-trading concern changed its transportation technology, introduced similar economic uncertainty.[25] These concerns were aggravated in the 1870s by the substantial losses to epidemic disease that the Prairie peoples had recently suffered.[26]

Many of these anxieties of the Aboriginal peoples came out in speeches made by two Plains Cree chiefs at a private caucus of First Nation leaders during the negotiations for the Treaty of Fort Carlton (Treaty 6) in 1876. Mistawasis, an old and respected chief, sought to counter younger leaders who were opposed to treaty, saying:

I have heard my brothers speak, complaining of the hardship endured by our people. Some have bewailed the poverty and suffering that has come to Indians because of the destruction of the buffalo as the chief source of our living, the loss of the ancient glory of our forefathers; and with all that I agree, in the silence of my teepee and on the broad prairies where once our fathers could not pass for the great number of those animals that blocked their way; and even in our day, we have had to choose carefully our campground for fear of being trampled in our teepees. With all these things, I think and I feel intensely the sorrow my brothers express.

I speak directly to Poundmaker and The Badger and those others who object to signing this treaty. Have you anything better to offer our people? I ask, again, can you suggest anything that will bring these things back for tomorrow and all the tomorrows that face our people?

I for one think that the Great White Queen Mother has offered us a way of life when the buffalo are no more. Gone they will be before many snows have come to cover our heads or graves if such should be.

Mistawasis went on to remind his audience of the sufferings of the Blackfoot as a result of incursions of American whiskey traders, until "The Great Queen Mother, hearing of the sorrows of her children, sent out the Red Coats." Pressing his argument home, he continued, "I, for one, look to the Queen's law and her Red coat servants to protect our people against the evils of white man's firewater and to stop the senseless wars among our people, against the Blackfoot, the Peigans, the Bloods." They, the First Nations, could not prevent the coming of settlers, as the experience of "the great Indian nations in the Long Knives' country [U.S.] who have been fighting since the memory of their old men" demonstrated. North of the Medicine Line, in British territory where redcoats patrolled, things were different: "The prairies have not been darkened by the blood of our white brothers in our time. Let this always be so. I for one will take the hand that is offered. For my band I have spoken."[27] Concerns about population loss, resource depletion, and looming settlement combined to make a powerful argument for taking "the hand that is offered" by the queen's government.

What was the nature of the seven numbered treaties that were negotiated between 1871 and 1877? Many difficulties cloud efforts to reach a shared understanding of these pacts more than a century after their creation. In the first place, the Government of Canada has until very recently insisted on regarding only its own written version of the agreements as valid and trustworthy. However, there is considerable evidence that many things were said and promised in the treaty talks that

Ahtakakoop (seated left) and Mistawasis (seated right) were eloquent
pro-treaty advocates at the Fort Carlton talks in 1876.

never made it into the printed texts. In Treaty 1, for example, treaty commissioner Archibald had to make oral commitments, usually described as "outside promises," to secure a treaty, but the government for four years refused to honour these integral elements of the pact. Only in 1875 did Canada accept that the "outside promises" – oral commitments, in other words – were part of the treaty. Second, wherever significant oral history research has been done among Elders, an account that it is internally consistent to a surprising degree, but often at marked variance with the government's text, has emerged.[28] Finally, as noted later, even when negotiators on both sides used similar language during treaty talks, they meant quite different things because of the sharply different cultural backgrounds from which they came.

In large part because the two sides approached the negotiations with different purposes and assumptions, their understanding of them was different at the time and has remained unhappily so to this day. The government, though it did not recognize that Indigenous people possessed title to the lands in the way that a Euro-Canadian could possess title in a system of freehold tenure, pragmatically faced up to the fact that First Nations had some sort of claim to occupancy and use of the land. Unlike the French, the British had never denied Aboriginal interest in the lands. The British-Canadian position was that Indigenous people possessed what the courts in the later 1880s would define as a "usufructary right," or a right of usage. To the government, then, the numbered treaties were land surrender agreements in which the First Nations conceded whatever claims they had to occupancy and use in return for gifts and annual payments.

The Indigenous understanding was different. Though First Nations agreed with Sweet Grass that the territory was theirs and that no one could sell it out from under them, they did not hold to a concept of absolute property right in a European legal sense. The land and its resources were the creation of the Great Spirit, and the Native was but one inhabitant of the world with obligations to use its resources prudently and pass them on to succeeding generations undiminished. They could not negotiate surrender of title because they did not possess it. What the First Nations sought in the negotiations of the 1870s was the establishment of a relationship with the Dominion of Canada that would offer them assurances for the future, while agreeing to permit entry and some settlement of the region. To them, the treaties were intended to be pacts of friendship, peace, and mutual support; they did not constitute the abandonment of their rights and interests.

Differences of meaning and purpose often had their roots in language that had varied implications because of the different cultural backgrounds from which government and Native negotiators came. An example was the dominant metaphor, familial comparisons, that negotiators on both sides used. Both government

The treaty medal, which would have been stamped with the number
of the individual treaty in the 1870s, symbolized the alliance of the First Nations
and the Queen's government that was a vital component of the agreements.

commissioner and Plains leader talked of "the Queen Mother" and "her Indian
children." However, commonality of terms masked difference of meaning, for in
Plains and Victorian British societies the relations of child and parent were utterly
dissimilar. To the society from which government commissioner came, childhood
connoted submissiveness, obedience, and dependence, but in Cree society, for example, childhood was a time of great personal autonomy during which the young
could look to adults for protection and assistance as a right.[29] Careful examination
of the treaty talks, even as reported by a commissioner such as Alexander Morris,
reveals that when government negotiators used the metaphors of childhood it was
often in a context in which assertions of government authority and Aboriginal submission predominated. However, when Saulteaux and Cree leaders used similar
metaphors they never followed them up with references to submission on their part

and dominance by the queen's government. Another tragic example of misunderstanding occurred at Fort Pitt, the second part of Treaty 6, when Mistahimusqua
(Big Bear) told Morris that he wanted to "make a request that he will save me from
what I most dread, that is: the rope to be about my neck." Morris's interpreter translated "rope to be about my neck" as "hanging," thereby distorting Mistahimusqua's
meaning. Coming as he did from a Plains culture, Big Bear had in mind not the
hangman's noose but the horse's halter; he was saying metaphorically that he wanted to retain autonomy for his people, not that he contemplated actions that would
make him a candidate for execution.[30] The misunderstanding at Fort Pitt in 1876
was to dog Mistahimusqua's relations with the Canadian government, with disastrous consequences.

The differing purposes and assumptions of the two parties manifested themselves frequently both in the bargaining process and in the final product of the
negotiations. Government representatives came with instructions to secure Native
surrender of claim to the land cheaply, in return for initial sums and annual payments. Because they also recognized the need to assist the First Nations to provide
for alternative economic pursuits, they were prepared as well to negotiate limited
areas in which the Indigenous people could adapt to the sedentary agriculture that
must replace the migratory economy that was based on the disappearing bison.
First Nations, in negotiation after negotiation, pressed not just for larger payments
but also for more extensive tracts of land and promises of continuing assistance.
The result was usually an agreement, only imperfectly embodied in the government's text, that achieved at least a modicum of what both parties sought.

The divergent approaches of the two parties were best expressed in what each
proposed by way of reserves and aid. The First Nations' goals could be summarized
as relationship and reciprocity. As Mistawasis had said when he talked of taking
the queen's hand, he and his colleagues were interested in establishing a relationship with the queen's government through which they could count on assistance
in times of need and help in finding a new way to sustain themselves now that
the buffalo were disappearing. Because their culture always emphasized mutual-
ity and balance, they also hoped for concessions from Canada that would roughly
reciprocate the generous concession they were making to share their territory.[31]
Envisaging the reserves as extensive homelands in which they might carry on their
traditional practices as long as possible, Native negotiators pressed for larger allotments for reserves than the commissioners were inclined to grant, and hammered
steadily away to gain promises of aid in times of distress and financial help in making a transition to agriculture. Negotiation of the easternmost of the numbered
treaties, Treaty 3, was protracted and difficult primarily because the Ojibwe of the

Fort Frances district insisted that the government emissaries must specify what areas Canada wanted for roads and other purposes. They clearly intended that they would retain control of the vast bulk of the lands. A similar gambit was employed by the First Nations of the Red River area in 1871 in the negotiation of what became Treaty 1.[32] The assumption on which the Indigenous people were operating was put most graphically by Poundmaker in the 1876 negotiation of Treaty 6: "The government mentions how much land is to be given us. He says 640 acres one mile square for each band. He will give us, he says." Poundmaker shouted, "This is our land, it isn't a piece of pemmican to be cut off and given in little pieces back to us. It is ours and we will take what we want."[33] Similar assumptions about Aboriginal entitlement to the lands they occupied underlay Saulteaux complaints at Treaty 4 talks in 1874 about the transaction between the Hudson's Bay Company and Canada by which Rupert's Land was purportedly transferred to the new Dominion.[34]

But when the government negotiators insisted on restricted areas as reserves, some Indigenous leaders, so anxious were they for a treaty, eventually capitulated. Their concession to the government was made somewhat easier by the answers they got to their expressions of concern that they not be interfered with in the practice of their traditional hunting and fishing pursuits. Commissioner Morris told the Native people at the negotiations of Treaty 3, the North-West Angle Treaty, "It may be a long time before the other lands are wanted, and in the meantime you will be permitted to fish and hunt over them." In these and other, even more explicit ways, the government commissioners sought to reassure First Nations that entering treaty would entail a minimum of economic and other change.[35] First Nations negotiators would have been impressed by Commissioner Morris's assurances that the treaty would not mean a major change to their practices. At Fort Carlton in 1876, for example, he assured the chiefs, "What I have offered does not take away your living, you will have it then as you have now, and what I offer now is put on top of it."[36] The government's commissioners usually attempted to keep the reserve lands small, and they were reluctant to make extensive promises of aid in distress and assistance with adjustment.[37]

Because the Indigenous leaders saw the treaties as establishing a relationship that would guarantee them assistance in adjusting to the new order in the West, it was they who were mainly responsible for the inclusion of many of the terms that promised continuing assistance. It was the Native negotiators who suggested the treaty obligations to supply farm stock, implements, and supplies.[38] It was the chiefs' clear perceptions of their needs, and their determination to secure the fulfilment of as many of them as they could before agreeing to treaty, that lengthened the negotiations and led the commissioners to complain of the Natives' stubbornness and outrageous demands. That was the government's perception of the First Nations' determined effort to obtain what they thought they needed: agreement that traditional pursuits could be carried on; an alternative land base; assistance in both instruction and equipment to make a transition to a different economy; and promises of aid in times of crisis such as famine and epidemic.

The terms of the treaties included a neat blend of what government and Indigenous leaders wanted. The seven treaties of the 1870s that covered an area from the Lake of the Woods to the Rocky Mountains, and from the forty-ninth parallel in the south to the middle of the three future provinces on the north, promised "reserves for farming lands," annual payments in compensation for the lands surrendered, livestock, seed, ammunition, twine, promises of assistance, and even in Treaty 6 the maintenance of a medicine chest in the house of the agent. In return, the chiefs, according to the government's text, agreed to "cede, release, surrender and yield up to the Government ... all their rights, titles and privileges whatsoever, to the lands" covered by the treaties. And the First Nations were required to "hereby solemnly promise and engage to strictly observe this treaty, and also to conduct and behave themselves as good and loyal subjects of Her Majesty the Queen."[39]

The two parties' fundamentally different purposes in making treaty were even embodied in the text of the agreements. Treaty 6, for example, clearly expressed the government's intent to secure the surrender of whatever claim or interest the Indigenous people had to the lands: "It is the desire of Her Majesty to open up for settlement, immigration and such other purposes as to Her Majesty may seem meet, a tract of country, bounded and described as hereinafter mentioned, and to obtain the consent thereto of her Indian subjects inhabiting the said tract, and to make a treaty and arrange with them." But the very same paragraph – indeed, the same sentence – went on to say that another purpose of Treaty 6 was to ensure "that there may be peace and good will between them and Her Majesty, and that they may know and be assured of what allowance they are to count upon and receive from Her Majesty's bounty and benevolence."[40] Given that sort of wording, and given the culturally based differences of meaning in the language both sides used, it was not surprising that officials and chiefs emerged from the negotiations with different understandings of what had transpired. First Nations thought that they had concluded treaties of friendship and mutual assistance, while agreeing to the entry into their lands at some future date of agricultural settlement. The government in Ottawa believed that the treaties secured the Natives' surrender of whatever claim they had to the vast lands of western Canada.[41] These differences were to cause much difficulty in the future.

In the two decades leading up to Treaty 7 of 1877, important changes occurred in the relationship between Euro-Canadians' government and the Native peoples of western Canada. Canada was established in 1867, and its borders extended westward between 1869 and 1877. This process sparked a major Native resistance to the assertion of Canadian authority in Red River in 1869, thereby frightening the government and spurring it to establish its control of the region after this setback was overcome by negotiation and compromise. Ottawa moved into the West in advance of settlers with institutions of government, an agency for policing, and a treaty-making process that it thought extinguished whatever rights to absolute possession of the territory that Indigenous people had. For First Nations, the coming of civil administration was largely irrelevant, the arrival of the North-West Mounted Police welcome, and the making of treaty somewhat confusing though apparently satisfactory in its results. To them it appeared that they had negotiated a relationship with the Great Queen's government that would ensure that their way of life would not be interfered with, that they could continue for some time to enjoy their traditional avocations, that they would be protected and assisted in times of crisis, and that they would be provided with lands and other means to make a successful transition from a hunting to an agricultural economy. They had been assured emphatically and repeatedly that they could rely on the "bounty and benevolence" of the queen's government. The most troubling aspect of the events of the 1870s was not the entry of the policeman or the coming of the treaty commissioner; what worried the Natives was the disappearance of the buffalo and, in the case of leaders such as Mistahimusqua, uncertainty about how bounteous and benevolent the government in Ottawa would be.

CHAPTER TEN

The North-West Rebellion

The rebellion that broke out in the spring of 1885 has been the subject of a great deal of misunderstanding and myth-making. Among the many distorted views of that event, none is more ingrained than the notion that insurrection was the consequence of the meeting of two distinct ways of life.[1] According to this view, both the Red River Resistance of 1869 and the trouble in the Saskatchewan country in 1885 are best understood as the lamentable consequences of the meeting of a sophisticated society and more primitive peoples. Both, it is argued, represented futile attempts by technologically backward peoples to resist the march of more advanced societies. In Saskatchewan in 1885, the Métis and First Nations used force to defend a fading way of life against the expansion of commerce and agriculture. Led by Louis Riel, the Métis precipitated a rebellion in which some of the Indigenous nations joined, both groups being motivated by a desire to repel the advance of agriculture. Later, Métis historian Howard Adams promoted a modified version of this interpretation. In Adams's treatment, the united western force that opposed eastern business interests and government was made up of Métis, First Nations, and oppressed small farmers.[2] Such interpretations, while seductive in their simplicity, fail to appreciate the complexity of the events and the variety of the motives of the actors in the North-West Rebellion.

A proper understanding of these events requires careful consideration of at least three distinct elements. These are the First Nations, the Métis communities of the Saskatchewan, and Louis Riel. The behaviour of each was quite distinguishable from that of the others, particularly in the preliminary stages of the armed struggle. And, in the case of the First Nations, there were important differences among the various nations: the use of force was confined to the more northerly bands. It is impossible to understand why some Cree killed people, while others remained quiet, without analysing the situation in which the western nations found themselves between the signing of Treaty 7 in 1877 and the outbreak of violence in 1885. And it is impossible to appreciate why a peaceful Métis struggle for redress of grievances culminated in rebellion without careful examination of both the people who had grievances and the individual whose leadership they sought. Such an analysis will demonstrate that there was no First Nation rebellion in 1885; there were only sporadic and isolated reprisals by small groups from some bands. It will also illustrate that Louis Riel was the spark that caused the mixture of Métis and government to explode.

If any people in the North-West Territories had reason to rebel in the 1880s it was the First Nations.[3] They had seen the basis of their economy shattered in the 1870s, and then watched in the 1880s as the new relationship with the Dominion of Canada that they had negotiated in the 1870s failed to provide them with the relief and assistance on which they had counted. Moreover, they watched as Ottawa deliberately and systematically violated its treaty promises in order to coerce them into adopting the government's plans for settlement rather than following their own. Finally, they endured great hardship as Ottawa implemented policies of retrenchment that bore savagely on them. The underlying cause of First Nations' problems was the disappearance of the bison. It had come under greater pressure after the 1820s, as the Métis increasingly shifted into the provisioning trade for the Hudson's Bay Company and attempted to satisfy the expanding market for buffalo robes. Other factors that accounted for the depletion of the herds included the arrival of modern weapons, such as the repeating rifle, and the completion of the transcontinental railway in the United States, which brought to the plains the "sports" hunter whose only interest was the acquisition of a trophy. Buffalo hides were also in demand in eastern factories for use in the belts that drove machinery.

One final factor was American policy towards the Native Americans south of the forty-ninth parallel. In the 1860s and 1870s the United States was still engaged in military campaigns against various western nations. Among the most spectacular of these was the ill-fated foray of General G.A. Custer and the Seventh Cavalry, which resulted in their annihilation at the hands of Sitting Bull, Crazy Horse, and their warriors on the Little Big Horn River in 1876. The aftermath was the flight of Sitting Bull and hundreds of his followers across the "medicine line," as the international boundary was called by First Nations who recognized its importance in demarcating a land of refuge from a territory in which they could be hunted.

Sitting Bull's presence in what is today southwestern Saskatchewan added to the strain on the food resources of the region and encouraged the American military to undertake operations designed to compel him to stay in Canada or starve him into submission in the United States.[4] At times in the late 1870s American forces burned the prairies in an effort to prevent the southern bison herd from migrating into Canada, where it might help to sustain the fugitive Sioux.

The result of this combination of factors was the near-extinction of the bison by the 1880s.[5] Of the herds that had impeded travellers on the Prairies and parkland for days at a time in the 1840s, mere hundreds were known to exist by the end of the 1870s. In 1879 a Hudson's Bay Company man wrote in shock of "the total disappearance of buffalo from British territory this season." By 1884 only three hundred bison hides were sold at St. Paul, and by 1888 an American game report said that "only six animals were then known to be in existence!"[6] The horror of starvation, never totally absent from Native societies, now became all too familiar in the lodges of both Plains and Woodlands bands.[7] Indian Commissioner Dewdney in 1879 reported that the Blackfoot "were selling their Horses for a mere song, eating gophers, mice, and for the first time have hunted the Antelope and nearly killed them all off ... Strong young men were now so weak that some of them could hardly walk. Others who last winter were fat and hearty are mere skin and bone."[8] A Mounted Police veterinarian who observed Mistahimusqua's (Big Bear) following near Fort Walsh in 1882 described them as "literally in a starving condition and destitute of the commonest necessaries of life."[9]

The devastating hardships that the Plains peoples faced as a result of the disappearance of the bison were compounded by the government's response. As the First Nations, especially the Cree, moved southward into the Cypress Hills in search of game and a base from which to pursue the buffalo herds, the Canadian authorities became increasingly alarmed. When the Cree, led by Piapot, Little Pine, and Big Bear in particular, began to press for contiguous reserves in the region of the Hills, Ottawa's man on the spot became determined to prevent such a concentration. The fact that all three of these Cree leaders had refused to adhere to Treaty 6 when it was signed in 1876, and that Big Bear in particular had expressly rejected submission to Canadian law, made their actions a source of concern to uneasy officials.[10] The disappearance of the bison and the consequent hardships provided North-West Territories Lieutenant-Governor Edgar Dewdney with his opportunity.

Dewdney, who was also commissioner of Indian Affairs for the territories after 1879, could use the Natives' plight to defeat their diplomatic campaign for the creation of an Indian territory and to disperse them into other parts of the territories where they might be more easily controlled.[11] In deliberate violation of treaty

provisions that covered at least Piapot and Little Pine, Indian Affairs officials refused them the reserves they requested in the south. At the same time, the government used denial of food aid to the starving bands as a weapon to drive them out of
the Cypress Hills. In 1882 they were informed that they would get no more rations
in the Cypress Hills, and in 1883 the Mounted Police post Fort Walsh was closed.
The bands were forced to make their way north to lands in the Saskatchewan country. One by one the recalcitrants accepted reserves; even Big Bear entered treaty in
1882 and in 1884 seemed about to accept a reserve well away from Little Pine and
Poundmaker in the Battleford district in order to secure assistance for his starving people.[12] Piapot was moved, amidst much hardship to his followers, to the
Qu'Appelle Valley. But these apparent retreats by Piapot and Mistahimusqua were
merely a strategic withdrawal, not a surrender.

Over the next few years the Cree chieftains tried to unite the Plains Indians so as
to force a revision of the treaties. The first step by the treaty chiefs was to complain
to the Crown that the treaties were not being honoured, apparently in the belief that
Victoria or her Canadian government would remedy the shortcoming once they
were informed of it. At Fort Carlton in 1881, Chief Mistawasis, one of the powerful
proponents of entering treaty in 1876, informed Lord Lorne, the governor general
and, not insignificantly, son-in-law of the Great White Queen in London, of the
hardship the Cree had suffered: "Many a time I was very sad when I saw my poor
people starving, and I could do nothing for them." His colleague Chief Ahtakakoop
added, "I remember right at the treaty it was said that if any famine or trouble came
the Government would see to us and help."[13] As it became ever clearer that treaty
sceptics such as Mistahimusqua had understood the queen's Canadian government
better than some others, Plains leaders shifted to a diplomatic campaign to unite
the First Nations and pressure Ottawa for improvements. Piapot in the south and
Big Bear and Little Pine in the Saskatchewan district attempted to persuade various
bands – even such traditional enemies as the Blackfoot and Cree – to combine in
a united front in their dealings with the federal government. Gradually, through
personal appeals and the use of thirst dances that were designed to unite different
groups through communal ritual observances, headway was made on this diplomatic offensive. In the summer of 1884 an Indian Council was held at Duck Lake
by leaders of twelve bands to protest the snail-like pace at which the government
was honouring its treaty promises on agricultural assistance. This was evidence of
the success that Big Bear and some others were achieving in their drive to secure
reserves in the same areas and other revisions of the treaties. These consummate
diplomats were confident that the following spring, 1885, would see the triumph of
their strategy when the Blackfoot joined them in a council on Little Pine's reserve.

Relations were good between North-West Mounted Police and Plains Indians
in the early years of contact after 1874.

The reason for the reliance of senior chiefs such as Piapot and Mistahimusqua on diplomacy instead of more warlike preparations was simple: they were bound by their treaty promises. This was true in at least two senses. First, during the 1870s most of them had faced the question of what posture to adopt towards the oncoming numbers and power of Canadian society. Would it be resistance or cooperation? When they took treaty they opted for cooperation; they chose to share their lands and resources rather than to resist the Canadians. Second, their taking of treaty occurred within a framework of spiritual practices – most notably the pipe ceremony that preceded most treaty talks – that signified that their discussions and agreements were overseen by the Great Spirit. To break commitments made in such a solemn manner for anything but the most dire of reasons was dishonourable and offensive to everything in which the First Nations believed. Consequently, when it became unmistakable that Canada was not living up to its treaty commitments, they reacted with protest and pressure. Such, at any rate, was the strategic choice of senior leaders such as Big Bear and Piapot.[14] The problem was that their younger followers were becoming impatient with the slow pace at which the diplomatic campaign was proceeding. So far as the elder leaders' chosen path of peaceful diplomacy was concerned, progress could not come too soon. During the winter of 1884–5, the worst on record for agriculture, younger warriors were becoming very restive.

Indian Affairs officials such as Edgar Dewdney had not been sitting idly by while the Cree attempted to do again by diplomacy what they had tried but failed to accomplish in the Cypress Hills in the late 1870s. Dewdney used a policy of "no work, no rations" to try to force First Nations into adopting agriculture speedily and to assert the government's control. At the same time, his officials and the Mounted Police did whatever they could to interfere with the movements of the First Nation diplomats. Where possible, they prevented chiefs from travelling to councils or disrupted council meetings. They also instructed their agents and farm instructors to use rations to force a speedy transition to agriculture. In the south, some chiefs were taken by the new railway to visit Regina and Winnipeg so that they would become acquainted with the numbers and power of the newcomer population.

This tendency towards coercion was made all the more painful for western First Nations by Ottawa's decision after 1883 to implement a policy of retrenchment that would necessitate a reduction in assistance to First Nations. A combination of renewed recession and mounting demands on the government treasury for the completion of Canadian Pacific Railway created a strain on the federal budget that led to cuts in many government departments, including Indian Affairs. Officials on the spot warned the department that such measures were false economy, but Macdonald's deputy minister was convinced by a quick tour of the region he made in 1883 that such reductions were possible. And the prime minister was too busy with other matters and too little informed about western affairs to overrule his senior bureaucrat. Such parsimony was as unwise as it was inhumane, given the situation that prevailed among First Nations of the western interior in 1883 and 1884.

Ironically, these economies were ordered at the same time as the Indian Affairs department began to divert an increasing share of its budget to education. Prior to the 1880s, nothing that could be called a First Nation educational policy existed. In eastern Canada there were schools that were run by representatives of missionary organizations, and in Ontario there were even a few boarding schools for Natives.[15] On the Prairies and in British Columbia that same chaotic approach to First Nation schooling had been allowed to develop. Missionary societies on their own initiative had set up schools associated with their mission stations. Many of these rudimentary efforts were day schools presided over by ill-trained, and worse paid, missionaries who had far too many other duties to worry unduly about the abysmal attendance and poor academic showing of their students. A few missionaries had also begun to experiment with boarding schools in the West. By the 1880s a hodgepodge of schools had developed in the region west of Ontario: there were day schools to which the government sometimes made small grants that paid much of the teachers' stipends; and less frequently there were also boarding schools to which the government rarely contributed anything. Between 1878 and 1883 the government embarked on an extension of the day schools and the creation of a wholly new system of industrial schools. In 1883–4 costly "industrial" schools that were designed to teach First Nations trades and agriculture were opened in Battleford, Qu'Appelle, and High River in the North-West Territories.[16] The financial impact of these schools, which were expensively built and maintained, was significant in an Indian Affairs department that was already under financial pressure as a result of the policy of retrenchment.

Indian Affairs Commissioner Dewdney had one final weapon that he proposed to use to cow and control the First Nations of the plains and Pacific in the mid-1880s. Convinced that the policy of harassing Indigenous diplomats and applying pressure by restricting the flow of rations was only partially successful, Dewdney urged Macdonald to adopt a policy of "sheer compulsion" in dealing with the leaders of those bands who refused to behave as the department desired.[17] His efforts to prevent leaders from meeting in 1884 had been thwarted by the small numbers of officials and police, and the absence of legislation enabling them to control Indians' movement. More police would be recruited by 1885, and the Indian Act was amended to authorize officials to arrest Natives who were on reserves other than their own without department permission, and to outlaw the potlatch of the Pacific First Nations. Dewdney was confident that, when these amendments came into effect in 1885, he would be equal to the challenge posed by the likes of Big Bear, Piapot, and Little Pine.

While Big Bear had been manoeuvering and Dewdney had been countering, increasing dissatisfaction had arisen within some of the Cree bands, discontent that threatened to supplant the traditional leadership and rise up against government authority. While such experienced leaders as Big Bear and Piapot understood the need for a united front and the futility of armed action, some of their younger followers did not. Or, if they did, they inclined to the view that it would be better to meet extinction fighting than starving. These less experienced men found it hard to bear the suffering caused by want and the indignities resulting from the actions of overbearing bureaucrats with stoicism. By 1883 their anger was approaching

the boiling point, and in the summer of 1884 there were confrontations on reserves, such as that of Yellow Calf in the Qu'Appelle area, between hungry Natives
and outnumbered policemen. In such disputes it was all that cooler, more mature
heads could do to prevent the slaughter of the constable or agent. Another near-
conflagration occurred in the "Craig incident" of 1884, when police and Indian
Affairs officials foolishly barged into a thirst dance in the Battleford area in search
of suspects. Big Bear complained at the 1884 council in Duck Lake that he was
losing control of his band to more militant young men, such as Little Poplar, who
advocated an all-out war as an alternative to diplomacy.

All the same, the older chiefs remained committed to a peaceful strategy, as they
explained during a revealing meeting that some of them had with an Indian Affairs
official at Fort Carlton in August 1884. After listing a number of specific grievances
related to treaty commitments, they added that "requests for redress of these grievances have been again & again made without effect. They are glad that the young
men have not resorted to violent measures to gain it ... [I]t is almost too hard for
them to bear the treatment received at the hands of the Government after its 'sweet
promises,' made in order to get their country from them. They now fear that they
are going to be cheated." They told the official that they would "wait until next summer to see if this council has the desired effect, failing which they will take measures to get what they desire. (The proposed 'measures' could not be elicited, but
a suggestion of the idea of war was repudiated.)"[18] The Cree chiefs could not have
been clearer about their peaceful intentions.

Though it did not have to be that way, it was in fact the grievances of the Métis, in
combination with the influence of Louis Riel, that brought armed rebellion to the
Saskatchewan country in 1885. The mixed-descent population of the region were
largely Manitoba Métis who had migrated westward in search of a new home in
which they could pursue their customary life of hunting, fishing, casual employment, and some agriculture. In the 1870s, while settlers were establishing the nearby town of Prince Albert, some 1,500 Métis founded villages such as St. Laurent
and Batoche in the South Saskatchewan Valley.

Both the Métis and the Euro-Canadians of the Saskatchewan had grievances
with the federal government in the 1880s. The non-Native farmers objected to the
slowness of the land registry system, the failure of the transcontinental railway
to make its expected way through their region, and the hardships resulting from
several bad seasons. They responded by participating in the 1884 formation of
the Manitoba and North West Farmers' Union, and joining with the Métis in a
campaign to pressure the federal government to deal with their problems. The

Métis not only shared in the settlers' disgruntlement with government and economic adversity but also had additional concerns of their own. As usual, land was
at the heart of most of their grievances.[19] As in Manitoba earlier, the Saskatchewan
Métis feared that the arrival of a land registration system from Ottawa might jeopardize their customary title to river-lot farms. They could not get assurances from
an ominously silent federal government that their title would be respected. Some
of them also believed that they had a claim for compensation for loss of Aboriginal
title in the territories. They argued that the Dominion had by treaty dealt with the
First Nations' title to the lands, but not theirs. Before extensive development occurred, Canada should recognize in Saskatchewan, as it had in Manitoba, that the
Métis shared in Aboriginal title, and should compensate them for their loss of this
interest in the land. And, finally, some of the Saskatchewan Métis argued that they
or their children had unresolved claims against the Dominion for land grants as
a result of the promises made to future generations of Métis in the Manitoba Act
of 1870. The problems the Métis experienced in advancing their case in the early
1880s were similar to those that non-Native farmers encountered: Ottawa never
seemed to deal with their complaints. In part the problem was that federal politicians were preoccupied with other, to them more important, matters. Additionally,
the ministers responsible for western matters, David Macpherson and later Sir John
Macdonald, knew little about western problems. In Macdonald's case the problem
was still further compounded by his age. Old Tomorrow was getting on. He was sixty-
three when he returned to power in the general election of 1878; he was running
out of energy. And he had little sympathy for the Métis. Macdonald mistakenly
believed that much of the talk of land compensation from the Métis was nonsense
that had been inspired by non-Native land speculators who were stirring up the
people of Batoche or St. Laurent. So far as a repetition of the Manitoba Act's promise of land to mixed ancestry people by virtue of their partial First Nation ancestry
was concerned, Macdonald was having no part of such schemes. The promise of the
Manitoba Act had been a disaster to fulfil, not least because the slowness, dishonesty, and incompetence of federal officials delayed the distribution of land so long
that many Métis gave up and sold their land scrip for a pittance to speculators.
Macdonald was, if possible, even more unsympathetic than he was uninterested
in the complaints from the Saskatchewan country.

The response of both Métis and settlers to their failure to get the federal government to deal with their grievances was a decision to ask Louis Riel to return to
Canada from south of the border to lead their movement. Both parties were clear
that what they wanted was Riel's experience and skill in dealing peacefully with an
unresponsive government. To obtain his help with their movement for redress of

grievances, they sent a party south to Montana at the beginning of June 1884 to ask him to come to their assistance. Had they thought about his response to their request for any length of time, they might have been troubled about what they were doing. "God wants you to understand that you have taken the right way," Riel told the delegates from the Saskatchewan, "for there are four of you, and you have arrived on the fourth of June."[20]

What Riel's cryptic response to the invitation imperfectly disguised was the fact that the Louis Riel who accepted the invitation in June of 1884 was a very different man from the Riel who had led the resistance fifteen years earlier. Riel had felt himself ill used by the Canadian government in 1870. Forced to flee, denied the amnesty he had been promised, elected to parliament but unable to take his seat for fear for his life, Riel was finally banished from the country for five years in 1875. The distressing events of the 1870s had unhinged him mentally. Riel was now convinced that he had a divine mission. Like the poet-king of Israel, David, whose name he adopted, he had been chosen by God. His mission was to prepare the world for the second coming of Christ and the end of life on earth by transferring the papacy from Italy to the new world, replacing the Bishop of Rome with the Ultramontane Bishop of Montreal, and ultimately locating the Holy See at St. Vital, his home parish in Manitoba. The Northwest was to become a new homeland in which the oppressed peoples of Europe could join the Métis and First Nations to live in peace during a millennium that would precede the final end of the world.[21]

Like most prophets, Riel found himself without honour in his own land once he began to act on the revelation of his divine mission. He spent two periods of incarceration in asylums for the mentally ill in Quebec in the 1870s and was told upon release that his cure would last only if he avoided involvement in matters that excited him. He moved to the United States, married, became an American citizen and participated in American politics, and settled down to the life of a mission schoolteacher in the West. However, he had not forgotten his mission; he continued to look for a sign that it was time for its fulfilment. When, on 4 June 1884, four delegates from the Métis of Saskatchewan invited him to return with them, he knew that it was the divine signal he sought.

In the initial months after his return to Canada with his wife and children, Riel played the role he had been asked to rather than the role he knew God ultimately intended for him. He served as an adviser and organizer of legal protests, attending meetings and helping with the preparation of yet more petitions to Ottawa. He was even at Duck Lake at the time of the chiefs' council in 1884, but although he met with Mistahimusqua, there is no record that he sought to incite either the Cree or his own followers to acts of rebellion. It was only gradually during the winter of 1884–5 that his purpose became known to the Oblate priests with whom he was in frequent contact. One of them claimed that Riel said that he had personal claims – no doubt based on the terms of the Manitoba Act – that the federal government should redress. The priest informed Ottawa, but the prime minister declined to play the game of bribery, if that was the game that Riel intended.[22] But as the clerics became aware of Riel's peculiar religious ideas, they became convinced that he was heretical if not completely deranged. They would be the first in the community to turn against him; they would be followed during that winter by the non-Native settlers and anglophone Métis along the Saskatchewan who set their face against the conversion of the movement from peaceful protest to armed struggle.[23]

It was clearly Riel – not the community at large, not even the Métis as a group – who pushed events in the direction of rebellion in the early weeks of 1885. For many months he had simply advanced the existing agitation; a petition of December 1884 did not include his own exalted claim for a land grant to the Métis by virtue of their sharing in the Aboriginal title to the country. By March, Riel was poised to attempt a re-enactment of the strategy that had worked so well in 1869. His pretext was the lack of response from Ottawa. In fact, in January the federal government decided to appoint a commission to inquire into the grievances of the Métis,[24] and while they made that decision known to Riel through an intermediary, they did not follow up their actions until two months later when the members of the commission were appointed. By that time Riel had raised the stakes, proclaiming a provisional government, of which he would be the prophet and Gabriel Dumont the adjutant-general. The insurgents demanded the surrender of Fort Carlton and its police detachment.

If Riel thought he was re-enacting the events at Red River in 1869, he miscalculated. The two situations were starkly different. In 1869 he had enjoyed clerical support and the backing of a reasonably united community. In 1885 the priests turned against him, and the settlers' support evaporated along with that of the anglophone Métis. It might have been possible in Rupert's Land in 1869, especially after McDougall's abortive proclamation of Canadian authority, to argue that there was a vacuum of legal authority that justified a provisional government. In 1885 there was little doubt that Canada was the effective government in the North-West Territories. Red River had been distant and vulnerable, partly because Ottawa feared that the Americans had designs upon the region and partly because of the season in which the Resistance occurred. Batoche in 1885 was geographically more remote but in actuality more accessible, thanks to the nearly complete Canadian Pacific Railway. If the Dominion chose in 1885 to crush Riel rather than negotiate, his rising was doomed. That, of course, was precisely what Canada decided to do.

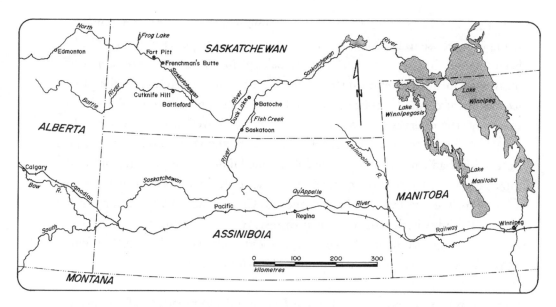

The North-West Rebellion, 1885

It was largely a matter of coincidence – certainly not a matter of design – that a series of First Nation actions occurred about the same time that Riel and the Métis confronted the police.[25] In the camp of Big Bear, effective power had shifted to the young men in the warrior society by March 1885. This transition, by no means unusual in the fluid and subtle political systems of Plains First Nation communities, meant that the authority of the elderly diplomat, Big Bear, was greatly lessened, while the ability of men such as his son Imasees and the war chiefs Little Poplar and Wandering Spirit to carry the band on their own more warlike policy was increased. Irritation had been building up against some of the non-Native men at Frog Lake, where Big Bear's band was established, and when news arrived of a Métis victory over the police at Duck Lake, some of the young warriors attacked the Hudson's Bay Company storekeeper and the Indian agent. Big Bear attempted to restrain them when he became aware of what was going on, but before he could make peace prevail nine whites lay dead.

The incident, essentially a bloody act of reprisal against unpopular officials, became unjustifiably known as the Frog Lake Massacre. That it was nothing of the sort was illustrated by the fact that not all the Euro-Canadians were killed; one Company man and two women were spared, thanks in part to Big Bear. Moreover, though these people were prisoners in Big Bear's camp for weeks, they were not harmed at all. If the death of nine people and the humane treatment of three others constitute a massacre, then, and only then, was Frog Lake a massacre.

But the impression that prevailed at the time was that the Plains nations were rising in response to the Métis initiative. The rout of the police at Duck Lake had been followed by the "massacre" at Frog Lake. Panic set in, nowhere more obviously than in the Battleford district, where settlers fled for refuge to the fort. A few days before trouble broke out, the industrial school principal noted during his visit to nearby reserves that the "Indians appear to be well disposed toward white men."[26] Yet when groups from Poundmaker's band who were travelling to the post in search of badly needed food looted abandoned homesteads near the fort, in the minds of the settlers and the government these relatively innocent events became a "siege" of the fort by Poundmaker and the Cree. Again, it was nothing of the sort, as Poundmaker's retreat to his own reserve clearly illustrated. Nonetheless, the Canadian government believed, and set about convincing others, that the entire Northwest was threatened by a combined Métis-Indian rising.

Canada's military response was devastating and indiscriminate. In all, some eight thousand troops, militia, and police were dispatched into the region along three routes: from Qu'Appelle north against the mixed-ancestry community in the valley of the South Saskatchewan; from Swift Current north to "relieve" Battleford; and from Calgary north to Edmonton. The only fighting of any consequence occurred at Fish Creek, Batoche, and Cut Knife Hill. At Fish Creek, Dumont persuaded Riel to let him attack the military column from hiding, but then nullified the advantage of surprise by prematurely revealing his position. The final stand came at Batoche, where the Métis dug rifle pits and established fortifications from which they rained a withering fire on their attackers. Unfortunately for the Métis, the defenders quickly exhausted their ammunition and were reduced to using makeshift projectiles. The attacking Canadian forces, both troops and militia, greatly outnumbered the few hundred armed Métis. Moreover, they were equipped with ample arms and ammunition, not even counting the Gatling gun that the American military had thoughtfully provided for field testing or the steamer that the commander attempted to use as a diversionary naval force. Finally, the ill-disciplined militiamen, tired of three days of feinting and long-range firing, and fed up with their general's cautious probes of Batoche, ignored their orders and overran the rifle pits.

Louis Riel, who had behaved throughout the encounters at Duck Lake and Batoche as though he was conducting a religious service rather than leading a revolt, surrendered. The truth was that, at least in his own mind, his was a religious cause. He could not fail because he was carrying out God's mission. If the deity had arranged for a defeat, it could only be because Riel was to make his case at a trial after the surrender. Dumont, practical fighter that he was, lit out for the United States.

The other military actions of the North-West campaign involved Poundmaker and Big Bear. When Colonel Otter's column "relieved" Battleford, its leader decided to set off in search of Poundmaker, whom all held responsible for the "siege" that had never happened. Otter caught up to Poundmaker's people at Cut Knife Hill and attacked. He and his men soon found themselves in trouble as the Cree fired from protected positions at the soldiers who were silhouetted on a hillside. The troops were astounded when they were able to retreat in an orderly fashion without suffering further losses. What they did not know was that Poundmaker had persuaded his men not to pursue and inflict any more damage on Otter's battered soldiers.

Big Bear and his followers spent much of May evading yet another Canadian force led by T.B. Strange in the bush country north of Frog Lake. The aftermath of the "massacre" had been the gradual restoration of the old leader's authority, and he used his control to follow his traditionally pacific paths. He allowed a frightened contingent of police to vacate Fort Pitt safely, and then he tried to take his people away from all trouble, including advancing troops. Strange caught up to Big Bear once, to his sorrow, near Frenchman's Butte, in the Fort Pitt area. Strange had to withdraw to Fort Pitt. Eventually, after Big Bear had led the soldiers on a merry chase in the northern bush, his forces began to melt away. Finally, Big Bear returned to the Fort Carlton area and surrendered early in July. With Riel and Poundmaker already in custody, Big Bear's surrender marked the end of the rebellion.

What was at least as significant as who participated in the rising was who did not. Piapot in the Qu'Appelle area did not take up arms, perhaps because the government quickly stationed troops on his reserve to discourage his men from violence. At Round Lake, near Broadview, Assiniboia, the Presbyterian missionary noted that the Natives became excited and prepared to leave only when they heard that "the soldiers are comming [sic] & will take us prisoner & we would rather fight & die on the battle field than to go away as a prisoner." However, when he assured them that if the troops came and took the braves they would have to imprison the missionary as well, "I was not a little astonished to see them take my advice & remain at home."[27] In other words, First Nations in Assiniboia either chose or were persuaded by the presence of troops not to join in the rising.

Nor did the Blackfoot Confederacy in the southwest take up arms. Part of the explanation lies in how weakened the southern nations were by hardship, hunger, and disease by 1885. Here, again, the pacific influence of older chiefs such as Crowfoot and the sense of commitment to treaty obligations were part of the explanation. But so, too, was the southern First Nations' familiarity with non-Natives and their power. The Blackfoot, four of whose chiefs had earlier travelled by train to Regina and Winnipeg at Dewdney's invitation, appreciated the general significance of the

Oblate missionary Albert Lacombe and translator Jean L'Heureux
accompanied Blackfoot chiefs who did not participate in the North-West
Rebellion to the prime minister's residence in Ottawa in 1886.

large numbers of Euro-Canadians and the military potential of the railroad.[28] The
non-participation of the southern nations, arguably the people who had suffered
most since the making of the treaties and the disappearance of the bison, was further evidence that the events of 1885, whatever Edgar Dewdney said they were,
were not a First Nation rising.

Nonetheless, Dewdney and the government chose to portray the events as a
First Nation rebellion and to use that excuse to complete the "subjugation" of the
Plains Cree that they had begun in the late 1870s.[29] Although there was no reliable
evidence that Poundmaker was responsible for the "siege of Battleford" or that Big
Bear was the architect of the "Frog Lake Massacre," both leaders were prosecuted
and convicted of treason-felony. In vain, Mistahimusqua pleaded in his remarks
prior to sentencing:

Indian Commissioner Edgar Dewdney, here proudly photographed with Chief Piapot and some of his band, shrewdly stationed armed forces on the reserve to discourage participation in the 1885 rebellion.

When white men were few in this land, I gave them my hand in friendship. No man can ever be witness to any act of violence by Big Bear to any white man. Never did I take the white man's horse. Never did I order any one of my people to one act of violence against the white man.

I ask for pardon and help for my tribe. They are hiding in the hills and trees now afraid to come to white man's government. When the cold moon comes the old and feeble ones, who have done no wrong, will perish. Game is scarce. Can not the men who speak for the White Mother send a pardon to my tribe and send them help?[30]

The incarceration of Big Bear and Poundmaker in a penitentiary in Manitoba, of course, made certain that the movement for revision of the treaties would not resume. Both were released before serving all of their three-year sentences; each died within a year of release. The Cree and other Plains First Nations suffered reprisals from Indian Affairs for years afterwards.[31] In addition to Big Bear and Poundmaker, forty-two other First Nations men were convicted of various offences for actions that had occurred during the insurrection. Students of the trials of the First Nation defendants have concluded that they were much less carefully handled than those of the Métis and non-Native defendants.[32] The explanation of the unfairness of the First Nation trials lies in a combination of Dewdney's desire to use the courts to complete the cowing of the leaders and the prejudice of Euro-Canadian juries.

It is an interesting comment on the preoccupations of historians that it has been the trial of the Métis leader that has captured most attention. It is often claimed that Riel's trial was a travesty of justice. Critics object that he should not have been charged with high treason, because he was an American citizen; that he should not have been tried before a magistrate, because he faced a capital charge; that he should have been granted a change of venue to Manitoba, where he would have been entitled to some French-speaking jurors rather than the six English-speaking Protestants who decided his fate during the tense days of July 1885. And, finally, most observers have argued that Riel was insane and should, consequently, not have been found guilty, or, if convicted, should have had the sentence of death commuted. These criticisms are unfounded.

The charge of treason was valid, as was the venue and composition of the court. Anyone residing, even temporarily, within a jurisdiction owes a sort of allegiance and obedience to the legitimate authority of that territory. Riel owed obedience to the laws and queen of Canada when he came into the country in 1884.[33] Riel was not entitled under territorial law to a change of venue to another province; Regina was a legal, if not entirely appropriate, site for his trial. Where else in the territories should the trial have occurred? Battleford? Prince Albert? And there was no doubt

Chief Poundmaker was one of the Cree chiefs unfairly tried
and imprisoned after the rebellion in 1885.

NOTICE.

———◆———

WHEREAS, the troubles in the North have necessitated the bringing of large bodies of troops into the country to suppress the troubles, and punish those causing them, and when these troops meet any Indians off their Reserves they may be unable to tell whether they are hostile or friendly, and may attack them ;

AND WHEREAS, runners are constantly being sent by Riel throughout the country spreading lies and false resports, trying to induce different bands of Indians to join him, by threats and otherwise ;

AND WHEREAS, it is the intention of the troops to arrest and punish such runners wherever the same may be found, and it will be necessary for them, in order to accomplish this, to arrest all Indians, or any suspicious persons whom they may see, in order to ascertain whether or not they are runners from Riel ;

AND WHEREAS, it is expedient that all good and loyal Indians should know how to act under the present circumstances so as to secure their own safety and the good will of the Government ;

Now, this is to give notice that all good and loyal Indians should remain quietly on their Reserves where they will be perfectly safe and receive the protection of the soldiers ; and that any Indian being off his Reserve without special permission in writing from some authorized person, is liable to be arrested on suspicion of being a rebel, and punished as such.

ANY LOYAL INDIAN who gives such information as will lead to the arrest and conviction of any such runner from Riel, or any hostile bands of Indians, will receive a reward of Fifty Dollars ($50.00.)

E. DEWDNEY,
Indian Commissioner.

Regina, 6th May, 1885.

This "emergency measure" during the troubles in 1885 evolved into the infamous pass system, which had no legislative foundation.

Cree chiefs Big Bear and Poundmaker in captivity. Poundmaker's braids were spared because
of his close relationship with Blackfoot chief Crowfoot, who enjoyed government favour.

that Magistrate Richardson was entitled to hear the case, even if it must be admitted
that he did not sparkle on the bench. There was a precedent for conducting a capital
trial before a territorial magistrate and jury of six.[34]

The most tangled issue surrounding Riel's trial and conviction was his mental
health. That he was mentally ill, perhaps even insane, seems indisputable. However,
his lawyers' opportunity to argue for a not-guilty verdict on this basis was largely
wiped out by Riel's public protestations to the court that he was not insane and
by his cogent closing address to the jury. Riel opposed the insanity plea because
he believed that he was the instrument of a great cause that deserved its day in
court. To have agreed to a plea of insanity would have been to deny the validity and
importance of both his and the Métis cause. Riel was mentally ill, but his lawyers
were unable to plead effectively that he should be acquitted on grounds of insanity.
Accordingly, once the jury found him guilty, the presiding judge had no choice but
to impose the ultimate sentence. The only possibility of avoiding execution, given
the charge and the verdict, lay in the jury's recommendation of clemency.

Only the federal government could recommend commutation of Riel's sentence to life imprisonment. And within Quebec a demand began to develop for

clemency once Ontario extremists began to demand the carrying out of the sentence in terms that were offensive to the French-speaking Catholics of Quebec. It was not that Quebec sympathized with Riel or supported his actions; it was rather that Ontarians had converted him into a symbol of Quebec itself by demanding his blood not as a Métis traitor, but as a French and Catholic rebel.[35] But if Ottawa was to accede to Quebec, on what grounds could it do so?

Many people, then and since, were prepared to come forward with arguments that they thought justified commutation. Some argued that the rebellion had been justified by the federal government's neglect. Obviously, no government – certainly not Sir John Macdonald's – was going to accept such an argument. It is a painful but real fact of life that the only thing that justifies rebellion is success. The successful revolutionary is a statesman, the unsuccessful a criminal. A suggestion that Riel should receive clemency because his offence was a *political* crime received a similarly chilly reception from Ottawa. Such a category of offence did not exist, and no conventional government was interested in creating one. One person's political crime was another's act of treason. That left only the insanity argument.

The insanity issue came in two phases: the trial and the prelude to execution. If Riel had been found legally insane at the trial, he would have been acquitted by reason of insanity. But the nineteenth-century criteria of legal insanity were extremely narrow and rigid. The test boiled down to the question, "Did the accused know right from wrong when he or she committed the act?" Doctors who examined Riel found that, though he held strange ideas on political and religious issues, he did know right from wrong. He was not *legally* insane. However, there was an additional point. If Riel had become insane since his conviction, it would be inhumane to execute him. The federal government explored this possibility with a medical commission that, though not unanimous, concluded that the condemned prisoner in the Regina jail was not insane. (The federal government misrepresented the views of one of the doctors to strengthen its case, thereby earning the opprobrium of later commentators.[36])

Advocates were running out of arguments, and Riel out of time. Since there were no medical grounds for commutation, since there were no effective arguments in favour of clemency, and since Ontario was demanding the carrying out of the sentence even more vehemently than Quebec was insisting on commutation, Macdonald and the federal cabinet concluded that the stern course of justice should be followed. The prime minister did not doubt Riel's guilt and the justness of the sentence, and he believed that no matter what his government did, it would be damned by some group. If they were damned if they did and damned if they didn't, then he was damned well going to do what he personally believed was right. The federal government announced that it would not interfere. And on 16 November 1885, Louis Riel was hanged.

In a sense Riel never died. Though they took down his body and transported it to St. Boniface where a grieving Métis community interred it in the cathedral cemetery, he lived on. Riel became a symbol of many causes in the century after his execution. To the French-speaking people of Quebec he immediately became a token of their own vulnerability in a Confederation dominated by English-speaking Protestants. They reacted by electing a so-called *parti national* government in 1886. In the twentieth century Riel has served as a representative figure for western politicians such as Saskatchewan's Ross Thatcher, who have exploited his tragic life to make their case against an unresponsive federal government. "Whether we realize it or not, we of 1968 face a situation which is similar in some respects. If Riel could walk the soil of Canada today, I am sure his sense of justice would be outraged as it was in 1885," intoned Premier Thatcher.[37] Pierre Trudeau also exploited the Métis martyr by holding him up as an example of where intolerance towards ethnic and racial minorities can lead. As he said at the unveiling of a monument to Riel in Regina in 1968, "We must never forget that, in the long run, a democracy is judged by the way the majority treats the minority. Louis Riel's battle is not yet won."[38] And in the 1960s Riel was adopted and patronized by non-Native, middle-class student radicals who found him an acceptable substitute for the Cuban Revolution's Che Guevara. He has been the subject of innumerable stories, plays, and one important opera. Canadians find Riel – or, more accurately, their own concerns that they project onto Riel – endlessly fascinating.

The Native communities have had a more difficult time deciding how to handle the historical memory of Riel. For a time the Métis embraced him as the principal symbol of their problems at the hands of an unsympathetic government and community. In the early 1970s the Association of Métis and Non-Status Indians of Saskatchewan even petitioned Ottawa for a pardon for Riel, but later they withdrew their request, arguing that it was not Riel but the federal government that needed a pardon. In the 1990s the separatist Bloc Québécois picked up Riel's case and argued for a federal pardon. So, too, did the 1996 *Final Report* of the Royal Commission on Aboriginal Peoples, although for far less cynical or political reasons. Most Métis in western Canada still admire Louis Riel greatly.

No corresponding fascination has developed with those who lost the most by the North-West Rebellion, the First Nations. Tekahionwake, better known to her

Euro-Canadian audiences as E. Pauline Johnson, evinced the ambivalence about 1885 among First Nations in her poem "A Cry from an Indian Wife," one of many poems she recited during her successful lecture tours early in the twentieth century:

> Go; rise and strike, no matter what the cost.
> Yet stay. Revolt not at the Union Jack,
> Nor raise Thy hand against this stripling pack
> Of white-faced warriors marching West to quell
> Our fallen tribe that rises to rebel.[39]

Non-Native Canadians have opted to ignore the First Nations and 1885. One can point to a National Film Board account, *Ballad of Crow Foot*, or a major novel on *The Temptations of Big Bear*, or a television miniseries on Big Bear, but not to any pattern of using leaders such as Poundmaker or Big Bear as symbols of various causes.[40] It is almost as though a great amnesia descended on Canadians as a result of the crushing of First Nation leadership after the rising of 1885. There was no Indian rebellion in the Saskatchewan country in 1885; there were scattered and isolated acts of violence by angry young men who could no longer be restrained by cooler heads. The First Nations did not rebel. Yet they have suffered the most.

CHAPTER ELEVEN

The Policy of the Bible and the Plough

After the rebellion of 1885, Ottawa continued to move towards coerced assimilation of Natives. To Canadians and their national government, First Nations were largely irrelevant. They no longer played a critical role in commerce save in the North, were not considered vital as military allies, and were even less useful for purposes of exploration and mapping than previously had been the case. Ottawa thought it obvious that the best Aboriginal policy was one that eliminated First Nations, not by violence but by assimilation to a Euro-Canadian pattern. The "great aim of our legislation," Sir John Macdonald noted, "has been to do away with the tribal system and assimilate the Indian people in all respects with the inhabitants of the Dominion, as speedily as they are fit for the change."[1]

Canadian policy after Confederation became steadily more interfering and coercive as Ottawa became increasingly impatient about the slow pace of Indians' "civilization" and "assimilation." The 1876 Indian Act maintained the provision for elective band councils that the 1869 act had instituted, to the annoyance of the eastern First Nations, but did so now on a voluntary basis. When First Nations demonstrated their opposition to this interference in their political affairs, the measure was amended in the 1880 revision of the Indian Act to make it possible for the Department of Indian Affairs to impose an elected band council on First Nations whether they preferred traditional, non-elected leadership or not. The 1880 act, which formally established the Department of Indian Affairs (DIA), applied to all status or registered Indians, that is, to all who were recognized by the department. In 1884 the so-called Indian Advancement Act augmented Ottawa's powers yet again by authorizing the superintendent general to depose chiefs whom he considered unfit or unable to discharge their duties. Finally, eastern bands were offered a further inducement to take up the opportunities of citizenship in the 1885 Franchise Act, which extended the right to vote in federal elections to adult male band members east of Lake Superior. These provisions were designed to undermine traditional forms of self-government and to permit active intervention in band matters.

First Nations resisted these attempts at interference in their political affairs. Between 1857 and 1920, only 250 individuals opted for full citizenship and loss of Indian status by means of enfranchisement.[2] It was the very fact that eastern First Nations refused to adopt the elected councils under the 1880 act, or, if they did, proceeded to elect their hereditary leaders, that prompted the reintroduction of compulsion in subsequent amendments. And on the Six Nations reserve near Brantford, Ontario, a conflict between elected and hereditary leaders developed that was to divide the First Nation community, lead to endless political agitation and litigation, and culminate in the Natives' unsuccessful appeal to the Assembly of the League of Nations at this meddling in their internal affairs.[3] Similarly, few eastern First Nations people used the ballot the Franchise Act of 1885 offered them, and in 1898 it was withdrawn.

Next to political control, Ottawa was most interested in reshaping First Nation attitudes towards land and land ownership. In the late years of the nineteenth century, western lands were considered particularly important for the settlement of the expected millions of immigrants as agriculturalists. Their successful accommodation was vital to Canada's success, as a 1905 poem entitled "The New Race" implied:

> And still the tide flows westward,
>   Toward the land of the setting sun;
> And the call goes forth into all the world,
> Until now, where the smoke of the wigwam curled,
>   A new life has begun.
> For see! 'Tis the birth of a nation!
> And the men who will mingle now
> The blood of the nations of every land,
> Are founding a race, 'neath whose sovereign hand
>   The knee of the world shall bow.[4]

Such naively imperialist expectations boded ill for western First Nations.

The artist's portrayal of the contrast between indigent Natives and "pioneers" typified attitudes towards Plains nations after the onset of western settlement.

As had already become apparent in the contests in Upper Canada before Confederation, First Nations regarded communal land-holding as essential to the preservation of their identity. The location ticket, the means by which reserve lands held in common would disappear as First Nation individuals were enfranchised, reappeared in the 1876 Act. An eastern male band member who had demonstrated that he lived as a Euro-Canadian did could receive a ticket for an individual plot and, after three years' probation, be enfranchised and receive absolute title to the land. An analogous program of encouraging western First Nations to hold their lands "in severalty" rather than in common was introduced in the 1880s. "The policy of destroying the tribal or communist system is assailed in every possible way," explained Indian Commissioner Reed, "and every effort made to implant a spirit of individual responsibility instead."[5] Prime Minister Macdonald approved of this cultural objective, and also noted that subdivision of reserves into individual plots would identify "surplus" lands that might then be made available to incoming members of the poet's "new race."[6] The department soon learned that the First Nations opposed the subdivision of reserves for fear "that the Government will deprive them of the residue of their lands, should there be any, after the location titles have issued for the lots allocated to individual Indians, and that the latter will become subject to taxation, as are the lands of white people in municipalities."[7] This assault on First Nation land-holding never succeeded to any great extent.

Not all government initiatives aimed at interference and coercion; some were protective in inspiration. The protective approach was a logical outgrowth of the Euro-Canadians' view that the Aboriginal peoples were retarded in their development and required protection from rapacious members of the newly dominant society. As Sir Hector Langevin put it during the debate on the 1876 act, "Indians were not in the same position as white men. As a rule they had no education, and they were like children to a very great extent. They, therefore, required a great deal more protection that [sic] white men."[8] This attitude explained why the Indian Act relegated First Nations to the legal status of "ward," with the DIA playing the role of surrogate parent.

The act forbade liquor sales to Native people, barred those who were not members of a band from its reserve after nightfall, and prohibited the presence of First Nation women in bars. Such limitations were intended to protect women from unscrupulous white men who sought their sexual services, and they were an indirect acknowledgment of the growing problem of the prostitution of Native women, particularly in the towns of western Canada. Reserve lands had to be protected, as the Royal Proclamation of 1763 had also figured, from crooked settlers and venal First Nations by making it impossible to sell or mortgage them. So that Aboriginal people who adapted to agriculture would be protected from unscrupulous whites who might try to cheat them when buying their foodstuffs, they were required to obtain a permit from the agent to sell their produce. In the process, of course, the degree of control the Indian agent could exercise over them would increase.

The protective impulse, as the pass system so graphically showed, usually gave way to coercion. The use of passes in western Canada was instituted, at least in part, to control the movements of First Nations during the tense spring and summer of 1885. (See image on page 200.) Under the pass system, Indians were prohibited from travelling off their reserves without written authorization of their agent, who would usually issue a pass only on the recommendation of the farm instructor. The pass system was used to protect reserve residents whom the department thought should be kept away from corrupting non-Natives and to thwart the movement of

Hayter Reed was much fonder of Plains costume
than he was of Plains culture and autonomy.

First Nation politicians among the reserves. It was also used to discourage parental visits to boarding schools and to promote certain DIA cultural policies.[9]

The pass system, however, was never very effective.[10] It was not often enforced in the 1880s, and by 1893 was virtually a dead letter. First Nations knew, as did the police and the department, that there was no legal basis for interfering with them, and by 1891 the Mounties decided that they would no longer enforce it because of its lack of legitimacy.[11] In any event, it was often a simple matter for reserve residents to evade the agent or even to defy him. Reed explained to the minister of the interior that he instructed agents to "issue passes to Indians who they know will leave in any case, and so preserve an appearance at least of control, and a knowledge of their movements."[12] Although passes were still in occasional use in parts of the West down to the 1940s, the system was never generally, or effectively, applied.[13] Police prudence and First Nation defiance prevented it.

Measures to control the availability of alcohol and to protect Aboriginal women from prostitution contributed to the strengthening of the powers of the Indian agent. Like the North-West Mounted Police officer, the agent was given the powers of a magistrate in 1881, making him investigator, prosecutor, and judge in his dealings with alleged miscreants. The following year, another amendment prohibited appeals from rulings of police magistrates and justices of the peace.[14] The opportunities for abuse of power were simply too great to be resisted. And the fact that First Nations, especially those in western Canada, were not accommodating themselves to the government's desire that they be assimilated made it all the more tempting to apply coercion. Protection of peoples relegated to child-like status in the eyes of the government led inescapably to compulsion.

The quintessential manifestation of the paternalistic mindset, and the clear proof of First Nation resistance, was found in 1884 changes to the Indian Act. The amendments, which came into effect in 1885, attempted to control people's movement and curtail such cultural practices as the Sun Dance and Thirst Dance of the southern prairies by prohibiting Natives from being on a reserve other than their own without department approval. These festivities were at one and the same time important elements of Plains nations' political and religious life, for these bands drew no distinction between the realms of the sacred and the secular. However, missionaries objected to the practices and successfully pressed for their prohibition.

Similar treatment was meted out in the 1884 amendments to the Pacific coastal First Nations. The amendment threatened anyone "who engages or assists in celebrating the Indian festival known as the 'Potlach' or in the Indian dance known as the 'Tamanawas'" with a jail term.[15] The immediate cause of the potlatch ban was a request by Indigenous converts, but behind it also lay missionary antipathy.[16]

Clerics intuited, if they did not comprehend, the importance of the potlatch to the coastal First Nations. Its ethos was the antithesis of the individualism and competitive accumulation that underlay Euro-Canadian society, as well as an important part of an alternative religious and social system. As the missionary William Duncan observed, the "potlatch was 'by far the most formidable of all obstacles in the way of the Indians becoming Christian, or even civilized.'"[17]

It was one thing to legislate, another to enforce. From a variety of evidence it is clear that the prohibitions against both the prairie dances and the coastal potlatch were largely unenforceable. Even with the pass system and agents who had the powers of magistrates, it was often impolitic for a handful of police and agents to try to compel large numbers of First Nations to forego practices that they considered central to their way of life.[18] Even amendment of the Indian Act in 1895 to bring prairie dancing within the prohibitions of the legislation by outlawing ceremonies that involved the mutilation of humans or animals, or even the giving away of "money, goods or articles," did not stop the summer ceremonials. When the First Nations were determined to dance, as the Blood who followed Red Crow were in 1900, there was nothing an agent could do to stop them. In the chronicles of the Blood people, 1900 was recorded as the year when "Yellow Buffalo Stone Woman put up the Sun dance by force."[19] Other times, guile worked as well as "force." On the Poundmaker and Little Pine reserves, which were contiguous, the Cree held their dances right on the boundary of the two reserves. Since the bands were not leaving their reserve for another, the agent and police could not use the Indian Act to deter them.[20] Throughout the West the dancing went on surreptitiously, even among First Nations who claimed to have converted to Christianity, for no other reason than that such practices were central to Plains Indian culture.[21] In the 1920s the deputy minister of DIA was still inveighing against traditional dancing; the First Nations kept on dancing.[22]

A similar pattern of response was found on the Pacific. There was only one conviction under the 1884 potlatch prohibition, and that was immediately quashed by a judge who ruled that the law was excessively vague. The more carefully phrased amendment in 1895 enjoyed occasional enforcement in some parts of British Columbia, but the effectiveness of the prohibition depended more on the zeal of the agent than the force of the law. "There is no decrease in the number of potlatches held," an agent reported in 1912, and no potlatcher served a prison sentence for his or her activities until 1920.[23] There was a brief and unsuccessful attempt by the department to enforce the ban in 1913, and a short-lived crackdown in 1922–3 stopped the festivities for a few years.[24] But by 1927 those First Nations who still wanted to potlatch were back at it. It took the economic stress of the Depression

Piercing, a sacrificial element of the Thirst Dance and the Sun Dance,
aroused missionary ire and attracted legislative prohibition.

and the influence of acculturation to put an end to it temporarily in the 1940s.[25] It
says a lot about the ineffectiveness of such culturally oppressive policies as the potlatch ban that potlatching died out earlier in Alaska, where there was no American
law against the practice, than it did in BC.[26]

The legislation against the potlatch and the prairie dances were merely parts of
an extensive attack on Aboriginal cultural practices carried out in the name of protecting them and moulding them to Euro-Canadian ways. Efforts to curb the abuse
of women through prostitution were motivated by humanitarian desires, but they
could have the effect of interfering with sexual behaviour that differed sharply from
the monogamy and continence that the Euro-Canadians preached, even if they did
not always follow it.[27] Similarly, a ban on polygamy was a well-intentioned attempt
to protect the Euro-Canadian's notion of the family unit, even if the familial and
social situations in which some Natives found themselves made multiple brides
sensible and socially useful. The Indian Act's tracing of First Nation descent and
identity through the father was the unthinking application of European patrilineal
assumptions by a patriarchal society; but it accorded ill with those First Nations,

such as some Northwest Coast nations or any of the Iroquoian, in which identity flowed through the female side of the family. All these attempts at cultural remodelling also illustrated how the first step on the path of protection seemed always to lead to the depths of coercion.

Politicians and bureaucrats thought that these coercive policies were but temporary measures that would be needed only until the great social curative in which Victorians believed so fervently could do its work. Education was held to be the universal panacea for all kinds of social and economic problems in the nineteenth century. Prime Minister Macdonald acknowledged this implicitly in his defence of the 1885 grant of the vote to eastern First Nations: "So I say that the Indians living in the older Provinces who have gone to school – and they all go to school – who are educated, who associate with white men, who are acquainted with all the principles of civilization, who carry out all the practices of civilization, who have accumulated round themselves property, who have good houses, and well furnished houses, who educate their children, who contribute to the public treasury in the same way as the whites do, should possess the franchise."[28] In 1892 the superintendent general said "that the sacred trust with which Providence has invested the country in the charge of and care for the aborigines committed to it carries with it no more important obligation than the moral, social, literary and industrial training of the Indian youth of both sexes." Money spent on Aboriginal education was "well spent," for it would mean "not only the emancipation of the subjects thereof from the condition of ignorance and superstitious blindness in which they are, and their parents before them were sunk, but converting them into useful members of society and contributors to, instead of merely consumers of, the wealth of the country."[29]

Experience in Upper Canada had already demonstrated both that First Nations desired access to education for their children, and that day schools were not effective. In the treaties of the 1870s, many western groups had been promised that they could have schools on their reserves when they wanted them, and in the years following the making of the numbered treaties some steps were taken to support the schools that missionaries had already established or wished to erect near or in Aboriginal settlements. In the 1880s the educational policy for western Canada and British Columbia shifted from day schools to boarding institutions.[30]

The theory behind residential schooling had not changed since Ryerson's day: it was still an experiment in social engineering. As the DIA 1889 Annual Report put it: "The boarding school disassociates the Indian child from the deleterious home influences to which he would otherwise be subjected. It reclaims him from the uncivilized state in which he has been brought up. It brings him into contact from

The Qu'Appelle industrial school, established in 1883, was one of the first residential institutions.

day to day with all that tends to effect a change in his views and habits of life. By precept and example he is taught to endeavour to excel in what will be most useful to him."[31] The underlying purpose of residential schooling was what the Americans called "aggressive civilization."[32]

Initially, First Nations welcomed offers of education for their young in western Canada as they had in the East. They understood the significance of the coincident arrival of whites and disappearance of bison: they would have to adjust to new ways and to new methods of earning a living. A young Assiniboine who "at the age of twelve years ... was lasooed, roped and taken to the Government School" later recalled that he had been sent to school to acquire "the whiteman's magic art of writing, 'the talking paper.'"[33] But First Nations wanted enough schooling to enable them to cope with the new order; this was not what they got. From 1883 onward the federal government established "industrial schools" off the reserves at which children would be educated and trained far from parental and band influence. As a federal cabinet minister explained in the Commons: "If these schools are to succeed, we must not have them too near the bands; in order to educate the children properly we must separate them from their families. Some people may say that this is hard, but if we want to civilize them we must do that."[34] A parallel system of boarding schools, which were less ambitious and less well financed than the industrial schools, persisted after 1883. Industrial and boarding schools both aimed at the assimilation of the status First Nation children.

The residential schools were operated in uneasy tandem by government and the missionary societies of the Catholic, Anglican, Methodist, and Presbyterian churches. Part of the unease arose from denominational rivalries between churches in various locations. More stemmed from the tug of war over funds between Indian Affairs and the missionaries. Although it was originally the department's intention to concentrate its efforts among western First Nations in the industrial schools, finances made it impossible to do so. The industrial schools were very expensive, and parliament was forever complaining about the heavy costs of Indian Affairs. In 1892 an attempt was made to control expenses by shifting to a new financing system, but costs continued to spiral well beyond the results that school inspectors could turn up in their annual visits. Moreover, both teachers and officials encountered substantial First Nation opposition to residential schooling. In some cases parents complained that their children worked too long in fields and shops, while learning too little in classes. In other cases they objected to the harsh discipline, including corporal punishment, and the poor food. By the early twentieth century the escalating death rates in the schools were becoming a public scandal as well as a reason for both parental and student refusal to cooperate with residential schools. Not even the 1894 Indian Act provision that permitted the minister to issue compulsory schooling regulations was able to keep some of the schools full.

The department's response was to contemplate exerting even more control over students. As early as 1892 Indian Affairs considered the establishment of "colonies" where graduates of the industrial and boarding schools might be sent to keep them longer from the influence of home and reserve. One such farming community was set up in the File Hills area of southern Saskatchewan at the turn of the century, and others were contemplated. Although the File Hills experiment lasted almost to mid-century, it by no means realized the complete assimilation of the "colonists" that was intended.[35] It was also significant that, although File Hills was envisaged as the first of a series of such colonies, no others were created.

Because the industrial schools proved little better in educating children than the boarding schools, Ottawa shifted away from the costly experiment. The Liberal government in power after 1896 was particularly unsympathetic to ambitious plans to train children in trades and agriculture in the industrial schools, the minister responsible for them saying flatly that "the attempt to give a highly civilized education to the Indian child ... was practically a failure. I have no hesitation in saying – we may as well be frank – that the Indian cannot go out from school, making his own way and compete with the white man."[36] The federal government reduced funding to the schools, looked for ways to close some and move their students to "new, improved day schools," and in 1910 reduced its pedagogical aim for both industrial and boarding schools. While the original intention of the founders of industrial schools had been to prepare youths to live and compete with non-Native Canadians, henceforth the schools would seek "to develop the great natural intelligence of the race and to fit the Indian for civilized life in his own environment."[37] Indian Affairs finally gave up the distinction between industrial and boarding schools in 1923, when both types of schools were amalgamated into a single category known as "residential schools." By then the system had grown quite large. Where in 1883 there had been three government-financed industrial schools and an unknown number of boarding establishments run by the churches, by 1907 there were twenty-two industrial and fifty-three boarding schools. At its height the system would number eighty government-approved and church-operated institutions. The system still reached only a minority, probably about one-third, of eligible school-age Indigenous children, however.[38] These schools would persist till the 1960s.

The failure of First Nation education in general, and residential schooling in particular, was attributable to government parsimony and First Nation resistance. Ottawa was not prepared to pursue assimilation through education if the struggle was going to be lengthy and expensive. From 1892 onward it tried regularly to shift an ever larger share of the cost of running these schools onto the shoulders of the school children and missionary organizations that, for their part, were becoming increasingly disillusioned with Natives, schools, and their government partners. The government preferred, as in the compulsory attendance provisions, to move to coercion rather than to invest in the schools to such an extent that First Nation communities would want to send their children there. But First Nations did not want to, because the schools were ineffective, harsh, and unsafe, and they interfered with the development of the child into a being with a sense of identity and a place in society. Most graduates found there was no work for them; many returned to the reserves and psychological limbo. Stoney Chief John Snow's "family ... had a tradition of respect for education ... and we children were encouraged to get as much as we could stand."[39]

First Nations resisted coercive education in a variety of ways.[40] Most simply they refused to surrender their children to the school and Indian Affairs authorities, no matter what police officers or agents said. Those who were still migratory or semi-migratory, as was often the case on the west coast, could simply remove themselves from the reach of those who enforced the compulsory attendance provisions. The parents could disrupt the school by making unauthorized visits or by failing to return their children after holiday visits home. On the Blackfoot reserve in 1895 an Indian Affairs employee was killed and the missionary-principal of the school forced to flee in fear for his life.[41] At the Kamloops school, the Shuswap chiefs came

The contrast between Quewich and his children, who were students of the Qu'Appelle
industrial school around 1900, was portrayed by the Department of Indian Affairs
as evidence of the successful assimilative strategy of residential schools.

to the school and drove out an instructor who had abused a girl. When the offender returned the next year in clerical garb, the "chief came and really raised hell with him, told him 'I don't care if you come camouflaged in a priest suit ... we told you to leave. We don't want you back. Get!'"[42] The children were even more effective at resisting. They could – and did – misbehave, violate rules, refuse to learn, defiantly continue to speak their own languages in spite of official prohibitions, run away, and, in the ultimate case, indulge in acts of arson against the property and violence against the staffs of the schools. Some of the escapes were spontaneous, others carefully and elaborately planned. In some cases the runaways got far away, occasionally never to return; but others ended in death, as the fleeing children died of exposure or by drowning.[43]

While some students of these residential schools were thoroughly converted by the experience, many more absorbed only enough schooling to resist still more effectively. It would be from the ranks of former residential school pupils that most of the leaders of First Nation political movements would come in the twentieth century. Unfortunately, yet another large group – probably more than one-quarter of the pre-1914 students – succumbed to disease during or shortly after their stay at the schools. By any reasonable standard of evaluation, the residential school program from the 1880s to the 1960s failed dismally.

Closely related to schooling was a series of policies designed to encourage First Nations, especially those of the western interior, to adopt agriculture. There was little awareness that the government was attempting to modify the economic activity of a distinctive group of people, a process that in Western Europe had taken centuries to accomplish. In an era in which there was little understanding of cross-cultural differences, officials usually assumed that the shift to agriculture, though certainly not easy, could with good will and effort be accomplished in fairly short order. The fact that the period when many of these policies were getting under way, 1883–90, was among the worst climatically in prairie history simply compounded the problem.[44]

The agricultural program for western reserves consisted mainly of instruction on reserves.[45] Farm instructors were supposed to teach both by example, on their own "home farm" near the reserve, and directly to the Native people, on reserve lands. However, too often Indian Affairs failed to provide instructors who were familiar with western conditions, neglected to furnish implements and seed in time, and became impatient when reserves showed little progress in adverse climatic conditions. The fact that Ottawa cut back the budget for agricultural instruction as well as rations in 1883 did not help the situation, either.

The situation, though not entirely the fault of the department, was greatly compounded by its behaviour. Certainly the government devoted considerable attention

Anglican Canon Edward Ahenakew, a product of residential schooling, was both
a devout Christian and a strong proponent of Aboriginal history and culture.

to providing advice until the 1890s. The number of instructors rose from twenty-
four in 1880 to a high of forty-five in 1890 before dropping to thirty-five in 1895.
When Euro-Canadian instructors from central Canada encountered problems in
dealing with western problems, Ottawa even hired a number of Métis, including
one who joined in the insurrection in 1885.[46] Aside from the climate, the greatest
obstacle the program faced was the department's attempt to impose its will on First
Nations in the West. When Ottawa began in the later 1880s to push for the subdivision of reserve lands into individual lots and to discourage large-scale farming,
Native people resisted. They recognized that advocacy of holding land "in severalty" was part of a plan to extinguish Aboriginal identity and reserves.

At the same time, the DIA's insistence on a "peasant farming" policy from 1889
to 1897 simply discouraged First Nation initiative. Ottawa claimed that it wanted
to prevent Native people from farming on a large scale with labour-saving machinery because eventually they would have to work without the aid of instructors who could service complicated implements. "The general principle is not to
allow them machinery to save them work which they should with hands available

on Reserves, do by help of such simple implements as are alone likely for long enough, to be within their reach," explained the Indian commissioner.[47] But the real reason was that department officials in the West did not want First Nations to advance to anything beyond subsistence peasant status.[48] Part of the explanation was ideological: Hayter Reed believed that there was an iron law of social evolution according to which societies had to go through successive stages of savagery, barbarism, and civilization. These phases were associated with hunting-gathering, peasant agriculture, and commercial farming and other forms of production. But there was a political explanation, too. Since non-Native farmers in the neighbourhood of reserves resented what they regarded as subsidized competition from First Nations, their resentment was a factor in making politicians anxious to limit Native production for markets that were still mainly local. Western settlers made their objections to Aboriginal competition in the small markets for produce in such places as Battleford and Fort MacLeod known to press and politicians.[49] Since the sale of produce required a permit from the agent, and since DIA officials were susceptible to political pressure from members of parliament who voiced settler complaints, it became all too easy for department officials to reject requests from reserve farmers who wanted to sell produce to buy machinery. And those who wanted to borrow money for implements, as some eastern Natives did, found that the Indian Act's prohibition on mortgaging reserve lands prevented their acting like the acquisitive capitalists the department claimed it wanted them to become.[50]

The frustrating case of a Dakota band in Manitoba showed the effect of these forces. The Oak River Dakota were successful farmers in the 1880s, but succumbed in the 1890s to obstacles placed in their way by the department. DIA officers often refused permission to buy machines in line with the "peasant farming" policy. In response the Dakota reduced their operations to what could be farmed without machinery. Since it was no longer economic to grow wheat in such small quantities, they dropped out of market-oriented grain production and became the sort of subsistence farmers, or peasants, that the department apparently wanted. In the process they removed themselves from competition with their non-Native neighbours and consigned themselves to a marginal existence.[51]

Another community in Treaty 4 took a different route to a similarly dismal end. Wahpeemakwa, or White Bear, adhered to Treaty 4 in 1875 and thereafter selected land in the Moose Mountain region of southeastern Saskatchewan that was unsuitable for dryland farming. Instead, he and his followers organized a mixed economy of hunting, fishing, and selling tanned hides, seneca root, and handicrafts to the nearby settlers. Clearly, Chief White Bear had no interest in a program of the Bible and plough, for he and those in his band who thought like him eschewed farming,

The "policy of the Bible and the plough" included the encouragement of agriculture,
in this instance on a reserve in western Canada.

had nothing to do with Christian missionaries, and refused to send their children
to residential school. For pursuing an economic strategy that, although totally at
variance with DIA wishes, was successful, Ottawa deposed White Bear and replaced him with a more compliant man. When the old chief's supporters refused to
cooperate with the department after the deposition of their leader, Indian Affairs
was compelled to backtrack and reinstate Wahpeemakwa. Shortly afterwards he
died, and a few years after that, as settlers began to flood into the region, Ottawa arranged to take suspicious surrenders of the nearby Ocean Man and Pheasant Rump
reserves and move their populations onto White Bear.[52] The result of this chicanery
was internal conflict and economic stagnation that beset the reserve through most
of the twentieth century.

Although reserve agricultural production in the West was regularly described
in the annual reports of the Department of Indian Affairs as promising, little progress was to be seen a generation after the agricultural policies had been instituted.
Bands on occasion won prizes at agricultural exhibitions, but their total crop production remained far below that of their non-Native neighbours in the Northwest
Territories.[53] (Ironically, while following the chief's alternative economic strategy,
White Bear's band did better economically than surrounding settlers.) An exception to the generally depressing picture of economic failure gradually emerged in

Treaty 7 in southern Alberta, where First Nations slowly and with considerable difficulty adjusted to the emerging ranching economy. Though these Blackfoot had been among the most desperate in 1879 when the buffalo resource failed, by 1896 they were moving towards prosperity.[54] There were too few such cases.

Sometimes First Nations found that their land was literally disappearing as they tried to utilize it for new economic purposes. The underlying problem here was that the title to reserve lands did not belong to the Native bands but to the Crown in the person of the Department of Indian Affairs. And, while the department legally stood in a trustee relationship to its Native "wards" and was obligated to administer a band's resources in the best interests of the group, sometimes the officials disposed of land in a manner that was the antithesis of Aboriginal interests. Particularly after 1896, when climatic conditions improved and large numbers of immigrants began to flood the prairie region, demands arose for the transfer of Native lands to homesteaders. It was a tiresomely familiar argument, based in equal parts on Christian notions of stewardship and capitalist desires for acquisition, that First Nations were not entitled to lands unless they "improved" them. Although the official stance of the government was that the Natives owned the lands and could not be dispossessed, in practice the DIA often transferred lands suitable for farming and mining from them to homesteaders and speculators.[55] The unhappy bands of Ocean Man and Pheasant Rump were two examples. There were many others, including the Kahkewistahaw reserve, whose surrender the Indian Claims Commission described in 1997 in scathing terms.[56]

These incursions, too, First Nations frequently opposed. Kahkewistahaw, an elderly chief in Treaty 4 reminded Indian Commissioner David Laird that he had predicted when the treaty was made in the 1870s that the white man would want all the land. "Did I not tell you a long time ago ... that you would come and ask me to sell you this land back again, but I told you at that time, No."[57] The Metlakatla converts who followed William Duncan resisted a government surveyor, as did Ojibwe on Manitoulin Island, for fear that survey was merely a prelude to usurpation.[58] In the Nass Valley, the Nisga'a lectured an 1887 royal commission on conditions on the Northwest Coast about non-Natives who talked about "giving" First Nations lands for reserves. "How can they give it when it is our own? We cannot understand it. They have never fought and conquered our people and taken the land in that way, and yet they say now that they will give us so much – our own land."[59] And the Blood nation fought ferociously with officials in 1907 and 1918 to prevent land surrenders.[60] But impecunious band members frequently found the cash that surrenders promised them impossible to resist.

In cases where First Nation resistance proved formidable, Ottawa was always ready to reach for the tools of compulsion. In 1895 it amended the Indian Act to authorize the DIA to rent out reserve lands at the request of an individual band member, without the group's permission. Further amendments, known as the Oliver Act after the minister of the day, in 1911 allowed companies and municipalities empowered by statute to do so to expropriate reserve land for public works, and established mechanisms for the department to remove First Nations from reserves adjacent to or within towns of more than eight thousand. Less than a decade later it was used by the Indian agent to threaten the Chippewas of Sarnia into making a "voluntary surrender" of a large portion of their reserve near Sarnia.[61] During World War I, under an ill-starred "Greater Production Campaign," Indian Affairs was given the power to help themselves to both reserve land and band funds to carry out farming projects designed to increase crop production for the war effort.[62] After the war, further assaults on reserves were made in the interest of providing agricultural lands for the Soldier Settlement Board.[63]

The erosion of First Nation resources with the connivance of the department was extensive in the period of rapid western Canadian development. By one estimate, one-quarter million acres, about half of the reserves in the southern Saskatchewan portion of Treaty 4, were sold in the thirty years after heavy immigration began, some of it under conditions that either were fraudulent or bordered on fraud.[64] In the 1980s efforts would be made to restore some of the lands, successfully in the case of the White Bear reserve in southeastern Saskatchewan. Ontario bands who refused to sell off valuable timber lands were pressured by the department to drop their sense of responsibility to future generations and grab the cash in the present. When two new transcontinental railways were under construction through western Canada during the first generation of the twentieth century, several First Nations found their lands coveted for townsites, and some of them agreed to sell.[65] On the more positive side, the Blackfoot in the Calgary area sold almost half their reserve for more than $1 million, and used the funds to finance their own social security, health care, housing, and economic development programs.[66] Few of the bands who surrendered land were so fortunate.

Another area in which there was little progress after the 1880s was treaty-making. That First Nations who had made treaty in the 1870s rejected the department view that their lands had been alienated was public knowledge. Piapot, for example, made a point of telling missionaries in 1895, "Jamais je n'ai consenti à vendre nos terres aux blancs."[67] But Native remonstrances were ignored when Ottawa began to consider new treaties for more northerly regions. Once again, although First Nations in the North sometimes indicated a desire to be taken into treaty, it

was not until non-Native economic activity encroached on the region that government took steps to conclude agreements. It was the gold strike in the Klondike in
the later 1890s, and fear that Natives in northern BC "were liable to give trouble
to isolated parties of miners or traders who might be regarded by the Indians as
interfering with what they considered their vested rights" that led in 1899–1900 to
Treaty 8, which covered northern Alberta and Saskatchewan, northeastern British
Columbia, and part of the Northwest Territories.[68] After the turn of the century,
economic conditions among the First Nations of the Far North would have justified the institution of treaties and government programs of economic development,
and Ottawa was lobbied to make treaty with the peoples on the Mackenzie. But
it was not until 1920, "when oil gushed forth from Indian land at Fort Norman,"
that Ottawa acted.[69] In 1921 Treaty 11 was signed to establish Canadian title to
the more northerly portion of the Northwest Territories. Treaty 9 (1905) covered
northern Ontario, while Treaty 10 (1906) dealt with those portions of northern
Saskatchewan that were not included in Treaties 6 and 8.[70]

The northern treaties differed little from the numbered treaties of the south.[71]
The annuities were larger, but the formula for alienation and promises of continued use of the land and its resources in a traditional mode were included. Treaty
8 differed somewhat from the earlier treaties in its provision that individuals or
individual families as well as bands could take advantage of the allocation of one
square mile for a family of five or 160 acres for an individual, and individuals were
explicitly promised that they could have their plots elsewhere than on or contiguous to the reserve.[72] Negotiators also, apparently, promised "non-interference with
the religion of the Indians" who feared the assimilative efforts of residential schools
would be applied to them after they entered treaty.[73] Few of these oral promises
were honoured in later years. Of course, the northern First Nations, who believed
the treaties established a kin-like relationship of friendship and mutual assistance
with the government, were shocked by the treatment they received.

The policies pursued in the boreal region of the North by an aloof and insensitive government were depressingly reminiscent of those that had failed in the South.
Although there was not, for obvious reasons, a major effort at agricultural instruction, there was extension of the residential school system to the region. In the North,
many of the schools in the early period were merely expansions of existing boarding
schools, and that approach may have mitigated somewhat the impact of the educational program. But as the twentieth century wore on, more numerous and more
elaborate schools were established in cooperation with the Oblates and Anglicans.

Nor were the promises to respect First Nations' pursuit of the traditional economy honoured. The Native people were brought willy-nilly under federal, provincial,

and territorial game regulations, including well-intentioned efforts in the 1920s to conserve the few remaining bison that included the establishment of Wood Buffalo Park as a preserve for the shaggy beasts. As the hunting and fur-gathering economy of the Mackenzie District went into serious decline in the 1920s, Aboriginal people had to starve while the bison multiplied in what had been their hunting territory. To the chief of a band near the park it was puzzling. "I'm hungry and my children too and I come upon one of the Government buffalo. One or the other has to die because I don't want myself or my children to starve to death simply because this Government buffalo mustn't disappear from the region. Which of us is to disappear first? I would like an answer, is it me or the buffalo?" The government's implicit answer to that question was found in its consideration of a proposal to issue hunting permits to "big game hunters with wealth" who would "possibly pay a thousand dollars for the privilege of shooting a buffalo in order to secure a good head."[74] To complete Ottawa's betrayal of First Nations of the boreal North, when Canada transferred jurisdiction over Crown lands and natural resources to the Prairie provinces by the Natural Resources Transfer Act in 1930, Indian Affairs made no effective provision to ensure that the provinces would respect Aboriginal and treaty rights, including rights of hunting and fishing.

As the unfortunate First Nations of the North learned during the northern resource boom of the 1920s and 1930s, Ottawa experimented with many programs without much success in the period down to the Second World War. Treaty-making continued, not in any provident way, but in response to immediate needs created by economic development. Although the government often began its relationship with the First Nations in a spirit of paternalism, with a desire to protect, it usually ended up employing coercive methods with results that severely harmed the interests of the Aboriginal people. The obscenity of protecting bison in Wood Buffalo Park while nearby Native people starved was merely a latter-day manifestation of an attitude that had led to interference with Indigenous self-government and plans for their own economic development in the South.

In British Columbia between the 1880s and 1920s, what became known as "the BC land question" taught similar lessons. The problem with Aboriginal lands in British Columbia was that the federal and provincial governments were never able to agree on the application of the 1871 terms of union that required Ottawa to apply a policy "at least as liberal" as had been pursued by the colony and the province to make available lands to carry out such a policy. Various commissions tried over the decades to allocate reserves to those First Nations that did not have them, with BC and the federal government invariably disagreeing. Before the Great War a joint body, the McKenna-McBride Commission, was established to tackle the question. Its 1916 report disappointed BC bands, for it proposed having some of the existing reserve lands surrendered for the benefit of settlers, with First Nations being compensated with a larger quantum of poorer and less well-located lands. Their travail over lands prompted British Columbia's First Nations to protest to Ottawa and London, and also to begin to organize politically to fight the implementation of the McKenna-McBride recommendations. Their efforts secured a joint parliamentary committee in 1926–7, which heard their representations and then dismissed almost all of them. The Department of Indian Affairs, apparently tired of BC's and other Native groups' political opposition, secured an amendment to the Indian Act in 1927 that outlawed giving or raising money for pursuing a Native land claim. The addition made it almost impossible for Native bands to hire lawyers or conduct political campaigns.[75]

As the aftermath of the BC land question showed in 1927, when protection slid into interference, persuasion was dropped for aggressive efforts. Shortcomings in policy were blamed on the victims, for reasons that anthropologist Noel Dyck has explained: to those determined to tutor Natives to change, acts of resistance "seemed to fulfil the prophecy of tutelage by demonstrating aboriginal peoples' need for guidance."[76] It is doubtful that these attempts at social engineering produced lasting cultural change, though they contributed to the demoralization of First Nations. An equally graphic example of the slide towards coercion was the evolution of provisions for the enfranchisement of Aboriginal peoples. The theory was that as Indians were educated, they would opt for full citizenship status, gaining the franchise and taking their share of reserve land with them as an individual freehold. But First Nations refused to apply for full citizenship; theirs was a response of passive resistance. Under an amendment introduced in 1920, any Native over the age of twenty-one whom the superintendent general thought fit for enfranchisement could, with two years' notice, be stripped of his (and his wife's and children's) status by the federal cabinet. Once again, First Nations protested this gross political interference; once again they were ignored, until a change of government brought about repeal of the compulsion in 1922. However, when the Tories returned to power under R.B. Bennett, they reintroduced compulsory enfranchisement in a 1933 amendment, although this time with recognition of treaty rights in the form of a statement that enfranchisement could not be imposed on any adult male in violation of treaty promises. Such actions were as revealing of the drift of government policy and First Nation resistance to directed cultural change as the potlatch laws or the attempts to "detribalize" western nations by subdividing their reserve lands.

These compulsory enfranchisement provisions showed that Ottawa still aimed at the peaceful elimination of Indians as a legal and social fact. As the department's deputy minister, D.C. Scott, explained in 1920,

> I want to get rid of the Indian problem. I do not think as a matter of fact, that this country ought to continuously protect a class of people who are able to stand alone ... But after one hundred years, after being in close contact with civilization it is enervating to the individual or to a band to continue in that state of tutelage, when he or they are able to take their position as British citizens or Canadian citizens, to support themselves, and stand alone. That has been the whole purpose of Indian education and advancement since the earliest times ...
>
> ... Our object is to continue until there is not a single Indian in Canada that has not been absorbed into the body politic, and there is no Indian question, and no Indian Department.[77]

As an American Bureau of Indian Affairs official was to observe a couple of decades later, the purpose of Canadian Indian policy, including the policy of the Bible and the plough, was "the extinction of the Indians *as Indians*.[78] Official thinking had not moved very far from the early nineteenth-century belief that complete assimilation was "the only possible euthanasia of savage communities."

CHAPTER TWELVE

Residents and Transients in the North: Relations to the 1960s

The first key to understanding the relations between the various Indigenous societies and visitors in the Far North is that non-Natives tend to be transients in the North while Indigenous people are permanent residents. "Transients," a northern scholar noted, "dominated the non-Native society in the Yukon, limiting the prospect for extended personal contact between the races, and ensuring that stereotypic images would dominate Native-white reaction to the people and the land."[1] Also important, if we wish to comprehend the pattern in the relationship, is the fact that the Government of Canada showed little interest in or responsibility to the Aboriginal peoples of the North until relatively recent times. Relations between Natives and newcomers in the North have passed through many phases: from the earliest contacts between explorers and Inuit; through eras of intense interaction in whaling, fishing, and mining; to the outreach of the Canadian state, tentative and half-hearted at the beginning of the twentieth century, more sure and certain from the middle of the century onward. Through all of this, the reality that underlay and gave some order to the apparently random and chaotic interactions between the Indigenous societies and the peoples that the Inuit called *kabloona* was Native residency, outsider transiency, and government indifference. After each foray by mariner, fur trader, miner, or missionary, it was the Inuit or Subarctic First Nations that had to greet the strangers and cope with the changes they introduced, as well as pick up the pieces after the most recent southern or European enthusiast had gone home.

The Aboriginal groups that played host with weary regularity for two hundred years from the late eighteenth century onward consisted of both northerly First Nations

and Inuit. The Indigenous peoples, who have appeared on the forested, or southerly, side of the treeline before in this account, were mostly Athapaskan peoples such
as Hare, Dogrib, or Chipewyan, nations that nowadays prefer to be known as Dene
(the people) in most of the Canadian North, with distinctive groups in the Far West
such as Tlingit, Tagish, or Tutchone. The other Aboriginal community found to the
north of the treeline was composed of many groups who speak various forms of
Inuktitut. These peoples, Inuit (the people), are the most recent Aboriginal arrivals
in the territory that is now Canada, having come from Siberia in a series of migrations over a lengthy period. According to leading experts Robert McGhee and
David Damas, all the Inuit in Canada are now believed to be "descended biological-
ly and culturally from the Thule people who first swept across the area from Alaska
after the tenth century. The Thule culture is the historical factor that explains the
biological, linguistic, and cultural similarities of all Eskimo [Inuit] between Bering
Strait and Greenland."[2]

Well before Europeans ventured into Arctic waters, these people had established
themselves across the Far North, from Greenland to Alaska, in an Inuit archipelago
of peoples who usually could understand the Inuktitut dialect of their nearest kinfolk, though not very easily the speech of more remote groups. Anthropologists
have suggested a number of groupings or categories for the Canadian Inuit. One of
the simplest describes them, beginning in the east, with Labrador Inuit along the
Labrador coast to Hudson Bay; the Central Inuit, who include western Hudson
Bay and parts of the Arctic coast; the Banks Island Inuit on Banks and Victoria
Islands, as well as other large islands off the central Arctic coast; and the Inuvialuit,
or Western Inuit, found along the Arctic coast of what is now the most westerly
portion of the Northwest Territories (NWT) and Yukon. Other classifications
break the population into smaller, more geographically defined groups, such as the
Ungava Inuit in northernmost Quebec, the Baffin Island Inuit, or Copper Inuit,
who are associated with the Coppermine and Cambridge Bay areas. The Caribou
Inuit once ranged through the Barren Grounds region west of Hudson Bay. Notable
is the recent arrival of the Inuvialuit, who moved into the western Arctic from
Alaska early in the twentieth century after the Mackenzie Inuit were drastically
reduced by epidemics. While the Inuit population at contact with Europeans is
impossible to determine, and in spite of severe losses to disease over the centuries,
the 2011 census found that they numbered 59,445.[3]

The most obvious features of the Inuit, ones on which newcomers never failed to
comment, were the product of their successful adjustment to the harsh and inhos-
pitable lands they occupied. They had created distinctive technology in such fields
as housing (where the Inuktitut term for dwelling, *igloo*, became the descriptor

newcomers used for the snow houses that Inuit constructed), clothing (parka and mukluks), transportation (*komatik* or sleigh, *umiak* and *kayak* for round or slender skin-covered watercraft), and art, particularly carving. As hunters and fishers they relied usually on sea mammals and seals. Indeed, it was Labrador Inuit who introduced European whalers to their distinctive whaling technology in the fifteenth century in the Strait of Belle Isle and off Labrador before the time of Jacques Cartier.[4] As later observers were to report, the hunting requirements in the North made the Inuit, particularly the males who did the hunting, extraordinarily perceptive readers of snow and ice conditions, weather patterns, and the behaviour of animals, both maritime and terrestrial. In terms of their spiritual relationship to the world, the Inuit, like Dene and First Nations in more southerly regions, belonged to the animistic tradition. Much of their art, particularly their small sculptures, recorded and propitiated powerful spirits in the world around them.

Although the most northerly Dene and some Inuit shared some social and economic traits, there was long-standing rivalry between them. One manifestation of the bitter enmity between the Dene and Inuit was the term that until relatively recently was applied by southerners to the Inuit. "Eskimo" is believed to be a derisive term meaning "eaters of raw meat" in some First Nation language. As was often the case with hunter-gatherers who shared a frontier of resources, they sometimes competed viciously for resources. One of the early European explorers, Samuel Hearne, was appalled by the cold-blooded massacre of five tents of Inuit by his guide Matonabbee and his Dene companions in the summer of 1771. For their part, the Dene showed no remorse for their actions and regarded Hearne contemptuously for his gentler feelings.[5] What underlay the bitter relations that led to such occurrences was the economic reality that some Inuit and First Nations competed for unpredictable game resources in a difficult environment.

Both Inuit and northern Dene found themselves confronted by the first wave of European contact, the forays of a succession of explorers and cartographers. Unlike Hearne, who laboured in a series of overland treks to find the Arctic Ocean principally for commercial reasons related to Hudson's Bay Company trading strategy, most of the early explorers after the Norse era were seeking a northern water passage from aboard ship. From the fifteenth century onward, British mariners in particular sought the fabled Northwest Passage through Arctic North America to the Pacific Ocean and trade opportunities in Asia and the south Pacific. These ambitions led the likes of Martin Frobisher to undertake three voyages to the eastern Arctic in the 1570s, John Davis to make three more in the 1580s, and Henry Hudson to go farther in 1610 and reach the bay that since has borne his name. Most of these early maritime ventures led to little involvement with the Indigenous population, although Frobisher in the sixteenth century and, as noted, Hearne in the late eighteenth century were exceptions. Hearne's travail, which he recorded in a published travel account, revealed the dependence that all explorers who ventured onto land had on the Indigenous population of the North. After two unsuccessful attempts, during the second of which he was "plundered" by Natives, Hearne came to rely on a Dene leader, Matonabbee, for his third, successful attempt to reach the Arctic Ocean overland.

Matonabbee provided a plain example of one of the most important reasons why Native assistance was critical to explorers' chances of success. "The misconduct of my guides, and the very plan we pursued ... in not taking any women with us on our journey," Hearne reported the guide as saying, were the principal reasons his first two ventures had failed. Women were essential in northern travel to carry most of the packs, leaving the men free to hunt and travel quickly if necessary. If the hunters were successful, "who is to carry the produce of their labour?" Women, Matonabbee explained, "were made for labour; one of them can carry, or haul as much as two men can do. They also pitch our tents, make and mend our clothing, keep us warm at night; and in fact there is no such thing as travelling any considerable distance, or for any length of time in this country, without their assistance."[6] Whether Matonabbee had the reason precisely correct or not, there was no doubt that successive European explorers were heavily dependent on Native knowledge, skill, and strength.

When the British government renewed the search for the Northwest Passage in the nineteenth century, it created a series of probes by British explorers. The fate of John Franklin, who sailed in 1845, illustrated well the perils of exploring without Native assistance, for he and his two ships never returned after the crews apparently left their vessels and attempted to journey overland. The search for Franklin that ensued produced several more explorations of the Arctic mainland, however. For example, the Schwatka expedition of 1878–80 relied heavily on Inuit skills and labour in an overland trek to Starvation Cove. The Europeans understood the superiority of Inuit fur clothing to cloth, recognized that "Inuit survival technique was invaluable" when one of them went through the ice, depended on Inuit hunters to get food for their starving dogs at one point, and constantly looked to their Inuit guides for advice on where to chop through the ice to make a water hole.[7] Much later, in 1927, a young English adventurer, Edgar Christian, left a poignant account of the painful trail to a death by starvation by three would-be trappers on the Thelon River. Nowhere in Christian's diary is there any mention of Native people after the luckless trio reached their wintering site, and it is highly likely that absence of Native help and a grisly end were closely connected.[8]

In their differing ways and eras, Hearne, Franklin, and Christian all illustrated the close connection between reliance on the local Aboriginal population and success on ventures in the North. This dependence lasted well into the twentieth century, when Arctic exploration was now often motivated by intellectual as well as economic reasons. Of the Fifth Thule Expedition of 1921–4, for example, Joe Curley, an Inuk, recalled that his family had had to care for two of the venturers over one winter because they were helpless in the North. Or, as Curley expressed it, "they were poor ... They were poor like little orphan boys."[9] In any event, because of the episodic and brief nature of explorers' contact with northern Indigenous peoples, the exploration phase had limited impact on Native-newcomer relations in the Far North. In the twenty-first century, federal government personnel working closely with Inuit informants located the final resting places of Franklin's ships, the *Erebus* and *Terror*, in 2014 and 2016, respectively.[10]

The second non-Native transients who began to visit regularly by the early nineteenth century shared a maritime approach and base of operations with the earlier explorers. However, the whalers would have more impact on northern Aboriginal peoples because their contacts and interactions in many cases were more prolonged than those of explorers. The Inuit had long hunted the massive mammals for their meat, oil, and bones. Meat provided sustenance; oil, heat and light; and bones, both utilitarian items such as sleigh (*komatik*) runners and raw material for works of art. The American and European newcomers who began to invade the whale fishery in the Atlantic and Davis Strait regions in the sixteenth and seventeenth centuries, and the Bering Sea by the 1850s were less interested in whale meat, but extremely covetous of whale oil and other materials. Whale oil was a popular source of energy and light until more easily obtained petroleum products began to supplant it in the North American market from the middle of the nineteenth century onward. However, baleen, the cartilaginous material that hung in strips inside the mouths of the bowhead whale in particular remained commercially important until well into the twentieth century. A strong but pliable material that was applied in situations in which flexible steel and (after the Second World War) plastics would later be used, baleen was ideal for a wide range of products from fishing rods and buggy whips to corset stays and skirt hoops. So important was it as a commercial product that whale hunters in the later stages of the fishery at the end of the nineteenth century sometimes discarded all of the whale except the flexible material. The bowhead made the whaling industry extremely lucrative in the nineteenth and very early twentieth centuries.

Whaling was a highly regionalized industry. In the early centuries, Basque whalers had worked the waters off Labrador; the next major site of whalers' operations was in the Davis Strait from the seventeenth century onward. This eastern whaling activity was supplemented for almost a century in the western Arctic, when New England whalers began to visit the Beaufort Sea region in the late years of the 1880s. Beaufort Sea whaling introduced much closer Inuit-whaler relations, for the remoteness of the western Arctic caused whalers there to overwinter rather than returning to their home base. Some overwintering had occurred earlier in the eastern Arctic, but the intensity of relations in the Beaufort Sea industry made whalers' sojourns there especially important. Herschel Island, in particular, became a winter haunt of New Englanders, and by the end of the nineteenth century, missionaries in Yukon were decrying the effect that these visitors were having on Inuit health and sexual conduct. The interactions between Natives and newcomers in Beaufort Sea whaling lasted only until the period of the Great War, but these patterns were by then being replicated in the eastern Arctic. In the latter half of the nineteenth century and first two decades of the twentieth century it was common for American, British, and European whaling vessels to winter over, often in Hudson Bay, to take advantage of whale hunting along the floe edge as spring approached. Whaling in the eastern Arctic, too, declined after the First World War, but some whaling persisted until the late decades of the twentieth century.

The role of the Inuit in the American and European whaling industry was multifaceted and important. Besides providing assistance, food, and companionship for winterers, Inuit communities also were the source of pilots, hunters, and workers who extracted the most commercially valuable portions of the whale once the giant mammals were taken. Close interaction dated from 1846, when Inuit in Cumberland Sound for the first time on record helped a visiting British vessel take a whale.[11] When ships were frozen in for the long winters, relations became particularly intense and influential. A New England whaling captain, George Comer, had what is probably a typical experience of relations with the Inuit during a voyage to Hudson Bay he undertook from 1903 to 1905.[12] Less than a week after Comer rendezvoused with "our natives" in Fullerton Harbour, he had commissioned "six native boats" for whale-hunting. After freeze-up he and his men relied on caribou skin coats and boots made by Inuit women. By the week before Christmas, "some of the natives are building their snow houses near the vessel." During the winter there was a great deal of socializing, including Comer's relationship to Niviatsianaq, a female Inuk whom he did not acknowledge as his partner though others referred to her as "Shoofly Comer." And in the spring they prepared for whaling at the floe edge, the encampment busily "shoeing the boats with bone from the jaws of a whale." Native women "made up the deer [caribou] skins into sleeping bags," and the sails for the small boats they would use for floe whaling were made with "the

Whaling and other maritime ventures in the North often led to trade, as between these Inuit and the crew of the *Karluk* off Point Barrow, Alaska, in 1913.

native women doing the sewing."[13] In every imaginable aspect of whaling and its attendant activities, the Inuit were indispensable to Comer, and no doubt to most non-Native whalers who visited these waters.

The impact on Inuit of the whalers' presence was, as usual, mixed. Clearly, Inuit enjoyed both the economic and the social benefits of interaction. Much later Nutaraq, a female Inuk, recalled the allure of whalers' visits to the eastern Arctic: "At first we'd see only the smoke out on the horizon; then after a long while under the smoke you'd see the ship. I remember how excited the adults would be – because now they would get tobacco, they would get tea, they would get bannock, all the good things they'd been missing all winter."[14] Whalers provided employment, valuable trade goods, and even entertainment. Captain Comer did not use the wax cylinders of his gramophone only to record Inuit songs; he also amused the Inuit aboard ship with "a concert from the graphaphone" from time to time.[15] Music serves to mark another type of impact. Whalers "brought new music; the accordion rang out from ships afloat or wintering over. Even today's young people sing *O Isaccie!* and the slightly ribald lyrics ('Isaccie's little penis is terribly ticklish'), set to the music of *O Susannah!* They brought wage labour, new diseases, and new genes. The relationship between Inuk and whaler was close and intimate; it is a rare Inuk

When southern mariners wintered over in the Arctic, interaction, such as
this at a Christmas party aboard the *Neptune* in 1903, greatly increased.

who has no whaler ancestor."[16] There were the usual negative products of interaction, too. Violence and abuse occurred sometimes, notably at Herschel Island, and disease was the constant companion of the European and Euro-American visitors. Clearly the disease, lechery, and violence of the whalers on Herschel Island in the Beaufort Sea contributed substantially to the drastic dwindling of the Mackenzie Inuit in the late years of the nineteenth century.[17] With the Inuit, as with so many Aboriginal groups, the absence of acquired immunity or resistance meant that these diseases wreaked havoc. In the twentieth century, tuberculosis was a fatal visitor in many parts of the Arctic North. By 1900, according to one expert, the Inuit population had been reduced by about one-third by diseases.[18]

Although there was little that Inuit could do to counter the communicable diseases, they could and did resist other impositions by whalers. In the Ungava region of what is now Quebec, local Inuit on one occasion sunk a whaling ship because the whalers had killed too many of the caribou on which they relied. On another occasion, in the Richmond Gulf region, "some whalers terrorized the Inuit until the women promised to make mitts for them. They made special mitts with no thumb piece, and tied them tightly around the whalers' wrists. The whalers were then helpless and their guns were taken away."[19] If the negative aspects of contact with the whalers outweighed the potential economic and social benefits, the Inuit always had the option of absenting themselves and avoiding interaction with the visitors. Obviously, the prevalence of such avoidance behaviour is not recorded and cannot be evaluated. On balance, it would seem likely that the harmful consequences of relations with visiting whalers were at least equal to the benefits.

There were similarities between the impact of the whalers and the damage wrought by the next group of strangers to invade the North in pursuit of its natural riches. Miners, particularly at first in Yukon, had an influence out of all proportion to the normal duration of their stay in the North. Both the background to and impact of the Klondike gold rush in the late 1890s reveal this pattern of Native-newcomer relations in the North. Thousands of prospectors and hangers-on trekked the "Trail of '98" and entered Yukon on their way to Dawson City and the Klondike, bringing disease, alcohol, and exploitation of the Indigenous population, especially women, during the short, intense rush. An episode involving the violent deaths of two non-Native prospectors at the hands of the Nantuck brothers, two Tagish men in southern Yukon, serves as a reminder of the way in which so much of Native-newcomer relations are distorted by the lens of Euro-Canadian documentation and interpretation. For a long time the general belief among non-Natives was that these two deaths were senseless acts of violence that frightened and mystified non-Natives. However, more recent oral history research by anthropologist Julie Cruikshank has revealed a deeper and more complex explanation for the bloody event. According to informants in the community, a couple of years before the prospectors' deaths, another non-Native had abandoned a cache of equipment and supplies, including some white powder that locals mistook for flour. When some of them died from food baked from the powder, which was in fact a poison, the man who had left the noxious substance was viewed as a murderer. The two non-Native prospectors who entered the territory subsequently were viewed as "kin" of the miscreant, and, as kin, they were expected to make good the wrong. However, when they had failed to do so during prolonged visits and tea-drinking with the Nantuck brothers, they were put to death.[20]

The prelude to the gold rush, as well as relations on the route and in the gold fields, left a lasting impression on Native-newcomer relations. Because the Klondike rush was preceded by incidents between Natives and interlopers in northern British Columbia, the 1898 rush also led to the making of a new treaty, Treaty 8, in 1899–1900.[21] This opportunistic reaction by Ottawa, which hitherto had evaded making treaty with northern Native peoples in order to avoid financial obligations to them, was merely a precursor to government responses elsewhere in the North.[22] Discovery of oil at Norman Wells on the Mackenzie River in 1920 was followed by negotiation of Treaty 11 in 1921, and the strategic demands for an important commodity such as oil awakened by the outbreak of the Second World War led to the Canol project, the construction of an oil pipeline from Norman Wells to Whitehorse. In the same era, American concerns about secure transportation during wartime between Alaska and the lower states induced Canada and her southern neighbour to agree to the construction of the Alaska Highway by the U.S. Army Corps of Engineers from northern BC through Yukon to Alaska.

All these "megaprojects," as a later age would term these economic developments, involved a disruptive invasion of the North by outsiders that temporarily unsettled and adversely affected the Indigenous population. For the most part, the real northerners were excluded from the creation of an industrial North in the twentieth century. Southern economic activity increasingly focused on mining and minerals in both Yukon and the Northwest Territories, as gold, uranium, and base metals all attracted southern investment and engineers in the period after the Great War. The "boom and bust" nature of Yukon mining especially would turn the flow of non-Natives into the region on and off, maintaining the tradition of non-Native transiency that characterized the North. To a lesser extent the same was true of mineral development in the NWT, although in the easterly territory what was most noteworthy about the twentieth-century economic development was the extent to which it was an activity dominated by outsiders for the benefit of outsiders. By 1938 the value of minerals produced in the NWT for the first time exceeded the value of fur production in the territory, but there was not yet a single person of Native ancestry employed in mining or prospecting there.[23]

Although the fur trade had always been designed for the benefit of outsiders, from the middle of the nineteenth century it provided economic benefits for Native peoples as well for close to a century. The northern fur trade can be dated from the 1840s, when traders began to operate in parts of what later would be known as western Yukon. Like European traders in many other parts of the continent, these newcomers had to fit themselves into a pre-existing Aboriginal trading network, a point that was brought home painfully to the Hudson's Bay Company in 1852 when a party of Chilcat made a long journey to the new HBC post, Fort Selkirk, for the express purpose of destroying the site and maintaining Chilcat monopoly over southern Yukon commerce.[24] Other aspects of the commercial relationship in the North were less drastic, but the subarctic fur trade was always rather volatile, subject to fluctuations in price and demand that made it a somewhat problematic kind of connection for First Nations merchants. However, the Hudson's Bay Company's presence in the North, which was increasingly challenged by other trading companies and individual traders from the late nineteenth century onward, provided a degree of stability and economic security for those First Nations who were in a commercial relationship with the venerable firm. As historical geographer Arthur J. Ray has argued convincingly, HBC's practice of assisting its Native partners in hard economic times was the precursor to a state-operated system of social security, the company a vital stopgap that prevented many Natives from starving to death thanks to Canadian government indifference until well into the twentieth century.[25] Of course, the HBC benefited, too, from the federal government's notorious reluctance to become directly involved with the peoples of the northern territories that Canada had acquired from Britain in the nineteenth century.

The Arctic fur trade involving Inuit commercial partners took off after the Great War. In the eastern Arctic the interwar period, from about 1920 to 1940, was the era when white fox pelts were in heavy demand in European markets. The Arctic, or white, fox trade provided Inuit with an excellent economic opportunity, and the entry of some trade rivals to the HBC created temptations to play one merchant off against the other. Non-Native traders were soon complaining that Inuit were skilful and ruthless at switching trade partners every year to maximize their access to trade goods and minimize their obligations to their merchants. As one HBC post keeper put it in 1922, "These people are evidently used to the custom of changing masters every year and cannot be depended upon to stick to any one company, especially when there is another company at hand to issue free grub, free rifles and ammunition as well as pay $25.00 for one fox."[26] However, during the harder times of the 1930s, many northerners found themselves again relying on the Hudson's Bay Company in its role as welfare dispenser; by the late 1930s it was also distributing government rations and medical aid. The northern fur trade, always an unstable and uncertain economic pursuit, would go into apparently permanent decline in the 1950s.

Missionaries, who were vociferous in their complaints about newcomers' mistreatment of Arctic Natives, took a lively, if paternalistic, interest in both Inuit and Indians. Anglican missionaries were especially prone to see non-Native interlopers – whether whalers, miners, or traders – as a corrupting influence. One of them, for example, listed among his "Particulars Regarding Copper Indians" for the Diocese of Yukon, that these Natives "are fairly intelligent, and were quite honest before they were influenced by the white men."[27] Although the Anglicans tried to maintain a denominational monopoly in Yukon and tussled aggressively with the Roman Catholic Church in the Northwest Territories, they were not the first Christian missionaries in the North, not even in their cherished home base of Yukon. Both the Society of Jesus and the Sisters of Saint Ann had served briefly in Yukon in the 1890s before abandoning that field to the aggressive Anglicans. The honour of being the first to carry the cross to Inuit and northern Indians belongs, in fact, to the Moravian Brethren, who established themselves at Nain on the Labrador coast in 1771 to evangelize and also to carry on a trade designed to underwrite their missions. Their creation of mission posts at several Labrador sites drew some of the Inuit south to these locales, the better to trade with the German missionaries. Although the attraction of Moravian missions for trade purposes declined in the nineteenth century, their centres remained significant places of social development, which included the emergence of a mixed-ancestry community who identified with non-Natives. They called themselves "settlers," but the Labrador Inuit term for them was *kablunanajok*, "one who resembles a white man."[28]

In the central and eastern Arctic it was the Roman Catholics, represented by the Oblates of Mary Immaculate, and the Church of England's Church Missionary Society (CMS) that divided the territory's souls between them. As a consequence of the Anglican-Catholic contest for Native adherents, denominational hot spots emerged in a few widely scattered locations. These were places, such as Moose Factory on James Bay or Aklavik near the Beaufort Sea, where denominational rivalry led both churches to establish missions, schools, and hospitals. While the duplication of social services no doubt benefited the Inuit or Indian population in the

favoured region – and there are clear examples of Natives playing one denomina-
tion off against the other for material gain[29] – it meant that large areas of the Arctic
North were left unserviced, most regrettably in the area of health care. In fairness to
the missionaries, it must be noted that from the 1890s it was they who for decades
pressed an uncooperative Government of Canada to take a more active role in the
Far North. However, successive deputy superintendent or superintendent generals
of Indian Affairs – from Hayter Reed in 1897 to Frank Pedley and Frank Oliver in
1909 – rebuffed entreaties from missionaries.[30] As the minister in 1909, Oliver told
an Anglican cleric that Canada would not provide medical care for Yukon Indians
or educate them. They would, he declared, earn a living better "if left as Indians."
Consequently, unable for a long time to secure government direct involvement in
providing services to northern Natives, missionaries had to do the best they could
on their own, scrapping all the while between themselves. A National Film Board
video, *Coppermine*,[31] captures the good and the bad of missionary involvement in
the North: a CMS man and an Oblate struggle for adherents, while the federal
government – despite repeated missionary entreaties – refuses to provide the medical equipment that might have saved a young Inuk from death from "ship cold,"
tuberculosis.

As might be expected of such an ambivalent role, the lasting effect of northern
missionaries on the Inuit and Indians is hard to assess with any precision. That
individual missionaries cared passionately about the material and spiritual welfare
of the Natives – in noteworthy contrast to the uninterested government, it should
be added – is beyond argument. Christian missionaries, whatever their denominational selfishness and their tendency to denigrate Aboriginal spiritual practices,
at least cared about the well-being of the Natives to whom they ministered. And
the response of the Inuit and First Nations populations? That, as usual, is harder
to gauge. That there were numerous conversions among Inuit, as, for example, at
Pond Inlet, where those who parted ways with their shaman, the *angakok*, in favour
of "coming up Jesusy," as they put it, is a clear matter of record.[32] And down to the
late twentieth century, a tradition introduced to the Labrador coast by Moravian
missionaries of calling bingo numbers in German persisted.[33] In the North, perhaps
even more so than in other regions of the country, the true and enduring legacy of
missions to the Native people of Christian evangelization was difficult to measure.

As the experience of whaling, mining, fur-trading, and missionary transients in
the North had demonstrated, the Government of Canada was a most reluctant –
and late – entrant into a relationship with the Inuit and Subarctic First Nations. In
fact, until the middle of the twentieth century, Ottawa's interest in the Aboriginal

peoples of the Far North could reasonably be described as episodic and transitory. The United Kingdom had transferred jurisdiction over the Arctic islands to Canada, but the Dominion showed little interest in taking up responsibilities in the North, especially if the assertion of title involved commitments to Native peoples. As noted, both Deputy Minister Hayter Reed and a later minister, Frank Oliver, steadfastly maintained that Canada was uninterested in making treaty with First Nations in Yukon, believing that they would be "best left as Indians" from a federal, fiscal point of view. The only incidents that altered that thinking were intrusions into the North by Americans that might threaten Canada's feeble hold on the region. Accordingly, the Klondike gold rush in 1898 was the occasion, not just for the conclusion of Treaty 8, but also of the effective assertion of Canadian control by mounted police in dealing with American prospectors and adventurers. Similarly, the 1903 voyage of the *Neptune*, the government vessel whose crew photographed the Inuit at a shipboard Christmas party, was in northern waters to assert Canadian control of the region in the presence of American whalers and American vessels.[34] Canadian concern with effective assertion of sovereignty led in 1922 to establishment of three mounted police detachments on the Arctic "to protect our rights against foreigners; to protect our fisheries, and to take care of our property generally."[35]

Canadian anxiety about sovereignty began to have a direct effect on the Inuit the following year, when Ottawa chose to prosecute a number of them charged with murder at Herschel Island. The zeal with which the government prosecuted this case – the judicial party that went to Herschel Island that summer was accompanied by a hangman and wood to construct a gallows – was in sharp contrast to the leniency with which it had dealt with the murderers of two scientists in 1912 and two Oblate missionaries in 1913. The 1912 deaths were not prosecuted, and the murderers of the priests, who argued that one of the priests had threatened them with his rifle, were convicted of manslaughter and sentenced to two years' labour at the police post. In the later Herschel Island case, however, concerns about sovereignty led the Government of Canada to prosecute zealously, gaining convictions, and hanging the unfortunate Inuit. Slightly later, the Inuk who killed a non-Native in the eastern Arctic was also subjected to the full rigour of Canadian justice, convicted of manslaughter by a jury composed of the crew of the ship that had brought the presiding magistrate and counsel to Pond Inlet for the trial, and taken south to a prison for ten years.[36] In 1924 Canada brought the Inuit under the administration of the superintendent general of Indian Affairs. All the same, the Indian Affairs minister conceded in 1925, "The Eskimos have not received very much attention at the hands of this government, but we are becoming more alive to our responsibilities in that regard."[37] For most purposes the Inuit were expected to look to one or more of the northern triumvirate – police, HBC trader, or missionary.

That the Canadian government's concern and solicitude for Inuit were not genuine was demonstrated during the following decade in a chapter of burlesque federalism that could only have occurred in Canada. The question was, simply, Which level of government, provincial or federal, had jurisdiction over Inuit? Were they, as generations of Canadians have puzzled about a myriad of topics, a federal or provincial responsibility? More specifically, did Inuit fall under section 91 (24) of the British North America Act (later, Canada Act 1867)? The question became more than academic during the 1930s, when severe economic hardship among Inuit drew the Quebec and Canadian governments into contention to see which of them could evade financial liability for aid that was dispensed in the North. In 1929 the province and federal government had agreed that Ottawa would aid Inuit in northern Quebec, with the province reimbursing it for the expenditure, but in 1932 Quebec objected to the arrangement and said that Inuit were the responsibility of Ottawa under section 91(24) of the BNA Act. Since the dispute could not be settled by negotiation, resort was made to the courts, the case reaching the Supreme Court of Canada in 1937. The federal lawyers relied on anthropological and historical evidence to demonstrate that Inuit were not Indians, but the court decision, rendered in 1939, ignored the scholars. Since, the highest court ruled, Ottawa had often looked after Inuit and since most people regarded Inuit as a tribe or nation of Indians, they were henceforth to be treated as "Indians" under the Canadian constitution.[38] Aside from maintaining the surveillance of the Eastern Arctic Patrol of the Royal Canadian Mounted Police, the Canadian government did little after 1939 to exercise the jurisdiction the court had assigned to it. The Hudson's Bay Company largely remained what authority there was in the North, and in instances of conflict between company and government it was the latter that backed down.[39]

From 1947 onward, with waning and waxing government support over the years, the Canadian Rangers acted as another assertion of Canadian sovereignty in the North. Serving as Canada's "eyes and ears" in remote regions such as the Far North, the Rangers have been the boots-on-the-ground expression of the country's concern about sovereignty, security, and stewardship in the North. For these members of the army reserve, their mission is highly personal. As one of them expressed their feelings, "We don't want other people intruding on our land without us knowing about it." The Rangers have proved an economical and effective instrument for carrying out Canada's perpetual concern for guarding its sovereignty in the North for seven decades.[40] As in so many other branches of Native-government relations, the Second World War dramatically changed matters. It was not so much that Canada began to accept any more responsibility in the North, but rather that an influx of southerners into the region revealed and publicized the poor state of many Inuit communities and government neglect. Canadian and American armed forces personnel who were in the eastern Arctic to build a series of air bases that formed an aerial staging route for air transportation to Europe, brought back stories of abysmal living and health conditions in many Inuit communities. The ensuing publicity caused the Government of Canada to conduct investigations into the state of affairs, resulting in reports that documented the deficient medical and educational services for Inuit in the North.[41] However, when Canada began to issue relief, it did so through the Hudson's Bay Company, and a timorous Ottawa lacked the will to compel the company to distribute the aid to all needy Natives, rather than just those who patronized the HBC. "Government relief was thus a direct subsidy to this trading giant."[42] Similarly, when Inuit mothers became some of the first beneficiaries of the nascent welfare state that Canada hesitantly began to erect in 1944–5, their family allowance, or "baby bonus" as it was colloquially known, came from 1945 onward in the form of a voucher that had to be cashed at the HBC store for goods from an approved list.[43] On the other hand, Inuit health care became the responsibility of the newly created Department of National Health and Welfare. Slowly during the 1950s and 1960s, federal government services of many kinds would begin to be provided in the Arctic.

Not all the federal government's attentions were beneficial, clearly. The continuing preoccupation with sovereignty led during the 1950s to one of the most traumatic events in Inuit-government relations, the episode often referred to as "the High Arctic exiles."[44] Migration had always been practised by Inuit pursuing economic and social advantages, of course. The whaling families who built their snow houses and wintered alongside the frozen-in whaling ships from outside were only one example. After the Second World War, migration to the settlements to be close to health care and children who now were being educated in day and residential schools was another.[45] However, in the 1950s an unprecedented type of coerced or manipulated migration occurred in the case of northern Quebec Inuit. Between 1953 and 1955 the Government of Canada moved a number of Inuit families from Port Harrison (Inukjuak), Quebec, to Grise Fiord at the southern tip of Ellesmere Island and Resolute Bay. At the time, the government said that its motive was to provide a land that could support the Inuit better, but suspicions have always existed that the relocation was part of a government effort to strengthen its claim to northern islands. Over time, Inuit leaders familiar with the case have become increasingly convinced that their people were exploited for strategic reasons and experienced severe want in their new locations.

Canada's newly developed welfare state entered the North during and
after the Second World War. At the Hudson's Bay Company store at Read Island,
NWT, in 1950, a family receives its Family Allowance in store goods.

   The official record is mixed, providing support to both sides of the argument,
but Inuit oral evidence is almost uniformly condemnatory about governmental
motives and the impact on the Inuit. In 1993 Inuit witnesses persuaded the Royal
Commission on Aboriginal Peoples that they had a strong case for redress, and the
commissioners recommended an apology and compensation for the wrong. At the
same time, the highly respected federal bureaucrat Gordon Robertson, who served
as Commissioner of the Northwest Territories and deputy minister of Northern
Affairs and Natural Resources from 1953 to 1963, has lent his support to those
who argue that the reason for relocation was compassion.[46] A troubling chapter
in the post-war story of Inuit government relations has become vexed, tangled,
and almost incapable of resolution in a manner that will satisfy scholarly and Inuit
political opinion. Ironically, it appears that oral history evidence in the eastern
Arctic at the end of the twentieth century had the opposite effect to the impact of

interviews about community memory of events in southern Yukon at the end of the nineteenth. In the case of the Nantuck brothers in the Klondike gold rush era, oral history clarified and corrected a documentary account, but in the case of the High Arctic exiles sixty years later, oral accounts and documentary evidence are apparently hopelessly snarled.

Inuit and northern First Nations began to have an impact on the non-Native majority in the rest of the country after the Second World War. Not only were they in strategically important locations during the war, but their homeland was in the middle of the potential ground of conflict in the Cold War era in which the United States and USSR squared off across the North Pole with intercontinental ballistic missiles, nuclear-laden bombers, and high-speed jet interceptors. The Cold War would lead to the construction of a northerly string of radar stations, the DEW, or Distant Early Warning, Line, in the Canadian Arctic, a radar tripwire to detect the anticipated Russian bombers or missiles. What the Inuit made of such military insanity – the official deterrent strategy of the American-led forces of "the West" in this era was known as MAD, for mutual assured destruction – is not clear.

Nor is it likely that Inuit realized the degree and swiftness with which they and their homeland were becoming part of the iconography of a blossoming English-Canadian nationalism after 1945. A popular radio serial in the era before the arrival of Canadian television was *Sergeant Preston of the Yukon*, in which square-jawed and white-skinned police and their faithful canine companions ("On, King! On, you huskies!" Preston urged over the yelps of his dog train at the start of each week's program)[47] dispensed justice and compassion to all throughout the North. Late in the 1950s, Tom Lehrer, a Harvard statistician and part-time satirist, linked the Inuit and the prospect of a Cold War holocaust: "We will all go together when we go, / Every Hottentot and every Eskimo. / When the air becomes uranious, / We will all go simultaneous. / Yes, we all will go together when we go."[48] Also from the 1950s onward, Inuit sculpture and printmaking began to enjoy acclaim and commercial success. Largely promoted by a sympathetic southerner, James Houston, northern communities, with government encouragement, organized Inuit art cooperatives that marketed soapstone carvings and beautiful prints based largely on Inuit spiritual concepts throughout North America and Europe. By the 1960s the Inuit, or, as would have been said at the time, Eskimo carving was as recognizable a symbol of Canadianism as the maple leaf or the totem pole.

By the 1950s and 1960s, the Canadian state was represented by the Arctic trinity: police, missionary, and bureaucrat. They supplanted the old threesome of fur trader, missionary, and police, underscoring both the drastic decline of the fur trade by

Ironically, an Inuk woman contemplates purchasing frozen food,
which her people used to acquire out of doors.

the 1950s and the expanding role of the Canadian state. Southern communications
such as the Canadian Broadcasting Corporation brought urban, bourgeois culture
and the ravenous demands of the advertising world to an unsuspecting Arctic.
From the 1960s onward it was clear that the original northerners responded to
this cultural, economic, and political onslaught with bemusement and increasing
resolve to take control of the forces of change and make them work for the benefit
of Inuit people for a change. There were some like Anthony Apakark Thrasher, a
self-described "skid-row Eskimo," who were destroyed by the alcohol that came
with the *kabloona*. He described "the Eskimo people" as resembling "the sun spots
which sometimes appear on the lens of an astronomer. We are in the way, we blur
the picture the white man has of the future of the North." He hurt, but was philosophical: "I have pains in my head from Skid Row beatings and too much drink
and my stomach hurts from the wrong kind of food. It's funny, but I can't get angry,

even though they put me in a cage. Eskimos don't get angry over something they can't control or understand."[49] Others were like Minnie Aodla; swept up in the early 1950s by the southern treatment program for Inuit suffering from tuberculosis, she combined her sunny personality with her iron will to fashion a career for herself, first as an interpreter for Indian and Northern Affairs Canada, and later as a writer and journalist specializing in northern themes.[50]

Others responded in ways that were geared more to protest and organized resistance. Abraham Okpik foreshadowed what would become a political movement in 1962 in an essay titled "What Does It Mean to Be an Eskimo?":

> We the Eskimo people, where do we come from and how did we get here? This is a big question to us all even in the white man's way of thinking or learning. We are still a mystery to them, but our ancestors are the ones who we give praise to for all that they have achieved, to live, to feel, to survive for centuries before the white people came. Some of the kablonat came with good intentions to teach us a better way to live; some came to destroy our livelihood and our culture ...
>
> There are only a very few Eskimos, but millions of whites, just like the mosquitos. It is something very special and wonderful to be an Eskimo – they are like the snow geese. If an Eskimo forgets his language and Eskimo ways, he will be nothing but just another mosquito.[51]

In 1971, led principally by the eastern Arctic Inuit, the Indigenous people of the Arctic established a new political organization, the Inuit Tapirisat of Canada, to represent them in their dealings with *kabloona* and their government. Only if and when the neglectful Government of Canada chose to listen seriously to such groups would relations in the North begin to change.

Part Three

CONFRONTATION

CHAPTER THIRTEEN

The Beginnings of Political Organization

By the second third of the twentieth century, changes in Indigenous policy were inevitable. Missionary organizations and Ottawa bureaucrats had come to recognize that directed change and economic development were not occurring as they wanted. Moreover, by the Depression decade, the decline in First Nation population that had been an unacknowledged factor in many of the policies had reversed. As numbers began to increase, schools that did not succeed and reserves shrunken by land transfers proved inadequate. The failure of the nineteenth-century policies and a rise in the numbers of First Nations people made attempts to redefine Indian policy unavoidable. And, as that process began on the governmental side of the relationship, coincidentally among the Native population there was a growing restlessness and a desire to control their own affairs.

The people responsible for the "policy of the Bible and the plough" had begun to have doubts even before the Great War. To some of the church groups it was obvious, in the words of the Presbyterian who directed his church's schools, that "instead of gaining ground for the last twenty-five years, we have been losing." The layman in charge of the Church of England's missionary efforts in Canada in 1908 described the industrial schools as "a very expensive farce" because of their dismal pedagogical showing.[1] On the government side, both politicians and bureaucrats were sceptical that reserves, missions, and Christian schools were having their desired effect. A senior official noted in 1898, "Experience does not favour the view that the [reserve] system makes for the advancement of the Indians." And Deputy Superintendent General of Indian Affairs Frank Pedley defended a decision in 1908 not to allocate more federal money to residential schools by saying, "It is clear that the present system with its large expenditure has not operated as was expected towards the civilization of the aborigines."[2]

A compounding factor was the attitude of Euro-Canadians in an era of advancing agricultural settlement. Such people increasingly regarded the presence of First Nations as simply an obstacle to their realization of dreams of material wealth. As a member of the Alberta Attorney General's office put it, Albertans "with whom I have spoken are not, I would gather, very much in sympathy with the Indian, nor with the efforts to better his condition. They look upon him as a sort of a pest which should be exterminated."[3] In Sydney, Nova Scotia, in 1916, the Mi'kmaq band's reserve was relocated from a downtown location against their will, under the draconian powers of the Oliver Act, because of attitudes that differed little from those of the Albertans. Such hostility also helped to propel the search for a new policy in the twentieth century.

The fact that First Nations were declining in numbers counteracted the pressure for policy reform that stemmed from disillusionment and racial hostility. The combination of undermining the economy of the western nations, encroaching upon the land base of many bands that had reserves, and forcing a switch in both housing and dietary styles from the traditional to a poor version of the Euro-Canadian's had the effect of continuing the decimation of First Nations. As had always been the case, the single greatest destroyer of the Indigenous population was disease. And the most destructive disease was tuberculosis, to which Natives still largely did not have an acquired immunity.[4]

Diseases were probably worst in the overcrowded dormitories of the residential schools, most of which were tightly sealed to conserve energy.[5] The fondness of school administrators for brass bands also contributed to the efficiency with which these schools disseminated diseases of the pulmonary system. A great deal of publicity was given this problem by the investigations and writings of a federal medical officer, Dr. P.H. Bryce, who revealed the scandalous health conditions in the boarding and industrial schools. As the deputy minister of the department was to concede on the eve of the Great War, "It is quite within the mark to say that fifty per cent of the children who passed through these schools did not live to benefit from the education which they had received therein."[6] Because of health problems, poor diet, inadequate housing, and low incomes, the First Nation population continued to dwindle through the late nineteenth and early twentieth centuries. This demographic pattern probably explained much of the delay in shifting to new policies. For example, although there was a serious attempt to phase out residential schools in favour of "new, improved" day schools in the first decade, partly because

Some of the students (far left, and centre) in this Sarcee school classroom
wear bandages that indicate they are tuberculosis sufferers.

of health considerations, denominational opposition prevented the change. And so
the dismal pattern of poor schooling and dwindling First Nation numbers continued for the first three decades of the century.

At the end of the 1920s or beginning of the 1930s, the decline was reversed and
Canada's recorded First Nation population began to increase. A census taken in
the early 1930s showed that, apparently for the first time since Confederation, the
population of registered, or status, Indians had increased.[7] During the Depression
decade, the First Nation population climbed back above the 110,000 level; it would
increase slowly till mid-century, when it would accelerate once more.[8] A growing
First Nation population meant that policies predicated on the eventual disappearance of Indigenous peoples had become fatuous. Increasing numbers also meant
that the department's highly paternalistic programs, such as selling off reserve
land and keeping children in residential institutions for prolonged periods, were
becoming expensive. The minister responsible for First Nation matters said in
1941 that "the fundamental difficulty which faced the Department in connection
with Indian education," for example, was "an increase in the Indian population
which made an increase in the cost of education, based on the per capita grants
to residential schools, a matter of serious moment to the financial programme of
the Department."[9]

Often, as in the case of these Six Nations chiefs in council, traditional First Nations political
structures persisted in the face of Department of Indian Affairs disapproval.

The final factor that combined with the churches' doubt and government's fiscal
anxiety was the emergence of political protest. In many ways, especially in the sense
of long-term effectiveness, this would be the most significant of the factors. As has
already been noted, First Nations throughout the country had not acquiesced in the
increasingly paternalistic and authoritarian policies that were put in place from the
1850s onward. But in the twentieth century, political movements would become
better organized and more effective in bringing First Nation grievances to the attention of the government and the Canadian public. Although the bureaucrats and
politicians continued to act until the 1960s or 1970s as though Indigenous peoples
were childlike and incapable of influencing policy for the better, First Nations eventually forced an unresponsive Ottawa to pay them heed.

Political confrontation did not begin with the largest group of Indigenous people
to have come recently into close contact with Euro-Canadians, the First Nations and
Métis of the West. The First Nations of the western interior certainly had as many
grievances and problems after the 1880s as did the peoples of the Pacific coast, but
for a long time they were demoralized by the aftermath of the Rebellion of 1885.

Both the western First Nations and the Métis were adversely affected by heavy agricultural settlement after 1895, becoming steadily more impoverished and marginalized. There were occasional attempts by government and church to resettle Métis groups in new locations in which they might have a chance to start anew, but for the most part these experiments enjoyed little success. Both Métis and Prairie First Nations would be a long time in recovering sufficiently from the traumas of the late nineteenth century to mount an effective political challenge.

Because of their particular problems over land, noted earlier, it was the First Nations of British Columbia who led the political movements of the early twentieth century. Those special circumstances concerning Native lands in British Columbia were two in number: the extent of reserve lands, and Aboriginal title.[10] The first arose from the confrontation of dominion and province over what lands should be provided from provincial Crown lands for reserves, a dispute that dated from the 1870s and culminated in the McKenna-McBride Commission. This commission's recommendations concerning BC reserve lands were so threatening that they helped to provoke the first province-wide Native political organization to fight them. However, prior to that phase, disagreements over Aboriginal title had also sparked protest. Since colonial British Columbia had never dealt with First Nations for any but fourteen small parcels on Vancouver Island, the situation after Confederation, as the Dominion put it in 1877, was that "Indian rights to soil in British Columbia have never been extinguished."[11] BC First Nations were quite clear about their unextinguished title, however. When an official with the Northwest Coast Commission, one of the succession of government bodies created to grapple with the BC land question, told some Nisga'a that the queen owned the land, an Elder demanded, "Who is the chief that gave this land to the Queen? Give us his name. We have never heard it."[12] Leaders of the Port Simpson Tsimshian asserted in 1909, "This country was our world and from time immemorial our forefathers taught us by legend and tradition and actual possession that the land was ours."[13] A 1910 memorial from a group of interior nations to the prime minister said that when strangers "first came amongst us ... they found the people of each tribe supreme in their own territory, and having tribal boundaries known and recognised by all ..."[14] It was the growing sense among First Nation leaders in British Columbia that their title was not recognized by the expanding settler society, as well as the marathon dispute over reserve lands, that provoked political organization on the West Coast at an early date.

When the BC First Nations began to organize to pursue their claims early in the twentieth century, a pattern that was to become very familiar developed. In 1906 Joe Capilano, a chief of the Squamish people whose territory was threatened by the growing city of Vancouver, carried the protests of his people against encroachment to the throne itself. Although this attempt produced no change in the attitudes of governments in Canada, it did help to galvanize BC Native peoples into political organization.[15] In 1909 twenty nations petitioned the monarch and formed a body called the Indian Tribes of the Province of British Columbia. The Nisga'a of the Nass River Valley established the Nisga'a Land Committee and in 1913 forwarded to Ottawa the "Nisga'a Petition" outlining their claim and asking for its adjudication by the Judicial Committee of the Privy Council. However, since the JCPC was an appeal body and the northern First Nation refused to submit their case to a Canadian court in the first instance, a lengthy stalemate ensued. In 1916 the Nass people joined with southern bands and the Interior Salish to found the Allied Tribes of British Columbia under the leadership of Haida Methodist clergyman Peter Kelly and Roman Catholic layman Andrew Paull. The Allied Tribes pressed the federal government for settlement of both land questions for a decade. In 1924 Ottawa refused to bargain further on the issue of reserve allotments and decided to implement the Reserve Commission's report of 1916. In 1927 a Special Joint Parliamentary Committee sat to consider BC claims. This body, which heard Paull and Kelly speak on behalf of the Allied Tribes, concluded that BC's First Nations had "not established any claim to the lands of British Columbia based on aboriginal or other title" and decided that the matter was ended (save for the aftermath that saw the Indian Act amended to deter the pursuit of land claims).[16]

In addition to the land issue in British Columbia, the continuing interference by Indian Affairs with the internal political matters of bands across the country was rousing ire that would lead to political protest and organization. Leaders reacted with frustration and anguish to the economic marginalization resulting from settler pressure and political oppression from Ottawa. Chief William, leader of an interior group in British Columbia, complained to a newspaper as early as 1879 that his people's problems were causing them to denounce him as inert and useless. "I am old and feeble," wrote the chief, "and my authority diminishes every day. I am sorely puzzled. I do not know what I say next week when the chiefs are assembled in a council. A war with the white man will end in our destruction, but death in war is not so bad as death by starvation."[17] Many nations experienced continued interference from the Department of Indian Affairs from the 1890s onward, as Ottawa applied ever more coercion to First Nations. The Okanagan, for example, sparred with the department over who would sit as chief from the late 1890s to the period of the Great War, culminating in the band's formation of an Okanagan Indian Rights Defence League.[18] In eastern Canada, particularly in Ontario, some of the Iroquois groups were embroiled in disputes over their political autonomy that would fester for decades. The Six Nations community near Brantford had

Great War veteran Lt. F.O. Loft organized the first national political
organization of status Indians, the League of Indians of Canada.

attempted to maintain its own judicial and legislative institutions in spite of efforts
of the provincial and federal governments to subject the reserve residents to the exclusive jurisdiction of Euro-Canadian law.[19] Their Mohawk cousins at Akwesasne,
near Cornwall, similarly tangled on and off from the late 1890s onward with the
Department of Indian Affairs over governance. Most Mohawk wanted hereditary
chiefs and council selected according to their traditional Great Law of Peace, but
Ottawa repeatedly attempted to impose the elective institutions it had been promoting since 1869.[20] Some of these disputes would end up at the League of Nations
in the 1930s, and Mohawk traditionalists have never accepted Canadian jurisdiction. In the short run, however, in the early decades of the twentieth century, such
clashes also contributed to the growing pressure within First Nations to organize
themselves politically.

In the interwar period, First Nations in several regions joined British Columbia in
organizing to exert political pressure on the government. They included an Ontario
Mohawk leader, Lieutenant F.O. Loft, who held a meeting to establish a League of
Indians of Canada at Sault Ste. Marie in the autumn of 1919.[21] Loft, a veteran of the

Great War, was an example of the considerable contribution that First Nations from all parts of the country had made to the Dominion war effort, as well as a manifestation of their understandable tendency afterwards to claim a right to be heard. Indian Affairs records showed that over four thousand status Indians voluntarily enlisted for service, representing approximately 35 per cent of First Nation men of military age.[22] Reserve communities also were generous contributors to the Red Cross and other agencies that supported war work. After the Great War, traditional arguments that Indigenous people had no grounds for complaint because they had made no recent contribution to the development of the country could hardly be sustained in the face of their recent sacrifice. As Loft said in a letter that he sent to leaders in the central and Prairie provinces, "As peaceable and law-abiding citizens in the past, and even in the late war, we have performed dutiful service to our King, Country and Empire, and we have the right to claim and demand more justice and fair play as a recompense." Loft also demonstrated that First Nations outside British Columbia understood the importance of land issues. His letter argued that First Nations should seek "absolute control in retaining possession or disposition of our lands."[23]

Gradually, in the 1920s, the League became dominated by western First Nations.[24] Meetings in 1920 and 1922 protested against the restrictions of the pass system and demanded programs to assist the Indigenous people in their development. Although the western movement's first leaders were Christian converts from the residential schools such as the Blood Mike Mountain Horse and the Cree clergyman Edward Ahenakew, who gave it a moderate cast, the western protest began to shift towards a more forceful assertion of traditional rights and demands for assistance. By the 1930s Prairie First Nations were pressing for better schooling and agricultural assistance, while asserting their right to follow traditional rituals: "Resolved that as Canada has freedom of religious worship we Indians would earnestly petition you to grant our request to worship in our own way and according to our past customs the Most High God that created the world and all the beasts thereof and everything that pertaineth thereof, especially as we do not see anything according to our past customs, and especially that we should not be prohibited from holding our ancient Sun Dance, which should be called the Thirsty Dance and the Hungry Dance; a religious ceremony which has been dear to us for centuries and is still dear to us."[25] These sentiments were reminiscent of what Bull Shield, a member of a Blood sacred society, told a policeman: "The Horn Society is as good as the Bible."[26]

There is evidence that Ottawa's continuing attempts to discourage the observance of rituals that distracted First Nations from immediate economic needs

This fund-raising poster of the Canadian Patriotic Fund, as patronizing
and offensive as it was, underscored the immense contribution
that First Nations were making to the Great War effort.

and deterred their assimilation were often unsuccessful. When the residents of
Poundmaker reserve in Saskatchewan built a meeting hall, they constructed it "across
the creek and out of sight of government health officials. Periodically, big feasts and
dances were held there by the community."[27] On the Pacific coast, potlatching went
on in spite of a brief crackdown by Ottawa in the early 1920s.[28] As an Ojibwe had told
a Jesuit in the mid-nineteenth century, "As there are many species of plants, birds,
fishes and animals, each one with its own peculiarities, so there are different kinds
of men, each one with its own blessings from the Great Spirit. We are not fools. We
have our wisdom given to our Ancients by the Great Spirit, and we shall cling to
it."[29] In the twentieth century, by means of political organization, Indigenous people
across the country were making such views heard anew.

Western First Nations' tendency to organize and resist culminated in the formation of new bodies, the Indian Association of Alberta (1939) and the organization that evolved into the Federation of Saskatchewan Indians (1944).[30] (Once
again, key figures in these advances towards political assertiveness were products
of the residential schools, men such as the clergyman Eugene Steinhauer in Alberta
and the Cree John Tootoosis in Saskatchewan.) The two bodies that these men
helped to create in their home provinces would be important to First Nation political struggles of the later twentieth century. The Manitoba Indian Brotherhood
emerged a little later, with a former residential school student, David Courchene,
as its first president in 1968. Developments in British Columbia in the 1930s and
1940s paralleled those in the western interior. There, too, the leading spirits in the
spreading political movement were products of the Christian schools. Two of the
most noteworthy BC leaders were Andrew Paull, a man from a Squamish reserve
who had been educated by the Oblates, and the Reverend Peter Kelly, a Haida
Methodist missionary, both of them active in the Allied Tribes of BC until it collapsed after failing to persuade the parliamentary committee of the validity of their
Aboriginal title in 1927. Neither the 1927 Indian Act prohibition on fund-raising
nor the stresses of Depression and the Second World War stopped BC Natives from
organizing. In 1931 the Native Brotherhood of British Columbia (NBBC) was established, and during the rest of the 1930s it spread southward down the coast
from its northern centres of strength, eventually establishing itself in the southern
interior as well. In 1942, thanks largely to Paull, a Kwakwaka'wakw-dominated economic organization called the Pacific Coast Native Fishermen's Association (1936)
amalgamated with the NBBC. Soon afterward Paull spearheaded the formation of
the North American Indian Brotherhood (NAIB), which, in spite of its name, was
principally an effort to forge a national First Nations political organization. Wags
described the NBBC as "a body without a head" and the NAIB as "a head without

a body."[31] In the 1940s Paull reached out to the young movements in the Prairie region and to sympathetic groups in Ontario and Quebec, but did not succeed for the time being in persuading them to support a national, united front for dealing with Ottawa. In the name of the NAIB, Paull asserted both land claims and more general issues before the joint parliamentary committee that sat from 1946 to 1948 to consider changes in the discredited Indian Act.

Other developments that had a dramatic impact on western First Nations in particular helped to force reassessment of policy. Perhaps the most important was the transfer in 1930 of jurisdiction over Crown lands and natural resources from Ottawa to the three Prairie provinces. The transfer agreements included an important statement that reaffirmed treaty rights to hunting and fishing, albeit in a more restricted way. The Act promised that "the said Indians shall have the right, which the province hereby assures them, of hunting, trapping and fishing game and fish for food at all seasons of the year on all unoccupied Crown lands and on any other lands to which the said Indians may have a right of access."[32] While this clause was an important confirmation of the right to hunt and fish regardless of provincial game laws, it also constituted a diminution of what had been promised in treaties because the transfer agreements limited the exercise of the right to occasions when Natives hunted or fished "for food." Moreover, the unilateral transfer to the provinces of jurisdiction over lands and resources constituted amendment of the numbered treaties without the agreement of the other party to the pact, the First Nations. In any event, the three provinces sought in a myriad of ways to evade their responsibility, and, often in response to Euro-Canadians' political pressure, attempted to subject Prairie Nations to the restrictions of their game and fishing laws. Western First Nations consistently rebuffed these attempts, and the result was thousands of prosecutions for hunting and fishing, and a heightening of the frustration and anger that fuelled political organization.[33]

The Depression decade that saw the transfer of Crown lands to the western provinces was an interregnum in policy-making between the experiments with coercion in the 1920s and the determination in the later 1940s to work out a new approach. The explanation of the inactivity of the 1930s resides largely in the economic depression that beset the country and distracted its governments. While the province of Alberta proved an exception to the general picture of inactivity by its appointment of the Ewing Commission that investigated Métis complaints and its creation of Métis reserves or settlements at the end of the decade, other parts of the country and the federal government left Natives to get through the troubled 1930s as best they could.[34] Naturally, the programs that supported them were subject to frequent budget cuts, and these reductions served only to discredit still further

existing policies by making them less effective and more hated. For many communities, especially on the parched and bankrupt Prairies, the decade was a period
of acute suffering. The Indian agent at Duck Lake, Saskatchewan, reported in 1933
that some families on two of the reserves in his agency wanted to shift their children from on-reserve day schools to distant residential schools. When he asked
them their reasons, "in most cases the reply was, 'We are poor (hardup) and cannot
clothe our children properly, during the winter months.'" Some families "had a hard
time providing sufficient food for their families."[35]

The Second World War seemed for a time to have blown apart Canadian Indian
policy as it crushed the Axis powers. There was a link between the two. After all, in
the midst of a war against institutionalized racism and barbarity, it was impossible
not to notice that the bases of Canadian Indian policy lay in assumptions about
the moral and economic inferiority of particular racial groupings. The horrors of
the war, in conjunction with the widening influence of the relativism of the social
sciences, seriously discomfited Canadians when, on rare occasions, they looked at
the way in which they were treating the Aboriginal peoples of their country. The
fact that, once again, Natives volunteered in exceptionally large numbers, although
not at as high a level as in the Great War, meant that service also strengthened First
Nations' claims to consideration. Military service, the discrediting of racism, and
the increasing influence of the social sciences combined to alter Euro-Canadians'
perceptions of Canada's Indigenous peoples. In 1950 Alfred L. Kroeber, an eminent
American anthropologist, boasted that his discipline's development of the concept
of culture had brought about "the toppling of the doctrine of racism – that bland
assumption of race superiority which is so satisfying emotionally to most people
and so unwarranted."[36]

While Kroeber was speaking specifically of his own discipline, Canadian public
opinion, at least as judged by the popular press, lent some support to the idea that
the hold of racism was weakening noticeably among the general public. Analysis
of the way in which popular magazines presented Indigenous people reveals that
the period from about 1930 to the 1960s was one of transition, during which condescending humanitarianism began to be supplanted by growing realization of
the problems faced by First Nations and concern about the ways in which non-
Natives were implicated in those problems.[37] In the 1940s, thanks in no small part
to Indigenous service in the war, the public's perception of First Nations evolved
to warrior and then victim.[38] Canada's Indigenous peoples were beginning to move
out of the "era of irrelevance" to policy-makers in which they had been cast by the
majority population in the nineteenth century.

One sign of First Nation "emergence from 'irrelevance'" was a search for a workable policy. As early as the 1930s minority voices were questioning aspects of the policy of the Bible and the plough. In 1938, for example, when member of parliament A.W. Neill, who had been an Indian agent on Vancouver Island, attacked critics of the potlatch in the Commons, he was joined by J.S. Woodsworth and several BC Cooperative Commonwealth Federation members.[39] In the early 1940s, the increasing assertiveness of First Nations leaders such as Andy Paull in British Columbia and Jules Sioui in Quebec also led bureaucrats to rethink their policies.[40] The upshot of the wartime experiences, coming on top of the mounting disillusionment in government and church circles, was the appointment in 1946 of a special joint committee of the Senate and House of Commons "to examine and consider the Indian Act ... and amendments thereto and suggest such amendments as they may deem advisable." An Alberta member of parliament claimed during a sitting of this joint committee that, "the Canadian people as a whole are interested in the problem of the Indians; they have become aware that the country has been negligent in the matter of looking after the Indians and they are anxious to remedy our shortcomings. Parliament and the country is [sic] 'human rights' conscious."[41] If the hearings of the special committee from 1946 to1948 were remarkable for the opportunity they gave the newly organized First Nations to express their opinions, the subsequent legislation was notorious for ignoring what they had said. Organizations from British Columbia, Alberta, Saskatchewan, Manitoba, and Quebec were particularly forceful in their condemnations of departmental political interference in band affairs, involuntary enfranchisement, inadequate economic assistance, schooling, and failure to adhere to the terms of the treaties. On the whole, First Nations sought changes that would enable them to advance economically and re-establish control of their own affairs, without assimilating and giving up status.[42]

In 1948 the committee recommended a complete revision of the Indian Act to remove many of its coercive methods without altering its assimilative purpose.[43] The committee report assumed that the work of assimilation and integration was well advanced, and that all that was required was a little more time and less bureaucratic intervention in First Nation communities. The legislation, which was based on both the committee's recommendations and suggestions from the Indian Affairs Branch of the Department of Citizenship and Immigration, and was finally passed in 1951, adopted the same assumptions and goals. While many of the most obnoxious features, such as involuntary enfranchisement and prohibitions on consumption of alcohol, were deleted, and while the department's ability to interfere politically was reduced somewhat, the general outlines of the policy remained unchanged. The 1951 act assumed that the purpose of Indian policy was the end of Indians, as they became assimilated and chose to integrate themselves into the economic, political, and social life of Canada. As a leading authority has written, the 1951 act merely "returned to the philosophy of the original [1876] Indian Act: civilization was to be encouraged but not directed or forced on the Indian people."[44] After the fine sentiments in 1946, and after the committee had listened to scores of leaders, little of what they said was incorporated into legislation. All the same, a future national leader believed that the 1951 amendment "did lay the foundation for change and flexibility in Indian-Government relations."[45]

Through the 1950s, First Nations had to contend with a perpetuation of the regime that assumed their infantile character and sought their emergence into Euro-Canadian adulthood. One manifestation of that continuity was the federal government's emphasis on integration, particularly in schooling, rather than segregation. This ideological shift was a reflection of a new emphasis on training First Nations people for citizenship. They were now perceived as citizens-in-training or potential citizens.[46] Another way in which policy appeared to change while staying constant in its objective was the expertise on which Indian Affairs now relied. From the late 1940s onward, the department was increasingly less likely to look to church officials for information and guidance; now it was ever more enamoured of the research and policy suggestions that medical researchers and social scientists provided.[47] The goal, however, was still the absorption of First Nations into the general citizenry. Although policy was much better funded in the 1950s, it changed relatively little in its purpose. Education, which was increasingly being carried out in provincial schools as Indian Affairs tried to shift from segregated and residential schooling to integrated education, still attempted to assimilate the Aboriginal child. And it continued to fail.[48] Only a small minority of First Nation children graduated from the schools, fewer still from post-secondary institutions; but some of those who did emerged with a burning desire to change the state in which Indigenous people had to live.

During the 1950s and 1960s, changes in public attitudes also occurred that helped to bring on another attempt at policy revision. During the resource-based boom that fueled much of the prosperity Canada enjoyed until the recession of 1957, Euro-Canadian enterprises began to penetrate Indian Country in a way that they had not since the expansion of agricultural settlement in the late nineteenth century. Exploration for raw materials and energy heightened interest in areas of the country that had hitherto been considered economically marginal. For example, as Canada's Crown uranium corporation, Eldorado, expanded its operations in northern Saskatchewan, it encountered large numbers of Natives who were still following a traditional economy. Similarly, hydroelectric projects and base-mineral mines in the Precambrian Shield area of northern Manitoba, Ontario, and Quebec caused provincial governments and entrepreneurs to take a much livelier interest in regions of the country that were noted for their Indigenous populations. If the Second World War's horrific revelations had brought Canada's First Nations "out of irrelevance" in a moral sense, then the post-war resource boom did the same thing economically.

Since little had changed in their position, First Nations remained disgruntled. Their political organizations continued as finances permitted to express that disenchantment, but their ability to affect policy formation remained limited. Nonetheless, at least some Euro-Canadians worried increasingly about First Nations policy. The reason for their concern had to do with more than the relevance of Native peoples to the country's economy. The post-war decolonization movement throughout the world raised questions among thoughtful Canadians about how long Canada could go on treating Indigenous communities as internal colonies. The civil rights movement of the 1960s in the United States posed similar riddles, while providing both Natives and non-Natives in Canada with object lessons in how to bring about change and what the consequences could be of refusal to change discriminatory policies directed against non-Caucasians. A future national leader said that the 1960s were "the decade in which we were rediscovered."[49]

The Trudeau government that was elected in 1968 under the slogans of the "Just Society" and "participatory democracy" was a response to, and was particularly imbued with, the idea that it was time for fairer treatment of a variety of disadvantaged groups. In the same period, surveys by social scientists of the conditions in which Natives lived provided proof that the policies, whether modified in method by the 1951 amendments or not, simply did not work. A prime example of the increased reliance on social scientists in policy-making was the Hawthorn Report that reported in the mid-1960s that change, including a change in approach, was necessary.[50] Harry Hawthorn and his colleagues coined a memorable phrase about First Nation status. Their report pointed out that First Nations endured inferior conditions but deserved better status: "Indians should be regarded as 'citizens plus'; in addition to the normal rights and duties of citizenship, Indians possess certain additional rights as charter members of the Canadian community."[51]

The consequence of Indigenous disgruntlement, the new-found articulateness of non-white peoples throughout the world, and increased awareness that existing policy did not work was a new initiative in the later 1960s to redefine policy. The Pearson government (1963–8) committed itself to revise the Indian Act after an elaborate series of consultations with Indigenous organizations.[52] The election of a new Liberal government headed by a man pledged to the creation of a "Just Society" and "participatory democracy" led to an expansion of the project to a full-blown search for a comprehensive, new policy towards Native peoples and to a renewed commitment to consultation. It would turn out, however, that Trudeau's strong liberal values were at one and the same time the most powerful force for policy change and the single greatest influence in favour of a policy that First Nation organizations would reject.

Trudeau's genuine commitment to popular participation in the policy-making process ensured that all those involved in the policy review that preoccupied parts of the bureaucracy through the winter of 1968–9 would make at least a show of consulting Native groups. But, at the same time, Trudeau's individualism left him unsympathetic to arguments for group rights, and his obsession with defeating the claims of French-Canadian nationalists for special status for Quebec made him anxious to avoid creating any precedents that recognized racial or ethnic groups in legislative or constitutional ways. Perhaps Trudeau's attitude was best expressed in two of his statements. In one he echoed former American president John F. Kennedy, saying "We will be just in our time" in response to historical arguments for redress of Natives' grievances.[53] Another Trudeau comment illustrated his opposition to special status and treaties: "It's inconceivable I think that in a given society, one section of the society have a treaty with the other section of the society. We must all be equal under the laws and we must not sign treaties amongst ourselves ... We can't recognize aboriginal rights because no society can be built on historical 'might-have-beens.'"[54] In other words, Trudeau was unimpressed by historical arguments that Canadians should make redress for past transgressions, and he perceived the body politic as composed of individuals who related to their governments as atoms or isolated entities rather than members of ethnic, racial, class, or regional collectivities. These views worked at cross purposes with Trudeau's commitment to consult the First Nation organizations. If they were consulted, they would make it clear how much they differed with the new prime minister.

But the consultations that went on in the name of participatory democracy were not genuine. The series of meetings that took place in 1968–9 were, to use a 1960s phrase, "a dialogue of the deaf." First Nation organizations had finally succeeded in 1961 in establishing a truly national body, the National Indian Council (NIC), thanks largely to the efforts of Prairie leaders. Perhaps even more important was the fact that, in the later 1960s, First Nation groups up to and including the NIC were beginning to receive better funding, and, with their better organization and funding, they now found themselves able to present their views in a series of cogent, effective arguments. They stressed that they remained committed to the twin

Telford Adams, George Manuel, A.H. Brass, Marion Meadmore, David Knight, and Joe Keeper
made up the Temporary Committee of the National Indian Council in 1961.

goals of advancement and retention of their identity. A common feature of their presentations was a demand that Ottawa create an Indian Claims Commission with power to settle the increasing number of claims that Native bodies were developing. Their model was an American commission that Washington had set up, and part of their argument for a Canadian version was a recommendation of the Joint Parliamentary Committee of the later 1940s in favour of such a body for Canada. They articulated these views and demands with great clarity and force between the summer of 1968 and the spring of 1969. The final consultation session at the end of April 1969, concluded with an agreement for the government to fund still more "future consultations." Though First Nations said they were discouraged by the slow pace of the talks, they also told the Indian Affairs minister, Jean Chrétien, "We are happy with the recognition of yourself that we in this meeting have entered into what you call a new era. Because for the first time our people as a whole are proposing to work with you on a basis of partnership rather than on a basis of directives from your officials. Our delegation is extremely pleased that this has occurred."[55] Within two months they would be very displeased.

On 25 June, the first anniversary of the Trudeau government's election, Chrétien rose in the House of Commons to release the long-awaited White Paper on Indian Policy.* It would turn out that it was as much the assumptions behind the white paper as its content that would cause the government its greatest problems. The *Statement of the Government of Canada on Indian Policy, 1969*, which claimed to be the product of "a year's intensive discussions with Indian people," argued that Canada's First Nations were disadvantaged because they enjoyed a unique legal status. The problems of poverty, high rates of incarceration, political impotence, and economic marginality were not attributable to insensitive government policies or generations of racial prejudice. It was not because First Nations lacked control of their own affairs or because they had been systematically dispossessed of their lands that they experienced severe economic and social problems. No. The explanation was that the law treated them differently, that they had a special status as Indians. The "separate legal status of Indians and the policies which have flowed from it have kept the Indian people apart from and behind other Canadians." Canada and First Nations had erred in travelling "the road of different status, a road which has led to a blind alley of deprivation and frustration." The white paper proposed that they change course to "a road that would lead gradually away from different status to full social, economic and political participation in Canadian life."

The language of the white paper made it clear that it was a path of the government's, not First Nations' choosing. "This Government believes in equality," and "Only a policy based on this belief can enable the Indian people to realize their needs and aspirations." To that end it recommended "that the legislative and constitutional bases of discrimination be removed" by abolishing Indian status, that for First Nations "services come through the same channels and from the same government agencies" as they do for other Canadians, and "that control of Indian lands be transferred to the Indian people." It proposed, accordingly, "that the Indian Act be repealed," that provinces "take over the same responsibility for Indians that they have for other citizens," and that the federal government "wind up that part of the Department of Indian Affairs and Northern Development which deals with Indian

---

* The term "white paper," though perhaps unfortunate given the subject matter, had no racial connotation. A white paper was simply a statement of preliminary government policy, issued after a series of consultations and prior to cabinet adoption of a plan for legislation. It was a stage in an elaborate process of review, consultation, and policy formulation that Trudeau had introduced after his election in 1968. It might as easily have been termed a "position paper" or "preliminary policy proposal," or, as was the case several years later with immigration policy, a "green paper."

Affairs." Indian status would be abolished, First Nations would relate to their governments as individuals in precisely the way that other citizens did, and as a collectivity they would function just like French Canadians or citizens of Ukrainian ancestry. "Today," intoned the white paper, Canada "is made up of many people with many cultures. Each has its own manner of relating to the other; each makes its own adjustments to the larger society." Indians, as Indians, would disappear; Indians would become just another element in a multicultural Canada. The federal government planned to assist the transition, said the white paper, with generous help, but within five years the Department of Indian Affairs was to disappear. So would First Nations as a special group.

The government thought this program was fair, a necessary step towards the "Just Society."[56] If some argued that such a treatment would be a violation of treaty obligations, the government had three answers. First, this policy was supposedly being adopted after consultations with the Indigenous people themselves. Second, the services that First Nations were receiving in the 1960s went "far beyond what could have been foreseen by those who signed the treaties." And, third, "once Indian lands are securely within Indian control, the anomaly of treaties between groups within society and the government of that society will require that these treaties be reviewed to see how they can be equitably ended." If critics argued that these changes would do away with Indian status and claims before they were satisfied, the white paper responded that "aboriginal claims to land ... are so general and undefined that it is not realistic to think of them as specific claims capable of remedy except through a policy and program that will end injustice to Indians as members of the Canadian community." It was true that Ottawa "had intended to introduce legislation to establish an Indian Claims Commission to hear and determine Indian claims. Consideration of the questions raised at the consultations and the review of Indian policy have raised serious doubts as to whether a Claim Commission as proposed to Parliament in 1965 is the right way to deal with the grievances of Indians put forward as claims."[57]

The white paper adopted government solutions and ignored First Nation proposals. The latter had said that they wanted economic and social recovery without losing their identity; the white paper proposed the extinction of their separate status as a step towards dealing with problems that Ottawa said were the consequence of a different status. First Nations had made it clear that they intended to hold the federal government to the commitments it had made in treaties, obligations that were embodied – often perversely – in the Indian Act. The white paper proposed to absolve the federal government of its commitments by revoking Indian status, eliminating the Department of Indian Affairs, and transferring responsibility for Indigenous matters mainly to the provincial governments. First Nations had been pressing for two decades for a claims commission that would respond to their argument that Aboriginal title justified extensive compensation for the loss of lands and resources; the proposed policy airily dismissed the concept of Aboriginal rights and explicitly rejected the establishment of an Indian Claims Commission. And all of this occurred after a year of supposed consultation; all this was done in the name of equality and justice.

The explanation for this grotesque conclusion to the policy review of 1968–9 is that the process of formulating policy became subordinated to the political needs of government. To a considerable extent the bureaucrats in Indian Affairs had opposed meaningful change, and throughout the policy review process they had given advice that would have resulted in traditional policies being recommended. The political operatives in the Prime Minister's Office and the Privy Council Office, impatient with the bureaucrats, seized control of the review. Since their most immediate constituency was the new prime minister, they shaped the proposals according to Trudeau's notions about individualism, equality, and the inappropriateness of recognizing ethnic and racial groups as collectivities. The brutal truth was that the series of consultations that had been carried out with First Nations never had any impact on the review of policy. At the end of April 1969, at the same time as Native leaders were congratulating Chrétien for listening to them and agreeing to continue the dialogue, officials were putting the final touches to a white paper whose assumptions, arguments, and recommendations were the antithesis of what First Nations had been saying. "The policy was a response to values within the policy-making arena, not to the basic problems facing Indians."[58]

It seemed that nothing had changed, not even in an age of "participatory democracy." When the final stage was reached, the process by which policy proposals were generated in 1969 paid no more heed to First Nation opinions and desires than earlier phases. The Joint Parliamentary Committee of 1946–8 had not been very responsive to Indigenous views, but that review had at least been honest. The parliamentarians and officials had made little pretence of being guided by First Nations' views. From the Native standpoint, the twentieth-century quest for a new policy that culminated in the white paper of 1969 seemed to show that nothing had changed in a century. The formulation of the first post-Confederation Indian legislation in 1869 had not involved First Nations at all; the development of the white paper of 1969 did not involve them in any meaningful way, either.

CHAPTER FOURTEEN

Land Claims and Self-Government
from the White Paper to *Guerin*

The Alberta chiefs led the reaction to the white paper by responding bluntly to its assumptions and arguments. Their 1970 reply referred to the concept that Hawthorn had articulated a few years earlier: First Nations people were not merely citizens, as Trudeau regarded them, but a distinct category of people within Canada who had special rights. They were "citizens plus." Perhaps more important, in the process of responding to the white paper, organizations like Alberta's were politicized to fight the federal government and found that they were sufficiently united to do so for the first time in a disciplined and effective way. The white paper thus initiated two decades of political and constitutional struggle by Native peoples. The Alberta chiefs argued that "the recognition of Indian status is essential for justice." Ottawa "must admit its mistakes and recognize that the treaties are historic, moral and legal obligations." The Alberta chiefs "are opposed to any system of [land] allotment that would give individuals ownership with rights to sell" and they "reject the White Paper proposal that the Indian Act be repealed" and "this proposal to abolish the Indian Affairs Branch." "Freedom depends on having financial and social security first."[1]

Another spectacular response came from Harold Cardinal, the Cree president of the Indian Association of Alberta, whose book *The Unjust Society* sarcastically dissected the white paper and the century of Indian policy that stood behind it. It was, said Cardinal, "a thinly disguised programme of extermination through assimilation" that was reminiscent of American policies of termination and much worse. He continued, "The Americans to the south of us used to have a saying: 'The only good Indian is a dead Indian,'" while the Canadian government believed "the only

Harold Cardinal (right front) was the author of *The Unjust Society*,
an effective polemic against the 1969 white paper.

good Indian is a non-Indian" and that to survive the Indian "must become a good little brown white man." Moreover, as Cardinal put it, "Talking and listening have been one-way streets with white men and Indians. Until very recently white men have expected Indians to do all the listening." First Nations were no longer willing to participate in this one-way conversation, he said: "We want the white man to shut up and listen to us, really listen for a change." Equally important, they no longer trusted non-Native politicians: "We will not trust the government with our futures any longer. Now they must listen to and learn from us."[2]

These were only the most eloquent of a series of denunciations that soon forced the federal government to beat a retreat from its white paper. The Union of Ontario Indians called the minister a liar; the Manitoba Indians issued their own Brown Paper to counter the analysis in the government's white paper; BC Natives weighed in; and gradually newspaper editorialists and academics swung into line by attacking the lack of consultation with First Nations and the call for their termination.

Although Chrétien and Trudeau started off defending the policy, they soon were pleading that it contained merely proposals for discussion, and in less than a year they recanted. In September 1969, Ottawa threw First Nations a sop by agreeing, finally, to the financial backing for Indian claims research that the organizations had been seeking for years. When that did little to still the outcry, which was amplified by angry reaction to the government's December 1969 appointment of a single Indian Claims Commissioner without authority to investigate claims based on Aboriginal title, the government began to move away from the policy in the white paper.

The next spring Trudeau said, "If the White people and the Indian people in Canada don't want the proposed policy, we're not going to force it down their throats." When he met the Alberta chiefs to receive the Red Paper in June 1970, the prime minister assured them that the government was prepared to participate in a dialogue for as long as the First Nations thought necessary. "You know, a hundred years has been a long time and if you don't want an answer in another year, we'll take two, three, five, ten, or twenty – the time you people decide to come to grips with this problem. And we won't force any solution on you, because we are not looking for any particular solution."[3]

The discordant notes of the white paper of 1969 continued to echo through the 1970s and into the 1980s. In the first place, the fraudulent consultations and ill-advised recommendations had planted deep suspicions among First Nations. They continued to suspect that Ottawa was attempting to implement, piecemeal, the 1969 policy of termination of status and transfer of responsibility for Indian matters to the provinces. The 1969 statement became a benchmark against which every initiative or proposal was measured, a crude litmus test into which every politician's speech was dunked for an instant reading. This distrust helped to embitter First Nation–government relations during the 1970s.

The other legacy of the white paper was the stimulus it gave to Indigenous politicization and organization. In their uniformly hostile reactions to it, Native leaders found a basis for a pan-Canadian unity they had long sought but failed to achieve. Moreover, in their first political test – the resistance to the white paper by the National Indian Brotherhood (NIB) and the various provincial federations – they had seen that unified and militant action worked. The granting of federal funding for claims research and Trudeau's renunciation of the white paper were interpreted as victories for organization. The white paper had given them a common enemy against whom to mobilize, and the prime minister's retreat had encouraged their troops. It would not be the last.

The key to understanding the events during the decade after the white paper fiasco of 1969 is the National Indian Brotherhood. The NIB was a spinoff of the National Indian Council (NIC), which the Federation of Saskatchewan Indians and other Prairie organizations had done much to found. Through most of the 1960s the NIC carried on low-key lobbying efforts and organized student exchanges and celebrations of First Nation culture. The NIC's highpoint, perhaps, was the Indian Pavilion at Expo '67, the world's fair in Montreal, which attracted a great deal of international attention. But the NIC was experiencing problems as well at the same time. It was troubled by tensions between treaty First Nations, principally from the Prairie provinces, and Métis and non-status Indians over the strategy to be followed. First Nations with treaties preferred to pursue claims on the basis of the treaty promises, but those without treaties (both Indians and Métis) found it more attractive to argue from a basis of Aboriginal rights. The latter group had never signed treaties that might be construed as having extinguished their primordial rights. In 1968 the NIC split into the National Indian Brotherhood and Canadian Métis Society. The NIB found itself propelled into national prominence and leadership of First Nation peoples largely as a consequence of the reaction to the white paper of 1969. But in the 1970s, especially during the leadership of George Manuel, a Shuswap from British Columbia, the body adopted a more political strategy in Canada while looking outward for international links and support. The NIB adopted a coherent program to present to the federal government, and also attempted to position the Canadian Native organizations in the worldwide decolonization movement. Manuel in particular subscribed to the notion that First Nations and other Natives around the world constituted a Fourth World of dependent peoples, internal colonies in a variety of modern states. Such a conceptual approach equipped the NIB advocates with an ideology to understand and present their case to the public, while providing it with allies internationally.[4] The other reason for the NIB's success in the 1970s was its successful campaign to wrest control of programs that affected Indigenous people from the federal government. A significant achievement of Manuel's early years in the NIB presidency was securing stable funding of the organization from Ottawa. Core funding assured financial support for the ongoing work of the NIB, and Department of Indian Affairs and Northern Development (DIAND) funding of research in support of claims provided a stability and impetus that no national Native political body had previously enjoyed.

Working from such a solid base, the NIB undertook a series of political initiatives in the 1970s, two of the more significant of which concerned social services and education. First Nation distrust of Ottawa, combined with well-established disenchantment with existing programs, pushed the NIB and provincial organizations, especially on the Prairies, to demand that Ottawa turn direction of welfare, child protection, and education programs over to them. These demands rarely met with success, and in some cases what can only be described as deliberate sabotage, by the department, of Indigenous-controlled social assistance and counselling programs occurred once management was surrendered.[5] The area of child welfare has been a particularly sensitive one because First Nations insist that their familial structures and child-rearing practices are different from those of the mainstream society. They oppose "adopting out," as they call the practice of sending Native children out of their communities for adoption, as usually happened when child-rescue and child-protection programs were under government administration.[6] In the 1960s and 1970s, these problems were aggravated by what became known as the Sixties Scoop: the adopting of Indigenous children in care by non-Native parents.

The First Nation experience in gaining control of the education of their young has been more successful. The abject failure of the government-controlled and church-administered educational system either to assimilate or to impart learning to Natives had become painfully obvious to all by the 1960s. First Nation groups were disenchanted, most missionary bodies wanted to retire from the field, and Ottawa was aghast at the rising costs of residential schooling.[7] By the end of the 1960s the residential schools were being phased out, some of them being turned into hostels in which children resided while attending neighbouring public schools. Since the alternative to residential schooling, integrated schooling in public schools, was proving to be neither more successful pedagogically nor more satisfactory to Native children, government was in a quandary.

Finally, in 1973, the federal government acquiesced to a demand by the NIB that it transfer control and funding to bands, endorsing a Brotherhood position paper on "Indian Control of Indian Education." While there were serious problems in beginning the real implementation of the policy and in carrying it through all levels of education, significant advances have been made over the past forty-five years, both in making the provincial schools more "user-friendly" to Native children and in expanding the system of First Nation–controlled schools. Particularly in the Prairie provinces, progress has been made in redesigning curricula to make them more reflective of and relevant to Native children, in finding or developing instructional materials that depict Natives as part of the visible world, in establishing special teacher-training programs, and, in some cases, in accelerating the hiring of Natives by both Native-controlled and regular school boards.

Contemporary developments were also working a fundamental shift in the handling of disputes over Native lands in the early 1970s. The resource-based economic boom that had being going on since the 1940s regularly caused both major corporations and governments to covet First Nation lands for resource developments and for the construction of infrastructure. A harbinger of this phenomenon was the construction of the Alaska Highway through northern British Columbia and Yukon to Alaska by the U.S. Corps of Engineers during the war, an intrusion that proved disruptive to the Natives of the region. After the war the discovery of enormous oil pools in Alberta, where Leduc #1 came on stream in 1947, drew hitherto remote groups, such as the Lubicon Lake Cree in northern Alberta, into a maelstrom of development activity. Similar upheavals were experienced in most provinces, such as those caused by uranium development by Eldorado Nuclear in Saskatchewan, or the Peace River hydroelectric power project in northern British Columbia. These examples of economic "progress" were harmful to First Nation and Métis communities because governments and corporations usually ignored their customary land rights in the rush for spoils, and the economic benefits of "progress" rarely came to the Native communities in anything but short-term or low-paying work.

These economic patterns combined in the 1970s with long-standing Aboriginal concerns to produce major changes in law and government policy that would affect First Nations for at least the remainder of the century. In Quebec, where the recently elected Liberal government of Robert Bourassa was promising to create 100,000 jobs by developing the hydroelectric potential of part of the James Bay watershed, the James Bay Cree decided to take a stand against a project that was slated to go ahead without dealing with their territorial rights. In 1972 a coalition of these Cree and Inuit from northern Quebec succeeded in temporarily stopping the project by securing a court injunction. Although the James Bay Corporation soon succeeded in having the ruling reversed, the brief victory was a shock to everyone concerned, a sharp reminder to deal with the Native peoples before trying to profit from the resources of their land.[8]

While negotiations were going on over this issue in Quebec, the Nisga'a of British Columbia finally had their decades-old campaign for recognition of their ownership of Nass Valley lands before the Supreme Court of Canada. Although the Nisga'a lost, they won, and they won for all First Nations that had not signed territorial treaties. In 1973, the court ruled against them in a split decision, three judges upholding the Nisga'a position, three arguing that their Aboriginal title had been extinguished, and one jurist deciding against them on a technical point. Although their appeal was rejected four to three, six of the seven judges did recognize in their ruling that Aboriginal title existed in Canadian law.[9] This outcome was an enormous legal advance, because hitherto Canadian law had rested on the 1888 decision in the St. Catharines Milling case, in which the Judicial Committee of the Privy

Council concluded that under the Royal Proclamation of 1763 Aboriginal rights to land consisted only of "a personal and usufructuary right, dependent on the good will of the Sovereign."[10] In the Nisga'a or *Calder* case in 1973, the highest court went much further when it implied that Aboriginal title was more than simply a right of usage. (Later in the 1970s, in the *Hamlet of Baker Lake* case, the criteria for establishing Aboriginal title were articulated: the claimants must be descended from an organized society that occupied the territory in dispute to the exclusion of all other peoples at the time of contact.)[11] The significance of what the Supreme Court did in 1973 was reflected in the bemused comment of Prime Minister Pierre Trudeau, he who had dismissed "historical might-have-beens" in 1969. To a delegation from the Union of British Columbia Indian Chiefs, Trudeau conceded a week after the *Calder* decision, "You have more legal rights than I thought you had."[12]

The consequences of the James Bay dispute and the Nisga'a ruling were dramatic. Late in 1975 Quebec signed the James Bay and Northern Quebec Agreement (JBNQA) with the Inuit and Cree litigants; this opened the way for what would turn out to be merely the first phase of James Bay hydroelectric development by surrendering 400,000 square miles in return for $150 million in grants and royalties over ten years, one-quarter of the royalties that Quebec would receive for the next fifty years, control of traditional Native sites that would not fall within the flooded area, and recognition of continuing hunting and fishing rights. The James Bay Agreement, in effect the first modern treaty, did not usher in a new golden age for the Quebec Cree and Inuit, but it did serve notice that a new era had arrived in government-Native dealings over resource-rich lands.[13] According to one authority, its implementation also fostered a regional sense of Cree identity where previously the Indigenous inhabitants had identified principally with their villages.[14]

The federal government responded creatively to the Nisga'a ruling. In 1973 Indian Affairs Minister Jean Chétien announced that henceforth Ottawa would deal with claims over lands not covered by treaty, and the following year the Office of Native Claims (ONC) was established to handle all aspects of the federal government's dealings over land claims issues. The government distinguished between comprehensive claims, which, like the Nisga'a or James Bay Cree cases, were assertions by First Nations that they held Aboriginal title to the lands in dispute, and specific claims, in which claimants had to establish that government had some "lawful obligation" to them that had not been discharged. Although specific claims could concern things other than land ownership, most specific claims that were handled by ONC from 1974 onward would be based on an allegation that Ottawa had not discharged an obligation arising from lands covered by treaty. The federal government would also fund research into claims by Native groups, an important consideration for many potential claimants. Once research was completed, a claimant would file its case with the Office of Native Claims, which would decide whether negotiation was in order and advise the government accordingly. If negotiations were deemed to be justified, the ONC would participate in the government bargaining team, and, if resolution was achieved, the ONC would assist with implementation of the settlement. Although the multiple roles played by the ONC would cause the claims resolution process to bog down in less than a decade, in the middle 1970s the future looked bright for Native claimants, whether they were asserting Aboriginal title to lands or alleging that there was an undischarged "lawful obligation" to them owed by the federal Crown.

These important breakthroughs in law and policy, like the political assertiveness of National Indian Brotherhood on funding, social programs, and education, led naturally to an emphasis on First Nation self-government. The linkage between claims resolution and self-government was even embodied in the Cree-Naskapi Agreement of 1984, which provided a measure of self-government in northern Quebec in concert with the James Bay and Northern Quebec Agreement. The evolution during the remainder of the 1970s and after towards greater emphasis on self-government was natural in two senses. First, if First Nations were going to administer policies that previously had been under government control, they would begin to regard bands and provincial federations as bureaucratic as well as political bodies. Second, First Nations had never conceded having surrendered powers of self-government to European powers. A succession of groups and individuals had insisted that they were not conquered peoples but groups who retained their right to decide their own affairs. The Six Nations had sternly pointed out this fact to British officials when the United Kingdom surrendered Iroquois lands to the Americans after the Revolution. From the first, attempts in the Province of Canada in the 1850s to empower civil government to interfere in internal band matters had evoked angry reactions from First Nations. And the Mohawk of the Brantford area had been locked in a battle from the nineteenth century well into the twentieth over whether their own traditional leaders or Ottawa's elected chieftains were the legitimate rulers of their community.

Similarly, as Canada extended its control westward after 1869, it was met by First Nation groups that insisted that no one – certainly not the Hudson's Bay Company – had the right to sell their lands or waive their right to manage their own affairs. Big Bear's comment at the making of Treaty Six in 1876 that he feared the rope around his neck was a metaphorical way of saying that he would not accept the imposition of Canadian law. BC First Nations in the 1880s had similarly expressed concern at the prospect of Canada's law being administered in their lands.[15] Throughout Canadian history, First Nations had insisted that they were not subjects but allies, and that they retained their rights of self-government even if they agreed to share their lands. As a chief of the Federation of Saskatchewan Indian Nations summarized the case, "Indian Nations are sovereign by virtue of their aboriginal rights to land. Those sovereign rights are a potent force forever ebbing and flowing on the tides of history. It is a force which cannot be restricted by political edicts or legal instruments. It transcends courts and political systems. It is the aboriginal inheritance."[16] When the National Indian Brotherhood embarked on a drive for self-government in the 1970s, it was simply expressing a well-established belief among First Nations.

Since the early 1970s the case for self-government has been advanced with varying degrees of success. Control over education and some aspects of welfare and child care have certainly been parts of a general thrust towards self-government. And the Department of Indian Affairs and Northern Development has always conceded that bands have at least a limited scope for self-regulation on the reserves by Band Council Resolutions, which have a force approximating that of statutes passed by other levels of government. But for a number of reasons self-government has largely remained something sought rather than achieved. The first is that there is no unanimity on what constitutes self-government and to whom it applies. Will First Nation legislative bodies have jurisdiction over everyone, or only Indians, while on the reserve? Will these bodies have jurisdiction over First Nation people when they are off Indian lands, for example, when they are residing in urban areas? What will happen if First Nation legislators attempt to regulate behaviour, whether of non-Indians in Indian territory or Indians outside Indian-controlled lands, and those people resist? How will disputes between individuals and First Nation governments be handled? Can First Nation governments be hauled before courts established by other levels of government? Can employees of bands bring their employers before a human rights tribunal or labour relations board if they feel aggrieved?

An illustration that some of these questions are real is the 1973 dispute between the Sagkeeng (Fort Alexander) First Nation and its teachers. Phil Fontaine, the young and determined chief of the band, decided that they needed to change the teachers in their schools. When he called Glenn Sigurdson, his former lawyer, and said, "I want to fire the teachers here at the Fort," Sigurdson responded, "Phil, small detail. You don't hire them." Fontaine observed, "Yeah, I guess that's a point. What if I just issue an order that they cannot come on the reserve?" "That should do it!" agreed the lawyer.[17] Not surprisingly, the teachers appealed to the Canada Labour Relations Board (CLRB), which in 1984 ruled against the Manitoba band's actions. At no time in the protracted proceedings did the band acknowledge the legitimacy of the tribunal to which the teachers took the case or their own obligation to Canadian labour relations and human rights legislation. Band leaders were fined and jailed for contempt of the Federal Court of Canada that ordered implementation of a CLRB ruling. The dispute was finally resolved when the band, which still refused to reinstate the teachers, agreed to pay four of them a total of $226,000 in compensation, and the teachers dropped a demand that they be given back their jobs.[18]

A second difficulty with winning acceptance for First Nation self-government is the fact that it runs up against the liberal democratic values of the majority population. Many non-Natives do not understand how sovereign First Nations within the country can operate in harmony with the existing system. Did Canadians not reject such a notion in the case of Quebec separatism, they ask? Many people, perhaps only at a subconscious level, reject political claims based on racial or ethnic and collective concepts because they understand civil society to be a collection of citizens who relate to government as individuals and are treated equally regardless of their place of residence or race or language. This barrier to the full acceptance of First Nation self-government is, in most cases, the product of a fundamental difference of political philosophy. It will take a great deal of effort and understanding to remove the obstacle.

Third, a major problem in advancing towards self-government has been economic. First Nations and both levels of government recognize that Native self-government without the resources to operate will prove a mockery. Consequently, First Nation, Métis, and Inuit organizations have insisted that discussions of increasing self-government be accompanied by the negotiated settlement of claims to land and resources that they have advanced. But few of the land claims have been settled, in part because the provinces have proven reluctant to make Crown lands available for concession to Native groups.

Finally, the campaign for self-government that the National Indian Brotherhood began in the 1970s has been sidetracked by protracted wranglings over constitutional renewal in the country at large. Ironically, the interminable arguments over patriation of an amending power and creation of a Charter of Rights, while they deflected the NIB's political campaign, ended up by giving both it and other Native groups a new basis from which to continue their struggle for political control over their own lives.

The search for a new constitutional formula sprang from Quebec separatism and Pierre Elliott Trudeau's battle against it – the reason he had entered federal politics in the first place. Trudeau believed that federalism was the ideal form of government for a vast, heterogeneous country such as Canada. He was equally implacable in his opposition to the modern force of nationalism and to the separatists in his home province. Trudeau believed that the existing constitution, especially its written portion then known as the British North America Act, was generally satisfactory. All that it needed was the addition of a formula for amending it within Canada (as a statute of the British parliament, the BNA Act could be amended only by the United Kingdom) and a bill of rights that would protect civil, political, and linguistic rights by moving these areas beyond the reach of the legislatures. Trudeau's answer to separatism was not greater power and autonomy for the French-Canadian homeland of Quebec, but the entrenchment of official bilingualism throughout Canada to make the whole country a congenial patrimony for all French Canadians. Although Trudeau worked consistently throughout his prime ministerial career at achieving his vision, he redoubled his efforts after the election of René Lévesque's Parti Québécois government in the autumn of 1976. A proposal for change in 1977–8 ultimately failed, but not before sparking a debate that engaged the leadership of the Native organizations.

The leaders of the National Indian Brotherhood recognized both that constitutional revision could affect their relationship to the federal government and that the process presented an opportunity to assert their role as another order of government. The NIB demanded that it be represented at forthcoming first ministers' meetings on the constitution, and, when the federal government offered only observer status, it boycotted the meetings in February 1979. In that year the NIB carried out a lobbying effort in Britain, whose parliament would have to put into legislation whatever Canadian politicians decided by way of constitutional changes, and at the same time obtained a commitment from the Liberal government that it would be given some form of limited participation in future constitutional talks scheduled for the autumn of 1979. Trudeau's electoral defeat in May 1979 made no difference to this important advance, for the new government headed by Joe Clark announced that it would honour the promise of Indigenous participation in any talks. However, since the new Conservative government seemed committed to avoiding conflict with the provinces, especially Quebec, the NIB was not likely to get a chance to participate in first ministers' talks.

A renewed opportunity was provided for First Nation assertiveness with Trudeau's unexpected return to power and the Quebec referendum campaign in the early months of 1980. The Grits' February victory reinstated a prime minister who was still determined to renew the constitution, and the federal Liberals' important contribution to the defeat of the anti-federal forces in the May referendum in Quebec emboldened Trudeau's supporters to make one final, determined effort to achieve constitutional change. During the course of the referendum campaign, many politicians from outside Quebec had pledged that defeat of the Lévesque government's proposal would lead to their cooperating in another attempt at constitutional renewal. Trudeau tried to call in those markers by initiating another round of talks on constitutional change in 1980–1.

To the intense disappointment of the NIB and other Native groups, the earlier promises of at least limited First Nation participation in these talks were not honoured. (During the period 1980–2 the NIB was reorganizing itself into the Assembly of First Nations, a title that reflected Indigenous peoples' view that their political organization represented nations that had a right to negotiate with other governments on terms of equality.) What was worse was that the western premiers took very firm positions against the inclusion of any protections in a new constitution for either First Nation self-government or Indigenous rights. The nadir of the First Nation cause seemed to be reached in November 1981, when nine of the ten provinces concluded a late-night agreement with federal representatives on an amending formula and the terms of a Charter of Rights and Freedoms, terms that left out any protection of either women's equality rights or Native rights. Prairie premiers' opposition forced Ottawa to drop a bid to recognize Aboriginal rights in the revised constitution.

By energetic effort, both the women's and Native organizations rescued something from the constitutional debacle during the winter of 1981–2. They lobbied ferociously to force the politicians to include protections for women's and Aboriginal rights in the Constitution Act, 1982, and eventually both succeeded. In the case of the Indigenous cause, lobbying succeeded in getting agreement to insert the sentence, "The existing aboriginal and treaty rights of the aboriginal peoples of Canada are hereby recognized and affirmed." And, even more important for the Métis, "aboriginal peoples" was defined to include "the Indian, Inuit and Métis peoples of Canada." Inclusion of the first sentence meant that these rights were placed beyond the reach of parliament and legislatures. What rights Inuit, First Nations, and Métis enjoyed in April 1982, when the new constitution was formally adopted, were enshrined in Canada's fundamental law. But there were problems. The first was that the adjective "existing" was restrictive; it was included so as to prevent resort to the courts in an effort to get a definition of "aboriginal rights" that was more extensive than politicians might be willing to embrace. The second difficulty was that no one knew what constituted "existing aboriginal and treaty rights." Therefore, it was also agreed that a series of conferences would be held with representatives of the Aboriginal peoples' organizations to define these "rights."

Assembly of First Nations representatives (L–R) Lou Demerais, Georges Erasmus,
Rob Robinson, and Harold Cardinal hold a press conference during the March 1984
first ministers' conference on Aboriginal constitutional issues.

The process of constitutional renewal, then, was both a distraction and a support
for the cause of First Nation self-government. The bruising battles over constitutional reform in 1978–9 and 1980–2 absorbed the time and money of the National
Indian Brotherhood and Assembly of First Nations. Though these struggles seemed
at first to have resulted in a terrible betrayal, they ended up giving protection to
Natives' "existing" rights and promising discussions to define what rights existed.
This inclusion gave the Native political bodies a platform from which to advance
their cause, and all three groups took full advantage of it to argue in favour of
self-government and other political objectives. At constitutional conferences in
1983, 1984, 1985, and 1987, representatives of the First Nations, the Métis (Native
Council of Canada),[19] and the Inuit argued that they were entitled to redress of their
land claims, respect for their treaties, and the right of self-government. Although
Trudeau argued heatedly at his final appearance at these conferences in 1984 that
the premiers should accept Native self-government in principle, leaving to later the
working out of the details of what the concept meant, the western premiers refused

to agree. At the 1985 conference the issue remained unsettled; and there was no progress at the conference in the spring of 1987. (Ironically, premiers who could not accept Native self-government in principle because they did not understand fully its implications, a few months later in 1987 would enthusiastically adopt the Meech Lake Accord, which contained commitments of astonishing vagueness to Quebec's "distinct society.")

However, if the cause of First Nation self-government stalled at the first ministers' conferences, it received further impetus elsewhere. In 1983 a Special Committee of the House of Commons on Indian Self-Government (the Penner Committee) unexpectedly produced a report that endorsed an expansive version of First Nation self-government.[20] Perhaps because the committee contained three non-voting members from Native political bodies and held extensive hearings at which many Native representatives testified, it produced a report that endorsed the expansion of the concept of Aboriginal right from the basis for claims to lands to a platform for political self-determination or self-government. The Indian Act had always purported to *confer* on bands the right to establish their own councils with limited powers, but the Penner Committee recommended that the right to self-government should be *recognized* by other governments and entrenched in the constitution. "Indian First Nations" would "form a distinct order of government in Canada." Such terminology signalled the adoption of the First Nation position that they were sovereign nations still possessing the power to regulate their own affairs. Thus, the Penner Committee conferred a legitimacy on First Nation self-government that it had not hitherto enjoyed in mainstream Canadian society, and not even the setbacks at the first ministers' conferences could diminish the moral and political significance of that advance.

While Native political organizations had been pursuing recognition of their rights of self-government in the political arena with mixed results, behind the scenes the cause of land claims in general had been experiencing a similar mixture of discouraging and, more occasionally, encouraging results. The most discouraging part of the claims resolution experience in the decade after the establishment of the Office of Native Claims in 1974 was the excruciatingly slow pace of resolving claims. The problem existed both with comprehensive claims, those based on an assertion of Aboriginal title, and with specific claims, the more limited category in which an undischarged "lawful obligation" on the part of the federal Crown was alleged to exist. By 1981 no comprehensive claims had been settled, unless the James Bay and Northern Quebec Agreement was counted as one, and thirteen other cases were waiting in line. On the specific claims side, things were no better by 1981: twelve had been settled, and 250 were in various stages of preparation or consideration. Another review of the claims process four years later found that the logjam had grown worse: six comprehensive claims were under negotiation, with fifteen more (thirteen of them from British Columbia) accepted for future negotiation, and seven under review by the ONC. As the chair of the committee that had reviewed the process in 1985 observed, "At the current rate of settlement it could be another 100 years before all the [comprehensive] claims have been addressed."[21]

What had gone wrong? Simply, the Office of Native Claims had become more a bottleneck than a passageway to resolution. In part the problem was that the ONC played the role of prosecutor, judge, and jury. The chair of the 1985 claims review panel perceptively noted, "The government decides which claim is accepted, how much money will be made available to the claimant group for research and negotiations, when negotiations will begin, and the process for negotiations. Except where court action threatens a major development project, the government's patience for negotiation appears unlimited." On the other hand, the "aboriginal party has few resources other than the intelligence, commitment, and skill of its leaders, who must sit across the table from the representatives of the Government of Canada, with their apparently overwhelming resources and power." Under the circumstances, it "is hardly surprising that the aboriginal groups have little confidence in the fairness of the process, or in the government's desire for early settlements."[22] Problems stemming from the inherent unfairness of the process were compounded by a legalistic approach by ONC, which sometimes used technical legal arguments concerning excessive passage of time and usually proved reluctant to accept oral history research results that were put forward to substantiate the claimant's case.[23] Finally, the ONC had arbitrarily set limits on access to the claims process. At first it would not negotiate more than three comprehensive claims at one time, although it raised the number to six as the backlog increased. On the specific claims side, the ONC simply refused to consider claims arising from pre-Confederation incidents.

Oka, or Kanesatake, illustrated some of the shortcomings of the claims process between 1974 and the mid-1980s. Since the middle of the nineteenth century, matters had gone from bad to worse for the people on the Lake of Two Mountains in southwestern Quebec. They were embroiled in a long-running dispute with the Sulpicians, who claimed to own the land they lived on, over use of resources, and their relations were exacerbated by the conversion of many of them to Methodism. Conflict became so heated, with arson directed at the Roman Catholic church in 1877 and prosecutions of Natives in retaliation, that the federal government sought by two different methods to eliminate the source of strife. First, the government encouraged the migration of Aboriginal people from Oka to more remote locations.

By and large, only the Algonkian groups, Nipissing and Algonkin, found this option attractive, and by Confederation most of them had gone to the upper Ottawa
Valley and Golden Lake west of Ottawa. The Mohawk, the remaining Aboriginal
group at Kanesatake, were not attracted by relocation to distant, forested regions
because they were traditionally less oriented to a hunting-gathering economy
than those who had departed. When some of their number accepted another
government offer to transfer to a newly created Gibson reserve in the Muskoka
district of Ontario in1882, most of them soon returned to Kanesatake. Relations
between Mohawk and missionaries were still bad, although they did manage in
the 1880s to cooperate in a reforestation project to plant what would become
known as The Pines.[24]

The government, having failed to end the problem by relocation, reverted to
its other method, resolution in the courts. With Ottawa picking up the tab for the
Mohawk, a case was got into court under the name of Corinthe, a First Nation
resident of Kanesatake. When the Judicial Committee of the Privy Council ruled
on the *Corinthe* case in 1912, they found, as the law of the time forced it to, that
an 1841 statute of the Province of Canada declared the Sulpicians to be the title-
holders. Speaking of the 1841 legislation, the law lords "thought that the effect of
this act was to place beyond question the title of the respondents [Sulpicians] to
the Seigniory," making it impossible for the Mohawk to "establish an independent
title to possession or control in the administration ... neither by aboriginal title,"
tradition, or trusteeship obligations on the part of the missionaries. The supremacy
of parliament – represented in this instance by the legislature of the Province of
Canada – trumped Aboriginal title and every other consideration.[25] Although the
Mohawk never accepted the validity of this ruling, the Sulpicians, townspeople of
Oka, and Government of Quebec acted through the rest of the twentieth century as
though there was no longer any question of title. Property was transferred from religious order to government, and parcels were sold to individual non-Natives who
established themselves throughout the territory that the Mohawk called Kanesatake. This distribution was legally possible because Kanesatake had never been set
aside by an Order in Council as an Indian reserve. In the late 1950s, the Town of
Oka authorized the building of a nine-hole golf course near The Pines, adjacent to
a graveyard that the Mohawk had used for close to a century. Through their lawyer,
the people of Kanesatake complained to a joint parliamentary committee in 1961
that land "once reserved for Indian use and profit is now reserved for golf," and
added that they "consider the building of the clubhouse directly adjacent to our
graveyard a desecration and an insult to our sensibilities."[26]

The creation of the Office of Native Claims appeared to breathe life back into the Mohawk case at Kanesatake and other Quebec locations. The Kanesatake community joined with their kin at Akwesasne and Kahnawake in 1975 to launch a comprehensive claim for a large tract that covered southwestern Quebec and stretched well up the Ottawa Valley. The ONC rejected this claim a few months later, arguing that Aboriginal title to this large territory had been extinguished, but implied that it would look favourably on "specific claims which the Mohawks of Oka, St. Regis, and Caughnawaga may have with respect to lands contiguous or near their existing reserves."[27] The Kanesatake Mohawk responded to this in June 1977 with a specific claim, and then waited for a ruling. Finally, in October 1986, the ONC brusquely rejected their specific claim with the statement that they had "not demonstrated any outstanding lawful obligation on the part of the Federal Crown." Again, the ONC softened the blow by adding that the government recognized "that there is an historical basis for Mohawk claims related to land grants in the 18th century," and said that it was "willing to consider a proposal for alternative means of redress of the Kanesatake Band's grievance."[28] Once more the Mohawk prepared to wait for this vague invitation to bring some results.

If the experience of the Mohawk of Kanesatake illustrated the problems that bands faced in attempting to get satisfaction from Ottawa on comprehensive or specific land claims, at least one other group scored a spectacular success through the courts that would transform the specific claims area totally. (In fairness, it ought also to be noted that in 1984 the government did reach agreement with the Inuvialuit, or Inuit of the western Northwest Territories, in what was known as the COPE comprehensive claim from the title of the group, Committee of Original People's Entitlement. The COPE settlement provided $45 million in 1977 dollars and 242,000 square kilometres to the Inuvialuit.) In 1984 the Supreme Court of Canada produced the *Guerin* decision in an action concerning the Musqueam band of British Columbia. The Musqueam alleged that their financial interests had not been well represented by their trustee, the Department of Indian Affairs, which had leased some of their land to a private golf course for below-market rent. What compounded the problem and irritated the First Nation was that for a long time they could not even get a copy of the lease. The Supreme Court agreed with a lower court that had awarded the Musqueam $10 million for the loss they had suffered. More important than the money, however, were two other aspects of the highest court's ruling. First, the *Guerin* decision established in Canadian law that the Royal Proclamation was deemed to apply retrospectively in every part of the country. Second, *Guerin* articulated the doctrine that First Nations, as wards of the federal

Crown, in law their trustee, could hold their trustee responsible for damages incurred by negligence in the administration of their affairs. The Crown had a fiduciary duty to First Nations, and could – as in the case of the Musqueam lease – be held liable for damages if it did not discharge that duty properly. This ruling opened up a vast area of potential litigation or argument with the Office of Native Claims, where now bands could argue that in incidents such as reserve surrenders where they had lost lands as a result of fraud or coercion by government officials, they were entitled to redress and compensation.[29] Even if the ruling did not make up for a decade of dissatisfaction with the ONC, it promised that the next decade of specific claims might be a lot more fruitful.

Progress was achieved in 1985 on the constitutional and legislative front, too, although in a somewhat roundabout way. The Charter of Rights and Freedoms that had been adopted in 1982 did not merely recognize and affirm existing Aboriginal and treaty rights. It also focused a spotlight on the Indian Act's discriminatory provisions. Since the 1850s, legislation governing First Nations had defined who was an Indian in a way that discriminated against women. Under the Indian Act, a First Nation woman who married a non-Indian lost her Indian status, and her children lost theirs too. Conversely, a First Nation man did not lose his status if he married a non-Indian woman; rather she became an "Indian." This gender discrimination had bothered many people for some time, particularly after the Supreme Court in the 1973 *Lavell* case upheld this discriminatory provision of the Indian Act. In 1975 a Maliseet woman, Sandra Lovelace, had taken her complaint against this gender discrimination to the Human Rights Committee of the United Nations. The Committee decided in 1981 that the Indian Act's provision barring Ms Lovelace from residence on the Tobique reserve was "an unjustifiable denial of her rights under" the United Nations' Covenant on Civil and Political Rights.[30] The UN decision was of limited practical value because of its unenforceability, but the Charter's prohibition of discrimination on the basis of gender made it essential that Ottawa grapple with the problem quickly. (The full implementation of the Charter was delayed until 1985 to give governments an opportunity to bring their legislation into line with the equality provisions in the 1982 document.)

The federal government concluded that it had no choice but to repeal the portion of the Indian Act that discriminated against First Nation women and their descendants, but many First Nation organizations were strenuously opposed. It was not so much that they favoured discrimination – though the heavily male character of their leadership caused some observers to wonder even on that point – as that they feared the consequences of making it possible for tens of thousands of people to reclaim Indian status. Some bands, especially in Alberta, were oil-rich and reluctant to share their wealth with a potential horde of returnees to the reserves. Others simply feared that they did not have enough land and other resources to cope with larger populations. Their efforts to persuade the federal government to put the financial resources in place to deal with larger band numbers before the discriminatory provision was repealed, of course, failed. Eventually, a compromise was worked out that satisfied the stringency of the Charter, though it did not please the First Nations. The discriminatory term would be repealed, and both women who had married non-Indians and their offspring could recover their status. But the question of determining if the portion of these people who had lost their status before 1985 would get band membership and services would be determined according to criteria that bands were invited to develop. It was a compromise that satisfied government but alarmed First Nations. Some leaders believed Ottawa had no right to tell them how to manage their internal affairs. Others were concerned about the precedent that the measure created by making a legislative distinction between Indian status and band membership.[31] Many other councils followed the wink-and-a-nudge that they got from Indian Affairs officials and drew up membership codes so stringent that they made admission to band membership and benefits extremely difficult.

The other setback that followed constitutional renewal was a split in 1985 in the ranks of the status Indians of Canada. The conferences leading up to and following from the making of the 1982 constitution made it ever clearer that there was a division of opinion and a clash of interests within the ranks of the national political body called the Assembly of First Nations. All the members of this organization were status Indians, but they differed in another important respect. Some of them, principally from the Prairie provinces and parts of the Territories, were descended from First Nations who had concluded treaties with the Dominion of Canada. They could argue for advances using a case built on either Aboriginal rights or treaty rights. But other First Nations had not made treaties that contained guarantees of educational and economic assistance. The only basis from which they could argue was Aboriginal rights. After the first ministers' conferences in 1983, 1984, and 1985 demonstrated that a case based strictly on "existing aboriginal" rights was getting nowhere, some First Nations wanted to shift strategy. When they could not persuade the AFN to go along with them, and when their representative, incumbent AFN chief David Ahenakew of Saskatchewan, was defeated by Georges Erasmus of the North West Territories, they left the Assembly and formed their own body, the

Prairie Treaty Nations Alliance. The difference of interest that underlay the division was real, and the decision of the Prairie First Nations to strike out on their own understandable, but the split, which was patched up later in the decade, temporarily weakened the Indigenous national political movement.

Another political problem of the 1980s that First Nations and other Native groups faced had nothing directly to do with the constitutional battle or the debate over Aboriginal versus treaty rights. The change in political fashions that occurred in the 1980s would have as powerful an impact on Indigenous people as on the population at large. These changes resulted in the election of more conservative governments and in a greater concern with deficit reduction. The combined effect of these ideological shifts was seen most clearly in the Native policies of the Tory government that was elected in September 1984.

The Mulroney government talked as though it were part of the neoconservative trend that had been noticeable in Western democracies for half a decade, though it behaved in office much as the discredited Trudeau Liberals had. The Conservatives' rhetoric about getting government off the back of business people and taxpayers tended to make Canadians think that they had put into power the Canadian equivalent of Britain's Margaret Thatcher or the United States' Ronald Reagan. The prime minister and his coterie encouraged this belief and sought to curry favour in the business community early in their mandate by appointing the deputy prime minister, Eric Nielsen of Yukon, to chair a task force to review a broad range of government programs and to report on their efficiency and the possibility of shrinking them. Relying strictly on a handful of bureaucrats and three outside consultants, and operating in great secrecy, Nielsen's group produced a preliminary report in April 1985 that concluded that Native peoples "were in a state of socio-economic deprivation," that federal programs were failing to change things, and that some spending on Natives went beyond the government's legal responsibilities.[32] The solution was to dissolve Indian Affairs, shifting some programs to other federal departments, and then transferring all of them to the provinces. The study group also recommended that comprehensive land claims were not to be proceeded with, though specific ones should, and that funding for the Native political organizations to support their policy development in all areas but the constitutional talks should be ended and the funds diverted to the bands. Core funding was also to be cut back. The only observable difference between the 1985 study group recommendations and the 1969 white paper was that the more recent effort recognized that Native groups would be opposed to it, because it proposed a media management strategy designed to minimize the public relations damage that it anticipated.

The reaction to the 1985 Nielsen report on Native policy was also reminiscent of the white paper of 1969. First Nations denounced the preliminary report when it was leaked in the spring of 1985 as a "restatement of the 1969 White Paper" that "singled out Indian people – already on the low rung of the country's economic ladder – as a target group for financial punishment." The Assembly of First Nations described the proposal to hand some programs over to other parts of the bureaucracy as "inviting the wolves to tend the sheep," and mainstream press reaction tended to be hostile, too.[33] The Prime Minister's Office moved swiftly to minimize the damage by stating flatly that the report was not government policy. It repeated the promises to respect First Nations' special relationship with government and their Aboriginal and treaty rights that Mulroney had made to Native leaders at a recent first ministers' conference, but the damage had been done. The Nielsen task force report rekindled the suspicions that had been aroused by the white paper of 1969, and, as an Assembly of First Nations official said, "A new generation of cynicism is born, and with good reason."[34] The last thing that Native-government relations needed in the mid-1980s was another dose of disillusionment and suspicion.

The drift of the Mulroney government's policy in the critical area of First Nation self-government hardly dissipated the cynicism of Native leaders. Here the standard for comparison was the Penner Report of 1983, which had been so supportive of the Native case for self-government. The Trudeau government had not committed itself to implementing the report, though it did say that it accepted its "general thrust." It had promised to introduce framework legislation for implementing self-government but failed to do so before its exit from office in 1984. When the Mulroney government began to formulate its policy on self-government in 1985, it appeared to revert to a pre-Penner approach to the subject. From the initiatives that Indian Affairs took, it looked as though the Department of Indian Affairs and Northern Development had turned the clock back to the 1978 policy of encouraging the adoption of municipal-style self-government at the band level. In 1985 Ottawa reached agreement with the Sechelt band in British Columbia, and at the end of that year concluded talks with several First Nations in Ontario for what became known as the Nishnawbe-Aski self-government agreement.[35]

From the First Nations' point of view, these initiatives were ominous. The style of government that the Sechelt accepted was essentially that of a municipality. Most First Nations regard such municipal-type governments as inadequate and dangerous. They are inadequate because they do not confer jurisdiction over a sufficiently wide range, a broad spectrum that First Nations believe they must control if they are to direct economic development and social programs in ways compatible with their values, aspirations, and judgment of what is likely to succeed. Self-government on the municipal model is also dangerous symbolically and as a precedent. In the Canadian constitution municipalities are the legal creatures of, and are answerable to, the provinces. Besides, the experience that most Aboriginal groups have had with provinces has been negative. As the Inuit explained in an advertisement in *The Times* of London during the lobbying over constitutional reform in 1980, "Provinces in Canada have power over lands, resources and local matters." Ottawa did not have a good record of "employing its powers on behalf of native peoples," but "the Federal responsibility has been the closest thing native Canadians have had to any guarantee of rights."[36] In the long shadow of the white paper and Nielsen task force report, Native organizations were understandably suspicious that acceptance of municipal-style self-government might be only the prelude to their being abandoned constitutionally by Ottawa and consigned to the provinces.

In the decade and a half between the white paper and the *Guerin* ruling, enormous changes occurred in Native-government relations in Canada. The experience of being promised consultation and then denied it in 1968–9 drove Native organizations together in powerful and effective national political bodies. Headed by a new generation of leaders, most of them relatively well educated and all of them articulate and committed, these organizations advanced the Native political cause dramatically. They defeated both the white paper of 1969 and the Nielsen task force proposals of 1985–6, and in between they managed to persuade the Penner Committee to endorse their concept of self-government. In the 1970s their united political action won them funding and greater influence, although they did not achieve the breadth of control and adequacy of funding that they considered necessary.

The First Nation political drive in the years after the white paper had its setbacks, too. Indian Affairs officials resisted most of their initiatives in the 1970s, and in 1978 these bureaucrats embarked on the promotion of a municipal style of First Nation government that probably constituted a danger to the Native cause in the long run. Furthermore, if Natives managed to convince the Penner Committee to endorse their notion of self-government, they were not able to persuade the Trudeau cabinet to commit itself fully to it. And, in spite of the landmark Supreme Court decision on the Musqueam case, the decade from the creation of the Office of Native Claims to *Guerin* produced dismal results on land issues. Perhaps more serious still was an economic development in the 1980s. The dramatic downturn in the economy that began in 1982 and lasted in most parts of Canada at least till 1984 dealt a crippling blow to Aboriginal peoples by hobbling a number of economic ventures that they had begun in the hopes of making themselves not just self-governing but also economically self-sufficient. In the Prairies, West Coast, and Far North, the recession lingered on well after 1984, holding back the economic development and muting the political militancy of those Native organizations that had been the most assertive during the Trudeau years. The slowdown did at least put an end to projects to build oil and gas pipelines that threatened the ecology of the Mackenzie Valley and the livelihood of the Dene and some Inuit. However, as Aboriginal communities knew from the 1930s, hard times for Canadians in general were usually desperate times for Indigenous people.

CHAPTER FIFTEEN

Meech, Oka, Charlottetown, Nass, and Ottawa: Relations 1968–2000

The social and economic conditions in which Indigenous peoples live in Canada – or, more accurately, exist – is a national disgrace. First Nation children are more likely than the general population to be born outside a stable family, are far less likely to complete enough schooling to obtain a job and become self-sustaining, are much more highly represented in the figures of unemployed and incarcerated people than the rest of the population, and have shorter life expectancy than most others in the country. What is worse is the fact that these conditions have existed for more than a century, and have been known by governments and churches to exist for most of that time. Ottawa and the missionaries have tried unsuccessfully to impose their programs of economic development on Indigenous peoples. Strangely, while in the 1990s Canadian politicians regularly boasted that "Canada is the best country in the world" according to a United Nations index of quality of life that was applied around the world each year, they ignored the Third World conditions in which Aboriginal peoples existed within Canada – despite an Indian Affairs study released in autumn 1998, which found that when the UN criteria and standards were applied to status Indians within Canada, on-reserve First Nations' quality of life was comparable not to the Canadian average but to Brazil's.[1]

Hypocritical governments often aggravate the socio-economic problems that Indigenous communities face, but Natives have begun to assert themselves about how economic development should take place. For example, in the 1988–9 fiscal year, the Mulroney government, under the flag of fighting the deficit, capped allocations for funding status Indian and Inuit students in post-secondary educational institutions, just as those communities were beginning to produce large numbers of

young people (and, sometimes, not so young people) qualified for the higher education that everyone recognized was vital to the advancement of themselves and
their communities. Native political organizations, through a variety of means, have
forced governments to listen to them on social and economic issues in large part
because economic development since the 1940s has focused on regions that are
occupied by Native groups, areas that often were not covered by the treaties of the
nineteenth and early twentieth centuries. Because Euro-Canadian entrepreneurs
and governments found that they wanted access to the resources in Indian and
Inuit country, and because Natives were insistent that they control change in their
regions, development has emerged as a major point of confrontation. Disputes over
economic development, as much as the political battles since 1969, have contributed to the Natives' emergence from their so-called age of "irrelevance."[2]

After 1985 the land claims issue continued to show how central the Indigenous
communities occupying lands frequently sought by resource companies were to
economic policy and the gross national product. In fact, there was a well-established
pattern of events that demonstrated the intimate linkage of economic development
policy and Native assertions of title to and control of land. In 1977, for example,
Thomas Berger, a judge of the BC Supreme Court who was sitting as a federal commissioner, reported on the impact of a proposed pipeline up the Mackenzie Valley,
and in the same year Ken Lysyk (then a law professor and later a judge of the BC
Supreme Court) conducted an inquiry into the likely effect of an Alaska pipeline
on the southern Yukon. Both men warned against rapid development that would
damage Native economies and ways of life. Lysyk argued that four years would
be necessary for the Natives to prepare for the impact of the construction of an
Alaskan pipeline, while Berger suggested that "a period of ten years will be required in the Mackenzie Valley and Western Arctic to settle native claims, and to
establish the new institutions and new programs that a settlement will entail. No
pipeline should be built until these things have been achieved."[3] As events turned
out, it was more the economic slowdown of the early 1980s than government policy that prevented construction of these pipelines, but the concerns that the Berger
and Lysyk inquiries had revealed underlined the fact that unresolved questions
about Native lands could retard economic development. The same point was made
in a confidential study that the firm Peat Marwick did for the Indian Affairs department in 1990. The consultants' study estimated that unresolved land disputes
in British Columbia were costing the province $125 million a year in foregone or
delayed investment, and projected an eventual cost of $1 billion "before a single
claim is settled."[4]

In spite of the pressures created by economic uncertainty, the pace of settle-ment of land claims after the Committee of Original People's Entitlement (COPE) comprehensive claim settlement in 1984 and the *Guerin* decision of 1985 remained frustratingly slow. The Office of Native Claims was eliminated in the mid-1980s and replaced with a Comprehensive Claims Branch and a Specific Claims Branch, but claims resolution did not improve substantially.[5] The two branches' slow pace, in combination with a growing number of bands whose research was by this time ma-turing into formal statements of claim, continued to create a backlog. By 1990 there were 371 specific claims lined up, with fifty more being added to the queue every year.[6] The number of comprehensive claims ripe for negotiation was smaller, but there, too, the backlog was growing. Problems were worsening in the comprehen-sive claims area because of the federal government's insistence on "final extinguish-ment," a provision that a settlement include a clause saying that it ended forever all claims concerning the territory. First Nations were becoming increasingly anx-ious in an era now influenced powerfully by the 1982 constitutional provisions that agreeing to such a blanket extinction of rights might harm future generations. The 1982 constitutional settlement, after all, affirmed their Aboriginal rights, un-defined, and the courts were defining new Aboriginal rights regularly by the end of the 1980s. What if agreeing to final extinguishment meant that their descen-dants would be barred from benefiting from an Aboriginal right that a future court would define and enshrine? Such concerns accounted in part for the rejection, in a plebiscite in 1990, of the Métis-Dene comprehensive claim settlement that dealt with a large portion of the western Northwest Territories. The Mulroney govern-ment responded to such anxieties by softening somewhat the federal government's demands for extinguishment, but in a post-Nielsen task-force era, suspicion and distrust of government continued to instil caution in Aboriginal political leaders.

In spite of these problems, successes were achieved on both comprehensive and specific claims after 1985. On the specific claim file, some of the changes that the Mulroney government made in 1991, including lifting the ban on dealing with pre-Confederation claims, facilitated settlement, but the Indian Claims Commission (ICC), despite the genuine commitment and strenuous efforts of the commission-ers and their staff, continued to be ineffectual. The ICC did not let the fact that it was merely a type of appeal body for specific claims that had been rejected by the Specific Claims Branch, or that it played only an advisory role in relation to gov-ernment, deter it from investigating and producing voluminous, well-documented reports on a number of cases. However, neither the Mulroney (1984–93) nor the Chrétien (1993–2003) governments would respond to the increasingly positive recommendations for settlement of a claim that issued from the ICC. Not even the commissioners' threat to resign en masse in 1997 produced much change for the better in government attitudes.

Among the most impressive and encouraging of the specific claims resolutions was one in Saskatchewan that was achieved apart from the procedures overseen by the Specific Claims Branch. The Federation of Saskatchewan Indian Nations (FSIN) had since the 1970s been negotiating with the federal and provincial governments for a package solution to the claims that over a dozen bands in the province had to lands they had been promised but never granted following treaty. This category, which became known as treaty land entitlement, or locally as TLE, was different from cases before Specific Claims and the ICC – usually claims, such as the Kahkewistahaw one in Saskatchewan, where the band alleged that it had been dispossessed of reserve lands by coercion or fraud, often with Indian Affairs involvement.[7] The TLE cases were claims in which the bands had never received the full quantum of reserve land to which their treaty entitled them. The Blakeney government (1971–82) in Saskatchewan and the Trudeau government (1968–79, 1980–4) had, after lengthy negotiations, reached agreement in principle on what was known as the "Saskatchewan formula," but it was never implemented. The onset of economic stagnation and the election of right-wing governments both provincially and federally combined in the 1980s with community resistance in rural Saskatchewan to stall the settlement. It was not, in fact, until the early 1990s, when Roy Romanow, once an influential minister under Alan Blakeney, returned his New Democratic Party to power in Saskatchewan, that agreement was reached with the Mulroney government on the eve of what would prove its crushing defeat in the federal election of 1993. During the remainder of the 1990s, the TLE bands and government undertook the gargantuan task of approving and implementing a settlement that would transfer over $450 million, most of it earmarked for land purchases, from government to Saskatchewan bands.[8]

Two claims of incredible complexity – Lubicon Lake and Temagami – that were neither precisely specific claims nor exactly comprehensive claims have festered and remained unhealed throughout three decades following the *Guerin* decision. The Lubicon Lake Cree in northern Alberta had never adhered to Treaty 8 (1899–1900), but when oil exploration began to invade their territory in the 1940s, they expressed an interest in joining in treaty and were promised a reserve.[9] For a variety of reasons this did not happen, and when an oil boom erupted in Alberta in the 1970s, the provincial government of Peter Lougheed showed little concern for the group, whose lands were being seriously affected by southern economic activity.

Chief Bernard Ominayak requested a reserve for the band, whose membership he estimated at over four hundred, but the province was opposed, claiming there were just a small number. In the 1980s the federal government proposed acceptance of the Lubicon as a band, but would not accept a population estimate that the group agreed to. Following the chief's call for a boycott of the 1988 Winter Olympics in Calgary, Ottawa agreed to terms. However, final agreement was not reached, and in 1989, under suspicious circumstances, a group that Ottawa termed the Woodland Cree were recognized by Indian Affairs as a "breakaway" band from the Lubicon. Miraculously, the Woodland Cree concluded a land claim settlement valued at $56 million with Ottawa by the end of 1990, but the dispute with the Lubicon remained unresolved through the 1990s. In the late years of the twenty-first century's second decade, the Lubicon case is still unsettled.

There were similarities between the Lubicon case and the Temagami dispute in Ontario. The Teme-Augama Anishnabai (Deep Water People, also known as Bear Island band) were not adherents to the 1850 Robinson treaties, but their homelands began to feel the effects of seasonal tourism and forestry by the beginning of the century. The band launched legal action in 1973 by getting a caution placed on all Crown lands in 110 townships in northern Ontario. The dispute is complex because two levels of government are involved, and competing interests representing the First Nation, pulp companies and the local workers who depend on them, private and commercial recreational users of the lakes of the disputed area, and environmentalists are all involved. The band has several times thought it was close to an agreement with the governments concerned, but no resolution has been achieved. Furthermore, the history of litigation arising over the dispute has been lengthy, complex, expensive, and confusing. A decision of the Supreme Court of Ontario against the band in 1984 was notorious for the harsh language with which Justice James Steele dismissed historical events before 1763. Legal fencing and continuing efforts to achieve settlement by negotiation continued on and off all through the 1990s.[10] As in the case of the Lubicon Lake Cree, the Temagami band still find that negotiations have proved frustrating. By the end of 2016, they had been suspended.

Some of the features that Lubicon Lake and Temagami shared illustrated how complicated claims could be. They both contained elements characteristic of comprehensive and specific claims: both were "missed" by nineteenth-century treaty makers; and both bands, in effect, were belatedly attempting to obtain what they would have been entitled to by earlier treaties. In both cases, complications arose from the involvement of two levels of government, where the attitudes and behaviour of Ontario and Alberta were typical of everything that made First Nations and Inuit wary of coming under provincial jurisdiction.

In other parts of the country, especially in British Columbia and the territorial North, at least there was no question that existing treaties, except for small patches on Vancouver Island and the northeast corner of British Columbia, had a bearing on claims of the First Nations. In Yukon and the Northwest Territories, too, federal freedom of action was untrammelled by provincial jurisdiction over Crown lands and natural resources although the political pressures that local and southern business interests could bring to bear were a factor that could not be ignored. That was a major reason why the first comprehensive claims settlements after James Bay in 1975 had occurred in the North. The COPE or Inuvialuit agreement (1984) had been followed by a deal with the Council of Yukon Indians (Agreement in Principle [AIP] 1988; Final Agreement [FA] 1990) that included financial compensation and territory. It was beginning to look as though the comprehensive claims file was enjoying a run of luck in April 1990, when the Dene and Métis signed an AIP valued by federal negotiators at $500 million. However, the deal came unstuck, as noted above, over the issue of final extinguishment, which was part of the deal. The AIP was never proceeded with, and five of the constituent elements sought individual pacts with government. In 1992 the Gwich'in signed an agreement covering their territory in the Upper Mackenzie Delta, in 1994 the Sahtu Dene and Métis of Great Bear Lake reached agreement, and other groups continued to negotiate through the 1990s. The issue of final extinguishment still looms as a deterrent to some.

The settlement with the Tungavik Federation of Nunavut (AIP 1990; legislation 1993; full effect 1999) provides fascinating parallels with and differences from the other comprehensive claims settlements in Yukon and the western part of the Northwest Territories.[11] The Inuit of the eastern part of the Northwest Territories were once considered the more politically backward of Aboriginal groups in the north. Part of the explanation for this reputation was that it had only been the 1950s when eastern Inuit communities came dramatically to southern attention because of a large number of highly publicized cases of starvation. However, some of the apparent difference between them and the Inuvialuit and Dene and Métis of the more westerly regions was a product of eastern Inuit preference for a quieter political style. Whereas Dene and Métis grabbed a lot of media and political attention in 1975 when they issued their provocative manifesto, *The Dene Declaration*,[12] the eastern Inuit opted for more cooperative and quieter tactics. However, they, too, began to participate in the northern political revolution in 1979, when the appointment of a sympathetic commissioner of the NWT and the election of a large number of pro-Aboriginal representatives to the territorial legislature led to the repudiation of the previously dominant pro-business and frequently anti-Native attitudes. They stunned the journalistic and political elites in 1982, when a plebiscite on whether

the Northwest Territories should be divided, as the eastern Inuit political leadership proposed, produced a record-high voter turnout and a four-to-one margin in
the east in favour of splitting NWT and creating a new territory, Nunavut.

Nunavut, which means "our land" in Inuktitut, was originally expected to be the
easterly half of a pair of territories, the other being Denendeh (land of the Dene)
in the west. However, it was the easterly group, the Inuit, who forged ahead to secure an agreement with the federal government to settle the comprehensive land
claim they had initiated in 1976 and to implement self-government. The agreement
was reached in 1990, confirmed by territorial voters in another plebiscite in 1992
that approved proposed boundaries for Nunavut, and authorized by federal legislation in 1993. When implemented on 1 April 1999 its wide-ranging provisions on
land and government created a unique territory in the eastern half of the Arctic.
Land and compensation provisions alone were breathtaking. The Inuit ceded "any
Aboriginal claims and title they may have to lands and waters in Canada," but "any
other existing or future constitutional rights that the Inuit may have are not affected" by the agreement.[13] The Inuit received $1.15 billion over fourteen years,
retained 18 per cent of the landmass involved, enjoyed subsurface rights to 10.5 per
cent (2 per cent of the total land mass), shared in royalties on minerals extracted in future from Crown lands, and, to cap it, participated in a new government.
Politically, Nunavut has a "public government," meaning that all residents who
meet the residency requirement are eligible to vote and stand for office. In reality,
the Inuit who constitute 80 per cent of the population dominate the territory, but
their history over recent decades suggests they will not act in an exclusive manner. Challenges face the young territory. Training the local population to staff the
governmental positions has required an enormous effort, the fruits of which have
not yet been evaluated. The Inuit population is extraordinarily young – 40 per
cent under fifteen – and has had low levels of school completion. And, as often
happens with large land claims, there is a complication with the Dene of northern
Manitoba and Saskatchewan, who have objected that some of the southerly portions of Nunvaut contain traditional hunting grounds of theirs. Although Nunavut
took more than a generation from initiation to implementation, it stands as one
of the great achievements of both Inuit political skill and Canadian innovation in
governance. The leaders of Nunavut learned the hard way what the Grand Council
of the Cree noted in 1986: "Negotiation of a claim settlement is only half the battle
and implementation is the other."[14]

Land disputes in British Columbia share a number of features with their northern counterparts, including taking a disturbingly long time to be resolved. Since
most of British Columbia, apart from the small Vancouver Island, or Douglas,

treaties of the colonial period and the portion covered by Treaty 8 at the end of the nineteenth century, is unceded Aboriginal territory, it is not surprising that there have been claims embracing the entire province. In fact, the total area claimed in British Columbia is greater than the province's, something that provokes hostile press comment, but is hardly surprising given the province's history. The two Aboriginal title disputes that attracted most attention in the 1990s were an interesting pair, Gitksan Wet'suwet'en, a court case, and the Nisga'a, a claim resolved by negotiation after an important legal history. The Gitksan case concerned traditional territories in north-central British Columbia occupied by related peoples, the Gitksan and Wet'suwet'en. Their court case attracted attention, first for their decision – highly controversial in some quarters – to have their "witnesses" tell their stories and songs in court to validate their assertions about the lands they had controlled from time immemorial. Equally controversial was the language of Chief Justice Alan McEachern in 1991, when he dismissed their case and oral history in terms reminiscent of those used by Mr. Justice Steele in the Teme-Augama Anishnabai litigation in Ontario.

After hesitations and various actions, the Gitksan proceeded alone to the Supreme Court of Canada, where in December 1997 they scored a landmark victory in what was now referred to as the *Delgamuukw* case, whose implications were as momentous as the 1973 *Calder* case had been. In allowing the appeal from the Supreme Court of British Columbia and ordering a new trial, the high court justices also upheld the validity and appropriateness of oral history evidence, ordering courts in future to take it into consideration along with other forms of evidence. The decision was a mammoth victory, not just for the Gitksan, who hoped to secure final resolution of their case by negotiation rather than another trial, but also for all Aboriginal litigants and claimants whose history, like that of the Gitksan, was recorded only in oral form as story, song, and dance. The *Delgamuukw* decision of the Supreme Court was also remarkable for its expansive definition of Aboriginal title, which read in part, "Aboriginal title encompasses the right to exclusive use and occupation of the land held pursuant to that title for a variety of purposes, which need not be aspects of those aboriginal practices, customs and traditions which are integral to distinctive aboriginal cultures. The protected uses must not be irreconcilable with the nature of the group's attachment to that land ... Aboriginal title is a right to the land itself."[15] The ruling represented a major victory for the Gitksan, and for other First Nations, but, as happened in the case of other First Nations, the federal government did not change its stance and the dispute has not been resolved.

"At 8:27 a.m., our canoe arrived," said Joseph Gosnell exultantly. "The journey our ancestors began more than a century ago ended."[16] And what a trip it had

been for the First Nation from the Nass River Valley in northern British Columbia!
From the time in the 1880s when Nisga'a paddled all the way to Victoria to request a treaty that would recognize their property and self-governing rights only
to be dismissed as having no more rights than "beasts of the field";[17] to the *Calder*
case, which was named for a descendant of one of those 1880s paddlers; to five-
year-long negotiations involving both the provincial government and Ottawa, once
British Columbia had given up (in 1991) its 120-year-long refusal to recognize the
legitimacy of Aboriginal title. The 1996 agreement confirmed Nisga'a control of
2,000 square kilometres of the 25,000 square kilometres they had claimed, provided
them with $200 million in compensation for riches extracted from their lands, as
well as a guaranteed share of the fishery's yield, a feature denounced by non-Native
critics as a "race-based fishery." What some other First Nations find disturbing about
the Nisga'a agreement is that, after 2000, federal and provincial income tax laws
will apply to all Nisga'a. After 1996, the Nisga'a agreement was the subject of coun-
terclaims by other First Nations who said some of the claim area contains lands
that were theirs, and by many non-Native British Columbians who objected to the
territorial, or compensation, or fisheries elements of the pact. However, in 1998
the agreement was ratified by the Nisga'a after considerable debate and over significant opposition, and in early 1999 by the legislature of British Columbia and parliament of Canada. The canoe had indeed landed after a long and difficult journey.

If land issues were complex and controversial, at least they were seldom as acrimonious as the continuing soap opera that first ministers' talks on the constitution,
including the issue of Aboriginal self-government, became after 1985. The 1987
First Ministers Conference on Aboriginal rights, the final of the series scheduled
pursuant to the 1982 constitutional arrangements, collapsed in acrimony. If that
were not enough of a disappointment for Native leaders, two months later the same
first ministers – this time without the Native politicians present – met at Meech
Lake, in the Gatineau Hills of Quebec, and swiftly agreed to a package of constitutional proposals that would, as Prime Minister Mulroney had promised he would
seek in the general election of 1984, lead Quebec to sign on to the 1982 constitution
"with honour and enthusiasm." The same ministers, including the usually obdurate
western premiers, who short weeks before had not been able to agree to entrench
explicitly the Aboriginal right of self-government because it was too vague for them
to grasp, now enthusiastically agreed to recognize constitutionally that Quebec was
"a distinct society" and its provincial government had the right and duty to promote that distinctiveness. The contrast between the treatment of Quebec and that
accorded to Aboriginal peoples was striking.

At first all the Native leaders could do was fume quietly about the treatment their communities had once more received on constitutional matters. The prime minister seemed unwilling to contemplate any further constitutional tinkering. If Mulroney spoke of the Meech Lake Accord at all in the first two years after it was agreed to in the spring of 1987, it was to discourage debate on its terms. The pact, he said on one occasion, was "a seamless web" that could not be altered in detail without being destroyed; another time he said the accord was "a done deal," obviously something beyond debate. Thus it seemed that there was nothing to do but wait out the three years prescribed by the 1982 amending formula during which all eleven senior legislatures had to ratify the terms until it became part of the fundamental law of the country. There had always been some opposition to the Meech Lake Accord because of a widespread fear that it would make the creation of new national social programs, such as day care, impossible, and its requirement that any territory wishing to become a province had to receive the unanimous approval of all eleven legislatures seemed as unfair as it did rigid. The latter requirement also was viewed as another slap at First Nations, for there were only two territories, Yukon and Northwest Territories, both of them heavily Native, that might some day seek provincial status. Still, there seemed little that could be done. By early 1990 all jurisdictions except Manitoba and New Brunswick had ratified the Meech Lake Accord. The only encouraging sign for opponents of Meech was Newfoundland and Labrador, whose new Liberal premier, Clyde Wells, had arranged for his legislature to rescind that province's approval of Meech on differences of political principle with the terms of the accord.[18]

Unexpectedly, the situation changed because the prime minister, who revelled in his reputation as a skilled negotiator because of his labour relations experience in Quebec, miscalculated his position. In early June, he summoned the first ministers to a special meeting at which pressure was brought to bear on the three holdout premiers.[19] McKenna of New Brunswick capitulated, Filmon of Manitoba promised only to take the deal to his legislature for its consideration, and Wells of Newfoundland gave an equivocal undertaking that was read as meaning his province would not stand as the lone opponent of the reform. Wells appeared to pledge that his province would sign on if Manitoba did, too. In an interview with the editorial board of the *Globe and Mail*, the prime minister was asked if he had been the victim of fleeting time. After all, if the accord were not ratified by all legislatures by 23 June, it would fail. Had he waited too long? On the contrary, he crowed. He and his advisors had dragged matters out to the last possible date to increase the pressure on Filmon and Wells. Tory strategists in Ottawa had picked the last possible date on which the conference could have ended and ratification by the provinces still be managed. "That's the day that I'm going to roll all the dice!" he boasted to the newspaper people.[20]

What Mulroney did not realize was that his high-risk strategy created an opportunity for First Nation political leaders to strike back. And when they retaliated, they did so with one of the most potent weapons that Native people had used since the 1830s to defeat efforts to coerce and mistreat them: passive resistance. Since there was a limited period in which the Manitoba government could carry out public consultations on the agreement, as it had pledged to do, and still push the pact through the legislature in time, any delay in Manitoba might prove fatal to Meech. After consultations with Native leaders and their legal advisers, Elijah Harper, then a New Democratic Party MLA in the Manitoba legislature, determined to do his bit to undo the deal concocted by Mulroney and the other premiers who cared so little about the Aboriginal agenda. As Harper later said, "We blocked the accord because it posed a threat to aboriginal people. Aboriginal people have no quarrel with Quebec. But we're a distinct society too, and we've fought for many years for the basic rights that Quebec takes for granted, such as participating in constitutional talks."[21] The measure could pass the Manitoba legislature only under expedited procedures that required the unanimous approval of members, and one MLA, Elijah Harper, was not prepared to approve. Day after day, as the clever politicians panicked and Mulroney dispatched negotiators to Winnipeg to offer concessions, including appointment of a royal commission on Native affairs, Harper sat in his place in the legislature, an eagle feather in his hand, and said no or just shook his head when the speaker asked if there was unanimous consent to proceed with consideration of the Meech Lake Accord. On 22 June 1990, it died at the hands of Elijah Harper and the Manitoba First Nation leadership.[22]

Reaction, both immediate and longer term, was explosive. The failure of Meech caused several Quebec members of parliament to defect and join a new sovereignty movement, the Bloc Québécois, headed by a former Mulroney minister, Lucien Bouchard, who had broken with Mulroney in the spring of 1990 over what he viewed as the watering down of the agreement. For his part, Mulroney chose to blame the defeat of the deal not on Elijah Harper and the Natives, but on Liberal premier Clyde Wells, whose legislature at the last minute saw what was happening in Winnipeg and desisted from carrying out re-ratification of the accord.

The Tory leader's spite could only be short-lived. He had to recognize that in the next round of constitutional negotiations, which could not be long delayed given the anger in Quebec at the rejection of the Meech Lake Accord, he would need their leaders. The next round would have to be a "Canada round," meaning that it must embrace the constitutional concerns of more than Quebec. Among the others who were included in the next phase, which produced the Charlottetown Accord in 1992, were the Aboriginal peoples, who did get some important recognition, however equivocally it was couched, in the agreement. For one thing, the 1992 deal included a "Canada Clause" containing a section that acknowledged that "the Aboriginal peoples of Canada, being the first peoples to govern this land, have the right to promote their languages, cultures and traditions and to ensure the integrity of their societies, and their governments constitute one of three orders of government in Canada."[23] Moreover, the first ministers and Aboriginal leaders at Charlottetown agreed that "the Constitution should be amended to recognize that the Aboriginal peoples of Canada have the inherent right of self-government within Canada" and "the recognition of the inherent right of self-government should be interpreted in light of the recognition of Aboriginal governments as one of the three orders of government in Canada." There were limits, however, on the proposed Aboriginal governments: their legislation "may not be inconsistent with those laws which are essential to the preservation of peace, order and good government in Canada." While Charlottetown recognized Aboriginal peoples' inherent right to self-government, it limited the scope of the proposed governments by denying them an international role ("have the inherent right of self-government *within* Canada") and posing "peace, order and good government" as a limitation on their jurisdiction.

Charlottetown represented enormous progress on Aboriginal self-government, but the accord did not survive. In the national referendum on the deal that was held in October 1992, almost no portion of the electorate, including most of the Native community, supported the pact. The Inuit in the Northwest Territories and Quebec gave the agreement their blessing, the Quebec Inuit by a four-to-one margin; the Métis in Manitoba supported it less enthusiastically; and the Huron (Wendat) in Quebec did as well. However, everywhere else Native voters joined non-Natives in rejecting the deal, and not a single Mohawk in Quebec voted in the referendum. Over all, only the Northwest Territories, Prince Edward Island, New Brunswick, and Newfoundland and Labrador, and Ontario (by a vote of 50.1 per cent) voted for the accord. Many voters, apparently, distrusted the language on Aboriginal self-government or their leaders who recommended support, or both. Certainly a large group of Aboriginal women, those represented by the Native Women's Association of Canada (NWAC), did not want Aboriginal self-government entrenched until they had some guarantee of continuation of gender equality rights. During the run-up to the Charlottetown negotiations, NWAC lobbied and even went to court to try to obtain separate representation at the talks, but neither the politicians nor the courts sustained them. Charlottetown had revealed a split along gender lines within the status Indian community in particular, a divide that had been opened by

dissatisfaction over Bill C-31 and then the leadership's preoccupation with constitutional matters rather than bread-and-butter issues (or bread, housing, and water
issues) that seemed more immediate and pressing to many Native women. These
differences, like the cause of entrenching Aboriginal self-government in the constitution, would have to wait, for large-scale constitutional reform seemed out of the
question in a Canada exhausted by close to two decades of argument over it.

There were other forms of Aboriginal right than self-government and places other
than the constitutional forum in which to advance the cause. In the 1990s the courts
proved a propitious place for Aboriginal rights of a non-political kind. The *Sioui*
case from Quebec, decided by the Supreme Court in 1990, upheld an Aboriginal
right to practise traditional ritual that had been recognized in a 1760 treaty between newly victorious British and the Huron after the capitulation of Montreal.
The Supreme Court found that the Aboriginal right of historian Georges Sioui and
his kin to carry out their "annual rites of purification" took precedence over Quebec
provincial law that prohibited cutting trees in a provincial park because the treaty
right to do so was one of those "existing Aboriginal and treaty rights" that the 1982
constitution "recognized and affirmed."[24] Also in 1990 the Supreme Court upheld
an Aboriginal right of a different sort, one that did not have treaty backing, in the
Sparrow decision. The highest court ordered a retrial for Ronald Sparrow, a member of the Musqueam First Nation in British Columbia, who had been convicted
of using a drift net larger than fishery regulations permitted. The judges concluded
that the right to fish was an Aboriginal right that legislatures could not abridge, unless acting to conserve the resource.[25] The ruling also clarified somewhat the adjective
"existing" in section 35 of the constitution: it meant not extinguished. This decision
was part of a rising tide of judicial support for Aboriginal rights, a swell that helped
in the autumn of 1990 to bring Nova Scotia and the Mi'kmaq to sign an agreement
permitting Native hunters to hunt moose when others were forbidden to do so.[26]
The Supreme Court would retreat somewhat from its expansive interpretation of
Aboriginal rights, particularly in the *Van der Peet* decision (1996), which defined
more precisely how an Aboriginal right could be identified judicially. However, the
progress that was made in the courts in the decade following the *Guerin* decision
was impressive.

Progress in the judicial realm in 1990 was more obvious than what happened in a
hitherto obscure patch of forest in southwestern Quebec that summer. On 10 July
1990 the mayor of the town of Oka requested that the Sûreté du Québec, the Quebec

provincial police, remove protesters who had occupied The Pines for months, by force if necessary. The immediate background was the occupation of The Pines by Kanesatake Mohawk who were determined to prevent the expansion of the golf course near their graveyard to eighteen holes, but the history of the confrontation stretched further back to the *Corinthe* decision of 1912, the 1841 statute that recognized Sulpician title, and even to an eighteenth-century dispute over ownership of the lands.[27] The police assault on The Pines on 11 July led to the death of a police corporal, an eleven-week standoff, the calling in of 2,500 Canadian Armed Forces personnel, outrageous interference with the civil liberties of reporters and sympathizers of the Mohawk, and, finally on 26 September, the end of the confrontation at Oka without further bloodshed.

The context of the 1990 Oka crisis did not just stretch backward in time; it spread outwards to other Native communities, too. In two other Mohawk communities in Quebec, the reserves of Kahnawake across the Mercier Bridge from Montreal and Akwesasne near Cornwall, there was a lengthy record of disputes and lawlessness between an increasingly angry Mohawk community and civil authorities. The Mohawk of Akwesasne and Kahnawake considered themselves sovereign, and those south of Cornwall claimed a right by the Jay Treaty of 1794 to pass back and forth across the international bridge without stopping for immigration or customs inspection.[28] By 1990 there had been many years of strife over tobacco smuggling through Akwesasne and sales of tax-free tobacco there and at Kahnawake, as well as increasing conflict between the latter community and Quebec authorities. Matters were further complicated at Akwesasne by bitter differences over on-reserve gambling, a right some Mohawk claimed they enjoyed as sovereign people. All three Mohawk communities were also fractured internally by divisions among followers of the traditional Longhouse religion and Christianity, as well as over governance. One faction recognized only leaders chosen by clan mothers according to the Iroquois Great Law of Peace, others favoured hereditary leaders selected by authority delegated under the Indian Act, and others supported the chiefs and councils elected in accordance with that act. These fissures made the Mohawk communities politically volatile and unstable, and their conflicts with non-Native governments made the Warrior Societies that existed at Akwesasne and Kahnawake scrappy. The Kahnawake Warriors had already closed down the busy Mercier Bridge that thousands of commuters relied on in 1988 in reaction to a police raid on a number of tax-free tobacco stores on the reserve. In the spring of 1990 there had been violent incidents within the Akwesasne community, as pro- and anti-gambling elements clashed in the night.

On-reserve gambling proved a divisive issue at the Akwesasne reserve in 1989.
Here Frank David and Lorraine Canoe urge their fellow Mohawk
to boycott a referendum on the issue.

It was because of these linkages and splits that the confrontation in The Pines quickly involved members from Akwesasne and Kahnawake. Members of the Akwesasne Warrior Society had helped to staff the blockade in The Pines in the early spring, when the occupiers refused to obey a court injunction of late April to take down their barricades. (Their refusal to respond to a second injunction on 29 June was the prelude to the 11 July police action.) Once the crisis erupted, the Kahnawake Warriors blockaded Mercier Bridge and dragged increasingly angry commuters into the dispute. The confrontations at Kanesatake and Kahnawake led to ugly clashes between Natives and non-Natives, particularly in the case of the south shore reserve. Townspeople in nearby Châteauguay engaged in threats and vigilante violence against Mohawk, and thugs from LaSalle, a neighbourhood on the north end of the bridge, threw rocks at cars containing old people, women, and children from Kahnawake who were attempting to leave via the bridge under an agreement negotiated between Mohawk and police. As ugly as many of the events arising from the Oka crisis were, the wonder is that so few people were hurt.

The aftermath, though not entirely negative, was disturbing in many respects. The governments of Quebec and Canada showed little awareness of how their negligence had helped to create the crisis, and little inclination to solve the root causes. Ottawa, although it had a fiduciary responsibility under the constitution to First Nations, quickly sided with Quebec. On 26 August Mulroney dismissed Mohawk assertions of Aboriginal sovereignty as "bizarre," and obviously the federal government exercised no restraint on soldiers and others who were interfering with freedom of movement, the right of assembly, and even the right of free speech. Although Ottawa said it would attempt to complete a land assembly that would resolve the disputes at Kanesatake, it did not succeed in doing so. The Pines, the graveyard, and the nine-hole golf course all stand as they were in July 1990. A number of Mohawk men were rounded up on 26 September when the last holdouts walked out of an addictions treatment centre into the arms of the army, but only a few dozen were tried, and only two convicted of relatively minor offences. Perhaps the longest-lasting result within Quebec was a growing animosity towards Native people on the part of the general population. Although Quebeckers liked to congratulate themselves on their supposedly better record of relations with Indigenous peoples than the rest of the country, the bigotry that had flared into violence at Châteauguay left lingering hard feelings.

Outside Quebec the aftermath was somewhat more positive, although the crisis caused some polarization of public attitudes into pro-Native and anti-Native camps across the land. One unforeseen result was that the government of British Columbia announced it would participate in discussions aimed at resolving comprehensive claims, a reversal of the province's position since the 1870s that it did not recognize the existence of Aboriginal title. Both the Oka crisis and the court's comments on Aboriginal title in the *Sparrow* decision were factors in the provincial about-face. In Saskatchewan, Premier Grant Devine also reversed his government's stance on the category of specific claims known as Treaty Lands Entitlement, paving the way for a resolution of that dispute by the autumn of 1992. A medium-term result of national significance was the creation in 1991 of the Royal Commission on Aboriginal Peoples (RCAP), something Mulroney had offered Elijah Harper and his supporters in June 1990 as the Meech Lake Accord lay dying in the Manitoba legislature.

The Garden River Ojibwe near Sault Ste. Marie in 1991 still remembered the Oka confrontation
that had pitted the Mohawk at Kanesatake against police and army.

Chaired by former Assembly of First Nations Chief Georges Erasmus of the
Northwest Territories and Quebec judge René Dussault, the commission was composed of both Native (Inuit, Métis, and Indian) and non-Native commissioners.
It undertook an ambitious research program and held extensive public hearings,
two practices that helped to make it one of the lengthiest and the most expensive
royal commissions in Canadian history. Its final report, issued in five fat volumes
in November 1996, emphasized both the past and the future of Indigenous peoples'
relations with non-Natives in Canada. It placed heavy emphasis on the history of
the relationship, stressing a number of traumatic experiences such as residential
schools, loss of lands, and the coerced relocation of Quebec Inuit in the 1950s by
Ottawa. Both the structure of the report and the public hearings showed that the
commissioners regarded the inquiry as an exercise in public education as well as
an investigation and public-policy exercise. The commission's recommendations
emphasized the future, advocating the establishment of a new relationship between
Aboriginal peoples and Canadians by means of a new royal proclamation for the

NATIVES FINALLY GET RESULTS FROM THE ROYAL COMMISSION ON ABORIGINAL PEOPLES

The final report of the Royal Commission on Aboriginal Peoples, issued in 1996,
did not impress many observers as likely to lead to practical solutions to Native problems.

twenty-first century, new governance institutions to enhance the Aboriginal communities' political voice, and greater Native control of their own affairs.

In two respects its recommendations were surprising and disappointing. First, the final report demonstrated a lack of interest in the situation of urban Natives, privileging reserve life and cultural persistence over the solving of socio-economic problems across the board.[29] The other disappointment was the Royal Commission's position on the residential school problem, which by the autumn of 1996 had become so notorious that most knowledgeable observers were ready for a full-scale attack on the individual and community problems the schools had bequeathed status Indians, Métis, and Inuit. After a fine historical analysis of the problems that residential schools had created, the report ended lamely with a recommendation that the federal government establish a public inquiry into residential school problems and means of solving their consequences.[30] Some critics were inclined to think that a public inquiry into residential schools had been part of the commission's mandate.

Other short-term results of the massive probe were also disappointing. Perhaps unfairly, many critics on Parliament Hill and in the press gallery professed to be shocked at the massive price tag that was attached to both the Royal Commission on Aboriginal Peoples and, more especially, many of its recommendations. In 1996 the country and its federal government had not yet quite turned the corner of the effort to get the government's deficit under control. After a decade of conflict and failure over efforts to remodel the constitution from Meech onward, the RCAP recommendations about a new royal proclamation and new institutions of government, which obviously would require constitutional amendments, seemed like non-starters. The minister of Indian Affairs, Ron Irwin, made it very clear by his unenthusiastic reaction to the report that he was not impressed by its ambitious recommendations. His deputy minister would later describe the commission's recommendations as "dead on arrival."[31] With a fiscally focused, right-wing opposition in the form of the Reform Party worrying its flank, the Chrétien government was not going to embark on anything ambitious in the Aboriginal peoples file before the general election it would hold in June 1997. Perhaps the commission could be dismissed as "unrealistic" in the short term. One of its commissioners, former Saskatchewan premier Alan Blakeney, had resigned from the commission in 1993, because it was fixated on general principles and spending a great deal of time exposing Native problems rather than focusing on specific solutions to actual challenges. However, in the longer term, and especially if the Royal Commission's research results pass scrutiny and endure, it will stand as an influential exercise in public education, similar in effect to Thomas Berger's Mackenzie Valley pipeline inquiry of the 1970s.[32]

Many of the themes that had been prominent in Native–non-Native relations after 1985 came together in an extraordinary period stretching from late 1997 to the end of 1998. As noted earlier, in December 1997 the Supreme Court of Canada handed down its important decision in *Delgamuukw*, the case involving the Gitksan claim in northern British Columbia. As important as the justices' verdict that the earlier decision should be set aside were other aspects of their ruling, precepts that are likely to influence both judicial and political developments well into the twenty-first century. The Court upheld the significance of oral history evidence, a clear sign that the judiciary was now willing to accord Aboriginal standards of reality and Aboriginal forms of history the same respect Euro-Canadian ones received. The *Delgamuukw* decision was a straight rejection of Euro-centric standards and criteria in the courts. It provided an expanded definition of Aboriginal title. And Chief Justice Antonio Lamer also urged both sides in the convoluted land case to avoid a retrial by working towards a negotiated resolution of the complex case. He practically pleaded with both sides – and, by logical and inevitable extension, with the larger Aboriginal and settler societies they represented – to recognize reality: "Let us face it, we are all here to stay," he wrote.[33] The implied message was clear: get on with resolving differences and building a healthier Canada. The Supreme Court sent the case back for retrial rather than settling the issues, and it has remained unlitigated for twenty years. The Supreme Court's message seemed to be picked up and amplified the next month, in January 1998, when the Government of Canada issued its formal response to the final report of the Royal Commission on Aboriginal Peoples (RCAP). The event was carefully staged in the Great Hall of the Canadian Museum of Civilization, an airy and spacious venue located in Gatineau that celebrated the architectural and other cultural achievements of the First Nations of the Pacific Coast. Indian Affairs Minister Jane Stewart was joined by her colleague Ralph Goodale, the "Interlocutor" for Métis issues in the federal government, and by representatives of the Assembly of First Nations (AFN), Métis Nation of Canada, Congress of Aboriginal Peoples, and Inuit Tapirisat of Canada. The Statement of Reconciliation that Stewart issued was reported to have been negotiated with Phil Fontaine, Grand Chief of the AFN. More important, it echoed elements of the RCAP report, such as the call for a new relationship between Aboriginal peoples and Canadians. "Today we are here to say that we have listened and we have heard," said Stewart "The time has come to state formally that the days of paternalism and disrespect are behind us and that we are committed to changing the nature of the relationship between Aboriginal and non-Aboriginal peoples in Canada." To that end Canada expressed its regret for damage done by its policies, especially the infamous residential schools, promised $350 million for healing programs to address that damage, and undertook to work with all the Native groups for a more harmonious future based on mutual respect.[34]

As encouraging as the federal government's Statement of Reconciliation was, it was typical of Native–non-Native relations at the end of the twentieth century in that it left many major issues unaddressed. While it went beyond the final report of the Royal Commission on Aboriginal Peoples on residential schools, promising financial aid for healing programs where RCAP had called for a public inquiry, in other important areas it fell strikingly short of what the commissioners had urged fourteen months earlier. There was no talk of a twenty-first-century royal proclamation to embody the renewed relationship, and the vexed question of Aboriginal self-government and its constitutional entrenchment was avoided. The Métis welcomed the statement's call for efforts to rehabilitate the historical image and standing of their hero, Louis Riel, but were less impressed with other aspects. Harry

Daniels of the Congress of Aboriginal Peoples pointedly observed at the ceremony that the non-status Indians and Métis still had not achieved a position like that of status Indians whose agenda was addressed regularly at least, if not usually effectively, by the government.

The January 1998 Statement of Reconciliation, with its good intentions and incomplete solutions, was symbolic of the state of Native–non-Native relations. Aboriginal self-government through constitutional amendment was viewed by government and non-Natives as a dead end, but Aboriginal groups still sought recognition of their inherent rights in this area. The scandal of residential schools was being addressed, but only at an individual or community level, not comprehensively. Given the failure of leadership by the federal government in dealing with individual complaints of abuse, the Christian churches continued to pursue a legal strategy of denying liability in the hope that the courts would force Ottawa to accept at least a share of responsibility. In 1998 a lower court ruling in a case involving the Alberni residential school on Vancouver Island apportioned liability between the United Church and Canada, beginning a legal process of fixing responsibility. However, Canada continued to evade grappling with the issue, and the expensive trail of litigation lengthened. By early 1999 there were 2,500 actions launched over residential school abuse of various types, and hundreds, if not thousands, more were maturing in law offices across the country. A surprise negotiated settlement of a case involving the Roman Catholic Williams Lake, or Cariboo, residential school in October 1998 created a spark of hope that painful and costly litigation might be avoided, at least in some instances. The reason for the unexpected resolution was that federal lawyers dropped their aggressive approach to claimants and entered into meaningful discussions with them. The school survivors responded positively, leading to the out-of-court settlement.[35] In the *Williams Lake* case both Roman Catholic agencies and the federal government were respondents. Did their newfound willingness to negotiate indicate a changed strategy on handling residential school cases? A federal government representative suggested it might, indicating to the *Vancouver Sun* that he expected the *Williams Lake* settlement to be the first of many, although it later appeared that he meant Ottawa would settle where there was a pre-existing criminal conviction of an abuser.[36]

The *Williams Lake* case and the Statement of Reconciliation were typical of many areas. For example, the government promised better treatment to the Métis, and by late 1998 courts in Manitoba, Saskatchewan, and Ontario seemed well on the way to establishing that the Métis had an Aboriginal right to hunt for food.[37] On the other hand, the *Dumont* case, a litigated Métis land claim in Manitoba that had been launched in the early 1980s still trundled along, and the provinces in which the courts found in favour of Aboriginal hunting rights for the Métis all appealed the lower court decisions. In Saskatchewan, in 1998, the Court of Appeal reversed the pro-Métis decision of the Court of Queen's Bench. Similarly, the courts had in the 1990s broadened the definition of other Aboriginal rights in the *Sparrow* and *Sioui* cases, but in 1996 the Supreme Court had appeared to narrow First Nations' ability to claim those rights by articulating stringent criteria for judicial recognition of Aboriginal rights in the *Van der Peet* decision. And then, in December 1997, the same jurists had delivered an expanded version of Aboriginal title. Which way would the courts move in the new century? To close out the eventful decade, in the autumn of 1999 the Supreme Court of Canada upheld Mi'kmaq fishing rights in *Marshall*, a case that turned on 1760–1 treaties.[38]

Other individual disputes also festered. The Innu in Labrador continued a long-standing resistance to low-level flights over their territories, and now they also were concerned about proposals from the Inco corporation and two levels of government to develop a massive nickel deposit near Voisey's Bay that initially did not take their territorial rights into account. In Ontario, what was known simply as Ipperwash continued to rankle with many First Nations. In 1995 provincial police had attacked occupiers of disputed land on Lake Huron, resulting in the death of Dudley George, a local leader. The reason that the incident lingered as an irritant in Native–non-native relations was that the provincial government steadfastly refused to accede to calls for a judicial inquiry to investigate what involvement the premier's office had had in the fatal affair. In the Prairies at century's end, even if there was encouraging progress on some specific claims such as Treaty Land Entitlement in Saskatchewan, and with judicial recognition in Manitoba of Métis Aboriginal hunting rights, old disputes such as the unfulfilled claims to reserve lands and compensation of the Lubicon Lake Cree persisted. And in British Columbia, the acrimonious debate on ratification of the Nisga'a agreement in 1998–9 did not augur well for the dozens of other comprehensive claims that First Nations and governments were trying to negotiate. On the other hand, the launch of Nunavut was a, perhaps, encouraging sign of the future. From one end of the country to the other, it was clear at the end of the 1990s that the future course of relations between Indigenous and settler societies in Canada remained, as usual, murky and unpredictable.

Part Four

RECONCILIATION?

CHAPTER SIXTEEN

Relations in the Twenty-First Century

In Native-newcomer relations, the two decades following the *Marshall* decision on Mi'kmaq treaty rights in some ways resembled a roller-coaster ride. Euphoria over the Supreme Court decision in 1999 gave way to angst about the stormy reception the decision received from non-Native fishers. Similarly, after sometimes uneasy relations between the Assembly of First Nations and the Jean Chrétien government (1993–2003) concerning litigation over allegations of residential school abuse, feelings relaxed and unease was replaced by a warm relationship under Liberal Prime Minister Paul Martin (2003–6) that led to an unprecedented agreement to tackle a range of social problems facing status Indian communities. Prospects for implementing the promises Martin made were dashed by the election of a Conservative leader, Stephen Harper (2006–15), who, with one brief exception, turned a cold face to Indigenous representations. And then the Conservatives were supplanted in the federal election of 2015 by a Liberal government, under Justin Trudeau, that promised a new relationship between government and Indigenous peoples. About the only part of Canadian society that was consistent in its dealings with Native peoples in the first years of the new century were the courts.

The Supreme Court of Canada's (SCC) ruling in *Marshall* set off an explosive reaction that exposed underlying tensions in the Maritimes. It would be more accurate to say the Court's *decisions*, because the outcry and confusion that followed the SCC's ruling in September 1999 led the Court to issue a second, clarifying ruling two months later. The decision that upheld Donald Marshall, Jr.'s right to fish for "a moderate livelihood" took many people by surprise. Among them, apparently, was the federal Department of Fisheries and Oceans, which responded slowly to the ensuing controversy. First Nations fishers reacted enthusiastically and took to the waters to harvest lobster, which was out of season.[1] Non-Native fishers, whose livelihood had been made precarious by the collapse of cod stocks and who found in the lobster fishery one of the few bright spots in their local economy, responded angrily to First Nation actions they viewed as jeopardizing their livelihood.[2] Incidents of threatened and actual violence between competing fishers on the water ended only with the onset of winter and the suspension of all fishing in the region. The Department of Fisheries and Oceans attempted to implement a strategy that involved government buying out the licences and equipment of non-Native fishers and supporting an expansion of the First Nation fishery. The program, though sensible on its own terms, did little to calm tempers. Over the next few years, the inherent moderation of Maritime people brought about a lowering of the emotional temperature, but the *Marshall* decision and its aftermath left lingering resentments on both sides.

At the other end of the country, the British Columbia Treaty Commission negotiation process avoided the type of fireworks that occurred in New Brunswick but, arguably, was no more successful than the federal government's response to *Marshall*. In 1992, responding to both the Supreme Court's comments about Aboriginal rights in the *Sparrow* decision and the heightened awareness of Aboriginal grievances after the Oka Crisis, the governments of Canada, British Columbia, and the provincial chiefs' association known as the First Nations Summit, established the British Columbia Treaty Commission to address the Aboriginal title issues that affected most of the land mass of British Columbia. The commission is not a treaty negotiator, but rather a facilitator whose role is to promote and help the parties to enter into discussions intended to lead to the conclusion of a territorial treaty. The treaty commission set up an elaborate six-stage framework, with stage one being the filing of a statement of intent to negotiate by a First Nation, stage five the negotiation of a final agreement, and stage six, the final stage, the implementation of the negotiated treaty following ratification by the several parties. In all, sixty-five of the province's First Nations, representing 104 of a total of 203 officially recognized bands, have participated or are participating in the British Columbia Treaty Commission process. To put it mildly, it has not gone well. A quarter-century after its start, and at enormous cost, the treaty commission process has facilitated only four agreements.[3] Maa-nulth First Nations on Vancouver Island, Tla'amin First Nation near Powell River, Tsawwassen First Nation just south of Vancouver, and Yale First Nation in the highly developed Fraser River Valley are the small minority who have made it to stage six. More than once, the BC treaty commission process has come close to breaking down completely.

The problems that the British Columbia Treaty Commission process has en-countered help to explain the complexity of modern-day treaty-making and the problems in Native-newcomer relations in the twenty-first century. Largely because of the long history of state denial of Aboriginal title in British Columbia, negotia-tors face a legacy of distrust and suspicion that can cause problems. As well, ne-gotiating treaties today in densely populated and economically highly developed regions in the southern part of the province is akin to trying to unscramble an omelette. The Tsawwassen First Nation territory is hemmed in by a BC Ferries ter-minal, the Roberts Bank Superport to accommodate ships taking coal and other products to export markets, and a large number of non-Native homes and busi-nesses, many of them spilled over from the mushrooming metropolis of Vancouver. Finally, particularly during the years of Stephen Harper's government, critics al-leged that federal government negotiators effectively had no mandate from their principal to conclude agreements. After more than two years under the govern-ment of Justin Trudeau, there is little evidence of changed attitudes and faster prog-ress. It is by no means clear that the British Columbia Treaty Process will survive. If it does not, what then will people and corporations in British Columbia do about unresolved Aboriginal title that clouds non-Natives' title to property and deters economic development?

A high-profile incident in Ontario in 1995 suggested what kinds of violence could occur when Aboriginal lands were in dispute. The Ontario case involved land on Lake Huron that the Government of Canada had taken from First Nations during the Second World War for military purposes. Prior to confiscation under the War Measures Act, Ottawa had tried and failed to purchase the land from the Kettle and Stoney Point community, promising to return the tract after the war. The return of land that was part of both Ipperwash Provincial Park and the Ipperwash military base did not occur, and its continuing appropriation was a major grievance for the Natives. Protesters took control of a grenade range in 1993 and later expanded their foothold into the nearby provincial park. On the Labour Day weekend in 1995 their numbers were reinforced by other members of the band. The Kettle and Stoney Point people maintained that they were attempting to repatriate a cemetery. As tensions developed, the premier of the province, Conservative Mike Harris, was heard to exclaim "I want the fucking Indians out of the park" at a meeting with provincial police commanders.[4] In the event, amidst confusion and miscommuni-cation, the police and protesters tangled. At the end of the confrontation, Dudley George, a member of the Stoney Point group, was dead.[5]

Although there was an immediate outcry and demand for an inquiry into what had caused Dudley George's death, the Harris government and its Conservative successor refused to call one. Only after the Conservatives were replaced by Liberals led by Dalton McGuinty in 2003 was Justice Sidney Linden commissioned to hold a judicial inquiry into the events at Ipperwash. Linden's exhaustive investigation led to the production in 2007 of a massive report that was critical of the provincial police, the Ontario government, and Ottawa for their handling of the dispute and protest. The report proposed a variety of steps to resolve the dispute, including the return of the disputed lands to the First Nation.[6] In fact, it would not be until April 2016, following the election of the Liberal government of Justin Trudeau, that the federal government arranged for return of the land.[7] As well, a provincial police sergeant, Kenneth Deane, was convicted of criminal negligence causing the death of Dudley George. The Ipperwash dispute underlined the serious consequences that Indigenous land claims could generate as well as the reluctance of governments to grapple with the issue once dispute turned into an organized protest.

A change of government of a very different sort led to another major setback for First Nations in the first decade of the twenty-first century. When Paul Martin, Jr., took over leadership of the Liberal Party and the prime ministry from Jean Chrétien late in 2003, it was a certainty that some of federal government's priorities would shift. Chrétien had devoted large amounts from the surpluses generated from 1998 onward to post-secondary research and education. Paul Martin wanted to give more attention and money to resolve some of the problems – to "close the gap" in the standard of living was the shorthand for what was intended – in Indigenous peoples' health care, education, housing, and economic development. After eighteen months of negotiations involving the provincial and territorial governments, as well as five national Aboriginal organizations, an agreement known as the Kelowna Accord was concluded in November 2005. The accord was a ten-year plan, involving a commitment of funding of $5 billion over the first five years, for Aboriginal social services. Although legislation to implement the ambitious agreement had not been passed by the time Martin lost power in a general election in early 2006, the defeated Liberals had made plans for implementation. Following the lengthy negotiations in 2004 and 2005, the Martin cabinet had twice discussed and approved the accord, and the department of finance had "booked" funds for it before parliament was dissolved in November 2005.[8] The new Conservative government led by Stephen Harper indicated in its first budget that it was rejecting the accord by allocating much less money for the causes Kelowna covered than the agreement had contained. As well, some rash Conservative politicians dismissed the accord as a hastily concluded pact scratched on the back of a napkin. The Kelowna Accord represented both a major opportunity lost and a harbinger of the difficult times ahead for Aboriginal peoples with a Harper-led Conservative government in power in Ottawa.

Indigenous peoples fared much better with jurists than with politicians in the first two decades of the twenty-first century. Aboriginal and treaty rights cases in the period from 2000 until 2016 built on the successes that First Nations, Métis, and Inuit had enjoyed in the courts under the new constitution adopted in 1982 and tested judicially from 1985 onward. Cases such as the *Guerin* decision in 1984 and *Sparrow* in 1990 began the process of defining what the phrase "existing Aboriginal … rights" meant in practice. In the 1990s, First Nations made progress in fleshing out the content of the "existing … treaty rights" that were constitutionally guaranteed by section 35 of the 1982 constitutional pact. Also important in the trend of high court decisions was the 1997 *Delgamuukw* ruling, which both established the validity of oral history evidence in law and continued the courts' process of defining "Aboriginal title." The nineteenth-century decision of the Judicial Committee of the Privy Council in *St. Catharines Milling* had defined that title as "a personal and usufructuary right dependent on the good will of the Sovereign." It was not until 1973 that another substantial step was taken, in the *Calder* decision, which confirmed that Aboriginal title was part of the common law. Finally, *Delgamuukw* advanced the definition further, with the chief justice of the Supreme Court declaring "Aboriginal title is a right to the land itself." As useful as these steps were, much still remained to be defined not just in Aboriginal title, but in "existing Aboriginal and treaty rights" in general, including those of Aboriginal people other than the First Nations.

The Métis made substantial strides in achieving judicial definition of their rights. They had always been the most vulnerable of the three Aboriginal groups because their status was ill-defined in law. In 1993, Steve Powley and his son Roddy killed a moose near Sault Ste. Marie and were charged with a conservation offence. They pled that their right to hunt for food was covered by section 35 of the constitution. At trial in 1998, the historic practices of the Métis of the region were examined in considerable detail, with the judge concluding that the Powleys' right to hunt was, indeed, an "existing" Aboriginal right and acquitting them of the charges they faced. The Crown appealed the decision to the Ontario Superior Court of Justice, then the Ontario Court of Appeal, and, finally, the Supreme Court of Canada. The Supreme Court in 2003 unanimously found in favour of the Powleys. The decision in the *Powley* case made it clear that the hunting right was site-specific, and the ruling did not necessarily apply more broadly to Métis communities elsewhere.[9]

In 2013, another Métis legal case, this one with deep historical roots, was resolved by the Supreme Court of Canada in a 6–2 decision. The dispute arose over the faulty implementation of the commitment in the Manitoba Act of 1870 to provide land to "children of the half-breed heads of families residing in the province" at the time of Rupert's Land transfer. The intention was to provide a land base for the Métis in anticipation of heavy non-Native settlement, and Prime Minister Macdonald defended the provision against criticisms by the Reform opposition by pointing out that Métis shared in "Indian title" and were entitled to have their prior rights recognized. For a number of reasons, some of them strongly suggesting fraud on the part of the government and local officials, many Métis did not receive their land grants.[10] The failure of the land-granting provision contributed greatly to the Métis economic problems throughout the twentieth century. Litigation started in the 1980s and later stalled, being revived in the early twenty-first century by the Manitoba Métis Federation (MMF). In 2013, the Supreme Court of Canada upheld the MMF argument, and in the spring of 2016 the recently elected government of Justin Trudeau signed a memorandum of agreement to negotiate a final settlement of the dispute. Needless to say, there was great rejoicing in the Manitoba Métis community.[11]

The final judicial victory the Métis achieved concerned their constitutional recognition. *Powley* had recognized their site-specific gathering rights, and the *Manitoba Métis Federation* case had resolved a long-standing grievance over lands. The *Daniels* decision settled questions about the standing of the Métis under the 1982 constitution. Section 35 specified "existing aboriginal and treaty rights" of "the aboriginal peoples of Canada" and said explicitly that the Métis were one of those "aboriginal peoples." But what did that statement mean in practice? (The case bore the name of Harry Daniels, a longtime Métis leader who died before the litigation was resolved.) The Federation and the Congress of Aboriginal Peoples, who represented non-status Indians, asked the Court to find that they fell within section 91(24) of the British North America Act, which assigned jurisdiction over "Indians and lands reserved for the Indians" to the parliament, in other words the federal government. They also asked that the Court declare that the Crown had a fiduciary duty towards them, and that the government was obligated to negotiate with them concerning their rights, interests, and needs. Unanimously, the Supreme Court came down in the affirmative on the first question, but declined to address the other two.[12] It was a significant, but incomplete, victory for the Métis: while their status was clarified definitively, they would still have to struggle to obtain the full range of rights to which they believed they were entitled.

Judicial advances for First Nations were similarly significant but qualified. Among the most important was recognition of the Crown's duty to consult Aboriginal peoples. In the *Haida* and *Taku River* rulings in 2004, as well as the *Mikisew* decision the following year, the Supreme Court of Canada found that the Crown was obligated to consult and, where appropriate, accommodate the Aboriginal parties when economic development on their traditional lands was being considered. A subsequent case produced a further explanation: "The duty to consult is part of the process for achieving 'the reconciliation of the pre-existence of Aboriginal societies with the sovereignty of the Crown.'"[13] Not surprisingly, these broad concepts have created a good deal of uncertainty, and advocates and courts have all been wrestling with the implications of "duty to consult" ever since.[14] It seems likely that the concept will take some time, and numerous higher court decisions, to clarify.

A more unqualified advance was the Supreme Court's landmark ruling on Aboriginal title in *Tsilhquot'in* in 2014. The case arose from provincially authorized lumbering operations in the central interior of British Columbia in the early 1980s, a region that was part of the traditional lands of the Tsilhquot'in. Like much of British Columbia, this region had never been covered by a territorial treaty, leading one of the six bands that constituted the Tsilhquot'in Nation to argue that the clear-cut logging that the province had authorized was illicit because the band still held Aboriginal title to the land. Although the band lost in the first trial and on appeal to the BC Court of Appeal, it succeeded at the Supreme Court of Canada in 2014. The Court found that the lands in question were indubitably those to which the band held title, and that the Crown had never extinguished that right. *Tsilhquot'in* advanced beyond the ruling in *Delgamuukw* because this time the highest court applied title to a specific area of 1750 square kilometres that the band had historically occupied and used. As had by now become customary, the Supreme Court also declared that the Aboriginal title was not absolute but, like Aboriginal rights such as Ronald Sparrow's right to fish, could be regulated and limited by government in pursuit of an important public objective and following proper consultation with and accommodation of the First Nation in question.[15]

A final case from the early decades of the twenty-first century was revelatory about both the law and federal government behaviour. In 2007, Dr. Cindy Blackstock, a Gitxsan academic with a profound interest in the rights and wellbeing of Indigenous children, lodged a complaint with the Canadian Human Rights Tribunal (CHRT) on behalf of the First Nations Child and Family Caring Society, which she led. Blackstock alleged that the federal government was guilty of discrimination because it did not provide funding for First Nations at the level that non-Aboriginal children enjoyed. She and her organization were then subjected to what can only be described as harassment by the government now headed by Stephen Harper. Federal core funding for the First Nations Child and Family Caring Society was terminated a month after the case was lodged with the CHRT, and Blackstock herself was subjected to surveillance by federal officials. The department of justice also sought to obstruct and delay the work of the human rights tribunal with a series of legal manoeuvres.

Nonetheless, in January 2016 the tribunal concluded that Ottawa had racially discriminated against more than 160,000 First Nations children and instructed government to correct the underfunding. Like First Nations who had succeeded in comprehensive claims earlier, Blackstock found that winning her case was just half the battle. Getting the decision implemented was the other half. Even the election of a Liberal government under Justin Trudeau that pledged to change how the government dealt with Indigenous peoples did not lead to satisfactory action. A year after its 2016 ruling, the Canadian Human Rights Tribunal issued another statement criticizing the federal government for inaction and calling on Ottawa yet again to implement fully its ruling.[16] Needless to say, government behaviour in the case Cindy Blackstock brought exacerbated tensions between government and Indigenous peoples.

The frustration Cindy Blackstock experienced in dealing with the federal government was widely shared. Indeed, anger and frustration underlay one of the most spectacular outbursts of social mobilization in Canadian history. In the autumn of 2012, four women in Saskatoon decided they had had enough of government tactics. Under the banner of Idle No More, they used social media to spread word of their cause and mobilize others to act in concert with them. What was striking about Idle No More (INM), however, was that it focused mainly on what it wanted to change. Rather than articulating a broad agenda of Aboriginal rights, it laid out no plans for conventional political action, and, most important, it vigorously eschewed any violent actions to deter the government behaviour they abhorred. The immediate objects of their opprobrium were two government measures in the House of Commons – Bill C-45 and Bill C-38 – which were typical products of Stephen Harper's governing style. The measures were what is known as omnibus bills, proposed legislation that gathers several legislative items into a single measure. Omnibus bills were hardly unknown in 2012; indeed, as far back as 1969 a fledgling minister of justice named Pierre Trudeau had begun to make his reputation in federal politics by shepherding an omnibus bill to overhaul Canada's criminal code through the Commons.

What was different about Harper's budget implementation bills in 2012 was their size and complexity. Each weighed in at about 450 pages and combined new provisions in a variety of areas. C-38, for example, contained a number of clauses that

"Restless."

opponents contended would weaken Canada's environmental regulatory regime. Also significant about the bills was the fact that the Tory government, in keeping with what by 2012 was a well-established pattern, gave the measures anodyne names. Bill C-45, for example, was labelled the "Jobs and Growth Act." In addition to opposing some of the specific contents, such as changes to environmental review procedures, opponents also criticized the omnibus bills as measures designed to obfuscate and thwart critical review of the government's legislative agenda and budget.[17] The four women who founded Idle No More decided to channel their concern about the jeopardy to the environment that C-38 in particular constituted into a consciousness-raising teach-in.[18]

In addition to the teach-in, which was held in early November 2012, Idle No More spawned a nation-wide and international movement of protest in a few short months. Using social media to inform and assemble people, the organizers conducted round dances in shopping malls and demonstrations in a number of places to get their message out. The dances were expressions of the pride in Indigenous culture and identity that, along with frustration and anger, fuelled Idle No More. Throughout the mobilization of Idle No More, they insisted on non-violent actions, kept their distance from established leaders of Indigenous political organizations, emphasized the primacy of treaties as a foundation of the Canadian community,

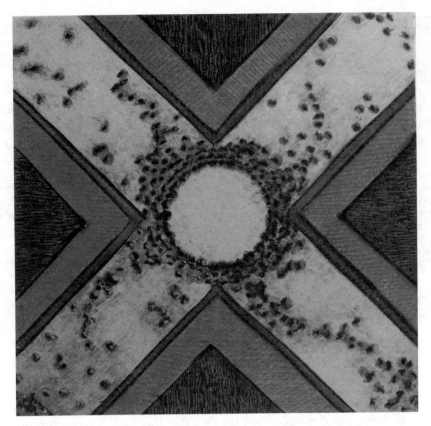

"Idle No More."

and criticized the federal government's attempt to erode legislative and regulatory protection of the environment. They tapped into the unease that by late 2012 was being felt in some sectors of Canadian society with the Harper government's un-critical promotion of petroleum development, including especially the oil sands in northern Alberta and pipelines to transport the heavy crude to American refiner-ies. Such was the power of social media that their movement took on a life of its own in only weeks. It appealed to young people in particular, but by no means were they the only ones swept up in it.[19]

In December 2012, Idle No More became ensnared in another protest that would sap the movement's momentum and enable the federal government to reassert its control of the situation. On 11 December, Theresa Spence, Chief of the James Bay Cree community of Attawapiskat in far northern Ontario, launched a hunger strike to protest Canada's mistreatment of Indigenous peoples, a resistance she said she was undertaking in the spirit of Idle No More. Her motivation was the abysmal conditions that beset the band that she led and the unresponsiveness of government in helping to deal with them. Unfortunately, she also issued demands that included that the prime minister and governor general meet with her and Aboriginal leaders to negotiate measures to deal with the problems. She believed firmly – and repeated the point frequently – that First Nations' treaties had been concluded with the monarch directly and that the queen or her representative in Canada, the governor general, should be involved. The difficulty for the governor general was that Canada was a constitutional, not an absolute, monarchy, and the queen's representative did nothing of a political nature except on the advice of his ministers. That approach was rooted in more than a century of the practice of responsible government.

For the governor general's first minister, Stephen Harper, Spence's obstinate insistence on involving the governor general was a golden opportunity to undermine her. His government had already released an auditor's report that seemed to the ill-informed to show that Chief Spence's band had been the recipient of lavish financial aid over the years. In fact, it showed nothing of the kind: the Attawapiskat band, like First Nations across the country, received funds to carry out tasks that for ordinary Canadians were provided by all three levels of government. As a result, the sums in the auditor's report were very large. All the same, the smear worked; non-Aboriginal support for Spence weakened substantially. After a flurry of action, federal ministers met with Aboriginal leaders on 21 December in a consultation that produced no firm commitments by government. In the process, the Tory leader had divided Aboriginal leadership, because some leaders, following Chief Spence, refused to participate because the governor general was not involved. The following day, Governor General David Johnston did meet with Aboriginal leaders in a purely ceremonial gathering at Rideau Hall. For Stephen Harper the results of the confrontation showed that he had won the trifecta: isolated and undermined Chief Spence, divided Aboriginal leaders, and distracted attention from the swelling Idle No More movement.[20]

For Indigenous people and the country at large, though, the outcome was more complicated. True, Chief Spence had unwittingly assisted the government and complicated the Idle No More movement. But Idle No More was not directly affected by the Spence debacle. The organizers, while making positive comments about Spence and her hunger strike, had carefully kept clear of her and avoided endorsing her cause or tactics. For her part, Chief Spence expressed her admiration of Idle No More but never claimed to be part of it or authorized by its leaders. All the same, a careless and hurried media tended to lump Chief Spence's fast and Idle No More together, just as they missed the key elements of the movement. Idle No More, as noted, was not a conventional Indigenous political movement nor did it adopt the usual methods. It had key tenets that it proclaimed repeatedly: the primacy of treaties, the necessity of stopping the erosion of the environment and environmental regulations, and the absolutely essential need to engage only in peaceful tactics. Observers also missed the fact that Idle No More was an expression of Indigenous pride and determination as well as its anger and frustration at the conditions in which Aboriginal people lived. Tapping into those emotions, especially among young people, ensured that Idle No More would endure after Theresa Spence and Stephen Harper ceased to be major political actors. Media analysts also usually missed, or downplayed, the reality that Idle No More was an implicit critique of Indigenous political leaders. Perry Bellegarde, National Chief of the Assembly of First Nations, had every reason to be uneasy about the implications of the emotions and objectives that Idle No More represented. It will be worth watching to see if events in the third decade and beyond of the twenty-first century give rise to a revitalization of Idle No More and the energy, joy, pride, anger, and determination it manifested in the autumn and winter of 2012–13.

In the roller-coaster ride of Native-newcomer relations in the years after 2000, the tale of efforts to secure redress and reconciliation for the ills left behind by residential schooling is an even more up-and-down story than most events within the theme. Although the efforts involved are usually grouped under the heading "reconciliation," it is more accurate to refer to "redress and reconciliation" because the champions of residential school survivors rightly knew that compensation for the material damage done to individuals was and is important. Indeed, redress for past wrongs might be almost as important as sincere efforts to heal social fissures.[21] Reconciliation cannot take place without accompanying redress because the historic victims of Native-newcomer relations in Canada have a lengthy list of accumulated grievances and claims that must be addressed before there can be reconciliation. It will not be possible to persuade them of the sincerity of the dominant society's efforts to forge a new relationship of mutual trust in the absence of material measures. Redress must accompany reconciliation if either or both is to succeed.

It was appropriate that the first group of Canadians to begin the long and daunting journey towards reconciliation over the malignant legacy of residential schooling was the Christian churches that had operated them in cooperation with the Government of Canada.[22] The Roman Catholic Church – or, more correctly, its many agencies – the Anglican Church of Canada, the United Church of Canada, and the Presbyterian Church in Canada were the principal ecclesiastical bodies involved. They had provided the leadership, some of the funding, and day-to-day operation of the schools while the federal government authorized the creation of schools, provided the lion's share of the funds, and was supposed to be responsible for oversight of the system. Just as the government shifted its policy from support of segregated schooling to integration after the Second World War, the churches went through transformations of their own in the same period. In particular, they became increasingly conscious of and concerned about the racism and ethno-centrism that underlay much of the secular and religious teaching they provided. They also moved from viewing Indigenous people as objects of evangelistic ef-fort on whom they worked to victims of social injustice with whom they should struggle for better treatment. By the 1970s, they were engaged in pro-Aboriginal solidarity movements such as Project North and the Aboriginal Rights Coalition. In the next decade, they began to act on their reflections on how they had evan-gelized. Beginning with an apology of the General Council of the United Church of Canada in 1986 for the patronizing style of their ministrations, all the church-es and principal agencies apologized for the residential schools specifically: the Oblates of Mary Immaculate in 1991, the Anglicans in 1993, and the Presbyterians in 1994. This process of public atonement culminated in a second apology by the United Church, this one specifically for its role in residential schools, in 1998. The churches, one of the two partners in residential schooling, had begun the process of reflection and response.[23]

The other partner, the Government of Canada, continued the process of reflec-tion in the 1990s with the appointment of the Royal Commission on Aboriginal Peoples (RCAP). Between 1992 and 1996, the commission contributed to public education about residential schools and their ills by means of both public hearings and its own research. The sessions that it held across the country brought press attention to survivors' stories of what they had endured in their school days, if only briefly. More enduring was the research into the role of the federal govern-ment in the operation of the schools that the commission initiated and publicized. Particularly in its final report, issued in November 1996, the Royal Commission on Aboriginal Peoples broadcast and documented how the schools had operated and what impact they had had on their inmates. The commission's recommenda-tions about residential schooling were anticlimactic: it proposed only that Ottawa conduct a public inquiry into the schools and that it "fund establishment of a na-tional repository of records and video collections related to residential schools." In its response to the commission's final report, the government of Jean Chrétien ignored the proposals on residential schools as, indeed, it did the commission's am-bitious recommendations on governance. In its January 1998 *Gathering Strength*, the federal government promised neither a public inquiry nor the creation of a record centre. It did, however, offer a $350-million grant to create and operate an Aboriginal Healing Foundation (AHF). At the release of *Gathering Strength*, Indian Affairs Minister Jane Stewart delivered an apparently heartfelt apology for residential schools that only partially satisfied the leaders of the Aboriginal political organizations. The AHF did important work helping individuals and communities deal with the damage that residential schooling had inflicted until its funding was terminated.[24]

Following the inadequate efforts of church and state it was the turn of the courts to wrestle with the consequences of residential schooling and the harms it had inflicted on students. Between the late 1990s and 2004, thousands of former students launched individual lawsuits against the government for abuse suffered at the schools. On the advice of counsel, survivors named the Government of Canada as the respondent in the litigation, but Ottawa immediately cross-sued the churches that had operated the schools, arguing that they were responsible for the lack of oversight that allowed the abuse to happen. This tactic drew the churches into the litigation, complicating proceedings and making them more costly for all concerned. Litigants quickly discovered that lawsuits could not bring them redress for cultural loss, including language, because Canadian civil law did not recognize that as compensable. They also found that the adversarial processes of civil law subjected them to withering cross-examination that often meant their revictimization and trauma. By 2004, when the individual legal actions numbered about 14,000 and had been joined by collective litigation known as class actions, the federal government began to rethink its tactics. The churches that were involved had been calling for years for a different approach, both in their own interest and for the sake of former students. When one of the class actions was certified in an Ontario court to proceed to trial, the federal government agreed with a proposal from the Assembly of First Nations to negotiate a comprehensive settlement of all the litigation, individual and class, that would prove less harmful to claimants. The result, finalized in 2006, was the Indian Residential Schools Settlement Agreement (IRSSA), the largest class-action settlement in Canadian history.[25]

The IRSSA, or Settlement Agreement, was wide-ranging and ambitious. When, after a period of court reviews necessitated by the fact that it was a settlement of class actions, it was implemented beginning in September 2007, it provided compensation, support for healing and commemoration, and the broad public inquiry that the Royal Commission on Aboriginal Peoples had called for in 1996. Compensating former students took two forms: a Common Experience Payment (CEP) that a survivor could get simply by proving attendance at one of the residential schools on an approved list, and awards under the Independent Assessment Process (IAP) that reviewed claims of serious physical and sexual abuse by means of an adjudicator who was instructed to avoid the most harrowing features of the adversarial court system. Money would be provided to continue the work of the Aboriginal Healing Foundation, and $20 million was set aside for projects to commemorate the schools. The most striking of the IRSSA's provisions, however, was the creation of a Truth and Reconciliation Commission (TRC) that over the course of five years was to investigate what the schools had done. It was to hold seven National Events, issue an interim report and then a final report, and establish a national record archives to house the records it would gather from a variety of government and church agencies as well as the records of its own public consultations.[26]

None of the Settlement Agreement's provisions was untroubled in its implementation. The grant to the Aboriginal Healing Foundation and the commemoration program were the least problematic. The AHF simply carried on operations at it had since 1998, in the process helping a lot of people and communities. The program to support commemoration, although it suffered delays that inconvenienced recipients of its grants, was carried out effectively, yielding many influential monuments, works of art, and even a ballet. The compensation provisions, however, were far more problematic. Among the problems were the lawyers for former students, who benefited enormously because they had been at the table when the IRSSA was negotiated. Lawyers also played a prominent role in the administration of the Independent Assessment Process, with some settling for the 15 per cent of the amount awarded by an adjudicator, many more charging their clients an additional amount permitted by the Settlement Agreement, and some bad apples outrageously exploiting the process for their personal gain. Publicity about the worst behaviour in the Independent Assessment Process did the reputation of the legal profession, probably never high among Canadians, no good at all. The Common Experience Payment was bedevilled by delays stemming mainly from the large number of survivors – far more than anticipated – who came forward to claim compensation for their attendance at residential schools. The Independent Assessment Process, which was expected to wind up operations only in 2017, was similarly challenged by the large numbers of claimants and the complexity of assembling all the evidence needed for a case from governmental and church sources. Approximately 37,000 of the estimated 100,000 surviving former students applied for compensation under IAP, although it was clear that a good number who were eligible to apply chose not to because of the delays and the stress that were unavoidable under the adjudication system.[27]

The problems that the commemoration program, the Common Experience Payment, and the Independent Assessment Process encountered, however, were minor compared to the challenges that the Truth and Reconciliation Commission had to confront. The people appointed to the commission in 2008 had promising credentials. The chair was Justice Harry LaForme of Ontario's Court of Appeal, and he was joined by Jane Brewin, a BC lawyer with experience investigating problems in custodial institutions, and Claudette Dumont-Smith, a health practitioner with a track record of service that included work with the Native Women's Association of Canada. Begun amidst high hopes at the end of June 2008, the TRC quickly ran into trouble. Within a few months it was obvious that the three commissioners were not working together harmoniously. When Justice LaForme resigned in the autumn he blamed the problems on the two women who, he charged, would not follow and support his lead. He said they wanted to decide things by vote, an approach he claimed was inappropriate. What Morley and Dumont-Smith wanted was a collegial approach, though they were prepared to accept the judge's leadership. The difficulty with LaForme's argument was that there was nothing in the provisions of the Settlement Agreement setting up the TRC that justified his interpretation of the chair's and members' roles. Morley and Dumont-Smith soldiered on, preparing materials for the new commission that would replace them, before resigning in 2009.[28]

The terrible events that befell the Truth and Reconciliation Commission were all the more unexpected and devastating because they followed shortly after an inspirational apology by the prime minister for the federal government's role in residential schooling. In fact, Stephen Harper closed his apology by hailing the commission as a "cornerstone of the settlement agreement" and "a unique opportunity to educate all Canadians on the Indian residential schools system." His apology, unlike the TRC, was not a part of the IRSSA. He had had to be dragged reluctantly to yield to pressure from Aboriginal political and survivors' organizations to issue a formal apology. Nonetheless, the statement he delivered in the House of Commons on 11 June 2008, with Aboriginal political leaders seated on the floor of the House, was eloquent and moving. Harper acknowledged the wrongs that had been done to Indigenous children in the schools, devoting half of his remarks to the revisionist interpretation of the history of Native-newcomer relations that the Royal Commission on Aboriginal Peoples had been the first state agency to articulate. The school system often "forcibly removed" children from their homes, "deprived [them] of the care and nurturing of their" families, and "inadequately fed, clothed and housed" them. He noted the fact that while some "former students have spoken positively about their experiences," those memories "are far overshadowed by

Stephen Harper apologizing for residential schools in 2008.

tragic accounts of the emotional, physical and sexual abuse and neglect of helpless children, and their separation from powerless families and communities." As
leader of the government, he said, he stood before them to "apologize to aboriginal
peoples for Canada's role in the Indian residential schools system," and went on
to say, "The government of Canada sincerely apologizes and asks the forgiveness
of the aboriginal peoples of this country for failing them so profoundly ... We are
sorry." The responses of the leaders of Aboriginal organizations, including Phil
Fontaine of the Assembly of First Nations, who had been instrumental in getting
the schools file to a resolution, reflected their appreciation of the apology.[29] The
public response, though sometimes mixed, was highly positive overall.

In keeping with the roller-coaster nature of Native-newcomer relations in the
first two decades of the twenty-first century, the euphoria turned to disappointment, disillusionment, and anger fairly quickly. Harper took a series of steps that
seemed to indicate that the apology had been the end of the residential school story
as far as he was concerned, not the first step on a journey towards reconciliation. He
closed the separate government department that had overseen residential school
matters, transferring its staff to the Aboriginal Affairs and Northern Development

department. His government's 2010 budget announced termination of funding
for the Aboriginal Healing Foundation. And a belated decision in 2010 to drop
his government's opposition to the United Nations Declaration on the Rights of
Indigenous Peoples was marred by an accompanying statement that insisted that
UNDRIP was read by the government of Canada as merely "an aspirational document" and a "non-legally binding document that does not reflect customary international law nor change Canada's laws."[30] Most shocking of all government actions,
though, was the federal department of justice's employment from late 2010 onward of a legal dodge known as "the administrative split." The term referred to the
fact that from 1969 onward, Ottawa had split the functions of former residential
schools in the North into custodial work carried out by hostels and pedagogical
work undertaken in nearby publicly supported schools. Now, for the first time, government lawyers argued that claimants that had been in the hostels from the 1970s
on were ineligible to apply for compensation under the Independent Assessment
Process. What was worse was that the courts and the IAP administration abided
by the federal ploy.[31] Many survivors who might have been impressed by the 2008
apology were thoroughly disillusioned by the government's behaviour following it.

On the other hand, the second Truth and Reconciliation Commission experienced mixed relations with the Stephen Harper government. While the commissioners battled over access to the "relevant documents" in government hands that
the Settlement Agreement said they were entitled to collect, in the final stages of
the new Commission's work Harper did agree to allow the TRC an additional year
and more funds to make up for the time lost and money expended on the first,
failed commission.[32] After an impressive "coming out" in its first National Event in
Winnipeg in June 2010, the commission ran into problems before regaining momentum. The commissioners certainly were an impressive trio: former Manitoba
Court of Appeal Justice Murray Sinclair was chief commissioner (not chair); lawyer
and former chief of an Alberta band Wilton Littlechild, and northern territories
journalist Marie Wilson were commissioners. Like the first TRC, the second reflected the same two-to-one composition favouring First Nations over non-Natives,
and the same preponderance of people with legal backgrounds. Both Sinclair and
Littlechild were trained in law, and Littlechild had also served in the House of
Commons. Although their work was not without occasional strains and friction,
the three worked effectively together, Littlechild and Wilson apparently content
to allow Sinclair to be the prominent leader and voice of the TRC. For his part,
Murray Sinclair had an ingratiating manner and warm sense of humour that made
him a hit with audiences. Between 2009 and 2015, the new commission held seven
National Events, two regional gatherings, and dozens of local events designed to

The TRC commissioners, (L–R) Marie Wilson, Murray Sinclair, and Wilton Littlechild, in 2009.

educate the public about residential schools and collect testimony from survivors and others who had been involved in residential schooling.

Like the Royal Commission on Aboriginal Peoples, among the most enduring products of the Truth and Reconciliation Commission were its reports. The other major contribution the TRC made was the creation of the National Centre for Truth and Reconciliation on the University of Manitoba campus. As far as the commission's reports are concerned, although the Settlement Agreement charged the TRC to produce an interim and a final report, the commissioners actually brought out three. Their interim report, *They Came for the Children,* was a short, hastily assembled document based principally on published and some archival sources. As well, in 2015 the commission released two versions of its final report. A summary final report that relied heavily on the oral testimony of former students was released in June and quickly published by a commercial publisher. The real final report, however, became available only in December 2015, in large part because extra time was required to translate the mammoth document into both official languages and three Indigenous languages.[33] Like RCAP's, the TRC's final report was a massive document of six volumes that weighed in at over 3,200 pages. And like the RCAP *Final Report*, the TRC's published legacy was presented within a historical

The TRC commissioners, (L–R) Wilton Littlechild, Murray Sinclair, and Marie Wilson, in 2015.

framework that adopted the revisionist version of Native-newcomer history that had been developed in the academy in the 1980s and that achieved consensus status among professional historians by the 1990s.[34] Indeed, the study of the past bulked large in the TRC's conclusions. About 70 per cent of its six volumes covered the history of one aspect or another of the schools, although the volumes on the Métis and northerners' experiences were skimpy and unimpressive. The general narrative history of the schools was contained in two "parts" of the first volume that totaled 1,888 pages. The booklet on the Métis, on the other hand, numbered but ninety-six pages.

The TRC's rationale for its heavy emphasis on history was simple: "Genuine reconciliation will not be possible until the broad legacy of the schools is both understood and addressed."[35] The past was not all negative, however. "If Canada's past is a cautionary tale about what not to do, it also holds a more constructive history lesson for the future. The Treaties are a model for how Canadians, as diverse peoples, can live respectfully and peacefully together on the lands we now share."[36] A proper understanding of the path to reconciliation, which the commission defined as the restoration and maintenance of respectful relations, also involved history. Referring to residential schools and the Sixties Scoop, the commission said, "Too many

Canadians know little or nothing about the deep historical roots of these conflicts. This lack of historical knowledge has serious consequences for First Nations, Inuit, and Métis peoples, and for Canada as a whole ... Too many Canadians still do not know the history of Aboriginal peoples' contributions to Canada, or understand that by virtue of the historical and modern Treaties negotiated by our government, we are all Treaty people. History plays an important role in reconciliation; to build for the future, Canadians must look to, and learn from, the past."[37]

In addition to its heavy emphasis on history, the Truth and Reconciliation Commission's *Final Report* was notable for its characterization of the residential schools and its prescription for curing the ills the schools had left behind. The TRC labelled the schools an exercise in "cultural genocide," a big step back from the term "genocide" with which Chief Commissioner Sinclair had flirted in 2012. It also insisted that Canada needed to use the provisions of the United Nations Declaration on the Rights of Indigenous Peoples (UNDRIP) as a framework for building reconciliation, and urged the government and the courts to follow the example of several of the Christian churches and renounce the obsolete Doctrine of Discovery, and the notion of *terra nullius* (unoccupied land) that usually accompanied it to deny Indigenous title to lands.[38] The commission's agenda for pursuing reconciliation was contained in ninety-four Calls to Action that it issued in its *Final Report*. Every major agency and institution in Canada – governments, churches, legal system, schools and universities, museums and archives, even the federal government's commemorative program in Historic Sites – were enjoined to take action. Not even the pope was spared: one Call to Action said the pope should apologize in Canada for the residential schools within one year.

As had been the case with RCAP's *Final Report*, the Harper government's reception of the TRC report was chilly. Although it did commit to provide the financial support for the National Centre for Truth and Reconciliation for which the TRC had called, it was otherwise silent. Prospects for the Calls to Action did not seem bright – another instance of the roller coaster heading down – until late 2015. Although the work of the commission played almost no role in the federal election campaign that took place in October, the result of a majority Liberal government headed by Justin Trudeau seemed to suggest better days ahead. Trudeau had promised during the campaign to implement all the Calls to Action if elected, and his government repeated the pledge in its first Speech from the Throne in December 2015. The new government did announce its unqualified endorsement of the United Nations Declaration on the Rights of Indigenous Peoples. Was the roller coaster headed up again? During the remainder of 2016 and into 2017, the signs emanating from the Liberal government were mixed. Rhetorically, the government was still committed to an ambitious plan to deal on a nation-to-nation basis with Indigenous peoples, and it did launch a commission of inquiry into missing and murdered Aboriginal women. But its minister of justice, Judy Wilson-Raybould, seemed to back away from the full implications of UNDRIP's "free, prior, and informed consent" provision in the latter part of 2016. And the Canadian Human Rights Tribunal in January 2017 marked the one-year anniversary of Dr. Cindy Blackstock's successful appeal on behalf of Indigenous children by criticizing the federal government for its failure to act on its earlier decision. Which way was the roller coaster headed?

In which direction will the roller coaster of Native-newcomer relations move in the coming years? Will there be sufficient consensus in public opinion to enable the government to move on the Truth and Reconciliation Commission's Calls to Action? Will the backlog of unresolved claims be attacked aggressively? Will relations between Indigenous peoples and settler Canada, whose devastating characteristics have been exposed repeatedly by public inquiries, begin to improve?

CHAPTER SEVENTEEN

Do We Learn Anything from History?

"While skyscrapers hide the heavens, / They can fall." The history of Native-newcomer relations in Canada demonstrates that the links between human groups, like the ties between humans and nature, are part of a single ecology. Today there is a growing understanding that the elements of a society are interdependent, bound together for good or ill. Slowly the awareness that one group's problem is everyone's is spreading. Economic disadvantages among Indigenous peoples are a drain on the whole community's wealth. Social ills in northern settlements, on reserves, and in the steadily expanding Native ghettoes that western Canadian cities harbour affect the general citizenry. Urban populations think they perceive rising crime statistics, and are fearful that Canada in the twenty-first century is about to experience the racial problems that fifty years ago confronted their southern neighbour. A 1988 report of the Canadian Bar Association on the criminal justice system's impact on Natives provided a measure of hope that something might be done, but little that was measurable was accomplished in the decades following, even though the Royal Commission on Aboriginal Peoples echoed the call for reform and many Canadians today are conscious that they should do something about the conditions in which too many Natives find themselves.

Perhaps it is worth asking if the history of five centuries of relations between newcomers and Indigenous peoples offers any clues for people in Canada, Native or non-Native, who are concerned about these ills. The philosopher Hegel once suggested that there is but one thing to be learned from history: "What experience and history teach is this – that people and governments never have learned anything from history, or acted on principles deduced from it." Later a highly unphilosophical American, Henry Ford, concluded, "History is more or less bunk." But, as one of Ford's contemporaries, George Santayana, argued, "Those who cannot remember the past are condemned to fulfil it."[1] Canadians who want to avoid a repetition of past mistakes in relations between First Nations and others might want to consider some of the lessons that can be gleaned from the past.

The most obvious conclusion about the history of Native-newcomer relations in Canada is that the motives the two parties have had for making contact have usually shaped their interaction. Europeans came to North America for three reasons in the fifteenth and sixteenth centuries: exploration, fish, and fur. The first contacts after the abortive Norse attempt at colonization occurred when fishers arrived on the Grand Banks off Newfoundland. The fishery led to the development, first as an ancillary enterprise and later as the main economic activity, of a trade in furs with the Indigenous population of the region. During the early sixteenth century Europeans also came in search of Asian gold and spices. By the seventeenth century explorers had realized that North America was not, as they had first thought, the "Indies," but a land mass between Europe and Asia. Now they bent their efforts to finding a passage through the new continent to the Orient. Finally, a massive European effort to spread Christianity in the seventeenth century brought missionaries to proselytize the Native peoples of North America. In sum, Europeans came to Canada for fish, fur, exploration, and evangelization.

For each of these purposes the Natives were indispensable, and the Indigenous peoples were prepared to cooperate in each of these activities. Fishing and fish-curing would have been impossible if the Aboriginal population had been hostile and driven the fishers off. In the fur trade, the First Nations' foodstuffs, transportation methods, and labour were vital for the success of the trade. North American sweet corn was a portable, protein-rich food that enabled trading parties to undertake long trips to fur-bearing regions; the canoe in summer and snowshoes in winter were essential for travelling in the interior; and the Natives caught, skinned, and processed the beaver pelts by wearing them next to their bodies as robes. In similar ways the Europeans found themselves dependent on the First Nations' knowledge and transportation technology when probing the continent in search of a passage to Asia. For the missionary, too, First Nation cooperation, food, transportation, and toleration of his presence were essential if the black robe was to win souls for Christ. In the fifteenth and sixteenth centuries, Natives had their own reasons for cooperating with the European newcomers along a frontier of commerce, exploration, and faith. The strangers had wonderful products of a more advanced technology than existed in North America. Iron revolutionized and simplified Indigenous people's hunting, warfare, and household chores. If toleration of black-robed shamans was a means to strengthen the commercial bonds with the men who made these products available, then the missionary presence would be endured. If cooperation in exploration also seemed expedient, then Natives would cooperate with the forays of the French explorers. They would always, however, try to prevent direct European contact with those peoples in the interior who supplied the best furs.

In this generally harmonious relationship there was no doubt about who was the dominant partner. The fact that French traders had to learn and use Indigenous languages, especially Huron in the early years, was one clear indicator of where the power lay. That trade had to conform to First Nation rituals was another sign that the newcomers were compelled to adapt to the patterns and values that they encountered. Ceremonies such as formal welcomes, feasting, gift exchange, and smoking the pipe were all employed to make kin of strangers, whether the Europeans understood the significance of ceremony or not. Cooperating in relations was all the easier to do because the Europeans regarded the First Nations whom they encountered along a frontier of commerce and faith as a means rather than an impediment to the realization of European objectives. The fact that newcomers lacked the numbers, as well as the motivation, to interfere with Indigenous society or attack First Nations directly also explains the relative harmony of early Indigenous-European relations. Not even French missionaries of the seventeenth century posed a direct threat to Indigenous culture, for Jesuits sought only religious conversion, not total assimilation. Still, it is true that there were negative consequences of contact for Aboriginal peoples. Most serious was disease, followed by more destructive warfare, and the debilitating effects of alcohol. The serious weakening, and eventually the dispersal, of the Huron Confederacy as a consequence of disease, internal divisions, and the attacks by the Iroquois is the clearest example of the dark side of relations in New France.

The first phase of mutually beneficial contact, in which non-directed cultural change occurred on both sides of the relationship, was modified significantly at the beginning of the eighteenth century. Europeans continued to pursue fish and converts, but they now knew that there was no accessible passage through the temperate part of America to Asia. Moreover, the commerce in furs changed greatly after 1700. The eighteenth century was an era of rivalry between Britain and France, and in the western hemisphere that contest was reflected in a struggle for control of North America. Neither European power wanted to field large numbers of its own troops, but the First Nations were on site, had vital navigational and martial talents, and were favourably disposed, thanks to the ties that had already been established by the fur trader and the missionary. From the Europeans' perspective, the edge of

contact in the eighteenth century changed from a commercial to an imperial frontier, the First Nations from trading partners to allies. The southwestern fur trade
became a means of maintaining alliances with Natives, and not, for the most part,
an economic pursuit in its own right.

The shift from a commercial to a strategic motive for contact did not seriously
disrupt the harmonious coexistence of First Nations and the French or *Canadiens*.
The topography of the continent had created the partnership of the French and
those Algonkians who controlled the fur regions oriented to the St. Lawrence watershed; the English had established business contacts with the Iroquoians and
other Natives of the regions that found their trade egress in the Hudson River.
When commerce gave way to imperial warfare, the same patterns persisted, as both
European powers lavished gifts on their First Nation friends to retain their support. But the French found it easier to hold the allegiance of their allies, because
the strangers in the valley of the St. Lawrence were still primarily merchants and
missionaries, rather than farmers and burghers.

Consequently, the Indigenous peoples regarded the French and *Canadiens* as
less of a threat to their traditional economy than the Anglo-Americans. On the
First Nation side, the contrast between American and Canadian experience was
manifested in the stereotype view that they held of the newcomers in the seventeenth century: they thought of "the Englishman as a farmer or town-dweller
whose activities gradually drove the original agriculturalists deeper into the hinterland, whereas the stereotype of the French was a trader or soldier."[2] The fact that the
French in Canada had dealt with First Nations along a frontier of commerce and
faith made it easier for them than it was for the British to win the support of First
Nation allies in the eighteenth century.

A consistent pattern developed during the century of struggle. From the initiation of the French strategy of encirclement by means of interior posts and Native alliances in 1700 to the death of Tecumseh in 1813, most First Nations found alliance
with the Europeans north of the St. Lawrence system more attractive than military
association with those in the Thirteen Colonies. This was true during the Seven
Years' War, when the French benefited from Native alliances while colonies such as
Virginia regarded the Indigenous peoples as another enemy. It was still true at the
end of that contest when Pontiac tried unsuccessfully to organize an Indigenous
resistance to the assertion of British and American rule. The same pattern held in
the American Revolutionary War, although the influences of geography and religion this time modified the patterns by inducing some Iroquois to seek neutrality.
Finally, the War of 1812 – the last phase of the century-long struggle – illustrated
the same alignment of forces. The overwhelming proportion of First Nations who

participated did so on the side of the British and Canadians. Alliance with the British in the War of 1812 offered Tecumseh and The Prophet the same chance that cooperation with France had given Pontiac earlier.

This second major phase of Native-European relations, the era of alliance, produced important developments of great relevance for both First Nations and Euro-Canadians in later ages. The first of these was the Royal Proclamation of 1763. The proclamation in the short term meant maintaining Indigenous support for Britain by not threatening their lands, and in the longer term formed part of the foundation of claims for land and self-government. After the conclusion of the Revolutionary War, the need to provide for angry warriors who insisted that they were allies, not subjects, of the British king led to the initiation of negotiations with First Nations in the lower Great Lakes region for peaceful access to tracts for both Native and settler Loyalists. The process of settling Upper Canada was at first carried on in a manner consistent with the proclamation policy, as was only to be expected in an era when the British and Canadians continued to regard First Nations as military allies and commercial partners. One sign of the continuity was the persistence of the use of ceremony in negotiations.

On the whole, the same pattern that had been observable in eastern Canada from the fifteenth century to Victoria's age was found in due course in the more westerly and northerly regions of what became the Dominion of Canada. In the Hudson's Bay Company lands, the imperatives of commerce led the English to cooperate with their First Nation trading partners, employing Indigenous ceremony to make and renew commercial relationships. In a second phase of the fur-trade frontier in the West, the intense competition between the HBC and the Nor'westers provided a brief economic golden age for both First Nations and Métis who traded with and provisioned the commercial interests. The struggle between these two companies for control of the region also produced what few instances of the Natives acting as allies that western Canadian history has. The same pattern, minus the military dimension, was found on the Pacific coast and in the British Columbia interior between the 1770s and 1850s. Here, too, the relationship that developed was a commercial one, whether the trade occurred aboard ships or at posts on land. It remained cooperative and mutually beneficial, and the changes induced among both parties were non-directed ones that did not seriously disrupt the respective societies.

In the nineteenth century a third phase of the relationship began – a phase that was to be anything but beneficial to the Indigenous peoples. Hitherto, Indians and Europeans had cooperated with each other along frontiers of commerce, faith, exploration, and alliance. In all these associations the two parties had found that they needed each other; in none had they had any reason to seek fundamental changes in each other. However, in the third era of the relationship, the association was not mutually beneficial, and one party did definitely try to coerce the other to change.

The onset of this troubled era was uneven across the country. In Maritime Canada it had already begun while interior First Nations were still fighting as allies against the Americans. Certainly for the Indigenous population of Newfoundland, it was a reality by the early nineteenth century. In the interior regions of present-day Quebec and Ontario, this third epoch began not long after the making of peace subsequent to the War of 1812 and with the Rush-Bagot Convention of 1817, which ushered in enduring peace between the United States and British North America in the interior. In the Pacific region, this third phase commenced with the arrival of prospectors, agricultural settlers, and missionaries in the late 1850s. And on the Plains and in the parklands immediately to the north of them, the Native became increasingly less relevant to the European population as the fur trade shifted northward. The arrival of missionaries in Red River in the 1820s and 1830s is one measure of the evolution, the decline of the bison in the 1860s and 1870s a second, and the completion of the transcontinental railway in the 1880s the final indicator of the change in the western interior. Across the continent in the nineteenth century, the commercial frontier shifted far to the north, the military preoccupations of the European powers declined, and the Natives increasingly were perceived as a "problem" by the now-dominant European population.

So far as nineteenth-century Canadians were concerned, the First Nations throughout southern Canada were now an impediment that had to be cleared away, much as the pine forests in the east had to be reduced before production of surplus wheat crops for export was possible. In the same era, a subtle but important perceptual shift occurred in British North America, one that tracked a similar change in the American republic in the eighteenth century. In the United States, by the time of the American Revolution non-Native people perceived Native Americans not as culturally different but as racially distinct or "other."[3] The change was important: seeing Indigenous people as racially separate and alien would underlie much mistreatment of the Native Americans by the state in the nineteenth century. To the north, in British North America, similar modifications of perception and attitude developed in the early and middle decades of the nineteenth century. For British North Americans, however, because of history, geography, and demography, the Native peoples north of the international border could not be cleared as bloodily as they were being removed at the same time in the United States.

Canadians, unlike their southern neighbours, had not learned to regard Natives as hostile forces to be crushed. Moreover, by the time the Dominion of Canada had to deal with First Nations in western Canada, a strong tradition of erecting political and legal institutions prior to intrusion by the general agricultural population had been established. In any event, the vast extent of the Dominion made destructive policies horrendously expensive and probably impossible to bring to completion. Finally, the sparseness of Euro-Canadian population in the West and North made such a bloody policy as problematical as history made it unacceptable. Even if the Indigenous peoples were now perceived as an obstacle, they could not be shifted by force.

The means to remove them was a coercive policy of land acquisition and directed cultural change. First in Upper Canada and then in the West, the proclamation policy of negotiating with First Nations for access to their traditional lands in advance of Euro-Canadian penetration was followed. Land surrender treaties – or what government interpreted as land surrender treaties – were intended to remove First Nations from resources that newcomers wanted to use in their own, exclusive, and frequently destructive ways. The second policy was a concerted effort to remove Natives from Canadian society as a distinctive racial and social type. As an American Indian Affairs official put it, the objective of treaties, reserves, and educational programs was "the extinction of the Indians *as Indians.*"[4] Schooling would assimilate them to Euro-Canadian values as it prepared them for husbandry, trades, or wage employment. Missionaries, Indian agents, and farming instructors would remove First Nations by changing them. Gradually Indigenous people would become enfranchised, taking their allotment of reserve land with them in freehold tenure. The reserves would dissolve as the distinctive Indians disappeared into Euro-Canadian society. This policy of directed change reached its nadir in the federal government's white paper of 1969, which claimed that First Nations' problems were a consequence of their distinctiveness, and recommended the dismantling of their special status.

These changes in Canada's attitudes and policies towards Indigenous peoples were the product of the changed relationship between a Euro-Canadian majority and the Native population. No longer was the First Nations' relationship with the newcomers that of dominant commercial partners who could compel the newcomer to learn their languages. Nor was it that of a military equal who could angrily inform a government emissary that his people were allies, not subjects, of the British Crown. The new situation reflected First Nations' dependence in an age when they were viewed as an obstacle to be removed from the newcomers' path. This destructive treatment was the consequence of the fact that the relationship was now between a dominant group and another people regarded as superfluous to the needs of the majority population.

Down to and through most of the third era, interactions in the Far North stood apart. For the Subarctic First Nations and the Inuit, the governing reality was that Europeans and Euro-Americans were transients, coming only for brief periods and specific economic reasons, while they, the Indigenous peoples, were permanent residents who coped with the newcomers when they came and mopped up the damage they had done once they left. The other ugly reality for northerners was that the southerners' government was usually uninterested in them and their welfare. A succession of developments demonstrated the impact of these realities. Whaling in both the western and eastern Arctic provided intermittent, though often intense, contacts between Inuit and outsiders until it fell into serious decline around the time of the Great War. Mining, whose commencement in the North can be dated from the Klondike rush in 1898, similarly erupted in the Aboriginal peoples' midst and then often sputtered out, at least for a time. Gold in Yukon, oil at Fort Norman, and gold, uranium, and base metals at various points in the territories all replicated the pattern of Indigenous residency and non-Native transiency for which the North has been notable. The enduring non-Native presence north of sixty took the forms of the fur trader, for a long time representing the Hudson's Bay Company, and Christian missionaries, principally Anglican and Roman Catholic.

Until the middle of the twentieth century the representatives of commerce and Christ were among the few who stayed for lengthy periods in the North and who took an interest in the welfare of the Inuit and northerly First Nations. Prior to the 1940s, when exposure of the deplorable conditions in which some Inuit lived forced the Government of Canada to take the provision of services seriously, Ottawa had sought to evade its responsibilities to northern Native peoples, except when such considerations as strengthening claims of Canadian sovereignty briefly moved policy makers to intervene. From the 1950s onward, concerns about sovereignty, the extension of the first stages of the Canadian welfare state, and strategic issues arising from the Cold War drew the federal government into a more extensive and systematic relationship with the Indigenous populations of the North.

Like the Inuit, First Nations in the south began to emerge from "irrelevance" to policy makers after the Second World War, and their emergence accelerated in the 1960s. The explanation was in part intellectual or ideological: wartime experiences and post-war intellectual fashions made the racist bases of government Indian policy increasingly untenable. First Nations emerged for economic reasons as well: they occupied territories that the dominant society now realized contained valuable and needed resources. Inuit were in strategically important locations, and growing knowledge in the south of the appalling conditions that prevailed in many northern communities drew government attention to Arctic regions. The explanation for growing attention to Native peoples and Native issues was also certainly political: First Nations now had effective political bodies that confronted and put pressure on the political parties to modify policies. Inuit soon would have similar political instruments.

In this fourth phase of relations – the era of Indigenous peoples' emergence from "irrelevance" to the larger population – no single type of relationship has developed. There is no consensus on either side of the relationship as to what should be done. On the Native side there are numerous reasons for division. Regional differences set the various Aboriginal groups apart. Historical distinctions are important, too. Those First Nations who have signed treaties have a contractual basis from which to litigate and agitate for compliance with promises made. Others who, for any number of reasons, never entered treaty with the Crown find that their most effective basis for action is the concept of Aboriginal status. Because of history and geography, the Inuit are a distinctive case. These differences have resulted in the fragmentation of Native political action into a multiplicity of organizations, with a resulting weakening of their political voice. On the non-Native side of the relationship, there also continues to be no unity. In a secular and urban age, the policy of the Bible and the plough is not acceptable to most Canadians. While the assimilative policy of the white paper still attracts liberal ideologues and secular missionaries, it offends champions of cultural and racial pluralism. Since the federal government adopted multiculturalism in 1971 and had the policy enshrined in the 1982 constitution, assimilators have had to face another barrier. On the non-Native side of the relationship, no consensus has developed to replace the nineteenth-century program of economic adaptation and assimilation. In the years after 2000, when the desire for redress and reconciliation was awakened, all parties are engaged in the effort to redefine the relationship.

What, if anything, can be learned from this historical record? First, that the relationship between the Indigenous peoples and non-Natives has been shaped by practical, often economic, factors. The record of Native-newcomer relations in Canada has been one moulded by the reasons that the various parties have had for making contact and maintaining relations. When their motives were complementary, the relationship was harmonious and the consequences mutually advantageous. The best example was the early fur trade era, in which the two groups cooperated for their mutual material advantage without inflicting hardship on each other. Conversely, when their motives were antagonistic or competitive, the relationship became unhappy and the consequences unfortunate. This tendency is found most starkly in the long third phase of the relationship, when the newcomers regarded the Natives not as commercial partners or military allies, but as obstacles to new forms of economic development. The result was the dispossession from the land of the Indigenous peoples, as well as coercive efforts to change them. The attempts have proven unavailing; all they have accomplished is the demoralization as well as impoverishment of the Native peoples and the creation of a climate of confrontation. If the Native and newcomer populations of Canada are to restore harmonious and mutually beneficial relations, they must find a new and complementary reason for interacting.

The historical record also indicates something about what ought not to be included in that new relationship. One and three-quarters centuries of attempts by Euro-Canadian society to define the role of Natives and to impose that destiny on them have added up to miserable failure. Aside from the effective removal of First Nations from most of their lands, none of the policies of the Bible and the plough have been successful. And now, with the recognition by the courts and governments of the validity of Aboriginal title in the hands of non-treaty Natives and the obligations of government's trustee relationship with those who made treaty, even that record of dispossession may be on the way to reversal. Attempts by governments, churches, and the general population at large to change First Nations, Métis, and Inuit into just another ethnic group in the multicultural mosaic have failed. It is past time that these policies were abandoned. As Chief Justice Antonio Lamer put it in 1997, "Let us face it, we are all here to stay."[5]

The reason that assimilationist policies have failed holds another clue to the direction in which a new relationship should be sought. To some degree these policies failed because they were perverted to other ends. The efforts in colonial New Brunswick to assimilate the Mi'kmaq failed because New Brunswickers diverted British donations to colonial development and exploited the apprenticeship programs to secure cheap labour. Perhaps more significantly, these policies failed in part because they were never adequately funded and supported. The attempt to encourage and facilitate western First Nations' shift to agriculture was sometimes met with enthusiastic cooperation by the Natives themselves. But in at least some instances, as in Manitoba's Oak River reserve, enthusiasm for agriculture was killed by bureaucratic obtuseness and racist assumptions. Elsewhere throughout the West in the 1880s and 1890s, the agricultural programs failed because they were not adequately funded and because governmental support and instruction were not maintained long enough to enable the Native population to make a satisfactory transition. Governments, especially when pressed for funds for development projects that the non-Native majority considered important, found it all too convenient to forget that they were asking First Nations to complete in a few years a transformation that had taken Europeans centuries. Racism, parsimony, and obtuseness go far to explain the failure of coercive assimilation in the third phase of the relationship. But none of these is the most important reason.

The policies that aimed at the conversion of Natives into Euro-Canadians have failed principally because Native peoples have resisted them tenaciously and persistently. Whether one looks at Upper Canada in the 1830s and 1840s, the Prairies in the 1880s and 1890s, or the North in the twentieth century, the record is the same. Native groups recognized the inevitability of change and sought only to control it so that it would not prove destructive to their identity and social cohesion. Upper Canadian First Nations agreed to support education with a portion of their annuities; they fought schooling when it turned out to be more concerned with turning their children into British Americans than into literate farmers. Western First Nations sought treaties to establish a relationship with government that would provide them assistance in a difficult transition; they resisted or lapsed into apathy when they realized that the government was more interested in assimilating them than in helping them.

To a considerable extent, the process of Native disillusionment is seen most clearly in their reaction to the attempts by government and churches to interfere with their traditional political institutions. The First Nations of Upper Canada complained about provisions in legislation of the 1850s that presumed to give administrators suzerainty over their councils. Big Bear attempted to put together a political front to confront the likes of Edgar Dewdney and Hayter Reed. For well over a century the Six Nations have resisted first colonial and then national governmental pretensions to be able to determine their political institutions. In the twenty-first century they are joined in this rejection of political interference by treaty First Nations, Métis and non-status Indians, and Inuit in the North. The record is absolutely clear and consistent: the Native peoples reject efforts to change them – whether economically, culturally, or politically – into imitation Euro-Canadians. Programs such as the white paper of 1969 that aim at such change will fail, as have all such earlier initiatives.

If there is a conclusion that can be drawn from these patterns in the historical record, surely it is that new policies that benefit Aboriginal peoples and non-Natives alike can be developed only within a real partnership. Now that there is greater awareness of the cost of history to Indigenous people, a program of redress and reconciliation is needed. And in pursuit of such a goal, only cooperative policies

that have the support of government, Native organizations, and the general population have any chance of helping Native groups to free themselves from their social
and economic morass. And real partnership has two aspects. First, there must be
meaningful consultation. Second, non-Natives must not only listen to Natives; they
must also agree to try solutions that the Aboriginal peoples consider desirable.

Meaningful consultation is not a process of discussion but the act of listening and considering seriously what is being said. The travesty of the "dialogue" of
1968–9 that preceded the white paper had a devastating effect on First Nations-
government relations. Not only was it dishonest to pretend to listen to Native leaders and then produce a document that reflected purely bureaucratic and political
considerations, it was also counterproductive. All that the duplicity accomplished
was the disillusionment and political unification of the Native peoples in opposition to the white paper. The decade of the 1970s was disfigured by the distrust that
the process leading up to the white paper, as well as the policy document itself,
engendered. And the making of the new constitution in 1980–2 was similarly
disillusioning for Native peoples. In spite of the professions that governments had
offered, in spite of the progress that supposedly had been made, when the first
ministers got together in the autumn of 1981, they betrayed the Aboriginal peoples.
And, finally, the Mulroney government's task force on public expenditure similarly
shut the Native people out of the evaluation of the policies that supposedly were for
their benefit. The era from Meech Lake to Charlottetown, 1987–92, saw improvements, but it was progress that came too late. By the time non-Native first ministers included Aboriginal leaders in constitutional discussions, disillusionment with
politicians had become so strong that Aboriginal voters joined non-Natives in rejecting the pact that had been fashioned at Charlottetown. The Royal Commission
on Aboriginal Peoples also had mixed results: in fashioning a response to its recommendations the Government of Canada worked closely with the Assembly of
First Nations, but largely froze the leaders of other Aboriginal political organizations out. The Truth and Reconciliation Commission's work has reinforced awareness of the doleful record and heightened demands for redress and reconciliation.

Meaningful consultation means more than just listening, however. It means listening with the intention of considering seriously what is being said, and with an
open mind as to its merits. George Manuel, chief of the National Indian Brotherhood
(1970–6), wrote scathingly of the usual way in which government "considered"
spending economic development funds in 1973: "Band councils have submitted
lists of thoroughly researched proposals, in consultation with professional economic advisers, for using the money for our own economic development. No dice. The
industries that have gotten federal support, set up on reserve land, have employed

no more than a token number of Indians in skilled or managerial positions. The department just cannot conceive of an Indian being able to run his own show."[6] A case study of the failures of the 1970s economic development program by two non-Native experts confirms what Manuel says: "Instead of beginning with a clear set of workable objectives that were consistent with what the people wanted, government agencies such as DIAND and Manpower almost always worked at cross-purposes, failed to monitor and assess their programs, and, worst of all, never really consulted with the people they were supposed to be serving. The outcome was that band members were rewarded for becoming dependent, stymied in their attempts to become independent, and left in a position where vulnerability to government cut-backs is now the one overriding feature of their lives."[7] Not consulting properly has resulted in the failure of programs, the frustration of bureaucrats, and the cynicism of Natives.

Surely there cannot be any defensible argument for refusing to consult Indigenous peoples about policy and allowing them to control the administration of the programs that are supposedly for their benefit? Can anyone point to the consequences of more than a century of paternalistic administration, in which programs were decided by people remote from the First Nations and administered by officials who were not answerable to them and argue that they were at all successful? In the face of the chilling statistics on school drop-outs, unemployment, poverty, ill health, family breakdown, incarceration, and early deaths, such an argument seems impossible. The record shows no reason to refuse Natives control over the development and administration of policies that affect them. They can hardly fail more abysmally than the thousands of Euro-Canadian politicians, bureaucratic planners, missionaries, and officials have during more than 180 years.

As initiatives as varied as the Mount Elgin manual labour school in Ontario in the 1850s and the Meech Lake Accord in the 1980s illustrate, policies affecting Aboriginal people that do not enjoy their confidence will not work, might not even be implemented. Dr. Lloyd Barber, a university administrator and Indian Claims Commissioner in the 1970s, explained how his experience made this lesson clear to him. Having watched government initiatives founder, he came to the conclusion that political groups like the Assembly of First Nations frequently resisted by refusing to cooperate. Barber drew the conclusion that "Indians have a capacity for passive resistance that makes Mahatma Gandhi look like an amateur."[8] Bureaucrats from Hayter Reed to D.C. Scott at least, who saw policies such as severalty and voluntary enfranchisement fail, would have to agree.

Perhaps more positively, there might be modest reason to hope that the shift to Native control of education and the administration of social policy provide proof that Aboriginal direction produces better results. By 1988 over two-thirds of the schools on reserve were band-operated.[9] Drop-out rates, while still too high, were coming down among the prairie communities with band-controlled schools or urban Native Survival Schools. First Nation and Métis children no longer leave Manitoba and the other Prairie provinces for adoption by non-Native Americans. Perhaps such initiatives provide a case for expanding the scope of Native peoples' control of the policies that affect them? If so, that in itself is an argument for greater Aboriginal self-government, an argument to which the two senior levels of government and the bulk of the Canadian population should listen. Aboriginal leaders, on the other hand, would find it advisable to sort out various issues involving the tactics that they use to induce non-Native politicians to consult them properly. Fortunately or unfortunately, in the Canadian system, whether or not a group can get politicians' attention depends on how successful they are in making their case to the general public. At present Canadian political leaders are dealing with the various Native communities within a model of interest-group politics. They regard the Inuit, Métis, and First Nations as specific interest groups and themselves as a broker adjudicating among the demands of many such groups. They are inclined to treat Aboriginal political organizations as they would the agrarian community or labour or manufacturers. Native leaders reject the interest-group or brokerage-politics approach and insist that they be dealt with on a nation-to-nation basis. So far, in spite of some rhetoric to the contrary, they have not succeeded, and there does not seem much likelihood that they will soon manage this. The way in which the governance recommendations of the Royal Commission on Aboriginal Peoples disappeared into political limbo underscore that sad reality.[10] That being the case, certain considerations follow. First, if Native causes are going to be treated as the demands of interest groups, then the more unified they are the better. One Native interest group will have more effect in negotiations than a series of Inuit, non-status Indian, Métis, and First Nation pressure groups. Second, the attitude of the general electorate will determine the extent to which the leaders of the senior levels of government respond positively to the pressure of Aboriginal groups. The fate of the ninety-four Calls to Action of the Truth and Reconciliation Commission will provide a gauge of how supportive non-Native Canadians are in the twenty-first century.

What is striking about Aboriginal-government relations now is that one of the smallest and most recently organized groups, the Inuit of the eastern Arctic, have been the most successful in pursuing their agenda of land claim and self-government. With dedication and persistence, the Inuit have worked steadily with the federal government to resolve these difficult problems, culminating in the Nunavut agreement that was implemented in April 1999. And what has been the political style of the leaders of the eastern Inuit? Repeatedly they have chosen to couch their analysis and proposals in low-key terms, and have sought to portray their objective as compatible with existing Canadian political norms, whether their aim represented dramatic departure from tradition or not. When the Dene and Métis of the western Northwest Territories adopted the Dene Declaration in 1975 to the plaudits of southern journalists and academics, the Inuit avoided the language of nationalism and worked quietly within the forum of the NWT legislature. In spite of enormous obstacles, they achieved resolution of their land claim and self-government in practice by the 1990s. When the Nunavut proposal was attacked as creating a "nation within a nation," Inuit leaders disarmed critics by saying that, on the contrary, the Inuit simply wanted into the Canadian political family. While the various Aboriginal political organizations must and will decide for themselves what strategies and practices they will adopt in the twenty-first century, consideration of the success that the Inuit of eastern Arctic enjoyed in the waning years of the last century might be in order.

George Manuel argued that First Nations will achieve political victories that do not entail political losses for the rest of the Canadian community. If, he has written, "we can resolve the contradictions between your values, white values, and our own, then our victory will be complete. And it will be *our victory*, not your loss. Indian victories only rarely demand that there be a loser."[11] Manuel was referring to the cooperative, consensual, non-competitive tradition of First Nation decision-making. He recognized that it was different from the adversarial, competitive, and, not infrequently, confrontational political style of the Euro-Canadian majority in Canada. The genius of the Inuit strategy has been that it enables southerners to see Inuit victory as a triumph that does not represent a loss for the rest of the country.

George Manuel's point also reminds us that Native-newcomer relations involve societies that differ in their values and aspirations. There is a society of skyscrapers and one that focuses on the heavens. Manuel says what First Nation leaders from Pontiac to Big Bear and the opponents of the white paper have said: while they want to cooperate with and benefit from Canadian society, they do not want to be submerged in it. They want to participate, not assimilate. They want to remain one of the many distinct entities – what one historian has called "limited identities"[12] – that make Canada the unique human community that it has become over the past five hundred years.

There have been some signs in recent years, in areas ranging from the trivial to the weighty, that suggest at least some elements of the Canadian citizenry, under at least some circumstances, are open to more tolerant, pluralist, and inclusive approaches to dealing with the diverse Indigenous communities within the Canadian polity and society. In the lightweight category, the House of Commons in 1994 responded to Native objections that a private member's bill proposing to designate ice hockey as Canada's national game ignored and obliterated lacrosse, a distinctive First Nation contribution, by changing the measure to specify hockey as Canada's winter game and lacrosse as the summer sport.[13] Also in the political realm, but perhaps of a different order of significance, two provinces in the 1990s forged new relationships with the Aboriginal groups in their jurisdictions. Ontario in 1991 signed a "Statement of Political Relationship" with the First Nations, while Quebec in 1998 unilaterally adopted guidelines for Aboriginal affairs, which were based on the Quebec Assembly's resolutions of 1985 and 1989 that recognized First Nations' "right to develop their identity, culture, economic base and self-sufficiency within Québec."[14] And in 2015, newly elected Prime Minister Justin Trudeau pledged to implement all ninety-four of the Truth and Reconciliation Commission's Calls to Action.

On the Aboriginal side of the relationship, the most eloquent statement of the new pride and growing confidence was found in the 1991 Canadian census, in which there was a dramatic jump in the number of respondents who reported Aboriginal ancestry. Whereas 711,720 people had responded positively to the question in 1986, five years later just over a million said that they had First Nation, Métis, or Inuit ancestors.[15] Since the 1996 census revealed that Aboriginal youth were far more numerous than non-Aboriginal young and that the Aboriginal birth rate was much higher, projections of a future Aboriginal population showed dramatic increases.[16] While the results of the Royal Commission on Aboriginal Peoples were disappointing, at least in the short term, the openness and inclusiveness of the Supreme Court of Canada in a succession of rulings from *Sparrow* and *Sioui* through *Delgamuukw* to *Tsilqot'in* to Aboriginal knowledge, to oral tradition and oral history evidence, suggested there were opportunities to make progress elsewhere in Canada's cumbersome system of government and law.

If Aboriginal peoples and the leaders of Canada's federal and provincial governments can build on the hopeful signs, the twenty-first century might see the restoration of healthy Aboriginal communities and vibrant relations between those communities and the rest of the people who reside in Canada. As the government of Canada's Statement of Reconciliation of January 1998 expressed the wish:

We envision a partnership not just between the federal government and Aboriginal people, men and women, Elders and youth, but one that also includes the provincial, territorial and local governments; national, regional and local Aboriginal leaders; the private sector; and other interested groups and organizations. This partnership must extend to include all Canadians, Aboriginal and non-Aboriginal alike.

...

Tradition and innovation need not be mutually exclusive. We have a rare opportunity to gather strength for a better future. In partnership, we can all succeed.[17]

That argument is as relevant and compelling in the second and third decades of the twenty-first century as it was in the last decade of the twentieth.

Notes

Preface to the Third Edition

1 James Clifford, "Introduction: Partial Truths," in *Writing Culture: The Poetics and Politics of Ethnography*, ed. James Clifford and George E. Marcus (Berkeley: University of California Press, 1986), 8.

1. Indigenous Peoples and Europeans at the Time of Contact

1 Cartier's narrative of 1534, Henry Percival Biggar, *The Voyages of Jacques Cartier* (Ottawa: King's Printer, 1924), 64–5.
2 Bruce G. Trigger, *The Indians and the Heroic Age of New France* (Ottawa: Canadian Historical Association, 1977), 3.
3 Michael J. Caduto and Joseph Burchac, *Keepers of the Earth: Native Stories and Environmental Activities for Children* (Saskatoon, SK: Fifth House, 1989), 25–6.
4 Bruce G. Trigger, *The Huron: Farmers of the North* (New York: Holt, Rinehart and Winston, 1969), 6. See also Kathryn Magee Labelle, *Dispersed But Not Destroyed: A History of the Seventeenth-Century Wendat People* (Vancouver: UBC Press, 2013), 10.
5 Jacques Rousseau and George W. Brown, "The Indians of Northeastern North America," *Dictionary of Canadian Biography*, vol. 1, *1000 to 1700* (Toronto: University of Toronto Press, 1966), 7.
6 Karen Anderson, *Chain Her by One Foot: The Subjugation of Women in Seventeenth-Century New France* (New York and London: Routledge, 1991), 5–6; Carol Devens, *Countering Colonization: Native American Women and Great Lakes Missions, 1630–1900* (Berkeley: University of California Press, 1992), 10–13.
7 Labelle, *Dispersed But Not Destroyed*, 17.
8 Reuben Gold Thwaites, ed., *The Jesuit Relations and Allied Documents*, 73 vols. (Cleveland: Burrows Brothers 1897), 6: 231, 243.
9 Labelle, *Dispersed But Not Destroyed*, 69–72.

10 Thwaites, *Jesuit Relations*, 43: 271.

11 Concerning campaigns to replenish population, sometimes called "mourning wars," see Daniel K. Richter, *The Ordeal of the Longhouse: The Peoples of the Iroquois League in the Era of European Colonization* (Chapel Hill: University of North Carolina Press, 1992), 32–5.

12 For an excellent brief explanation of "mourning wars" and torture, see Jon Parmenter, *The Edge of the Woods: Iroquoia, 1534–1701* (East Lansing: Michigan State University Press, 2010), xliii–xliv and 46–51.

13 See, for example, Trigger, *Farmers of the North*, 50–1.

14 Ibid., 51. On torture, see also Denys Delâge, *Bitter Feast: Amerindians and Europeans in Northeastern North America, 1600–64* (1985), trans. Jane Brierley (Vancouver: UBC Press, 1993), 64–6.

15 Trigger, *Farmers of the North*, 106–12.

16 Trigger, *Indians and the Heroic Age*, 8.

17 Lawrence C. Wroth, ed., *The Voyages of Giovanni da Verrazzano, 1624–1628* (New Haven, CT: Yale University Press, 1970), 134.

18 Cornelius J. Jaenen, "French Sovereignty and Native Nationhood during the French Régime," in *Sweet Promises: A Reader on Indian-White Relations in Canada*, ed. J. R. Miller (Toronto: University of Toronto Press, 1991), 25.

2. Early Contacts in the Eastern Woodlands

1 According to Eirik's Saga. See Magnus Magnusson and Hermann Pálsson, trans., *The Vinland Sagas: The Norse Discovery of America* (London: Penguin, 1965), 98–100.

2 James Axtell, "At the Water's Edge: Trading in the Sixteenth Century," in *Natives and Newcomers: The Cultural Origins of North America* (New York: Oxford University Press, 2001), 79; Marcel Trudel, *Introduction to New France* (Toronto: Holt, Rinehart and Winston, 1968), 253.

3 Olive P. Dickason, *Canada's First Nations: A History of Founding Peoples from Earliest Times* (Toronto: McClelland and Stewart, 1992), 12, 92.

4 Cartier's narrative of 1534, in Henry Percival Biggar, *The Voyages of Jacques Cartier* (Ottawa: King's Printer, 1924), 49.

5 Ibid., 53. For Henry Hudson's similar experience in James Bay in 1611, see Georg Michael Asher, ed., *Henry Hudson the Navigator* (1860; repr., New York: Burt Franklin, 1953), 114–15.

6 Cartier's narrative of 1534, in Biggar, *Voyages*, 56.

7 See the quotation at the beginning of chapter 1, this volume.

8 William J. Eccles, *The Canadian Frontier, 1534–1760* (New York: Holt, Rinehart and Winston, 1969), 15. See also Cornelius J. Jaenen, *Friend and Foe: Aspects of French-Amerindian Cultural Contact in the Sixteenth and Seventeenth Centuries* (New York: Columbia University Press, 1976), 12–13.

9 Axtell, "At the Water's Edge," 84.

10 Cartier's narrative of 1534, in Biggar, *Voyages*, 60

11 On the proper interpretation of *sauvage* as "forest dweller," see David Hackett Fischer, *Champlain's Dream* (New York: Simon and Schuster, 2008), 142–4.

12 Christian Le Clercq, *First Establishment of the Faith in New France*, ed. John Gilmary Shea, 2 vols. (New York: J.G. Shea, 1881), 1: 110–11.

13 Pierre-François-Xavier de Charlevoix, S.J., *History and General Description of New France*, 6 vols. (1743), trans. John Gilmary Shea (Chicago: Loyola University Press, 1870), 4: 198.

14 Gabriel Sagard-Théodat, *Le Grand Voyage au Pays des Hurons*, 2 vols. (Paris: Librairie Tross, 1865), 1: 67; George M. Wrong, ed., *The Long Journey to the Country of the Huron by Father Gabriel Sagard* (Toronto: Champlain Society, 1939), 74, 183.

15 William Francis Ganong, ed., *Description and Natural History of the Coasts of North America (Acadia)* (Toronto: Champlain Society, 1908), 440–1.

16 Henry Percival Biggar, ed., *The Works of Samuel de Champlain*, 6 vols. (Toronto: Champlain Society, 1922–6), 1: 98–101, 104. See also J.R. Miller, *Compact, Contract, Covenant: Aboriginal Treaty-Making in Canada* (Toronto: University of Toronto Press, 2009), 25–6; and Fischer, *Champlain's Dream*, 132–3. On fictive kinship and ceremony, see James Axtell, "Imagining the Other: First Encounters," in *Natives and Newcomers*, 28–31.

17 Emma Helen Blair, ed., *The Indian Tribes of the Upper Mississippi Valley and Region of the Great Lakes as described by Nicolas Perrot*, 2 vols. (Cleveland: Arthur H. Clark Company 1911), 1: 177. For other examples of First Nations' efforts to keep newcomers from establishing relations with interior groups, see Fischer, *Champlain's Dream*, 137, 242.

18 Kathryn Magee Labelle, *Dispersed But Not Destroyed: A History of the Seventeenth-Century Wendat People* (Vancouver: UBC Press, 2013), 3; Axtell, "Imagining the Other," 30.

3. Commercial Partnership and Mutual Benefit

1 Arthur C. Parker, "Iroquois Uses of Maize and Other Food Plants," in *Parker on the Iroquois*, ed. William N. Fenton (Syracuse: Syracuse University Press, 1975), 15.

2 See André Vachon, "Talon, Jean," *Dictionary of Canadian Biography* online, accessed 13 May 2016, www.biographi.ca/en/bio/talon_jean_1E.html.

3 Cornelius J. Jaenen, "French Sovereignty and Native Nationhood during the French Regime," in *Sweet Promises: A Reader on Indian-White Relations in Canada*, ed. J.R. Miller (Toronto: University of Toronto Press, 1991), 20.

4 David Hackett Fischer, *Champlain's Dream* (New York: Simon and Schuster, 2008), 475.

5 Reuben Gold Thwaites, ed., *The Jesuit Relations and Allied Documents*, 73 vols. (New York: Pageant Books, 1959), 5: 119–21.

6 Bruce G. Trigger, *Natives and Newcomers: Canada's "Heroic Age" Reconsidered* (Montreal: McGill-Queen's University Press, 1985), 225. See also Cornelius J. Jaenen, *Friend and Foe: Aspects of French-Amerindian Cultural Contact in the Sixteenth and Seventeenth Centuries* (New York: Columbia University Press, 1976), 23–4.

7 Chrestien Le Clercq, *New Relation of Gaspesia, with the Customs and Religion of the Gaspesian Indians* (1691), trans. and ed. William F. Ganong (Toronto: Champlain Society, 1910), 104–5. As the Mi'kmaq continued, "Besides, since we are wholly convinced of the contrary, we scarcely take the trouble to go to France, because we fear, with good reason, lest we find little satisfaction there, seeing, in our own experience, that those who are natives thereof leave it every year in order to enrich themselves on our shores. We believe, further, that you are also incomparably poorer than we, and that you are only simple journeymen, valets, servants, and slaves, all masters and grand captains though you may appear, seeing that you glory in our old rags and in our miserable suits of beaver which can no longer be of use to us, and that you find among us, in the fishery for cod which you make in these parts, the wherewithal to comfort your misery and the poverty which oppresses you."

8 Trigger, *Natives and Newcomers*, 192–3 and 219.

9 Kathryn Magee Labelle, *Dispersed But Not Destroyed: A History of the Seventeenth-Century Wendat People* (Vancouver: UBC Press, 2013), 14–15.

10 T.R.L. MacInnes, "History of Indian Administration in Canada," *Canadian Journal of Economics and Political Science* 12, no. 3 (August 1945): 387. Ramsay Cook, "The Social and Economic Frontier in North America," in *The Frontier in History: North America and South Africa Compared*, ed. Howard Lamar and Leonard Thompson (New Haven, CT: Yale University Press, 1981), 188–9, argues that much higher initial population figures should be used. Estimates of population at contact range up to three-quarters of a million. For thoughtful discussions of the difficulties of establishing pre-contact population figures, see Trigger, *Natives and Newcomers*, 231–42; and John D. Daniels, "The Indian Population of North America in 1492," *William and Mary Quarterly* 49, no. 2 (April 1992): 298–320.

11 Abbé Raynal, *A Philosophical and Political History of the Settlements and Trade of the Europeans in the East and West Indies*, 8 vols., trans. John Obadiah Justamond (London: A. Strahan and T. Cadell, 1788), 6: 514.

12 André Vachon, "L'Eau-de-Vie dans la société indienne," Canadian Historical Association, *Annual Report 1960*, 22–32.

13 Nancy Oestreich Lurie, "The World's Oldest On-Going Protest Demonstration: North American Indian Drinking Patterns," *Pacific Historical Review* 40, no. 3 (August 1971): 311–32. It is important to note that Lurie's analysis is based on evidence from a much later period, when conditions in which Native peoples and Europeans interacted had changed dramatically.

14 Thwaites, *Jesuit Relations*, 5: 49.

15 Raynal, *Philosophical and Political History*, 6: 514.

16 Brian J. Given, *A Most Pernicious Thing: Gun Trading and Native Warfare in the Early Contact Period* (Ottawa: Carleton University Press, 1994), 110.

17 Jaenen, *Friend and Foe*, 17.

18 Ibid., 33.

19 See Labelle, *Dispersed But Not Destroyed*, chaps 1–2.

20 José António Brandão, *"Your fire shall burn no more": Iroquois Policy toward New France and Its Native Allies to 1701* (Lincoln: University of Nebraska Press, 1997).

21 Thwaites, *Jesuit Relations*, 45: 41. The best account of the Huron dispersal is Labelle, *Dispersed But Not Destroyed*.

22 James Ronda, "The Sillery Experiment: A Jesuit-Indian Village in New France, 1637–1663," *American Indian Culture and Research Journal* 3, no. 1 (1979): 1–18. For examples of female assertiveness against the Jesuits, 1640–1740, see Annette de Stecher, "Wendat Arts of Diplomacy: Negotiating Change in the Nineteenth Century," in *From Huronia to Wendakes: Adversity, Migrations, and Resilience 1650–1900*, ed. Thomas Peace and Kathryn Magee Labelle (Norman: University of Oklahoma Press, 2016), 194.

23 These early reserves are summarized in George F.G. Stanley, "The First Indian 'Reserves' in Canada," *Revue d'histoire de l'Amérique française* 4, no. 2 (September 1950): 178–210. An excellent account of their role in European–First Nation diplomacy is Jean-Pierre Sawaya, *La Fédération des Sept Feux de la vallée du Saint-Laurent: XVIIe au XIXe siècle* (Sillery, QC: Septentrion, 1998).

24 Trigger, *Natives and Newcomers*, 108, 110, 117, and 162

25 William J. Eccles, *The Canadian Frontier, 1534–1760* (New York: Holt, Rinehart and Winston, 1969), 9.

26 Trigger, *Natives and Newcomers*, 224.

27 Ibid.

28 For a useful summary of Indian responses to Christian missions, see Cornelius J. Jaenen, "Amerindian Responses to French Missionary Intrusion, 1611–1760," in *Religion/Culture:*

Comparative Canadian Studies/Études canadiennes comparées, ed. W. Westfall and L. Rousseau (Ottawa: Association for Canadian Studies, 1985), 182–97.

29 Fischer, *Champlain's Dream*, 456; Thwaites, *Jesuit Relations*, 5: 203.

4. Military Allies through a Century of Warfare

1 Reuben Gold Thwaites, ed., *The Jesuit Relations and Allied Documents*, 73 vols. (New York: Pageant Books 1959), 5: 53. Allowance should be made for the fact that the author was not reporting events he had witnessed, but rather quoting others.

2 A perceptive, revisionist treatment, with particular reference to the Thirteen Colonies, is Francis Jennings, "Savage War," in *The Invasion of America: Indians, Colonialism, and the Cant of Conquest* (Chapel Hill: University of North Carolina Press, 1975), 146–70.

3 See James Axtell, "The White Indians," in *Natives and Newcomers: The Cultural Origins of North America* (New York: Oxford University Press, 2001), 189–213.

4 Daniel K. Richter, *The Ordeal of the Longhouse: The Peoples of the Iroquois League in the Era of European Colonization* (Chapel Hill: University of North Carolina Press, 1992), 32–5. See also ibid., 65–6, where Richter notes that contemporary observers by the 1660s believed that more than half the population of Iroquoia had originally been non-Iroquois.

5 Axtell, "The White Indians," 197–8, 206.

6 Thwaites, *Jesuit Relations*, 9: 269.

7 Cornelius J. Jaenen, *Friend and Foe: Aspects of French-Amerindian Cultural Contact in the Sixteenth and Seventeenth Centuries* (New York: Columbia University Press, 1976), 143.

8 Ibid., 122–3. For a revisionist interpretation of Mi'kmaq diplomacy and military contributions, see Daniel N. Paul, *We Were Not the Savages: A Micmac Perspective on the Collision of European and Aboriginal Civilization* (Halifax: Nimbus, 1993), chaps. 4–11.

9 Cadwallader Colden, *History of the Five Indian Nations of Canada*, pt. 1 (London: T. Osborne, 1747), 69. "Quatoghies" was the Onondaga name for the nation the French called Huron.

10 See J.R. Miller, *Compact, Contract, Covenant: Aboriginal Treaty-Making in Canada* (Toronto: University of Toronto Press, 2009), especially chaps. 2 and 3.

11 Jonathan Lainey, "Les colliers de wampum comme support mémoriel: le cas du Two Dog Wampum," in *Les Autochtones et le Québec: Des Premiers Contacts au Plan Nord*, ed. Alain Beaulieu, Stéphan Gervais, and Martin Papillon (Montreal: Les presses de l'Université de Montréal, 2013), 96–8.

12 André Vachon, "Talon, Jean," *Dictionary of Canadian Biography* online, accessed 12 May 2016, www.biographi.ca/en/bio/talon_jean_1E.html.

13 On the Great Peace, see especially Gilles Havard, *The Great Peace of Montreal of 1701: French-Native Diplomacy in the Seventeenth Century*, trans. Phyllis Aronoff and Howard Scott (Montreal: McGill-Queen's University Press, 2001).

14 Richard White, *The Middle Ground: Indians, Empires, and Republics in the Great Lakes Region, 1650–1815* (Cambridge: Cambridge University Press, 1991), 49.

15 Unidentified chief quoted in William J. Eccles, *Canada under Louis XIV 1663–1701* (Toronto: McClelland and Stewart, 1964), 4.

16 José Brandão and William A. Starna, "The Treaties of 1701: A Triumph of Iroquois Diplomacy," *Ethnohistory* 43, no. 2 (Spring 1996): 209–44.

17 Jaenen, *Friend and Foe*, 192.

18 Gideon Hawley to Eleazar Wheelock, 26 Nov. 1767, Wheelock Papers, Dartmouth College, 767626; quoted in Laura J. Murray, ed., *To Do Good to My Indian Brethren: The Writings of Joseph Johnson, 1751–1775* (Amherst: University of Massachusetts Press, 1998), 175.
19 Quoted in William J. Eccles, *The Canadian Frontier, 1534–1760* (New York: Holt, Rinehart and Winston, 1969), 158.
20 Leslie F.S. Upton, *Micmacs and Colonists: Indian-White Relations in the Maritimes, 1713–1867* (Vancouver: UBC Press, 1979), 26.
21 Ibid., 36 ("betrayed by our must trustworthy Indians"). Note that this is another instance of the inappropriateness of translating *sauvages* as "savages."
22 William C. Wicken, "The Treaties of Atlantic Canada," in *Aboriginal History: A Reader*, 2nd ed., ed. Kristin Burnett and Geoff Read (Don Mills, ON: Oxford University Press, 2016), 77, 80–5; Miller, *Compact, Contract, Covenant*, 62–4.
23 White, *Middle Ground*, 240–8, espec. 245.
24 Eccles, *Canadian Frontier*, 156.
25 D. Peter MacLeod, *The Canadian Iroquois and the Seven Years' War* (Toronto: Dundurn, 1996), 20–1, 99–100, and 155–6.
26 Quoted in Guy Frégault, *Canada: The War of the Conquest* (Toronto: Oxford, 1969), 96.
27 Adam Shortt and Arthur G. Doughty, eds., *Documents Relating to the Constitutional History of Canada 1759–1791* (Ottawa: King's Printer, 1907), 17. Article 40 of Capitulation of Montreal, 1759: "Les Sauvages ou Indiens alliés de Sa Mté tres [sic] chretienne [sic] seront maintenus dans Les Terres qu'il habitent, S'ils veulent y rester; Ils ne pouront [sic] Estres [sic] Inquietés Sous quelque prétexte que ce puisse Estre, pour avoir pris les Armes et servi Sa Mté très Chretienne. Ils auront Comme les Français, la Liberté de Religion et Conserveront leurs Missionaires ..."
28 The Royal Proclamation of 1763, in Clarence S. Brigham, ed., *Transactions and Collections of the American Antiquarian Society*, vol. 12, *British Royal Proclamations Relating to America, 1603–1783* (Worcester, MA: American Antiquarian Society, 1911), 212–13.
29 Ibid., 215–17.
30 Francis Jennings, "The Deed Game," in *The Invasion of America*, 128–45.
31 John Borrows, "Wampum at Niagara: The Royal Proclamation, Canadian Legal History, and Self-Government," in *Aboriginal and Treaty Rights in Canada: Essays on Law, Equity, and Respect for Difference*, ed. Michael Asch (Vancouver: UBC Press, 1997), 155–72, espec. 161–5. See also Miller, *Compact, Contract, Covenant*, 72–3.
32 Ibid., 155. For a similar interpretation from First Nations political organizations, see "From the Anishnabek, The Ojibway, Ottawa, Potowatomi and Algonquin Nations to the Parliament of the Dominion of Canada," *Ontario Indian* 3, no. 12 (Dec. 1980): 18–27. I am indebted to a colleague, Bill Waiser, who procured a copy of this item for me.
33 The legal issues are analysed in D.W. Elliott, "Aboriginal Title," in *Aboriginal Peoples and the Law: Indian, Metis and Inuit Rights in Canada*, ed. Bradford W. Morse (Ottawa: Carleton University Press, 1985), 56.
34 Alexander Henry, *Travels and Adventures in Canada and the Indian Territories between the Years 1760 and 1776*, ed. James Bain (1901; repr., New York: Burt Franklin, 1969), 42, 44.
35 White, *Middle Ground*, 284.
36 Henry, *Travels and Adventures*, 45.
37 White, *Middle Ground*, 257.
38 Quoted in Jaenen, *Friend and Foe*, 7.

39 Amherst to Bouquet, Bouquet Papers, British Library, Add. Mss. 21364; quoted in Robert
    S. Allen, "The British Indian Department and the Frontier in North America, 1755–1830,"
    Canadian Historic Sites, *Occasional Papers in Archaeology and History*, 14:33. See also Bernard
    Knollenburg, "General Amherst and Germ Warfare," *Mississippi Valley Historical Review*,
    41 (March 1955): 489–94; and Elizabeth Fenn, "Biological Warfare in Eighteenth-Century
    North America: Beyond Jeffery Amherst," *Journal of American History* 86, no. 4 (March 2000):
    1551–80, espec. 1552–8, 1565, 1574–6, and 1579–80.
40 Louis Chevrette, "Pontiac," *Dictionary of Canadian Biography* online, accessed 16 June 2016,
    www.biographi.ca/en/bio/pontiac_3E.html.
41 Quoted in Sydney F. Wise, "The American Revolution and Indian History," in *Character
    and Circumstance: Essays in Honour of Donald Grant Creighton*, ed. John S. Moir (Toronto:
    Macmillan, 1970), 182.
42 Quoted ibid., 185–6. Wise describes this as "a relatively light-hearted sample" of the propagan-
    dists' work (185).
43 Oneida to the New England Provinces, 19 June 1775; quoted in Murray, *To Do Good to My
    Indian Brethren*, 263. On the Oneida's sympathy for the Americans, see also Barbara Graymont,
    The Iroquois in the American Revolution (Syracuse: Syracuse University Press, 1972), 128.
44 Allen, "The British Indian Department and the Frontier in North America," 11. Johnson's ap-
    pointment as superintendent constituted the beginning of a "Department of Indian Affairs." See
    also Robert S. Allen, *His Majesty's Indian Allies: British Indian Policy in the Defence of Canada,
    1774–1815* (Toronto: Dundurn, 1992), chap. 2.
45 Graymont, *Iroquois in the American Revolution*, chap. 2.
46 Ibid., 221.
47 Quoted in Wise, "American Revolution and Indian History," 199.
48 Ibid., 200.
49 Brig. Gen. Allan Maclean, post commander at Niagara, to Sir Frederick Haldimand, 18 May
    1783, in *The Valley of the Six Nations*, ed. Charles M. Johnston (Toronto: Champlain Society,
    1964), 35–8. The excerpts quoted are from 36 and 37.
50 Elizabeth Elbourne, "Managing Alliance, Negotiating Christianity: Haudenosaunee Uses of
    Anglicanism in Northeastern North America, 1760s–1830s," in *Mixed Blessings: Indigenous
    Encounters with Christianity in Canada*, ed. Tolly Bradford and Chelsea Horton (Vancouver:
    UBC Press, 2016), 42–3.
51 White, *Middle Ground*, 454.
52 Allen, *His Majesty's Indian Allies*, 93.
53 John Leslie, *The Treaty of Amity, Commerce and Navigation, 1794–1796: The Jay Treaty* (Ottawa:
    Department of Indian and Northern Affairs Canada, 1979), 8–15. See also Audra Simpson,
    Mohawk Interruptus: Political Life across the Borders of Settler States (Durham, NC: Duke
    University Press, 2014), chap. 5.

5. From Alliance to "Irrelevance"

1 E. Palmer Patterson, *The Canadian Indian: A History Since 1500* (Don Mills, ON: Collier-
   Macmillan, 1972), 72.
2 J.R. Miller, *Compact, Contract, Covenant: Aboriginal Treaty-Making in Canada* (Toronto:
   University of Toronto Press, 2009), 82; G. Brown and R. Maguire, *Indian Treaties in Historical
   Perspective* (Ottawa: Indian and Northern Affairs, 1979), 22.

3 Robert S. Allen, *His Majesty's Indian Allies: British Indian Policy in Defence of Canada, 1774–1815* (Toronto: Dundurn Press, 1992), 84–5 and 111–13.

4 A useful of overview of British-Native-US relations in this period is Colin G. Calloway, *Crown and Calumet: British-Indian Relations, 1783-1815* (Norman: University of Oklahoma Press, 1987).

5 Quoted in Gerald M. Craig, *Upper Canada: The Formative Years, 1784–1841* (Toronto: McClelland and Stewart, 1963), 67.

6 Sandy Antal, *A Wampum Denied: Procter's War of 1812* (Ottawa: Carleton University Press, 1997), 23.

7 John Sugden, *Tecumseh: A Life* (New York: Henry Holt, 1998), 23.

8 Quoted in Allen, *His Majesty's Indian Allies*, 109. See also R. David Edmunds, "Tecumseh's Native Allies: Warriors Who Fought for the Crown," in *War on the Great Lakes*, ed. William Jeffrey Welsh and David Curtis Skaggs (Kent, OH: Kent State University Press, 1991), espec. 60, concerning Tenskwatawa's use of astronomical knowledge in a manner reminiscent of seventeenth-century Jesuits to win credibility with his followers.

9 Patterson, *Canadian Indian*, 84. See also Richard White, *The Middle Ground: Indians, Empires, and Republics in the Great Lakes Region, 1650–1815* (Cambridge: Cambridge University Press, 1991), 516.

10 General Hull quoted in George F.G. Stanley, "The Indians in the War of 1812," in *Sweet Promises: A Reader on Indian-White Relations in Canada*, ed. J.R. Miller (Toronto: University of Toronto Press, 1991), 110; Calloway, *Crown and Calumet*, 46, 193–205.

11 Antal, *A Wampum Denied*, 92–3 (Brock and Tecumseh meet); 156–7 (Britain and a Native state); and 252, 254–5, and 256–7 (First Nations leaders deciding strategy).

12 "Speech of Indian Chief 'Me-Tawth' [Metoss]" (1813), Women's Canadian Historical Society, *Transaction*, 4 (1903): 11–12. I wish to thank the Ontario Archives, who provided me with a copy of this document, and Dr. Cecilia Morgan, who advised me to look for it there.

13 Calloway, *Crown and Calumet*, 240–52.

14 Leslie F.S. Upton, *Micmacs and Colonists: Indian-White Relations in the Maritime Provinces, 1713-1867* (Vancouver: UBC Press, 1979), pts. 2 and 3; Daniel N. Paul, *We Were Not the Savages: A Micmac Perspective, 1713–1867* (Halifax: Nimbus, 1993), chaps. 6–13.

15 Upton, *Micmacs and Colonists*, 145; Paul, *We Were Not the Savages*, chap. 14.

16 The following synopsis is based on the excellent study by Judith Fingard, "The New England Company and the New Brunswick Indians, 1786–1826: A Comment on the Colonial Perversion of British Benevolence," *Acadiensis* 1, no. 2 (Spring 1972): 29–42.

17 The most authoritative source, on which this account is primarily based, Ingeborg Marshall, *A History and Ethnography of the Beothuk* (Montreal: McGill-Queen's University Press, 1996), does not take a precise position on the population question. She presents estimates from 500 to a bit less than 1,000 at contact as the most credible (281–4). The other source on which this account relies, Leslie F.S. Upton, "The Extermination of the Beothucks of Newfoundland," in *Sweet Promises: A Reader on Indian-White Relations in Canada*, ed. J.R. Miller (Toronto: University of Toronto Press, 1991), estimates the population at contact to have been approximately 2,000 (69).

18 Marshall, *History and Ethnography*, 205, 207, 208, 210, and 281.

19 J.R. Miller, "Great White Father Knows Best: Oka and the Land Claims Process," *Native Studies Review* 7, no. 1 (1991): 26–30.

20 Robert J. Surtees, "Indian Land Cessions in Upper Canada, 1815–1830," in *As Long As the Sun Shines and the Water Flows: A Reader in Canadian Native Studies*, ed. Ian A.L. Getty and Antoine S. Lussier (Vancouver: Nakoda Institute and UBC Press, 1983), 67. Arthur R.M. Lower,

Canadians in the Making: A Social History of Canada (Don Mills, ON: Longmans, 1958), 189–90; Miller, *Compact, Contract, Covenant,* 94.

21 Miller, *Compact, Contract, Covenant,* 95–9.

22 Donald B. Smith, *Sacred Feathers: The Reverend Peter Jones (Kahkewaquonaby) and the Mississauga Indians* (Toronto: University of Toronto Press, 1987), 124

23 Sir George Murray to Sir James Kempt, 25 January 1830, *Correspondence and Other Papers Relating to Aboriginal Tribes in British Possessions. 1834. British Parliamentary Papers* (Shannon: Irish University Press, 1969), no. 617, 88.

24 Robert S. Allen, "The British Indian Department and the Frontier in North America, 1755–1839," Canadian Historic Sites, *Occasional Papers in Archaeology and History,* No. 14 (Ottawa: Indian and Northern Affairs, n.d.), 91.

25 Charles White, *Account of the Regular Gradation in Man* (London, 1799), 135, quoted in Leslie F.S. Upton, "The Origins of Canadian Indian Policy," *Journal of Canadian Studies* 8, no. 4 (1973): 52.

26 For an example of the use of phrenology to "explain" the alleged fact "that all attempts to make gentlemen of them [Métis], have hitherto proved a failure," see J. Tod to F. Ermatinger, 20 March 1843, quoted in Jennifer S.H. Brown, *Strangers in Blood: Fur Trade Company Families in Indian Country* (Vancouver: UBC Press, 1980), 188–9.

27 Quoted in Smith, *Sacred Feathers,* 27.

28 "From the Anishinabek, the Ojibway, Potowatomi and Algonquin Nations to the Parliament of the Dominion of Canada," *Ontario Indian* 3, no. 12 (1980): 25.

29 Unidentified Mississauga, 1820, in D.F. McOuat, ed., "The Diary of William Graves," *Ontario History* 43, no. 1 (1951): 10. I am indebted to a colleague, James Ralph Handy, who made me aware of this item.

6. Reserves, Residential Schools, and the Threat of Assimilation

1 Sir James Kempt to Sir George Murray, 16 May 1829, *Correspondence and other Papers Relating to the Aboriginal Tribes in British Possessions. 1834. British Parliamentary Papers* (Shannon: Irish University Press, 1969), no. 617, 40–1.

2 Herman Merivale, *Lectures on Colonization and Colonies* (London, 1928), 511, quoted in Leslie F.S. Upton, "The Origins of Canadian Indian Policy," *Journal of Canadian Studies* 8, no. 4 (1973): 54.

3 A useful, brief survey of missionary efforts in Upper Canada is Elizabeth Graham, *Medicine Man to Missionary: Missionaries as Agents of Change among the Indians of Southern Ontario, 1784–1867* (Toronto: Peter Martin Associates, 1975). The Methodists are best examined in Donald B. Smith, *Sacred Feathers: The Reverend Peter Jones (Kahkewaquonaby) and the Mississauga Indians* (Toronto: University of Toronto Press, 1987). For the Jesuits, see Julien Paquin, S.J., "Modern Jesuit Missions in Ontario" (unpublished manuscript, Regis College Archives, Toronto) and [Anonymous] "Synopsis of the History of Wikwemikong" (unpublished manuscript, Regis College Archives, Toronto).

4 James Ralph Handy, "The Ojibwa: 1640–1840. Two Centuries of Change from Sault Ste. Marie to Coldwater/Narrows" (master's thesis, University of Waterloo, 1978), 91–7.

5 Minutes of a Speech, 19 July 1827, *Aboriginal Tribes in British Possessions,* 16–17.

6 Proceedings of a Council of the Chippewa Indians, 20 July 1827, ibid., 170.

7 Handy, "The Ojibwa," chaps. 9–12.

8 J.R. Miller, *Shingwauk's Vision: A History of Native Residential Schools* (Toronto: University of Toronto Press, 1996), 77–80.

9 *Christian Advocate and Journal*, 5 February 1830, 94, quoted in Graham, *Medicine Man to Missionary*, 19.

10 Graham, *Medicine Man to Missionary*, 73; "Brief Account of Kahkewaquonaby Written by Himself," box 8, file 2, 9, Peter Jones Collection, Victoria University Library, Toronto.

11 Hope MacLean, "The Hidden Agenda: Methodist Attitudes to the Ojibwa and the Development of Indian Schooling in Upper Canada, 1821–1860" (master's thesis, University of Toronto, 1978), 89.

12 Francis Bond Head, "Memorandum on the Aborigines of North America," Appendix A in *A Narrative* to Lord Glenelg, 20 November 1836 (London: John Murray, 1839), 1–2.

13 The best account is John Leslie, "The Bagot Commission: Developing a Corporate Memory for the Indian Department," Canadian Historical Association, *Historical Papers 1982*, 38–51, on which this summary is based.

14 A useful overview of the Upper Canadian boarding schools is found in Truth and Reconciliation Commission, *The Final Report of the Truth and Reconciliation Commission of Canada*, vol. 1, *Canada's Residential Schools: The History, Part 1, Origins to 1939* (Montreal: McGill-Queen's University Press, 2015), 69–82.

15 Miller, *Shingwauk's Vision*, 72–3, 76.

16 MacLean, "Methodist Attitudes," 144.

17 Miller, *Shingwauk's Vision*, 79–80.

18 Ibid., 84–6.

19 Egerton Ryerson, *Statistics Respecting Indian Schools with Dr. Ryerson's Report of 1847 Attached* (Ottawa: Government Printing Bureau, 1898), 73. I am indebted to Professor Donald B. Smith of the University of Calgary and to John Leslie of the Claims and Historical Research Centre of Indian and Northern Affairs Canada for supplying me with a copy of this report.

20 "Report of the Special Commissioners Appointed on the 8th of September, 1856, to Investigate Indian Affairs in Canada," *Journals of the Legislative Assembly of the Province of Canada*, vol. 16, appendix 21, 1858, unpaginated.

21 Chief Shingwauk to Lord Elgin, Royal Commission on Aboriginal Peoples, *Final Report*, vol. 1, *Looking Forward, Looking Back* (Ottawa: Indian and Northern Affairs Canada, 1996), 158.

22 "Petition of Chief Chingwauk," 10 June 1846, vol. 612, 115–19, reel C-13, 385, Records of the Department of Indian Affairs (RG10), Library and Archives Canada, Ottawa; J.R. Miller, *Compact, Contract, Covenant: Aboriginal Treaty-Making in Canada* (Toronto: University of Toronto Press, 2009), 110.

23 Lord Elgin to Lord Grey, 23 November 1849, in Arthur George Doughty, *The Elgin-Grey Papers 1845–1852*, 4 vols. (Ottawa: King's Printer 1937), 4 (app. 7): 1485, 1486. This account is based on Elgin's reports ibid., 2: 549, 553–4, and 563–4; 4: 1485–6; and also on Frank Tough, Jim Miller, and Arthur J. Ray, "Bounty and Benevolence: A Documentary History of Saskatchewan Treaties" (unpublished report for the Office of the Treaty Commissioner, Saskatoon, 15 March 1998), 63–77; and James Morrison, "The Robinson Treaties of 1850: A Case Study" (research report for the Royal Commission on Aboriginal Peoples, 1993).

24 W.B. Robinson to superintendent general, Indian Affairs, 24 September 1850, Alexander Morris, *The Treaties of Canada with the Indians of Manitoba and the North-West Territories* (1880; repr., Saskatoon: Fifth House, 1991), 17, 19.

25 John Leslie and Ron Maguire, eds., *The Historical Development of the Indian Act*, 2nd ed. (Ottawa: Department of Indian and Northern Affairs Canada, 1979), 23–4.

26 Ted Binnema, "Protecting Indian Lands by Defining Indian: 1850–76," *Journal of Canadian Studies* 48, no. 2 (2014): 15–24. I am grateful to Dr. Binnema, who provided the citation for this important article.

27 John F. Leslie, "Assimilation, Integration or Termination: The Development of Canadian Indian Policy, 1943–1963" (PhD diss., Carleton University, 1999), 3–6.

28 Quoted in George Manuel and Michael Posluns, *The Fourth World: An Indian Reality* (Don Mills, ON: Collier-Macmillan, 1974), 162.

29 Leslie and Maguire, *Historical Development*, 27. There are useful discussions of this important measure in John S. Milloy, "The Early Indian Acts: Developmental Strategy and Constitutional Change," and John L. Tobias, "Protection, Civilization, Assimilation: An Outline History of Canada's Indian Policy," both in *Sweet Promises: A Reader on Indian-White Relations in Canada*, ed. J.R. Miller (Toronto: University of Toronto Press, 1991), 146–7 (Milloy) and 130 (Tobias).

30 Account of the 15 May 1857 Legislative Assembly session, in the *Toronto Globe*, 16 May 1857, 2.

31 Tobias, "Protection, Civilization, Assimilation," 130.

32 "Minutes of Great Council, 20–29 September 1858," vol. 245, pt. 1, 145510-11, Records of the Department of Indian Affairs (RG10), Library and Archives of Canada, Ottawa.

33 Ibid., 145566.

34 Ibid., vol. 519, 83, R. Pennefather to Rev. A. Sickles, 10 November 1858. This was a response to the Oneida, who had raised objections similar to those quoted supra at n. 32. (ibid., vol. 245, pt. 2, 145787–90, memorial to Governor Head from the Oneida Indians of Munceytown, received 10 October 1858).

35 See Miller, *Compact, Contract, Covenant*, 104–6.

36 J. Michael Thoms, "Ojibwa Fishing Grounds: A History of Ontario Fisheries Law, Science, and the Sportsmen's Challenge to Aboriginal Treaty Rights, 1650–1900" (PhD diss., University of British Columbia, 2004), 125, 222–4.

37 Royal Commission on Aboriginal Peoples, *Looking Forward, Looking Back*, 146–7.

38 Smith, *Sacred Feathers*, 213–14.

39 Allan Sherwin, *Bridging Two Peoples: Chief Peter E. Jones, 1843–1909* (Waterloo, ON: Wilfrid Laurier University Press, 2012), 15. I am grateful to Dr. Donald Smith, who generously provided me with copies of an excerpt from this volume and the letter from a collection in the National Library of Scotland on which Dr. Sherwin based his statement.

40 Augustine Shingwauk, *Little Pine's Journal: The Appeal of a Christian Chippeway Chief on Behalf of His People* (1872; repr., Sault Ste Marie: Shingwauk Reunion Committee, 1991), 6–7. On the strategy of the Garden River First Nation in general, see the excellent study by Janet E. Chute, *The Legacy of Shingwaukonse: A Century of Native Leadership* (Toronto: University of Toronto Press, 1998).

7. The Commercial Frontier on the Western Plains

1 Arthur J. Ray, Jim Miller, and Frank Tough, *Bounty and Benevolence: A History of Saskatchewan Treaties* (Montreal: McGill-Queen's University Press, 2000), 3–5.

2 This description of the western and northern nations is based mainly on the excellent brief account in Gerald Friesen, *The Canadian Prairies: A History* (Toronto: University of Toronto Press, 1984), 23–7.

3 Ibid., 21.

4 Ray, Miller, and Tough, *Bounty and Benevolence*, 5–10.

5 William Waiser, *A World We Have Lost: Saskatchewan Before 1905* (Toronto: Fifth House, 2016), Introduction and chaps. 1–5.

6 Arthur J. Ray, *Indians in the Fur Trade: Their Role as Hunters, Trappers and Middlemen in the Lands Southwest of Hudson Bay, 1660–1870* (Toronto: University of Toronto Press, 1974), 69.

7　Arthur J. Ray, "Indians as Consumers in the Eighteenth Century," in *Old Trails and New Directions: Papers of the Third North American Fur Trade Conference*, ed. Carol M. Judd and Arthur J. Ray (Toronto: University of Toronto Press, 1980), 255–71.

8　Ray, *Indians in the Fur Trade*, 68.

9　Theodore Binnema, *Common and Contested Ground: A Human and Environmental History of the Northwestern Plains* (Toronto: University of Toronto Press, 2001), 89, 95, and 198; Waiser, *World We Have Lost*, 150–2.

10　Ray, *Indians in the Fur Trade*, 14, 16.

11　Binnema, *Common and Contested Ground*, 119–28; James Daschuk, *Clearing the Plains: Disease, Politics of Starvation, and the Loss of Aboriginal Life* (Regina: University of Regina Press, 2013), 36–40; Waiser, *World We Have Lost*, 217–21 and 362–4.

12　Ray, *Indians in the Fur Trade*, 188–92; Daschuk, *Clearing the Plains*, 68–70.

13　George Nelson, "Journals 6 July–22 Aug. 1822," entry of 10 July 1822, quoted in J.R. Miller, *Compact, Contract, Covenant: Aboriginal Treaty-Making in Canada* (Toronto: University of Toronto Press, 2009), 3.

14　Sylvia Van Kirk, *"Many Tender Ties": Women in Fur-Trade Society, 1670–1870* (Winnipeg: Watson and Dwyer, 1980), 4. The following account is based mainly on Van Kirk's study.

15　Jacqueline Peterson, "Many Roads to Red River: Métis Genesis in the Great Lakes Region, 1680–1815," in *The New Peoples: Being and Becoming Métis in North America*, ed. Jacqueline Peterson and Jennifer H.S. Brown (Winnipeg: University of Manitoba Press, 1985), 38–64.

16　Ray, Miller, and Tough, *Bounty and Benevolence*, 21–7.

17　Waiser, *World We Have Lost*, 234–6, 277–81, and 340–2; Daschuk, *Clearing the Plains*, 43, 47–8, and 65.

18　Quoted in Robin A. Fisher, *Contact and Conflict: Indian-European Relations in British Columbia, 1774–1890* (Vancouver: University of British Columbia Press, 1977), 42.

19　A good starting point for understanding this phase of relations in the West is John E. Foster, "Program for the Red River Mission: The Anglican Clergy 1820–1826," *Histoire sociale/Social History* 4 (November 1969): 49–75.

20　E. Palmer Patterson, *The Canadian Indian: A History since 1500* (Don Mills, ON: Collier-Macmillan, 1972), 122. See also J.R. Miller, *Shingwauk's Vision: A History of Native Residential Schools* (Toronto: University of Toronto Press, 1996), 66–72.

21　James Douglas, quoted in Van Kirk, *"Many Tender Ties,"* 1.

22　The case for division within the mixed-ancestry community at Red River has been argued most effectively by Frits Pannekoek, *A Snug Little Flock: The Social Origins of the Riel Resistance of 1869–70* (Winnipeg: Watson and Dwyer, 1991). A forceful restatement of the traditional views is Irene Spry, "The Métis and Mixed-Bloods of Rupert's Land before 1870," in Peterson and Brown, *The New Peoples*, 95–118; and a more detailed refutation is Gerhard Ens, *Homeland to Hinterland: The Changing Worlds of the Red River Metis in the Nineteenth Century* (Toronto: University of Toronto Press, 1996).

23　Allyson Stevenson, "The Metis Cultural Brokers and the Western Numbered Treaties, 1869–1877" (master's thesis, University of Saskatchewan, 2004), 33, 45, 48–9, 51–2, and 149–50.

24　Friesen, *Canadian Prairies*, 101 ("Hurrah for freedom! Free trade is here!"). The Louis Riel involved in the *Sayer* case was the father of the leader of the 1869–70 resistance.

25　Ray, Miller, and Tough, *Bounty and Benevolence*, 21–31 (quotation 26).

26　John S. Milloy, *The Plains Cree: Trade: Diplomacy and War, 1790–1870* (Winnipeg: University of Manitoba Press, 1988), especially the chapter on "The Buffalo Wars."

27 Petition of Blackfoot chiefs to Lieutenant-Governor Morris, n.d., Alexander Morris Papers, box 6, file 1265, Provincial Archives of Manitoba, MG 12, B 1. The Blackfoot Council took place in the autumn of 1875.

8. Contact, Commerce, and Christianity on the Pacific

1 Alan D. McMillan, *Native Peoples and Cultures of Canada: An Anthropological Overview*, 2nd ed. (Vancouver: Douglas and McIntyre, 1995), 185–219; Diamond Jenness, *The Indians of Canada*, 7th ed. (Ottawa: Supply and Services Canada, 1977), chap. 23.

2 An excellent, easily accessible introduction to their art is Judy Thompson, "No Little Variety of Ornament: Northern Athapaskan Artistic Traditions," in *The Spirit Sings: Artistic Traditions of Canada's First Peoples*, ed. Julia Harrison (Toronto: Glenbow Museum/McClelland and Stewart, 1987), 133–68.

3 See Wilson Duff, *The Indian History of British Columbia*, vol. 1, *The Impact of the White Man*, 2nd ed. (Victoria: Royal British Columbia Museum, 1969), chap. 1; Jenness, *Indians of Canada*, chap. 22.

4 *Historical Atlas of Canada*, vol. 1, *From the Beginning to 1800* (Toronto: University of Toronto Press, 1987), plate 14 ("Prehistoric Trade").

5 Jean Barman, *The West beyond the West: A History of British Columbia* (Toronto: University of Toronto Press, 1991), 14.

6 James R. Gibson, *Otter Skins, Boston Ships, and China Goods: The Maritime Fur Trade of the Northwest Coast, 1785–1841* (Montreal: McGill-Queen's University Press, 1992), 9.

7 McMillan, *Native Peoples and Cultures of Canada*, 188; Rolf Knight, *Indians at Work: An Informal History of Native Labour in British Columbia 1848–1930* (Vancouver: New Star Books, 1996), 35.

8 Helen Codere, *Fighting with Property: A Study of Kwakiutl Potlatching and Warfare, 1792–1930* (Seattle: University of Washington Press, 1966).

9 This account is based mainly on the excellent study by Robin A. Fisher, *Contact and Conflict: Indian-European Relations in British Columbia, 1774–1890* (Vancouver: UBC Press, 1977), espec. chap. 1. A second edition was published in 1992, but it contained no substantive changes.

10 Ibid., 23.

11 Duff, *Indian History*, 56.

12 Knight, *Indians at Work*, 75 re: copper.

13 Fisher, *Contact and Conflict*, 40 and 45–6 (quotation). See also Duff, *Indian History*, 57.

14 Quoted in Duff, *Indian History*, 59.

15 John Sutton Lutz, *Makúk: A New History of Aboriginal-White Relations* (Vancouver: UBC Press, 2008), 81–3.

16 Fisher, *Contact and Conflict*, 47–8.

17 Quoted ibid., 24.

18 James R. Gibson, "The Maritime Trade of the North Pacific Coast," in *Handbook of North American Indians*, vol. 4, *History of Indian-White Relations*, ed. Wilcomb E. Washburn (Washington: Smithsonian Institution, 1988), 381.

19 The best account of this period is Fisher, *Contact and Conflict*, chap. 2.

20 Margaret A. Ormsby, "Douglas, Sir James," in *Dictionary of Canadian Biography*, vol. 10, University of Toronto/Université Laval, 2003–, accessed 2 August 2017, http://www.biographi.ca/en/bio/douglas_james_10E.html. See also Paul Tennant, *Aboriginal Peoples and Politics: The Indian Land Question in British Columbia, 1849–1989* (Vancouver: UBC Press, 1990), chaps. 2–3.

21 J.R. Miller, *Compact, Contract, Covenant: Aboriginal Treaty-Making in Canada* (Toronto: University of Toronto Press, 2009), 147.

22 Ormsby, "Douglas."

23 Daniel Patrick Marshall, "Claiming the Land: Indians, Goldseekers, and the Rush to British Columbia" (PhD diss., University of British Columbia, 2000), chap. 6; Donald Hauka, *McGowan's War* (Vancouver: New Star Books, 2003), 84–93, 97–9; and "H.M. Snyder, letter to James Douglas, Fraser River, Fort Yale, 28th August 1858," *Native Studies Review* 11, no. 1 (1997): 140–5.

24 Adele Perry, *On the Edge of Empire: Gender, Race, and the Making of British Columbia, 1849–1871* (Toronto: University of Toronto Press, 2001), 14.

25 Duff, *Indian History*, 39.

26 John Douglas Belshaw, "Mining Technique and Social Division on Vancouver Island, 1848–1900," *British Journal of Canadian Studies* 1, no. 1 (1986): 53–4.

27 Quoted in Fisher, *Contact and Conflict*, 117.

28 Ibid., 107–8; Barman, *West beyond the West*, 79; Tina Loo, *Making Law, Order, and Authority in British Columbia, 1821–1871* (Toronto: University of Toronto Press, 1994), chap. 7; Lutz, *Makúk*, 131–9.

29 Cole Harris, *Making Native Space: Colonialism, Resistance, and Reserves in British Columbia* (Vancouver: UBC Press, 2002), chaps. 3 and 4.

30 Perry, *On the Edge of Empire*, 114; Barry Gough, *Gunboat Frontier: British Maritime Authority and Northwest Coast Indians, 1846–1890* (Vancouver: UBC Press, 1984), 24.

31 Lutz, *Makúk*, 101–2.

32 John Webster Grant, *Moon of Wintertime: Missionaries and the Indians of Canada in Encounter since 1534* (Toronto: University of Toronto Press, 1984), 125–6; David Mulhall, *Will to Power: The Missionary Career of Father Morice* (Vancouver: UBC Press, 1986), 8–9.

33 Jacqueline Gresko, "Paul Durieu, O.M.I.," *Dictionary of Canadian Biography*, vol. 12, *1891 to 1900* (Toronto: University of Toronto Press, 1990), 283. I am grateful to Dr. Gresko for this and many other helpful suggestions.

34 The best account is Jean Usher, *William Duncan of Metlakatla: A Victorian Missionary in British Columbia* (Ottawa: National Museum of Man, 1974).

35 Andrew Rettig, "A Nativist Movement at Metlakatla Mission," *BC Studies*, no. 46 (Summer 1980): 28–39.

36 Jan Hare and Jean Barman, "Good Intentions Gone Awry: From Protection to Confinement in Emma Crosby's Home for Aboriginal Girls," in *With Good Intentions: Euro-Canadian and Aboriginal Relations in Colonial Canada*, ed. Celia Haig-Brown and David A. Nock (Vancouver: UBC Press, 2006), 179–98.

37 Clarence Bolt, *Thomas Crosby and the Tsimshian: Small Shoes for Feet Too Large* (Vancouver: UBC Press, 1992).

38 Dave De Brou and Bill Waiser, eds., *Documenting Canada: A History of Modern Canada in Documents* (Saskatoon: Fifth House, 1992), 55.

9. Resistance in Red River and the Numbered Treaties

1 John S. Milloy, "The Early Indian Acts: Developmental Strategy and Constitutional Change," in *Sweet Promises: A Reader on Indian-White Relations in Canada*, ed. J.R. Miller (Toronto: University of Toronto Press, 1991), 151–2. See also John L. Tobias, "Protection, Civilization,

Assimilation: An Outline History of Canada's Indian Policy," ibid., 131; J.R. Miller, *Canada and the Aboriginal Peoples, 1867–1927* (Ottawa: Canadian Historical Association, 1997), 10.

2 "Report of the Indian Branch of the Department of the Secretary State for the Provinces, 1871," Canada, *Sessional Papers (No. 23), 1871*, 4.

3 Quoted in Doug Owram, *Promise of Eden: The Canadian Expansionist Movement and the Idea of the West, 1856–1900* (Toronto: University of Toronto Press, 1980), 49.

4 James G. Snell, "American Neutrality and the Red River Resistance, 1869–1870," *Prairie Forum* 4, no. 2 (1979): 193. I am grateful to Bill Waiser, who drew my attention to this article.

5 "Declaration of the People of Rupert's Land and the North West," Archives of Manitoba, MG3 A1–6, accessed 14 November 2016, http://manitobia.ca/content/en/records/RRS/RRS_1869_1207.

6 Quoted in George F.G. Stanley, *Louis Riel* (Toronto: Ryerson, 1963), 114.

7 33 Vict., c 3, section 31, *Revised Statutes of Canada 1985*, Appendix 8 (Ottawa: Queen's Printer, 1985).

8 Canada, Parliament, *Debates of the House of Commons*, First Parliament, Third Session, 2 May 1870, 1293.

9 Ibid., 4 May 1870, 1359.

10 Douglas N. Sprague, *Canada and the Métis, 1869–1885* (Waterloo: Wilfrid Laurier University Press, 1988), chaps. 6–9.

11 This interpretation, championed by Sprague, ibid., is vigorously opposed by Gerhard J. Ens, *Homeland to Hinterland: The Changing Worlds of the Red River Metis in the Nineteenth Century* (Toronto: University of Toronto Press, 1996) and by Thomas Flanagan, *Metis Lands in Manitoba* (Calgary: University of Calgary Press, 1991).

12 Alexander Morris to Macdonald, 16 January 1873, vol. 252, 113998–114003, Sir John A. Macdonald Papers, MG 26 A, Library and Archives Canada.

13 Confidential Memorandum re: discussion held during visit to Washington by David Mills, Minister of the Interior, 23 August 1877, C.O. 42, vol. 749, microfilm reel B-586, 401–25, Library and Archives Canada.

14 Alexander Morris, *The Treaties of Canada with the Indians of Manitoba and the North-West Territories* (1880; repr., Saskatoon: Fifth House, 1991), 272.

15 The following account is based mainly on J.R. Miller, *Compact, Contract, Covenant: Aboriginal Treaty-Making in Canada* (Toronto: University of Toronto Press, 2009), chap. 6; Treaty 7 Tribal Elders and Tribal Council with Walter Hildebrandt, Dorothy First Rider, and Sarah Carter, *The True Spirit and Original Intent of Treaty 7* (Montreal: McGill-Queen's University Press, 1997); and Richard Price, ed., *The Spirit of the Alberta Indian Treaties*, 2nd ed. (Edmonton: Pica Pica Press, 1987).

16 Report to government 1869, Records of the Department of Public Works, vol. 265, RG 11, Library and Archives Canada, quoted in Royal Commission on Aboriginal Peoples, *Final Report*, vol. 1, *Looking Forward, Looking Back* (Ottawa: Indian and Northern Affairs Canada, 1996), 165.

17 John L. Tobias, "Canada's Subjugation of the Plains Cree, 1879–1885," in Miller, *Sweet Promises*, 213; Gerald Friesen, *The Canadian Prairies: A History* (Toronto: University of Toronto Press, 1984), 137–8; Morris, *Treaties of Canada with the Indians*, 37. Concerning Commissioner Alexander Morris's concern about First Nation unrest, especially near Portage, see Morris to Macdonald, 7 February and 2 June 1873, vol. 252, 114028–32, 114133–7, Sir John A. Macdonald Papers, MG 26 A, Library and Archives Canada.

18 Hugh A. Dempsey, "One Hundred Years of Treaty Seven," in *One Century Later: Western Canadian Reserve Indians Since Treaty 7*, ed. Ian A.L. Getty and Donald B. Smith (Vancouver: UBC Press, 1977), 21.

19 Roderick Charles Macleod, *The North-West Mounted Police and Law Enforcement* (Toronto: University of Toronto Press, 1976), 3.

20 Canada, *Debates of the House of Commons*, 8 February 1877, 3.

21 *Oxford Dictionary of Quotations*, 3rd ed. (New York: Oxford University Press, 1979), 505.

22 Morris, *Treaties of Canada with the Indians*, 174; J.R. Miller, *Big Bear (Mistahimusqua)* (Toronto: ECW Press, 1996), 78–83.

23 Morris, *Treaties of Canada with the Indians*, 170–1.

24 G. McDougall to J. Ferrier, 17 December 1875, in Hugh A. Dempsey, ed., "The Last Letters of Rev. George McDougall," *Alberta Historical Review* 6, no. 2 (1967): 26. The most authoritative and up-to-date explanation for the decline and collapse of the bison is found in Geoff Cunfer, "Overview: The Decline and Fall of the Bison Empire," and Dan Flores, "Reviewing an Iconic Story: Environmental History and the Demise of the Bison," both in *Bison and People on the North American Great Plains: A Deep Environmental History*, ed. Geoff Cunfer and Bill Waiser (College Station: Texas A&M University Press, 2016), 1–29 and 30–47.

25 Frank Tough, *As Their Natural Resources Fail: Native Peoples and the History of Northern Manitoba, 1870–1930* (Vancouver: UBC Press, 1996), chap. 2.

26 James Daschuk, *Clearing the Plains: Disease, Politics of Starvation, and the Loss of Aboriginal Life* (Regina: University of Regina Press, 2013), 96–8.

27 Peter Erasmus, *Buffalo Days and Nights* as told to Henry Thompson (introduction by Irene Spry) (Calgary: Glenbow-Alberta Institute, 1976), 247–9. For similar sentiments by another influential chief at Fort Carlton, Ahtakakoop, see ibid., 249–50. Sweet Grass spoke similarly at Fort Pitt, and Crowfoot the next year at Blackfoot Crossing.

28 Miller, *Compact, Contract, Covenant*, 164–5; Price, *Spirit of the Alberta Indian Treaties*; and Tribal 7 Elders and Tribal Council with Hildebrandt, First Rider, and Carter, *True Spirit and Original Intent of Treaty 7*; Sharon Venne, "Understanding Treaty 6: An Indigenous Perspective," in *Aboriginal and Treaty Rights in Canada*, ed. Michael Asch (Vancouver: UBC Press, 1997), 173–207.

29 John L. Tobias, "The Origin of the Treaty Rights Movement in Saskatchewan," in *1885 and After: Native Society in Transition*, ed. F. Laurie Barron and James B. Waldram (Regina: Canadian Plains Research Center, 1986), 248; John L. Tobias, "Canada and the Plains Indians," *NeWest Review* (February 1987): 12–13.

30 Morris, *Treaties of Canada with the Indians*, 40; Tobias, "Subjugation of the Plains Cree," 215.

31 Jean Friesen, "Magnificent Gifts: The Treaties of Canada with the Indians of the Northwest, 1869–76," *Transactions* of the Royal Society of Canada, Series 5, vol. 1 (1986): 46.

32 Friesen, *Canadian Prairies*, 138–9.

33 Quoted ibid., 144.

34 Morris, *Treaties of Canada with the Indians*, 99–106.

35 Ibid., 58, 96, 231–3.

36 Ibid., 211. At the same talks, Morris offered assurances concerning gathering rights: "Understand me, I do not want to interfere with your hunting and fishing. I want you to pursue it through the country, as you have heretofore done." Ibid., 204.

37 The different approaches and objectives are summarized by John L. Tobias, "Indian Reserves in Western Canada: Indian Homelands or Devices for Assimilation," in *Approaches to Native*

History in Canada, ed. Delphin Andrew Muise (Ottawa: National Museum of Man, 1977), espec. 90–1.

38 John L. Taylor, "Canada's North-West Indian Policy in the 1870's: Traditional Premises and Necessary Innovations," in *Sweet Promises*, ed. Miller, 207–11.

39 On Treaty 6, see Morris, *Treaties of Canada with the Indians*, 352, 355.

40 Ibid., 351.

41 The different understandings have been documented for Treaties 6 and 7 in John L. Taylor, "Two Views on the Meaning of Treaties Six and Seven," in *The Spirit of the Alberta Indian Treaties*, ed. Price, 9–45.

10. The North-West Rebellion

1 The earliest, and still the best, treatment of the Rebellion as the clash of two ways of life is George F.G. Stanley, *The Birth of Western Canada: A History of the Riel Rebellions*, 2nd ed. (Toronto: University of Toronto Press, 1960). University of Toronto Press issued a new edition, with introduction by Thomas Flanagan, in 1992.

2 Howard Adams, *Prison of Grass: Canada from the Native Point of View* (Toronto: New Press, 1975). A revised edition, with the subtitle *Canada from a Native Point of View*, was issued in Saskatoon by Fifth House in 1989.

3 Essential to understand the limited role of First Nations in the Rebellion is Blair Stonechild and Bill Waiser, *Loyal Till Death: Indians and the North-West Rebellion* (Calgary: Fifth House, 1997).

4 Gary Pennanen, "Sitting Bull: Indian Without a Country," *Canadian Historical Review* 51, no. 2 (June 1970): 123–41.

5 Geoff Cunfer, "Overview: The Decline and Fall of the Bison Empire," and Dan Flores, "Reviewing an Iconic Story: Environmental History and the Demise of the Bison," in *Bison and People on the North American Great Plains: A Deep Environmental History*, ed. Geoff Cunfer and Bill Waiser (College Station: Texas A&M University Press, 2016), 1–29 and 30–47. In comparison to many other authors, Flores (41–2) de-emphasizes the role of the American military in the demise of the bison.

6 Stanley, *Birth of Western Canada*, 220, 221; Gerald Friesen, *The Canadian Prairies: A History* (Toronto: University of Toronto Press, 1984), 250.

7 James Daschuk, *Clearing the Plains: Disease, Politics of Starvation, and the Loss of Aboriginal Life* (Regina: University of Regina Press, 2013), 101–13.

8 Quoted in Noel Evan Dyck, "The Administration of Federal Indian Aid in the North-West Territories 1879–1885" (master's thesis, University of Saskatchewan, 1970), 28.

9 Quoted in J.R. Miller, *Big Bear (Mistahimusqua)* (Toronto: ECW Press, 1996), 90.

10 John L. Tobias, "Canada's Subjugation of the Plains Cree, 1879–1885," in *Sweet Promises: A Reader on Indian-White Relations in Canada*, ed. J.R. Miller (Toronto: University of Toronto Press, 1991), 216–17.

11 This account is based on Tobias, ibid., 216ff.; and Daschuk, *Clearing*, chap. 8.

12 Miller, *Big Bear*, 90–6.

13 Notes of Governor General Lorne's meeting at Fort Carlton, 1881, vol. 3768, file 33642, Records of the Department of Indian Affairs (RG 10), Library and Archives Canada.

14 Stonechild and Waiser, *Loyal Till Death*. Spiritual considerations might also have contributed to the law-abiding behaviour of Plains First Nations between treaty and 1885. Rod Macleod reports that the North-West Mounted Police did not fire a shot in anger at a First Nation person

or Métis before 1885. Roderick Charles Macleod, *The North West Mounted Police, 1873–1919* (Ottawa: Canadian Historical Association, 1978), 8. Macleod and another researcher have also found that settlers were five times as likely as First Nations people were to be tried on a criminal charge in the Territories between 1878 and 1885. Roderick Charles Macleod and Heather Rollason, "'Restrain the Lawless Savages': Native Defendants in the Criminal Courts of the North West Territories, 1878–1885," *Journal of Historical Sociology* 10, no. 2 (1997): 157–83.

15 J.R. Miller, *Shingwauk's Vision: A History of Native Residential Schools* (Toronto: University of Toronto Press, 1996), chap. 3.

16 Ibid., chap. 4.

17 Quoted in Tobias, "Subjugation," 221–2. On the policy in general, see William A. Waiser, *A World We Have Lost: Saskatchewan Before 1905* (Markham, ON: Fifth House, 2016), 506–8.

18 J. Ansdell Macrae to Department, 25 Aug. 1884, vol. 3697, file 15423, Records of the Department of Indian Affairs (RG 10), Library and Archives Canada.

19 Waiser, *A World We Have Lost*, 513–16.

20 Quoted in Friesen, *Canadian Prairies*, 227.

21 The best account of Riel's millenarian thought is Thomas Flanagan, *Louis "David" Riel: Prophet of the New World* (Toronto: University of Toronto Press, 1979).

22 Thomas Flanagan, *Riel and the Rebellion: 1885 Reconsidered* (Saskatoon: Western Producer Prairie Books, 1983), chap. 5. How accurate the priest's report was is impossible to determine.

23 Waiser, *A World We Have Lost*, 514–16 and 527.

24 "Claims of the Half-Breeds in Manitoba and the North-West Territories," Order in Council 135, 28 January 1885, in *Documenting Canada: A History of Modern Canada in Documents*, ed. Dave De Brou and Bill Waiser (Saskatoon: Fifth House, 1992), 140.

25 The following account relies heavily on Stonechild and Waiser, *Loyal Till Death*, and Waiser, *A World We Have Lost*, chap. 15.

26 Thomas Clarke, diary entries of 23–4 March 1885, file 1.1, A718, Thomas Clarke Papers, Saskatchewan Archives Board, Saskatoon office.

27 H. McKay to "Dear Sir," 13 April 1885, box 1a, file 18, Presbyterian Church Papers, Home Missions Committee, United Church of Canada Archives.

28 Hugh A. Dempsey, "The Fearsome Fire Wagons," in *The CPR West: The Iron Road and The Making of a Nation*, ed. Hugh A. Dempsey (Vancouver: Douglas and McIntyre, 1984), 65.

29 Tobias, "Subjugation," 230–2. On post-Rebellion trials and government reprisals, see also Waiser, *A World We Have Lost*, 557–69.

30 François Dufresne (as narrated to Humphrey Gratz), "Defence of Big Bear," *Western Producer*, 16 June 1983, 10–11.

31 For example, see H. Reed to E. Dewdney, 20 July 1885, with Dewdney's marginal minutes and Sir John Macdonald's comments, vol. 3710, file 19550–3, Records of the Department of Indian Affairs (RG 10), Library and Archives Canada.

32 See William A. Waiser, "The White Man Governs: The 1885 Indian Trials," in *Canadian State Trials*, vol. 3, *Political Trials and Security Measures, 1840–1914*, ed. Barry Wright and Susan Binnie (Toronto: Osgoode Society for Canadian Legal History, 2009), 451–82. See also Sandra Estlin Bingaman, "The North-West Rebellion Trials, 1885" (master's thesis, University of Regina, 1971); "The Trials of Poundmaker and Big Bear, 1885," *Saskatchewan History* 28, no. 3 (1975): 81–94; and "The Trials of the "White Rebels," 1885," ibid., 25, no. 2 (1972): 41–54; Flanagan, *Riel and the Rebellion*, 118.

33 D.H. Brown, "The Meaning of Treason in 1885," *Saskatchewan History* 28, no. 2 (1975): 65–73.

34 Flanagan, *Riel and the Rebellion*, 122–4, 126–9.

35 Arthur Isaac Silver, *The French-Canadian Idea of Confederation 1864–1900* (Toronto: University of Toronto Press, 1982), 153–79.

36 See espec. Flanagan, *Riel and the Rebellion,* chap. 7.

37 Quoted in Association of Métis and Non-Status Indians of Saskatchewan, *Louis Riel: Justice Must Be Done* (Winnipeg: Manitoba Metis Federation Press, 1979), vi.

38 John Robert Colombo, *Colombo's Canadian Quotations* (Edmonton: Hurtig, 1974), 597. I am indebted to Professor Donald B. Smith, who pointed out to me that Trudeau's speech at the unveiling of Riel's monument occurred in 1968, not 1969 as given in Colombo.

39 *Flint and Feather: The Complete Poems of E. Pauline Johnson (Tekahionwake),* 8th ed. (Toronto: Musson, 1922), 17. I am indebted to my late art history colleague, Peter Perdue, for bringing this poem to my attention.

40 Rudy Wiebe, *The Temptations of Big Bear* (Toronto: McClelland and Stewart, 1973); *The Ballad of Crowfoot,* directed and performed by Willie Dunn (1968, National Film Board); *Big Bear,* directed by Gil Cardinal (1999, Canadian Broadcasting Corporation).

11. The Policy of the Bible and the Plough

1 "Return to an Order of the House of Commons, dated 2 May 1887," Canada, *Sessional Papers (No. 20b) 1887,* 37. See also Macdonald's enthusiastic agreement "with Mr. Reed's suggestion that the Tribal system should be broken up as soon as possible – so that each individual Indian may be dealt with instead of through the Chiefs." Hayter Reed's memo of 20 July 1885, vol. 3710, file 19,550–3, Records of the Department of Indian Affairs (RG10), Library and Archives Canada.

2 Hana Samek, *The Blackfoot Confederacy, 1880–1920: A Comparative Study of Canadian and U.S. Indian Policy* (Albuquerque: University of New Mexico Press, 1987), 26.

3 E. Brian Titley, *A Narrow Vision: Duncan Campbell Scott and the Administration of Indian Affairs in Canada* (Vancouver: UBC Press, 1986), chap. 7.

4 Manseü-Scanian, "The New Race," *The Missionary Outlook* 24, no. 5 (1905): 58.

5 Reed to Superintendent General, 31 Oct. 1889, Canada, *Sessional Papers (No. 12) 1890,* 165.

6 Sarah A. Carter, "Two Acres and a Cow: 'Peasant' Farming for the Indians of the Northwest, 1889–1897," in *Sweet Promises: A Reader on Indian-White Relations in Canada,* ed. J.R. Miller (Toronto: University of Toronto Press, 1991), 356.

7 Reed to Superintendent General, 31 Oct. 1889, Canada, *Sessional Papers (No. 12) 1890,* x.

8 Canada, House of Commons, *Debates,* 1876, 752.

9 Sarah A. Carter, "Controlling Indian Movement: The Pass System," *NeWest Review,* May 1985, 8–9; F. Laurie Barron, "The Indian Pass System in the Canadian West, 1882–1935," *Prairie Forum* 21, no. 1 (1988): 25–42; J.R. Miller, *Canada and the Aboriginal Peoples 1867–1927* (Ottawa: Canadian Historical Association, 1997), 15.

10 See J.R. Miller, "Owen Glendower, Hotspur, and Canadian Indian Policy," in *Sweet Promises,* ed. Miller, 327.

11 Roderick Charles Macleod, *The North-West Mounted Police and Law Enforcement, 1873–1905* (Toronto: University of Toronto Press, 1976), 146.

12 H. Reed to T.M. Daly, 25 March 1893, vol. 14, file "Reed, Hayter 1893," Hayter Reed Papers, Library and Archives Canada.

13 Significantly, the printed "General Instructions to Indian Agents in Canada" that the Department issued in 1913 and reissued in 1933 nowhere mentioned passes. Blackfoot Indian Agency Papers, box 3, file 15, Glenbow Archives.

14 John Leslie and Ron Maguire, *The Historical Development of the Indian Act*, 2nd ed. (Ottawa: Department of Indian and Northern Affairs Canada, 1979), 79, 81.

15 Victoria c. 27, s. 3, *Statutes of Canada*, 1884.

16 Order in Council, 7 July 1883 (Gazetted 4 Aug.1883), vol. 54, no. 4355, Correspondence of the Secretary of State, Library and Archives Canada. Douglas Cole and Ira Chaikin, *An Iron Hand upon the People: The Law against the Potlatch on the Northwest Coast* (Vancouver: Douglas and McIntyre, 1990), 14–17.

17 Quoted in Robin A. Fisher, *Contact and Conflict: Indian-European Relations in British Columbia, 1774–1890* (Vancouver: UBC Press, 1977), 206–7.

18 For the prairie dancing issue in general, see K. Pettipas, *Severing the Ties That Bind: Government Repression of Indigenous Religious Ceremonies on the Prairies* (Winnipeg: University of Manitoba Press, 1994).

19 Hugh A. Dempsey, *Red Crow, Warrior Chief* (Saskatoon: Western Producer Prairie Books, 1980), chap. 19, espec. 213.

20 Interview with Gordon Tootoosis, Poundmaker Reserve, 7 May 1987.

21 Eleanor Brass, "Recollections and Reminiscences: The File Hills Ex-Pupil Colony," *Saskatchewan History* 6, no. 2 (1953): 67; *I Walk in Two Worlds* (Calgary: Glenbow Museum 1987), 13, 25.

22 Stan Cuthand, "The Native Peoples of the Prairie Provinces in the 1920s and 1930s," in *Sweet Promises*, ed. Miller, 389–90.

23 Cole and Chaikin, *An Iron Hand,* 83, 116.

24 See Tina Loo, "Dan Cranmer's Potlatch: Law as Coercion, Symbol, and Rhetoric in British Columbia, 1884–1951," *Canadian Historical Review* 73, no. 2 (1992): 126–65.

25 Cole and Chaikin, *An Iron Hand*, chap. 10.

26 Ibid., 175.

27 See Sarah Carter, *The Importance of Being Monogamous: Marriage and Nation Building in Western Canada to 1915* (Edmonton: University of Alberta Press, 2008), chap. 5, especially 152–4 and 167; *Capturing Women: The Manipulation of Cultural Imagery in Canada's Prairie West* (Montreal: McGill-Queen's University Press, 1997), 183 and 186–8.

28 Canada, House of Commons, *Debates*, 4 May 1885, 1575.

29 Canada, *Sessional Papers (No. 14) 1892*, x.

30 For overviews of residential schooling, see J.R. Miller, *Shingwauk's Vision: A History of Native Residential Schools* (Toronto: University of Toronto Press, 1996); John S. Milloy, *A National Crime: The Canadian Government and the Residential School System, 1879 to 1986* (Winnipeg: University of Manitoba Press, 1999); Truth and Reconciliation Commission, *Final Report*, 6 vols. (Montreal: McGill-Queen's University Press, 2015), espec. vols. 1, 2, and 5.

31 Canada, *Sessional Papers (No. 12) 1890*, xi.

32 N.F. Davin, (Confidential) "Report on Industrial Schools for Indians and Half-Breeds," 14 March 1879, vol. 91, 35428, p. 1, Sir John A. Macdonald Papers, MG 26 A, Library and Archives Canada.

33 Dan Kennedy [Ochankugahe], *Recollections of an Assiniboine Chief*, ed. James R. Stevens (Toronto: McClelland and Stewart 1972), 54–5.

34 Canada, House of Commons, *Debates*, 1883, 1377.

35 Canada, *Sessional Papers (No. 14) 1892*, 291; Brass, "The File Hills Ex-Pupil Colony."

36 Canada, House of Commons, *Debates*, 18 July 1904, 6948. Later (ibid., 6956) Sifton elaborated: "He has not the physical, mental or moral get-up to enable him to compete. He cannot do it."

37 Canada, *Sessional Papers (No. 27) 1911*, 273–4.

38 The Truth and Reconciliation Commission used Indian Affairs annual reports, which provide enrolment figures only for status First Nations children. This approach leaves out of the calculation non-status, Métis, and Inuit children, as well as status children who did not attend any school. Truth and Reconciliation Commission, *Final Report*, vol. 1, *The History, Part 1, Origins to 1939* (Montreal: McGill-Queen's University Press, 2015), 245: In 1934, "40% of *First Nations children enrolled in school* were attending residential school" (emphasis added). From vol. 1, *The History, Part 2, 1939 to 2000* (Montreal: McGill-Queen's University Press, 2015), 9: In 1944–5 the 8,865 in residential schools "accounted for 53.9% of the 16,438 *First Nations students enrolled in school* in Canada" (emphasis added). By the 1960s, the percentage has dropped because of the federal government's policy of integrated schooling. Ibid., 10. See also ibid., 55.

39 John Snow, *These Mountains Are Our Sacred Places: The Story of the Stoney People* (Toronto: Samuel Stevens, 1977), 109.

40 Miller, *Shingwauk's Vision*, chap. 12.

41 Ibid., 129–30.

42 "Sophie," quoted in Celia Haig-Brown, *Resistance and Renewal: Surviving the Indian Residential School* (Vancouver: Tillacum Library, 1988), 102.

43 Miller, *Shingwauk's Vision*, 365–8; Truth and Reconciliation Commission of Canada, *Final Report*, vol. 1, *The History, Part 2, 1939 to 2000* (Montreal: McGill-Queen's University Press, 2015), 336–66.

44 James Daschuk, *Clearing the Plains: Disease, Politics of Starvation, and the Loss of Aboriginal Life* (Regina: University of Regina Press, 2013), 131, 135–6, 150.

45 This account relies heavily on Sarah A. Carter, *Lost Harvests: Prairie Indian Reserve Farmers and Government Policy* (Montreal: McGill-Queen's University Press, 1990), a study principally of Treaty 4. An analysis with a similar interpretation that is broader geographically and chronologically in its coverage is Helen Buckley, *From Wooden Ploughs to Welfare: Why Indian Policy Failed in the Prairie Provinces* (Montreal: McGill-Queen's University Press, 1992). See also Carter's article, "Two Acres and a Cow."

46 Marion Joan Boswell, "'Civilizing' the Indian: Government Administration of Indians, 1876-1896" (PhD. diss., University of Ottawa, 1977), 218, 221.

47 H. Reed to T.M. Daly, 10 March 1893, vol. 14, 1349, file "Reed, Hayter 1893," Hayter Reed Papers, Library and Archives Canada.

48 Canada, *Sessional Papers (No. 12) 1890*, 162. See also Canada, *Sessional Papers (No. 14) 1892*, 193; Carter, *Lost Harvests*, 209–14, 235–6.

49 Canada, House of Commons, *Debates*, 19 May 1888, 1610 (Macdowall referring to a petition from Battleford); *Regina Leader*, 20 November 1884; *MacLeod Gazette*, 2 August 1895, editorial, "Indian Competition," in J.W. Tims Papers, box 4, file 51, Glenbow Archives.

50 Boswell, "'Civilizing' the Indian," 340–2.

51 Sarah A. Carter, "Agriculture and Agitation on the Oak River Dakota Reserve, 1875–1895," *Manitoba History* no. 6 (fall 1983): 4–8; Peter Douglas Elias, *The Dakota of the Canadian Northwest: Lessons for Survival* (Winnipeg: University of Manitoba Press, 1988), 60–1, 86–7, 111, 154–6.

52 This complicated story is reconstructed from the annual reports of the Department of Indian Affairs, 1881–1900, in *Sessional Papers*; and from "Moose Mountain Elections, 1888–1911," vol. 3940, file 121,698-13, Part A, Records of the Department of Indian Affairs (RG 10), Library and Archives Canada.

53 Canada, *Sessional Papers (No. 18) 1891*, 250–7.

54 Canada, *Sessional Papers (No. 14) 1896*, xxx. See also Samek, *Blackfoot Confederacy*, chap. 4.

55 David J. Hall, "Clifford Sifton and Canadian Indian Administration 1896–1905," in *As Long as the Sun Shines and Water Flows: A Reader in Canadian Native Studies*, ed. Ian A.L. Getty and Antoine S. Lussier (Vancouver: Nakoda Insitute and UBC Press, 1983), 132–6. See also Boswell, "'Civilizing' the Indian," 350–6.

56 The prairie surrenders have been documented in useful detail in a study for the Indian Claims Commission (ICC). Peggy Martin-McGuire, *First Nation Land Surrenders on the Prairies, 1896–1911* (Ottawa: ICC, 1998). Concerning the Kahkhewistahaw case, see Indian Claims Commission, "Kahkewistahaw First Nation 1907 Reserve Land Surrender Inquiry," *Proceedings* 8 (1998): 3–99.

57 Kakhewistahaw, quoted in S. Raby, "Indian Land Surrenders in Southern Saskatchewan," *Canadian Geographer* 17, no. 1 (1973): 46.

58 Jean Usher, *William Duncan of Metlakatla: A Victorian Missionary in British Columbia* (Ottawa: National Museum of Man, 1974), 125–6, 132–3; Julien Paquin, S.J., "Modern Jesuit Indian Missions in Ontario" (unpublished manuscript, Regis College Archives, Toronto), 248.

59 Chief David Mackay, quoted in Thomas Berger, *Fragile Freedoms: Human Rights and Dissent in Canada*, rev. ed. (Toronto: Clarke, Irwin, 1982), 230.

60 Samek, *Blackfoot Confederacy*, chap. 5.

61 "President of Board of Trade, Sarnia, to Duncan C. Scott, 16 Sept. 1918," vol. 1931, file 3368–3, Records of the Department of Indian Affairs (RG 10), Library and Archives Canada; "D.C. Scott to Chief Elijah Maness and Councillors, 29 Oct. 1918 and 2 Jan. 1919," ibid.; "Council of Chippewas of Sarnia to Inspector C.C. Parker, 19 Dec. 1918," ibid.; "C.C. Parker to D.C. Scott, 28 Feb. 1919," ibid.

62 Bruce Dawson, "'Better than a few squirrels': The Greater Production Campaign on the First Nations Reserves of the Canadian Prairies" (master's thesis, University of Saskatchewan, 2001).

63 Leslie and Maguire, eds., *The Historical Development of the Indian Act*, 97, 108–9; Titley, *Narrow Vision*, 40-3.

64 Raby, "Indian Land Surrenders," 39.

65 Ibid., 41–3; Hall, "Clifford Sifton," 134–5; Martin-McGuire, *First Nation Land Surrenders on the Prairies*, chap. 3.

66 Gerald Friesen, *The Canadian Prairies: A History* (Toronto: University of Toronto Press, 1984), 159.

67 Quoted in "Mission de Qu'Appelle," *La Bannière de Marie Immaculée*, 1895, 71. ("I never agreed to sell our lands to the whites.")

68 Commissioner of North West Mounted Police, 1898, quoted in *Treaty Number Eight* (Ottawa: Indian Affairs, 1900), 5; Arthur J. Ray, Jim Miller, and Frank Tough, *"Bounty and Benevolence": A History of Saskatchewan Treaties* (Montreal: McGill-Queen's University Press, 2000), 156–9.

69 René Fumoleau, *As Long as This Land Shall Last: A History of Treaty 8 and Treaty 11, 1870–1939* (Toronto: McClelland and Stewart, 1975), 19, on which this account of Treaty 11, unless otherwise noted, is based.

70 For Treaty 8 and Treaty 11 the best source is still Fumoleau, *As Long as This Land Shall Last*. Treaty 8 is also well covered in Ray, Miller, and Tough, *Bounty and Benevolence*, chap. 10; and Treaty 11 in Kerry Abel, *Drum Songs: Glimpses of Dene History* (Montreal: McGill-Queen's University Press, 1993), chap. 8. Treaty 9 is now best examined in John S. Long, *Treaty No. 9: Making the Agreement to Share the Land in Far Northern Ontario in 1905* (Montreal: McGill-Queen's University Press, 2010). And Treaty 10 is thoroughly examined in Anthony Gulig, "In Whose Interest? Government-Indian Relations in Northern Saskatchewan and Wisconsin, 1900–1940" (PhD diss., University of Saskatchewan, 1997).

71 For the four northern numbered treaties, see J.R. Miller, *Compact, Contract, Covenant: Aboriginal Treaty-Making in Canada* (Toronto: University of Toronto Press, 2009), chap. 7.

72 The essential terms of Treaty 8 are in Ray, Miller, and Tough, *Bounty and Benevolence*, tables A11 and A12, 244–8.

73 Richard Daniel, "The Spirit and Terms of Treaty Eight," in *The Spirit of the Alberta Indian Treaties*, 2nd ed., ed. Richard Price (Edmonton: Pica Pica Press, 1987), 79–82.

74 Quoted in Fumoleau, *As Long*, 356, 257.

75 Miller, *Canada and the Aboriginal Peoples*, 18–19. For the background to this complex issue, see Paul Tennant, *Aboriginal Peoples and Politics: The Indian Land Question in British Columbia, 1848–1989* (Vancouver: UBC Press, 1990), chaps 5–8.

76 Noel Dyck, *What Is the "Indian problem"?: Tutelage and Resistance in Canadian Indian Administration* (St. John's: Institute of Social and Economic Research, Memorial University, 1991), 95.

77 Quoted in Miller, *Compact, Contract, Covenant*, 223.

78 A.G. Harper, "Canada's Indian Administration: Basic Concepts and Objectives," *America Indigena* 5, no. 2 (1945): 127.

12. Residents and Transients in the North

1 Ken S. Coates, *Best Left as Indians: Native-White Relations in the Yukon Territory, 1840–1973* (Montreal: McGill-Queen's University Press, 1991), xxii.

2 Robert McGhee, "Thule Prehistory of Canada," in *Handbook of North American Indians*, vol. 5, *Arctic*, ed. David Damas (Washington: Smithsonian Institution, 1984), 376.

3 Statistics Canada, "Aboriginal Peoples in Canada: First Nations People, Métis and Inuit," accessed 14 December 2016, http://www12.statcan.gc.ca/nhs-enm/2011/as-sa/99-011-x/99-011-x2011001-eng.cfm.

4 Olive P. Dickason, *Canada's First Nations: A History of Founding Peoples from Earliest Times* (Toronto: McClelland and Stewart, 1992), 12, 24.

5 Samuel Hearne, *A Journey from Prince of Wales's Fort in Hudson's [sic] Bay to the Northern Ocean 1769, 1770, 1771, 1772* (1795), ed. Richard Glover (Toronto: Macmillan, 1958), 99–103. For another bloody example of Inuit-First Nation hostility, see Daniel Francis and Toby Morantz, *Partners in Furs: A History of the Fur Trade in Eastern James Bay 1600–1870* (Montreal: McGill-Queen's University Press, 1985), 75–7.

6 Hearne, *Journey from Prince of Wales's Fort*, 5.

7 Heinrich Klutschak, *Overland to Starvation Cove: With the Inuit in Search of Franklin 1878–1880* (1881), ed. and trans. William Barr (Toronto: University of Toronto Press, 1987), 12, 19, 29, 34, 45, 198, 197.

8 Edgar Vernon Christian, *Death in the Barren Ground*, ed. George Whalley (1937; repr., Ottawa: Oberon Press, 1980).

9 Dorothy Harley Eber, *When the Whalers Were Up North: Inuit Memories from the Eastern Arctic* (Montreal: McGill-Queen's University Press, 1989), xiii.

10 Parks Canada, "The Franklin Expedition," accessed 15 December 2016, https://www.pc.gc.ca/en/culture/franklin.

11 Mark G. Stevenson, *Inuit, Whalers, and Cultural Persistence: Structure in Cumberland Sound and Central Inuit Social Organization* (Toronto: Oxford University Press, 1997), 74.

12 George Comer's account was published as *An Arctic Whaling Diary: The Journal of Captain George Comer in Hudson Bay 1903–1905*, ed. William Gillies Ross (Toronto: University of Toronto Press, 1984).

13 Ibid., 51, 53, 71, 82, 110–12, 183.

14 Eber, *When the Whalers Were Up North*, 8–9.

15 Ross, *An Arctic Whaling Diary*, 53, 73.

16 Eber, *When the Whalers Were Up North*, xvii.

17 David Damas, "The Arctic from Norse Contact to Modern Times," in *The Cambridge History of the Native Peoples of the Americas*, vol. 1, *North America, Part 2*, ed. Bruce G. Trigger and Wilcomb E. Washburn (Cambridge: Cambridge University Press, 1996), 363.

18 Keith J. Crowe, *A History of the Original Peoples of Northern Canada* (Montreal: Arctic Institute of North America, 1974), 108.

19 Ibid., 105.

20 Julie Cruikshank, "Oral Traditions and Written Accounts: An Incident from the Klondike Gold Rush," *Culture* 9, no. 2 (1989): 25–31.

21 Arthur J. Ray, Jim Miller, and Frank Tough, *Bounty and Benevolence: A History of Saskatchewan Treaties* (Montreal: McGill-Queen's University Press, 2000), 156–9. Although Treaty 8 deals mainly with northeastern BC and northern Alberta, it was included in this study because the northwestern corner of Saskatchewan was also embraced by Treaty 8.

22 These other incidents are covered well by Coates, *Best Left as Indians*, chap. 3; and "On the Outside in Their Homeland: Native People and the Evolution of the Yukon Economy," *Northern Review*, no. 1 (Summer 1988): 73–89; and by Kerry Abel, *Drum Songs: Glimpses of Dene History* (Montreal: McGill-Queen's University Press, 1993), chap. 9.

23 René Fumoleau, *As Long as This Land Shall Last: A History of Treaty 8 and Treaty 11, 1870–1939* (Toronto: McClelland and Stewart, 1975), 337–8.

24 Coates, *Best Left as Indians*, 24–5.

25 Arthur J. Ray, "Periodic Shortages, Native Welfare and the Hudson's Bay Company 1670–1930," in *The Subarctic Fur Trade: Native Social and Economic Adaptations*, ed. Shepard Krech III (Vancouver: UBC Press, 1984), 1–20.

26 Hudson's Bay Company Archives, B455/a/3, 22 December 1922, quoted in Stevenson, *Inuit, Whalers, and Cultural Persistence*, 93. See also Damas, "The Arctic from Norse Contact," 367.

27 "Particulars Regarding Copper Indians," July 1908, box 14, file 7, Indian Matters 1908, 1909, Anglican Diocese of Yukon Records, Archives of Yukon.

28 Damas, "The Arctic from Norse Contact," 353–4. In the late twentieth century, Labrador settlers would rediscover their Aboriginality. See Evelyn Plaice, *The Native Game: Settler Perceptions of Indian/Settler Relations in Central Labrador* (St. John's: Institute for Social and Economic Research, Memorial University of Newfoundland, 1990).

29 J.R. Miller, "Denominational Rivalry in Residential Schooling," *Western Oblate Studies* 2 (1991): 145–8; *Shingwauk's Vision: A History of Native Residential Schools* (Toronto: University of Toronto Press, 1996), 349–50, 370, 394–5.

30 "Hayter Reed to Bishop Bompas," 19 March 1897, box 14, file 6, Indian Matters 1890s, 153,377, Anglican Diocese of Yukon Records, Archives of Yukon; A.E. O'Meara, "Notes of Interview [with F. Pedley and F. Oliver]," 26 February 1909, file 8, Indian Matters 1909, Anglican Diocese of Yukon Records, Archives of Yukon.

31 *Coppermine*, directed by Ray Harper (1992, National Film Board).

32 The phrase was noted by Henry Toke Munn, *Prairie Trail and Arctic By-Ways* (London: Hurst and Blackett, 1932), 247.

33 Crowe, *Original Peoples*, 140.

34 For an American whaling captain who resented intensely the Canadians' insistence on applying Canadian regulations and law to him and his ship, see Ross, *An Arctic Whaling Diary*, 146–7.

35 Minister of Justice Sir Lomer Gouin, quoted in R. Quinn Duffy, *The Road to Nunavut: The Progress of the Eastern Arctic Inuit since the Second World War* (Montreal: McGill-Queen's University Press, 1988), 4.
36 Duffy, *Road to Nunavut*, 4–5.
37 Charles Stewart, 10 June 1925, quoted ibid., 7.
38 Richard J. Diubaldo, "The Absurd Little Mouse: When Eskimos Became Indians," *Journal of Canadian Studies* 16, no. 2 (1981): 34–40.
39 Duffy, *Road to Nunavut*, 15–16.
40 P. Whitney Lackenbauer, *The Canadian Rangers: A Living History* (Vancouver: UBC Press, 2013), especially Introduction. The quotation appears on 2.
41 Duffy, *Road to Nunavut*, 16–17.
42 Ibid., 142.
43 Ibid., 145–6.
44 There is now a substantial, and sometimes controversial, body of literature on the topic. See Frank Tester and Peter Kulchyski, *Tammarniit (Mistakes): Inuit Relocation in the Eastern Arctic, 1939–63* (Vancouver: UBC Press, 1994); Royal Commission on Aboriginal Peoples, *The High Arctic Relocation: Summary of Supporting Information*, 2 vols. (Ottawa: RCAP, 1994); Gerard I. Kenney, *Arctic Smoke and Mirrors* (Prescott, ON: Voyageur Publishing, 1994); Alan R. Marcus, *Relocating Eden: The Image and Politics of Inuit Exile in the Canadian Arctic* (Hanover, NH: University of New England Press, 1995).
45 Truth and Reconciliation Commission of Canada, *Final Report*, vol. 2, *The Inuit and Northern Experience* (Montreal: McGill-Queen's University Press, 2015), 4.
46 See Robertson's foreword to Kenney, *Arctic Smoke and Mirrors*.
47 If the author may indulge in another personal recollection, a 1950s television commercial for Gillette razor blades had a non-Native northerner singing, "My trading post is so far north / TV ain't reached here yet. / But Eskimos and sourdoughs / Use blue blades by Gillette" between rounds of the Friday night boxing matches.
48 Tom Lehrer, "We Will All Go Together When We Go," 1959, *An Evening Wasted with Tom Lehrer*, Reprise Records, 1966.
49 Anthony Apakark Thrasher, in collaboration with Gerard Deagle and Alan Mettrick, *Thrasher ... Skid Row Eskimo* (Toronto: Griffin House, 1976), 154, 155.
50 Minnie Aodla, *Life among the Qallunaat* (Edmonton: Hurtig, 1978).
51 Quoted in Tester and Kulchyski, *Tammarniit*, 357–8.

13. The Beginnings of Political Organization

1 A.B. Baird, quoted in John Webster Grant, *Moon of Wintertime: Missionaries and the Indians of Canada in Encounter since 1534* (Toronto: University of Toronto Press, 1984), 191; S.H. Blake to F. Oliver, 29 December 1908, Special Indian Committee [Series 2–14], box 18, (copy), Papers of the Missionary Society of the Church in Canada [GS 75–103], General Synod Archives.
2 J.J. McKenna, quoted in David J. Hall, "Clifford Sifton and Canadian Indian Administration 1896–1905," in *As Long as the Sun Shines and Water Flows: A Reader in Canadian Native Studies*, ed. Ian A.L. Getty and Antoine S. Lussier (Vancouver: Nakoda Institute and UBC Press, 1983), 137; F. Pedley to Rev. L.N. Tucker, 21 March 1908, Special Indian Committee [Series 2–14], box 18, Papers of the Missionary Society of the Church in Canada [GS 75–103], General Synod Archives.
    From its inception in 1896, the Laurier government was doubtful about the value of residential schooling. See David J. Hall, *From Treaties to Reserves: The Federal Government and Native*

Peoples in Territorial Alberta, 1870–1905 (Montreal: McGill-Queen's University Press, 2015), 217, 233.

3 A.Y. Blair to S.H. Blake, 27 March 1908, Special Indian Committee [Series 2–14], box 19, Papers of the Missionary Society of the Church in Canada [GS 75–103], General Synod Archives.

4 George Jasper Wherrett, *The Miracle of the Empty Beds: A History of Tuberculosis in Canada* (Toronto: University of Toronto Press, 1977), 103–5; Maureen Lux, *Medicine That Walks: Disease, Medicine, and Canadian Plains Native People, 1880–1940* (Toronto: University of Toronto Press, 2001), 42–51.

5 J.R. Miller, *Shingwauk's Vision: A History of Native Residential Schools* (Toronto: University of Toronto Press, 1996), 130–4; Truth and Reconciliation Commission of Canada, *Final Report*, vol. 1, *The History, Part 1: Origins to 1939* (Montreal: McGill-Queen's University Press, 2015), chap. 16.

6 Duncan Campbell Scott, "Indian Affairs, 1867–1912," in *Canada and Its Provinces*, vol. 7, ed. Adam Shortt and Arthur G. Doughty (Toronto: Glasgow, Brook, 1914), 16.

7 *Annual Report of the Department of Indian Affairs for the Year Ended March 31, 1933* (Ottawa: King's Printer 1934), 54.

8 John F. Leslie, "Assimilation, Integration or Termination: The Development of Canadian Indian Policy, 1943–1963" (PhD diss., Carleton University, 1999), Table 1, Indian Population 1871–1963, 97.

9 "Memorandum re Deputation's Interview with the Honorable T.A. Crerar," Ottawa, 25 November 1941, E.E. Joblin Papers, box 1, file 1, United Church of Canada Archives.

10 This complex issue is best followed in Paul Tennant, *Aboriginal Peoples and Politics: The Indian Land Question in British Columbia, 1849–1989* (Vancouver: UBC Press, 1990).

11 Quoted in Wilson Duff, *The Indian History of British Columbia*, vol. 1, *The Impact of the White Man*, 2nd ed. (Victoria: Royal British Columbia Museum, 1969), 67. See also Hamar Foster, "We Are Not O'Meara's Children: Law, Lawyers, and the First Campaign for Aboriginal Title in British Columbia, 1908–28," in *Let Right Be Done: Aboriginal Title, the Calder Case, and the Future of Indigenous Rights*, ed. Hamar Foster, Heather Raven, and Jeremy Webber (Vancouver: UBC Press, 2007), 64–70.

12 Quoted in E. Palmer Patterson, "A Decade of Change: Origins of the Nishga and Tsimshian Land Protests in the 1880s," *Journal of Canadian Studies* 18, no. 3 (1983): 45.

13 "Port Simpson Tsimshian to Dear Sir," 30 January 1909, box 5, file 87, A. Sutherland Papers, United Church of Canada Archives.

14 Memorial of Shuswap, Okanagan, and Couteau Nations, quoted in Frank Cassidy, "Aboriginal Land Claims in British Columbia," in *Aboriginal Land Claims in Canada: A Regional Perspective*, ed. Ken Coates (Toronto: Copp Clark Pitman, 1992), 14.

15 Duff, *Indian History*, 69; E. Palmer Patterson, "Andrew Paull and the Early History of British Columbia Indian Organizations," in *One Century Later: Western Canadian Reserve Indians Since Treaty 7*, ed. Ian A.L. Getty and Donald B. Smith (Vancouver: UBC Press, 1978), 48–9; Keith Thor Carlson, *The Power of Place, the Problem of Time: Aboriginal Identity and Historical Consciousness in the Cauldron of Colonialism* (Toronto: University of Toronto Press, 2010), 265–9.

16 Duff, *Indian History*, 69 and note; Foster, "We Are Not," 80–2.

17 Chief William to *Victoria Colonist*, 7 November 1879, quoted in Elizabeth Furniss, *Victims of Benevolence: Discipline and Death at the Williams Lake Indian Residential School 1891–1920* (Williams Lake, BC: Cariboo Tribal Council, 1992), 9.

18　Duane Thomson, "The Response of Okanagan Indians to European Settlement," *BC Studies* 101 (Spring 1994): 113–15.

19　Sidney L. Harring, "The Liberal Treatment of Indians: Native People in Nineteenth Century Ontario Law," *Saskatchewan Law Review* 56, no. 2 (1992): 297–371. For Mi'kmaw resistance and political organization, see Martha Elizabeth Walls, *No Need of a Chief for This Band: The Maritime Mi'kmaq and Federal Electoral Legislation, 1899–1951* (Vancouver: UBC Press, 2010), 105–8.

20　Thomas Stone, "Legal Mobilization and Legal Penetration: The Department of Indian Affairs and the Canadian Party at St. Regis, 1876–1918," *Ethnohistory* 22, no. 4 (1975): 375–407. For resistance over governance issues on three Mohawk reserves, see Gerald F. Reid, "'To Renew Our Fire': Political Activism, Nationalism, and Identity in Three Rotinonhsionni Communities," in *Tribal Worlds: Critical Studies in American Indian Nation Building*, ed. Brian Hosmer and Larry Nesper (Albany: State University of New York Press, 2013), 37–64. I am grateful to Don Smith, who generously provided me with a copy of the Reid essay.

21　Peter Kulchyski, "'A considerable unrest': F.O. Loft and the League of Indians," *Native Studies Review* 4, nos. 1 & 2 (1988): 95–117.

22　Canada, *Sessional Papers (No. 27) 1920*, 13. It is highly probable that the official numbers underestimated even status Indians' contribution, and they did not capture the record of service by non-status Indians and Métis.

23　Quoted in Stan Cuthand, "The Native Peoples of the Prairie Provinces in the 1920s and 1930s," in *Sweet Promises: A Reader on Indian-White Relations in Canada*, ed. J.R. Miller (Toronto: University of Toronto Press, 1991), 381–2.

24　There is a good account of these developments in Jean Goodwill and Norma Sluman, *John Tootoosis*, 2nd ed. (Winnipeg: Pemmican Publications, 1984), chaps. 9 and 12.

25　Quoted Cuthand, "Native Peoples," 384. See also Goodwill and Sluman, *John Tootoosis*, 156.

26　Quoted in Hana Samek, *The Blackfoot Confederacy, 1880–1920: A Comparative Study of Canadian and U.S. Indian Policy* (Albuquerque: University of New Mexico Press, 1987), 132.

27　Cuthand, "Native Peoples," 390.

28　Anthropological Picture Collections Section, Royal British Columbia Museum, #250, 834, 2777 (examples only); Douglas Cole and Ira Chaikin, *An Iron Hand upon the People: The Law against the Potlatch on the Northwest Coast* (Vancouver: Douglas and McIntyre, 1990), 138–43; Mrs. Edward Joyce interview, tape 965–1, Sound and Moving Images Division, Provincial Archives of British Columbia.

29　Quoted in Julien Paquin, S.J., "Modern Jesuit Indian Missions in Ontario" (unpublished manuscript, Regis College Archives, Toronto), 58–9.

30　Laurie Meijer Drees, *The Indian Association of Alberta: A History of Political Action* (Vancouver: UBC Press, 2002), chap. 2. For the formation of the Union of Saskatchewan Indians, James M. Pitsula, "The CCF Government and the Formation of the Union of Saskatchewan Indians," *Prairie Forum* 19, no. 2 (1994): 131–51; and F. Laurie Barron, *Walking in Indian Moccasins: The Native Policies of Tommy Douglas and the CCF* (Vancouver: UBC Press, 1997), 64–81.

31　George Manuel and Michael Posluns, *The Fourth World: An Indian Reality* (Don Mills, ON: Collier-Macmillan, 1974), 97.

32　Quoted in Donald Purich, *Our Land: Native Rights in Canada* (Toronto: Lorimer, 1986), 83–4.

33　See Bradford W. Morse, ed., *Aboriginal Peoples and the Law: Indian, Metis and Inuit Rights in Canada* (Ottawa: Carleton University Press, 1985), 356–97.

34　Donald Purich, *The Metis* (Toronto: Lorimer, 1988), chap. 6.

35 Report of agent C.P. Schmidt, 12 July 1933, box 1, Duck Lake Agency Papers, Saskatchewan Archives Board.

36 Alfred L. Kroeber, *The Nature of Culture* (Chicago: University of Chicago Press, 1952), 139. The chapter in which this quotation appears, "A Half-Century of Anthropology," originally appeared as an article in *Scientific American*, September 1950.

37 Ronald Graham Haycock, *The Image of the Indian* (Waterloo: Waterloo Lutheran University, 1971), 91–2.

38 R. Scott Sheffield, *The Red Man's on the Warpath: The Image of the "Indian" and the Second World War* (Vancouver: UBC Press, 2004), espec. chaps. 1, 3, and 4.

39 Katherine Pettipas, *Severing the Ties that Bind: Government Repression of Indigenous Religious Ceremonies on the Prairies* (Winnipeg: University of Manitoba Press, 1994), 195–6.

40 Leslie, "Assimilation," 88–94.

41 Canada, Special Joint Committee of the Senate and the House of Commons [on] the Indian Act, *Minutes of Proceedings and Evidence*, vol. 2 (1947), 1673, J.H. Blackmore, 10 June 1947.

42 Jayme K. Benson, "Different Visions: The Government Response to Native and Non-Native Submissions on Education Presented to the 1946-48 Special Joint Committee of the Senate and the House of Commons" (M.A. memoire, University of Ottawa, 1991). I am most grateful to Mr. Benson, who provided a copy of his analysis. See also Ian V.B. Johnson, *Helping Indians to Help Themselves – A Committee to Investigate Itself: The 1951 Indian Act Consultation Process* (Ottawa: Indian and Northern Affairs, Treaties and Historical Research Centre 1984); and Leslie, "Assimilation," chap. 3.

43 The developments from the joint committee's report in 1948 to the passage of the revision are well covered in Leslie, "Assimilation," chap. 4.

44 John L. Tobias, "Protection, Civilization, Assimilation: An Outline History of the Indian Act," in *Sweet Promises*, ed. Miller, 140.

45 Manuel and Posluns, *The Fourth World*, 115.

46 Sheffield, *The Red Man*, chaps. 6 and 7; Leslie, "Assimilation," 203.

47 Ian Mosby, "Administering Colonial Science: Nutrition Research and Human Biomedical Experimentation in Aboriginal Communities and Residential Schools, 1942–1952," *Histoire sociale/Social History* 46, no. 91 (2013): 145–72; Hugh Shewell, *"Enough to Keep Them Alive": Indian Welfare in Canada, 1873–1965* (Toronto: University of Toronto Press, 2004), 208–15, 227, and 332; and Leslie, "Assimilation," 265–74.

48 Miller, *Shingwauk's Vision*, chap. 13.

49 Manuel and Posluns, *The Fourth World*, 156.

50 Harry B. Hawthorn, ed., *A Survey of the Contemporary Indians of Canada: Economic, Political, Educational Needs and Policies*, 2 vols. (Ottawa: Indian Affairs, 1966–7).

51 Ibid., 13 and 6.

52 Unless otherwise noted, this account is based on the excellent analysis in Sally M. Weaver, *Making Canadian Indian Policy: The Hidden Agenda 1968–1970* (Toronto: University of Toronto Press, 1981).

53 Quoted in J. Rick Ponting and Roger Gibbins, *Out of Irrelevance: A Socio-Political Introduction to Indian Affairs in Canada* (Toronto: Butterworths, 1980), 28.

54 Quoted in Purich, *Our Land*, 52.

55 Quoted in Weaver, *Making Canadian Indian Policy*, 148.

56 Canada, Department of Indian Affairs and Northern Development, *Statement of the Government of Canada on Indian Policy 1969* (Ottawa: Indian Affairs, 1969), 5–8.

57 Ibid., 11.
58 Weaver, *Making Canadian Indian Policy*, 197.

14. Land Claims and Self-Government from the White Paper to *Guerin*

1 Indian Association of Alberta, *Citizens Plus: A Presentation of the Indian Chiefs of Alberta to Right Honourable P.E. Trudeau* (Edmonton: Indian Association of Alberta, 1970), 4, 7, 9, 12, 19, 16.

2 Harold Cardinal, *The Unjust Society: The Tragedy of Canada's Indians* (Edmonton: Hurtig, 1969), 1, 11, 17.

3 Quoted in Sally M. Weaver, *Making Canadian Indian Policy: The Hidden Agenda 1968–1970* (Toronto: University of Toronto Press, 1981), 171. For the reaction in general, see chap. 7.

4 J. Rick Ponting and Roger Gibbins, *Out of Irrelevance: A Socio-Political Introduction to Indian Affairs in Canada* (Toronto: Butterworths, 1980), 203. See George Manuel and Michael Posluns, *The Fourth World: An Indian Reality* (Toronto: Collier Macmillan, 1974), espec. chap. 4.

5 This is what happened to the Calgary Urban Treaty Indian Alliance's programs in the early 1970s. See Joan Ryan, *Wall of Words: The Betrayal of the Urban Indian* (Toronto: Peter Martin Associates, 1978).

6 See Donald Purich, *Our Land: Native Rights in Canada* (Toronto: Lorimer, 1986), 218–19. See also Manitoba Métis Federation, "Position Paper on Child Care and Family Services (May 15, 1982)," *Native Studies Review* 2, no. 1 (1986): 125–39.

7 J.R. Miller, *Shingwauk's Vision: A History of Native Residential Schools* (Toronto: University of Toronto Press, 1996); chap. 13 deals with the winding down of the system.

8 J.R. Miller, *Compact, Contract, Covenant: Aboriginal Treaty-Making in Canada* (Toronto: University of Toronto Press, 2009), 257–63.

9 Christina Godlewska and Jeremy Webber, "The *Calder* Decision, Aboriginal Title, Treaties, and the Nisga'a," in *Let Right Be Done: Aboriginal Title, the Calder Case, and the Future of Indigenous Rights*, ed. Hamar Foster, Heather Raven, and Jeremy Webber (Vancouver: UBC Press, 2007), 3–7.

10 Quoted in Bradford W. Morse, ed., *Aboriginal Peoples and the Law: Indian, Metis and Inuit Rights in Canada* (Ottawa: Carleton University Press, 1985), 97.

11 Purich, *Our Land*, 57–8.

12 Quoted in Manuel and Posluns, *The Fourth World*, 225.

13 Boyce Richardson, *Strangers Devour the Land: A Chronicle of the Assault upon the Last Coherent Hunting Culture in North America, the Cree Indians of Quebec, and their Vast Primeval Homelands* (New York: Knopf, 1975).

14 Richard F. Salisbury, *A Homeland for the Cree: Regional Development in James Bay, 1971–1981* (Montreal: McGill-Queen's University Press, 1986), 8, 147–50.

15 E. Palmer Patterson, "A Decade of Change: Nishga and Tsimshian Land Protests in the 1880s," *Journal of Canadian Studies* 18, no. 3 (1983): 51.

16 Sol Sanderson, "Foreword," *The First Nations: Indian Government and the Canadian Constitution*, ed. Delia Opekokew (Saskatoon: Federation of Saskatchewan Indians, 1980), v.

17 Glenn Sigurdson, *Vikings on a Prairie Ocean: The Saga of a Lake, a People, a Family, and a Man* (Winnipeg: Great Plains Publications, 2014), 292.

18 *Globe and Mail*, 22 November 1984 and 29 March 1985; Saskatoon *Star-Phoenix*, 2 February and 4 December 1985.

19 The Métis and non-status Indian national organization had to initiate legal action before Ottawa would agree to its presence at the 1983 conference. See Purich, *Our Land*, 181.

20 House of Commons, Special Committee on Indian Self-Government, *Report* (Ottawa: Queen's Printer 1983). There is a useful series of analyses of this report by political scientist Paul Tennant, anthropologist Sally M. Weaver, and the team of political scientist Roger Gibbins and sociologist J. Rick Ponting in *Canadian Public Policy* 10, no. 2 (1984), 211–24, under the title "The Report of the House of Commons Special Committee on Indian Self- Government: Three Comments."

21 Murray Coolican, *Living Treaties: Lasting Agreements: Report of the Task Force to Review Comprehensive Claims Policy* (*Coolican Report*) (Ottawa: Department of Indian Affairs and Northern Development, 1985), 13.

22 Ibid., 78.

23 J.R. Miller, "Great White Father Knows Best: Oka and the Land Clams Process," *Native Studies Review* 7, no. 1 (1991): 39–40.

24 Ibid., 30–2.

25 Quoted ibid., 34.

26 Quoted ibid., 37.

27 Quoted ibid., 42.

28 Quoted ibid., 43. This apparently meant that the federal government was willing to attempt to reassemble the lands into a compact territory, perhaps to make it, finally, into a reserve.

29 Purich, *Our Land*, 19.

30 Quoted in Maureen Davies, "Aboriginal Rights in International Law: Human Rights," in *Aboriginal Peoples and the Law*, ed. Morse, 770–3, espec. 772; Purich, *Our Land*, 137.

31 A useful summary of Indian organizations' views is found in Joyce Green, "Sexual Equality and Indian Government: An Analysis of Bill C-31 Amendments to the *Indian Act*," *Native Studies Review* 1, no. 2 (1985): 85–93.

32 This account is based on the excellent survey by Sally M. Weaver, "Indian Policy in the New Conservative Government, Part I: The Nielsen Task Force of 1985," *Native Studies Review* 2, no. 1 (1986): 1–43.

33 Ibid., 20–1.

34 Quoted ibid., 29.

35 Purich, *Our Land*, 226.

36 Quoted in Peter Jull, "Aboriginal Peoples and Political Change in the North Atlantic Area," *Journal of Canadian Studies* 16, no. 2 (1981): 47.

15. Meech, Oka, Charlottetown, Nass, and Ottawa

1 *Globe and Mail*, 12 October 1998.

2 Of course, Indians, Inuit, and Métis were never "irrelevant" economically; they simply were relegated to the most marginal places in the economy, to roles where there was little they could do to affect policy. There is a growing body of revisionist literature on the role of Native peoples in the economy. See Carl Beal, "Money, Markets and Economic Development in Saskatchewan Indian Reserve Communities, 1870–1930s" (PhD diss., University of Manitoba, 1994); Steven High, "Native Wage Labour and Independent Production During the 'Era of Irrelevance,'" *Labour/Le Travail* 37 (Spring 1996): 243–64; Rolf Knight, *Indians at Work: An Informal History of Native Labour in British Columbia 1848–1930* (Vancouver: New Star, 1996); John Lutz, "After the Fur Trade: The Aboriginal Labouring Class of British Columbia, 1849–1890," *Journal of the*

Canadian Historical Association 3, no. 1 (1992): 69–93; Arthur J. Ray, *I Have Lived Here Since the World Began: An Illustrated History of Canada's Native Peoples* (Toronto: Key Porter, 1996); W. Keith Regular, *Neighbours and Networks: The Blood Tribe in the Southern Alberta Economy, 1884–1939* (Calgary: University of Calgary Press, 2009); and Frank Tough, *"As Their Natural Resources Fail": Native Peoples and the Economic History of Northern Manitoba, 1870–1930* (Vancouver: UBC Press, 1996).

3 Thomas R. Berger, *Northern Frontier/Northern Homeland: The Report of the Mackenzie Valley Pipeline Inquiry*, 2 vols. (Ottawa: Minister of Supply and Services, 1977), 1: xxxiv–xxv.

4 *Globe and Mail*, 22 October 1990. The newspaper obtained the report under the Freedom of Information Act.

5 A useful survey of comprehensive claims to about 2014 is Terry Fenge, "Negotiation and Implementation of Modern Treaties between Aboriginal Peoples and the Crown in Right of Canada," in *Keeping Promises: The Royal Proclamation of 1763, Aboriginal Rights, and Treaties in Canada*, ed. Terry Fenge and Jim Aldridge (Montreal: McGill-Queen's University Press, 2015).

6 Indian and Northern Affairs Canada, *Transition*, Special Edition, Feb. 1991 noted that nineteen comprehensive claims awaited settlement. During the winter of 1990–1 the federal government lifted the six-claim limit on the number of comprehensive claims it would negotiate at one time.

7 Indian Claims Commission, "Inquiry into the 1907 Reserve Land Surrender of the Kahkewistahaw First Nation" (Ottawa: Indian Claims Commission, 1997). For a study of surrenders that underlay some prairie specific claims, see Peggy Martin-McGuire, *First Nation Land Surrenders on the Prairies, 1896–1911* (Ottawa: Indian Claims Commission, 1998).

8 Government of Saskatchewan Release 92–561, "Treaty Land Entitlement Agreement Signed," 22 September 1992.

9 For background and events to about 1990, see John Goddard, *Last Stand of the Lubicon Cree* (Vancouver: Douglas and McIntyre, 1991). See also Christine Mary Smillie, "The People Left Out of Treaty 8" (master's thesis, University of Saskatchewan, 2005); "Saskatchewan Treaty Land Entitlement (TLE) Fact Sheet," Indigenous and Northern Affairs Canada, accessed 3 February 2017, https://www.aadnc-aandc.gc.ca/eng/1100100034825/1100100034826; and J.R. Miller, *Lethal Legacy: Current Native Controversies in Canada* (Toronto: McClelland and Stewart, 2004), 207–8. Events since 1990 are covered in newspaper, especially *Globe and Mail*, accounts.

10 Coverage of the Temagami dispute to the late 1980s can be found in Bruce Hodgins and Jamie Benidickson, *The Temagami Experience: Recreation, Resources, and Aboriginal Rights in the Northern Ontario Wilderness* (Toronto: University of Toronto Press, 1989). The Steele ruling is ibid., 268–9.

11 This account relies heavily on accounts, published and unpublished, by Peter Jull, who was intimately involved in many of the events, and to whom I am grateful for assistance and advice on this and many other topics. Among Jull's published analyses are "Building Nunavut: A Story of Inuit Self-Government," *The Northern Review* 1 (Summer 1988): 59–72; "Reflections on Regional Agreements: Yesterday, Today and Tomorrow," *Australian Indigenous Law Reporter* 2, no. 4 (1997): 476–93; and "'Them Eskimo Mob': International Implications of Nunavut, Revised 2nd edition," in *Seven Generations: An Information Legacy of the Royal Commission on Aboriginal Peoples*, CD-ROM (Ottawa: Public Works and Government Services, 1997). Also useful on the background is R. Quinn Duffy, *The Road to Nunavut: The Progress of the Eastern Arctic Inuit since the Second World War* (Montreal: McGill-Queen's University Press, 1988).

12 Mel Watkins, *Dene Nation: The Colony Within* (Toronto: University of Toronto Press, 1977). The Declaration is on 3–4.

13 Indian and Northern Affairs Canada release 1-9324, "Summary of Agreement."
14 Quoted in Evelyn J. Peters, "Protecting the Land under Modern Land Claims Agreements: The Effectiveness of the Environmental Regime Negotiated by the James Bay Cree and Northern Quebec Agreement," *Applied Geography* 12, no. 2 (1992): 142.
15 Supreme Court of Canada, *Delgamuukw v. British Columbia*, 11 December 1997.
16 *Globe and Mail*, 13 February 1996.
17 Thomas R. Berger, *Fragile Freedoms: Human Rights and Dissent in Canada*, rev. ed. (Toronto: Clarke, Irwin, 1982), 230.
18 Deborah Coyne, *Roll of the Dice: Working with Clyde Wells during the Meech Lake Negotiations* (Toronto: James Lorimer, 1992).
19 Coyne, *Roll of the Dice*, chap. 8, "The Seven-Day Dinner."
20 *Globe and Mail*, 20 June 1990.
21 Quoted in Jake MacDonald, "One Little Indian," *Globe and Mail West*, September 1990, 20.
22 Roy MacGregor, "The Feather, Elijah Harper and Meech Lake," *Windspeaker* 8, no. 8 (1990), accessed 27 January 2017, www.ammsa.com/node/17819. MacGregor's article originally appeared in *The Ottawa Citizen*. Coyne, *Roll of the Dice*, 139–40.
23 Clause 2(1)b of People and Communities section of the Charlottetown Accord.
24 Georges E. Sioui, *For an Amerindian Autohistory: An Essay on the Foundations of a Social Ethic* (Montreal: McGill-Queen's University Press, 1992), 110. See also Government of Quebec, *Rencontre*, Sept.–Oct. 1990, 3.
25 *Globe and Mail*, 1 June 1990.
26 Ibid., 23 September 1990.
27 J.R. Miller, "Great White Father Knows Best: Oka and the Land Claims Process," *Native Studies Review* 7, no. 1 (1991): 23–52. The best account of the 1990 crisis is Geoffrey York and Loreen Pindera, *People of the Pines: The Warriors and the Legacy of Oka* (Boston: Little, Brown, 1991).
28 In 1997 the courts rejected the argument based on the Jay Treaty, but upheld the right of trans-border passage as an Aboriginal right.
29 Alan C. Cairns, *Citizens Plus: Aboriginal Peoples and the Canadian State* (Vancouver: UBC Press, 2000), chap. 4. An overview and assessment is found in J.R. Miller, *Residential Schools and Reconciliation: Canada Confronts Its History* (Toronto: University of Toronto Press, 2017), chap. 2.
30 Royal Commission on Aboriginal Peoples, *Final Report*, vol. 1, *Looking Forward, Looking Back*, chap. 10, 333–409, espec. 382–6.
31 Harry Swain, *Oka: A Political Crisis and Its Legacy* (Vancouver: Douglas and McIntyre, 2010), 168–9.
32 The Royal Commission on Aboriginal Peoples *Final Report* (1996) and background reports are available on a CD-ROM, *For Seven Generations: The Report of the Royal Commission on Aboriginal Peoples*.
33 *Delgamuukw v. British Columbia*, reasons of Chief Justice Antonio Lamer, paragraph 186.
34 Canada, *Gathering Strength: Canada's Aboriginal Action Plan* (Ottawa: Public Works and Government Services, 1997). The government presentation opened with a "Statement of Reconciliation," which was followed by a "Statement of Renewal," and then "Canada's Aboriginal Action Plan."
35 Miller, *Residential Schools and Reconciliation*, chap. 4.
36 *Vancouver Sun*, 4 November 1998; Saskatoon *StarPhoenix*, 26 December 1998.
37 *Globe and Mail*, 22 December 1998; *National Post*, 22 December 1998.
38 Ken Coates, *The Marshall Decision and Native Rights* (Montreal: McGill- Queen's University Press, 2000); William C. Wicken, *Mi'kmaq Treaties on Trial: History, Land, and Donald Marshall Junior* (Toronto: University of Toronto Press, 2002).

16. Relations in the Twenty-First Century

1 Library of Parliament, "The Marshall Decision and the Atlantic Fishery," accessed 9 February 2017, https://lop.parl.ca/content/lop/ResearchPublications/tips/tip63-e.htm.

2 Ken Coates, *The Marshall Decision and Native Rights* (Montreal: McGill-Queen's University Press, 2000), xvii.

3 J.R. Miller, *Compact, Contract, Covenant: Aboriginal Treaty-Making in Canada* (Toronto: University of Toronto Press, 2009), 278–80; "Negotiations Update," accessed 14 February 2017, www.bctreaty.ca.

4 *Globe and Mail*, 28 November 2005.

5 P. Whitney Lackenbauer, *Battle Grounds: The Canadian Military and Aboriginal Lands* (Vancouver: UBC Press, 2007), 234–6. Terminology in this case can be confusing. The official name of the First Nation people involved was Kettle and Stony Point First Nation (KSPFN), but a group of them referred to themselves as Stoney Pointers. The elective leaders denied that the Stoney Pointers had a legitimate separate existence and showed little sympathy for them once they resorted to occupation.

6 Lackenbauer, *Battle Grounds*, 236–8.

7 Diana Mehta, "Federal Govt, Ontario First Nation Formally Sign Settlement over Camp Ipperwash," *Globe and Mail*, 15 April 2016. The federal government also paid compensation of $98 million.

8 J.R. Miller, *Residential Schools and Reconciliation: Canada Confronts Its History* (Toronto: University of Toronto Press, 2017), chap. 3; interview with Andy Scott, Fredericton, 1 November 2012.

9 "Powley Case," accessed 18 February 2017, http://indigenousfoundations.arts.ubc.ca/powley_case/. See also Arthur J. Ray, *Telling It to the Judge: Taking Native History to Court* (Montreal: McGill-Queen's University Press, 2011) chap. 5.

10 The case for "government lawlessness" in the administration of Métis lands was made by Douglas N. Sprague, *Canada and the Métis, 1869–1885* (Waterloo, ON: Wilfrid Laurier University Press, 1988). The counterargument is found in Tom Flanagan, *Métis Lands in Manitoba* (Calgary: University of Calgary Press, 1991). Sprague and Flanagan were expert witnesses for the Métis and the Crown, respectively.

11 Manitoba Métis Federation, "Land Claims," accessed 18 February 2017, http://www.mmf.mb.ca/land_claims_landing_page.php.

12 Supreme Court of Canada, *Daniels v. Canada*, 14 April 2016, accessed 18 February 2017, https://scc-csc.lexum.com/scc-csc/scc-csc/en/item/15858/index.do.

13 Supreme Court of Canada, *Behn v. Moulton Contracting Ltd.*, accessed 17 February 2017, https://scc-csc.lexum.com/scc-csc/scc-csc/en/item/13038/index.do.

14 Dwight G. Newman, *Revisiting the Duty to Consult Aboriginal Peoples*, rev. ed. (Saskatoon: Purich Publishing, 2014).

15 Supreme Court of Canada, *Tsilhquot'in Nation v. British Columbia*, accessed 20 February 2017, https://scc-csc.lexum.com/scc-csc/scc-csc/en/item/14246/index.do.

16 "Canadian Human Rights Tribunal Decision in First Nations Child and Family Caring Society of Canada application, 26 January 2016," file T1340/7008, accessed 21 February 2017, www.chrt-tcdp.gc.ca; "Information Sheet – By the Numbers, Canadian Human Rights Case on First Nations Child Welfare," accessed 21 February 2017, https://fncaringsociety.com/sites/default/files/By%20the%20Numbers%202017_0.pdf.

17 Ken Coates, *#Idlenomore and the Remaking of Canada* (Regina: University of Regina Press, 2015), xiii, xxi, and 216n57; John Ibbitson, *Stephen Harper* (Toronto: McClelland and Stewart,

2015), 352–3; Sylvia McAdam, "Armed with Nothing More than a Drum and a Song: Idle No More," in *The Winter We Danced: Voices from the Past, the Future, and the Idle No More Movement*, ed. The Kino-nda-mimi Collective (Winnipeg: ARP Books, 2014), 65–6. Ms. McAdam was one of the four founders of Idle No More.

18 According to Sylvia McAdam, the idea of a teach-in came from Sheelah McLean, a doctoral student in education at the University of Saskatchewan and the only non-Indigenous member of the quartet. The other founding members of the movement were Alex Wilson and Jessica Gordon. McAdam, "Armed," 66.

19 The principal events are covered in Coates, *#Idlenomore*, chaps. 1 to 4.

20 Coates, *#Idlenomore*, chap. 4. Coates accurately labels the chapter covering these events "The Ottawa Distraction and the Complicated Evolution of Idle No More."

21 I would to thank an anonymous reader for the University of Toronto Press who stressed the importance of redress as well as reconciliation during a pre-revision consultation.

22 The following account is based on Miller, *Residential Schools and Reconciliation*.

23 Ibid., chap. 1.

24 Ibid., chap. 2. The RCAP recommendations are found in *Report of the Royal Commission on Aboriginal Peoples* (Ottawa: RCAP, 1996), vol. 1, 385–6. Coverage of the AHF can be found in Miller, *Residential Schools and Reconciliation*, chap. 3.

25 Miller, *Residential Schools and Reconciliation*, chaps. 4 and 5.

26 Ibid., chap. 5.

27 Ibid., chap. 6.

28 Ibid., chap. 7.

29 Text of Prime Minister Harper's apology, 11 June 2008, http://www.aadnc-aandc.gc.ca/eng /1100100015644/1100100015649.

30 Government of Canada, Aboriginal Affairs and Northern Development Canada, "Canada's Statement of Support on the United Nations Declaration on the Rights of Indigenous Peoples," 12 November 2010, accessed 12 June 2015, http://www.aadnc-aandc.gc.ca/eng/1309374239861 /1309374546142.

31 Gloria Galloway, "Government Used Technicality to Disqualify 1,000 Residential-School Claims," *Globe and Mail*, 2 February 2016; Gloria Galloway, "Ottawa to Review Tactics Used to Reject Residential-School Claims," *Globe and Mail*, 3 February 2016; see also Akivah Starkman, *The Independent Assessment Process: Reflections* (np: Akivah Starkman, 2014), 37. Starkman served as an executive director of the office overseeing the Independent Assessment Process.

32 For the work and results of the second TRC, see Miller, *Residential Schools and Reconciliation*, chap. 8.

33 Truth and Reconciliation Commission of Canada, *They Came for the Children: Canada, Aboriginal Peoples, and Residential Schools* (Winnipeg: Truth and Reconciliation Commission, 2012); *Final Report of the Truth and Reconciliation Commission of Canada*, vol. 1, *Summary: Honouring the Truth, Reconciling for the Future* (Toronto: Lorimer, 2015); and *The Final Report of the Truth and Reconciliation Commission of Canada*, 6 vols. (Montreal: McGill-Queen's University Press, 2015).

34 See Miller, *Residential Schools and Reconciliation*, chap. 9.

35 *Final Report of the TRC*, vol. 5, *Legacy*, 8.

36 Ibid., vol. 6, *Reconciliation*, 34.

37 Ibid., vol. 6, *Reconciliation*, 4.

38 Ibid., vol. 1, *The History, Part 1*, 7; vol. 6, *Reconciliation*, 25–33. For Sinclair's earlier flirtation with the term "genocide," see Chinta Puxley, "Residential Schools 'An Act of Genocide,'" *Globe and Mail*, 18 February 2012, A11.

17. Do We Learn Anything from History?

1 *Oxford Dictionary of Quotations*, 3rd ed. (New York: Oxford University Press, 1979), 244, 216, 414.
2 Cornelius J. Jaenen, *Friend and Foe: Aspects of French-Amerindian Cultural Contact in the Sixteenth and Seventeenth Centuries* (New York: Columbia University Press, 1976), 192.
3 Alden T. Vaughan, "From White Man to Redskin: Changing Anglo-American Perceptions of the American Indian," *American Historical Review* 87, no. 4 (1982): 917–53.
4 A.G. Harper, "Canada's Indian Administration: Basic Concepts and Objectives," *America Indigena* 5, no. 2 (1945): 127.
5 Supreme Court of Canada, *Delgamuukw v. British Columbia*, reasons of Chief Justice Lamer, paragraph 186.
6 George Manuel, "Manifesto for Survival," *Macleans*, May 1973, 53. I should like to thank a student, Michelle Amy, who brought this item to my attention.
7 Paul Driben and Robert Sanderson Trudeau, *When Freedom Is Lost: The Dark Side of the Relationship between Government and the Fort Hope Band* (Toronto: University of Toronto Press, 1983), 10.
8 Larry Krotz, *Indian Country: Inside Another Canada* (Toronto: McClelland and Stewart 1992), 106.
9 Indian and Northern Affairs Communiqué 1–8831, "Policy for the Provision of Education Facilities and School Space Accommodation Standards: Backgrounder," 1.
10 In large part, the explanation of why the federal government did not proceed with RCAP recommendations is found in public opinion data, which in 1998 indicated that one-third (32 per cent) of respondents thought Aboriginal people were about as well off as other Canadians, about one-third (34 per cent) thought they were worse off, and one-quarter (26 per cent) thought they were better off. Eight per cent did not know. Support for more spending on Aboriginal people varied directly with the respondents' perception of how well off Aboriginal people were compared with Canadians in general. *Globe and Mail*, 23 February 1998.
11 Manuel, "Manifesto," 28.
12 Ramsay Cook, "Canadian Centennial Celebrations," *International Journal* 22, no. 4 (1967): 663.
13 Saskatoon, *StarPhoenix*, 28 April 1994. Consideration of the revised bill, with a former National Hockey League referee, Edmonton MP Bob Kilger, in the Speaker's chair, passed all stages in under two hours.
14 Ontario, "Statement of Political Relationship," 6 August 1991; Quebec Government Guidelines Concerning Aboriginal Affairs, *Rencontre*, March 1998, 12–13. I am grateful to Kerry Wilkins, Counsel to the Ontario Ministry of the Attorney General, who provided me with a copy of the Ontario pact.
15 *Globe and Mail*, 31 March 1993.
16 Ibid., 14 January 1998. Comparative (Aboriginal/non-Aboriginal) figures by age cohort were: ages 0 to 4, 12.4% / 6.7%; ages 5 to 9, 11.9% / 7%; ages 10 to 14, 10.7% / 7%; and ages 15 to 19, 9.4% / 6.9%.
17 Canada, *Gathering Strength: Canada's Aboriginal Action Plan* (Ottawa: Public Works and Government Services, 1997), 36.

Select Bibliography

Note on Primary Sources

It is impossible to list all the primary sources that are relevant to the study of the history of Native-newcomer relations in Canada. What follows is a comment on but a minute portion of the primary materials.

The most accessible primary sources for the New France period are travel accounts and reports of missionaries. Henry Percival Biggar, *The Voyages of Jacques Cartier* (Ottawa: King's Printer, 1924); Henry Percival Biggar, ed., *The Works of Samuel de Champlain*, 6 vols. (Toronto: Champlain Society, 1922–6); Gabriel Sagard, *The Long Journey to the Country of the Huron*, ed. George M. Wrong (Toronto: Champlain Society, 1939); and William Francis Ganong, ed., *Description and Natural History of the Coasts of North America (Acadia)* (Toronto: Champlain Society, 1908) are but three of the former genre. The records, charts, and pictorial renderings of Samuel de Champlain constitute another rich collection that is too voluminous to discuss here. The most renowned of religious records are the annual "public relations" exercises that the Society of Jesus produced to stimulate piety and generosity among their admirers. A particularly fine edition of these records for the seventeenth century is Reuben Gold Thwaites, ed., *The Jesuit Relations and Allied Documents*, 73 vols. (New York: Pageant Books, 1959). Other useful collections are cited in the bibliographical sections of standard works on New France.

Access to primary material for the period between the Royal Proclamation of 1763 and the middle of the nineteenth century is much more difficult. Until 1830 most of these records were produced by military administrators of the British imperial government, and most of them are unpublished. A useful path of entry to these important documents is the endnotes and bibliography of Robert S. Allen, "The British Indian Department and the Frontier in North America, 1755–1830," *Canadian Historic Sites, Occasional Papers in Archaeology and History* 14 (Ottawa: Indian and Northern Affairs, n.d.), 109–25, or the same author's *His Majesty's Indian Allies: British Indian Policy in Defence of Canada* (Toronto: Dundurn, 1992). Most of the religious and civil governmental material remains unpublished. However, biographical works, including the appropriate volumes of the *Dictionary of Canadian Biography*, are a good guide to the best sources.

For the period from Confederation onward, primary materials dealing with Native-newcomer relations are more voluminous and accessible. In particular, the records of the federal government and parliament provide useful insights on what policy was intended to do, and less revealing glimpses of the degree to which policy was effective. The Annual Reports of the Department of Indian Affairs were published in the *Sessional Papers* of parliament each year. Until the period of the Great War these annual surveys were very detailed and useful, but thereafter they became more abbreviated. The other principal records regarding policy are found in Hansard, the verbatim report of parliament's deliberations. Debates on amendments to the Indian Act or on particular problems such as Native destitution provide illuminating comments. There are also extensive published records of treaty-making, the most important of which have been condensed in Alexander Morris, *The Treaties of Canada with the Indians of Manitoba and the North-West Territories* (Toronto: Belfords, Clarke, 1880), which is available in a Fifth House reprint (Saskatoon, 1991).

The views of missionaries, officials, and First Nations people themselves can be sampled with relative convenience only by means of published primary documents and participants' reminiscences. An example of the useful published primary document is the "Speech of Indian Chief, 'Me-Tawth' [Metoos]," November 1813, Women's Canadian Historical Society, *Transaction*, 4 (1903): 11–12. Among reminiscences, the missionary memoir is the most common. Samples include Canon H.W. Gibbon Stocken, *Among the Blackfoot and Sarcee*, new edition (Calgary: Glenbow Alberta Institute, 1976) and Augustin Joseph Brabant, *Mission to Nootka 1874–1900: Reminiscences of the West Coast of Vancouver Island* (1900), ed. Charles Lillard (Sydney, BC: Gray's Publishing, 1977, first published 1900). Most Indian agents, police, and other officials were more inhibited than the clergy when it came to putting their views on the record, but useful exceptions to this constabulary and bureaucratic modesty are William May Halliday, *Potlatch and Totem, and The Recollections of an Indian Agent* (Toronto: Dent, 1935), Cecil Edward Denny, *The Law Marches West* (Toronto: Dent, 1939), and William M. Graham, *Treaty Days: Reflections of an Indian Commissioner* (Calgary: Glenbow Museum, 1991). It is worth noting that the Prairies, especially southern Alberta, and coastal British Columbia have produced more of this sort of material than the rest of the country.

Until fairly recently First Nation accounts of their experiences were rare, but that situation is happily changing very rapidly now. An early exception was Peter Jones, *Life and Journals of Kah-ke-quo-na-by (Rev. Peter Jones), Wesleyan Missionary* (Toronto: Wesleyan Printing Establishment, 1860). In the twentieth century it has largely been western peoples whose recollections have been published. Examples from British Columbia include *Guests Never Leave Hungry: The Autobiography of James Sewid*, ed. James P. Spradley (New Haven, CT: Yale University Press, 1969) and Charles James Nowell's *Smoke from Their Fires: The Life of a Kwakiutl Chief*, ed. Clellan S. Ford (New Haven, CT: Yale University Press, 1949). Dan Kennedy [Ochankugahe], a Prairie Assiniboine, published *Recollections of an Assiniboine Chief*, ed. James R. Stevens (Toronto: McClelland and Stewart, 1972), and a former resident of the File Hills Colony in Saskatchewan, Eleanor Brass, brought out *I Walk in Two Worlds* (Calgary: Glenbow Museum, 1987). Note should also be taken of Harold Cardinal's *The Unjust Society: The Tragedy of Canada's Indians* (Edmonton: Hurtig, 1969), which contains considerable autobiographical detail. A useful collection of documents that have some biographical material is Keith D. Smith, ed., *Strange Visitors: Documents in Indigenous-Settler Relations in Canada from 1876* (Toronto: University of Toronto Press, 2014).

Another heartening sign is the increasing effort that is being made to collect and disseminate Native recollections. A good deal of Indigenous oral history is contained in Margaret Whitehead, ed., *Now You Are My Brother: Missionaries in British Columbia*, British Columbia Sound Heritage Series (Victoria: Provincial Archives of British Columbia, 1981); and Penny Petrone, ed., *First People, First Voices* (Toronto: University of Toronto Press, 1983), collects material from a longer period and a more representative body of Natives. A variety of archival and museum programs that are designed to recover the voices of historically inarticulate Native peoples should lead to more such publications in the coming years.

Reference Works

Brigham, Clarence S., ed. *Transactions and Collections of the American Antiquarian Society.* Vol. 12, *British Royal Proclamations Relating to America, 1603–1783*. Worcester, MA: American Antiquarian Society, 1911.

Corbeil, Pierre, comp. *Recherches amérindiennes au Québec. Index des volumes I à XXVI, 1971–1996*. Montreal: Recherches amérindiennes au Québec, 1997.

Secondary Sources

Secondary works are so numerous that only a representative sample can be given here. The works listed below are selected in most cases with an eye to their accessibility as well as their scholarly merit. Those interested in pursuing individual topics are urged to consult the bibliographies and notes of these historical works.

Abel, Kerry. *Drum Songs: Glimpses of Dene History*. Montreal: McGill-Queen's University Press, 1993.

Adams, Howard. *Prison of Grass: Canada from the Native Point of View*. 2nd ed. Saskatoon: Fifth House 1989. First published 1975.

Allen, Robert S. "Big Bear." *Saskatchewan History* 25, no. 1 (1972): 1–17.

– "The British Indian Department and the Frontier in North America, 1755–1830." Canadian Historic Sites, *Occasional Papers in Archaeology and History*, No. 14. Ottawa: Indian and Northern Affairs, n.d.

– *His Majesty's Indian Allies: British Indian Policy in Defence of Canada, 1774–1815*. Toronto: Dundurn, 1992.

Anderson, Karen. *Chain Her by One Foot: The Subjugation of Women in Seventeenth-Century New France*. New York: Routledge, 1991.

Andrews, Isabel. "Indian Protest against Starvation: The Yellow Calf Incident of 1884." *Saskatchewan History* 28, no. 2 (1975): 41–51.

Antal, Sandy. *A Wampum Denied: Procter's War of 1812*. Ottawa: Carleton University Press, 1997.

Aodla, Minnie. *Life among the Qallunaat*. Edmonton: Hurtig, 1978.

Asch, Michael, ed., *Aboriginal and Treaty Rights in Canada: Essays on Law, Equity, and Respect for Difference*. Vancouver: UBC Press, 1997.

– *On Being Here to Stay: Treaties and Aboriginal Rights in Canada*. Toronto: University of Toronto Press, 2014.

Asher, Georg Michael, ed. *Henry Hudson the Navigator*. 1860. Reprint, New York: Burt Franklin, 1953.

Association of Métis and Non-Status Indians of Saskatchewan. *Louis Riel: Justice Must Be Done*. Winnipeg: Manitoba Metis Federation Press, 1979.

Axtell, James. *The Invasion Within: The Contest of Cultures in Colonial North America*. New York: Oxford University Press, 1985.

– *Natives and Newcomers: The Cultural Origins of North America*. New York: Oxford University Press, 2001.

Bailey, Alfred Goldsworthy. *The Conflict of European and Eastern Algonkian Cultures 1504–1700: A Study in Canadian Civilization*. 2nd ed. Toronto: University of Toronto Press, 1969. First published 1937.

The Ballad of Crowfoot. Directed and performed by Willie Dunn. National Film Board, 1968.

Barman, Jean. *The West beyond the West: A History of British Columbia.* Toronto: University of Toronto Press, 1991.

Barman, Jean, Yvonne Hébert, and Don McCaskill, eds. *Indian Education in Canada.* Vol. 1, *The Legacy.* Vancouver: Nakoda Institute and UBC Press, 1986.

Barron, F. Laurie. "The Indian Pass System in the Canadian West, 1882–1935." *Prairie Forum* 21, no. 1 (1988): 25–42.

– *Walking a Mile in Indian Moccasins: The Native Policies of Tommy Douglas and the CCF.* Vancouver: UBC Press, 1997.

Barron, F. Laurie, and James B. Waldram, eds. *1885 and After: Native Society in Transition.* Regina: Canadian Plains Research Center, 1986.

Beal, Carl. "Money, Markets and Economic Development in Saskatchewan Indian Reserve Communities, 1870–1930s." PhD diss., University of Manitoba, 1994.

Beaulieu, Alain, Stéphan Gervais, and Martin Papillon, eds. *Les Autochtones et le Québec: Des premiers contacts au Plan Nord.* Montreal: Les Presses de l'Université de Montréal, 2013.

Belshaw, John Douglas. "Mining Technique and Social Division on Vancouver Island, 1848–1900." *British Journal of Canadian Studies* 1, no. 1 (1986): 45–65.

Benson, Jayme K. "Different Visions: The Government Response to Native and Non-Native Submissions on Education Presented to the 1946–48 Special Joint Committee of the Senate and the House of Commons." MA mémoire, University of Ottawa, 1991.

Berger, Thomas. *Fragile Freedoms: Human Rights and Dissent in Canada.* Rev. ed. Toronto: Clarke, Irwin, 1982. First published 1981.

– *Northern Frontier, Northern Homeland: The Report of the Mackenzie Valley Pipeline Inquiry.* 2 vols. Ottawa: Minister of Supply and Services, 1977.

Big Bear. Directed by Gil Cardinal. Canadian Broadcasting Corporation, 1999.

Bingaman, Sandra. "The North-West Rebellion Trials, 1885." Master's thesis, University of Regina, 1971.

– "The Trials of Poundmaker and Big Bear, 1885." *Saskatchewan History* 28, no. 3 (1975): 81–102.

– "The Trials of the 'White Rebels,' 1885." *Saskatchewan History* 25, no. 2 (1972): 41–54.

Binnema, Theodore. *Common and Contested Ground: A Human and Environmental History of the Northwestern Plains.* Toronto: University of Toronto Press, 2001.

– "Protecting Indian Lands by Defining Indian: 1850–76." *Journal of Canadian Studies* 48, no. 2 (2014): 5–39.

Blair, Emma Helen, ed. *The Indian Tribes of the Upper Mississippi Valley and Region of the Great Lakes as Described by Nicolas Perrot.* 2 vols. Cleveland: Arthur H. Clark, 1911.

Bolt, Clarence. *Thomas Crosby and the Tsimshian: Small Shoes for Feet Too Large.* Vancouver: UBC Press, 1992.

Bond Head, Francis. "Memorandum on the Aborigines of North America." Appendix A. In *A Narrative* to Lord Glenelg, 20 November 1836. London: John Murray, 1839.

Boswell, Marion Joan. "'Civilizing' the Indian: Government Administration of Indians, 1876–1896." PhD thesis, University of Ottawa, 1977.

Brandão, José A. *"Your Fire Shall Burn No More": Iroquois Policy toward New France and Its Native Allies to 1701.* Lincoln: University of Nebraska Press, 1997.

Brandão, José, and William A. Starna. "The Treaties of 1701: A Triumph of Iroquois Diplomacy." *Ethnohistory* 43, no. 2 (1996): 209–44.

Brass, Eleanor. "Recollections and Reminiscences: The File Hills Ex-Pupil Colony." *Saskatchewan History* 6, no. 2 (1953): 66–9.

Brown, D.H. "The Meaning of Treason in 1885." *Saskatchewan History* 28, no. 2 (1975): 65–73.

Brown, George, and Ron Maguire. *Indian Treaties in Historical Perspective.* Ottawa: Indian and Northern Affairs, 1979.

Brown, Jennifer S.H. *Strangers in Blood: Fur Trade Company Families in Indian Country.* Vancouver: UBC Press, 1980.

Buckley, Helen. *From Wooden Ploughs to Welfare: Why Indian Policy Failed in the Prairie Provinces.* Montreal: McGill-Queen's University Press, 1992.

Caduto, Michael J., and Joseph Burchac. *Keepers of the Earth: Native Stories and Environmental Activities for Children.* Saskatoon, SK: Fifth House, 1989.

Cail, Robert Edgar. *Land, Man and Law: The Disposal of Crown Lands in British Columbia, 1871–1913.* Vancouver: UBC Press, 1974.

Cairns, Alan. *Citizens Plus: Aboriginal Peoples and the Canadian State.* Vancouver: UBC Press, 2000.

Calloway, Colin G. *Crown and Calumet: British-Indian Relations, 1783–1815.* Norman: University of Oklahoma Press, 1987.

Campbell, Maria. *Halfbreed.* Toronto: Seal Books, 1979. First published 1973.

Canada. *Gathering Strength: Canada's Aboriginal Action Plan.* Ottawa: Public Works and Government Services, 1997.

Carlson, Keith Thor. *The Power of Place, the Problem of Time: Aboriginal Identity and Historical Consciousness in the Cauldron of Colonialism.* Toronto: University of Toronto Press, 2010.

Carter, Sarah A. "Agriculture and Agitation on the Oak River Dakota Reserve, 1875-1895." *Manitoba History* 6 (Fall 1983): 2–10.

– *Capturing Women: The Manipulation of Cultural Imagery in Canada's Prairie West.* Montreal: McGill-Queen's University Press, 1997.

– "Controlling Indian Movement: The Pass System." *NeWest Review* (May 1985): 8–9.

– *The Importance of Being Monogamous: Marriage and Nation Building in Western Canada to 1915.* Edmonton: University of Alberta Press, 2008.

– *Lost Harvests: Prairie Indian Reserve Farmers and Government Policy.* Montreal: McGill-Queen's University Press, 1990.

– "Two Acres and a Cow: 'Peasant' Farming for the Indians of the Northwest, 1889–1897." In *Sweet Promises: A Reader on Indian-White Relations in Canada*, edited by J.R. Miller, 353–77. Toronto: University of Toronto Press, 1991.

Cassidy, Frank. "Aboriginal Land Claims in British Columbia." In *Aboriginal Land Claims in Canada: A Regional Perspective*, edited by Ken Coates, 11–43. Toronto: Copp Clark Pitman, 1992.

Christian, Edgar. *Death in the Barren Ground.* Edited by George Whalley. Ottawa: Oberon Press, 1980. First published 1937.

Chute, Janet E. *The Legacy of Shingwaukonse: A Century of Native Leadership.* Toronto: University of Toronto Press, 1998.

Coates, Ken. *#IdleNoMore and the Remaking of Canada.* Regina: University of Regina Press, 2015.

– *Best Left as Indians: Native-White Relations in the Yukon Territory, 1840–1973.* Montreal: McGill-Queen's University Press, 1991.

– "'Betwixt and Between': The Anglican Church and the Children of the Carcross (Chooutla) Residential School." *BC Studies*, no. 64 (Winter 1984–5): 27–47.

– *The Marshall Decision and Native Rights.* Montreal: McGill-Queen's University Press, 2000.

– "On the Outside in Their Homeland: Native People and the Evolution of the Yukon Economy." *Northern Review* no. 1 (Summer 1988): 73–89.

Coates, Ken, ed. *Aboriginal Land Claims in Canada: A Regional Perspective.* Toronto: Copp Clark Pitman, 1992.

Codere, Helen. *Fighting With Property: A Study of Kwakiutl Potlatching and Warfare, 1792–1930.* Seattle: University of Washington Press, 1966.

Colden, Cadwallader. *History of the Five Indian Nations of Canada.* Part 1. London: T. Osborne, 1747.

Cole, Douglas. *Captured Heritage: The Scramble for Northwest Coast Artifacts.* Vancouver: Douglas and McIntyre, 1985.

Cole, Douglas, and Ira Chaikin. *An Iron Hand upon the People: The Law against the Potlatch on the Northwest Coast.* Vancouver: Douglas and McIntyre, 1990.

Colombo, John Robert. *Colombo's Canadian Quotations.* Edmonton: Hurtig, 1974.

Cook, Ramsay. "Canadian Centennial Celebrations." *International Journal* 22, no. 4 (1967): 659–63.

– "The Social and Economic Frontier in North America." In *The Frontier in History: North America and South Africa Compared*, edited by Howard Lamar and Leonard Thompson, 175–208. New Haven, CT: Yale University Press, 1981.

Coolican, Murray. *Living Treaties: Lasting Agreements: Report of the Task Force to Review Comprehensive Claims Policy (Coolican Report).* Ottawa: Department of Indian Affairs and Northern Development, 1985.

Coppermine. Directed by Ray Harper. National Film Board, 1992.

Correspondence and Other Papers Relating to Aboriginal Tribes in British Possessions. 1834. British Parliamentary Papers. Shannon: Irish University Press, 1969.

Coyne, Deborah. *Roll of the Dice: Working with Clyde Wells during the Meech Lake Negotiations.* Toronto: James Lorimer, 1992.

Craig, Gerald M. *Upper Canada: The Formative Years, 1784–1841.* Toronto: McClelland and Stewart, 1963.

Crowe, Keith J. *A History of the Original Peoples of Northern Canada.* Montreal: Arctic Institute of North America, 1974.

Cruikshank, Julie. "Oral Traditions and Written Accounts: An Incident from the Klondike Gold Rush." *Culture* 9, no. 2 (1989): 25–31.

Cunfer, Geoff. "Overview: The Decline and Fall of the Bison Empire." In *Bison and People on the North American Great Plains: A Deep Environmental History*, edited by Geoff Cunfer and Bill Waiser, 1–29. College Station: Texas A&M University Press, 2016.

Cuthand, Stan. "The Native Peoples of the Prairie Provinces in the 1920s and 1930s." In *Sweet Promises: A Reader on Indian-White Relations in Canada*, edited by J. R. Miller, 381–92. Toronto: University of Toronto Press, 1991.

Damas, David. "The Arctic from Norse Contact to Modern Times." In *The Cambridge History of the Native Peoples of the Americas*, Vol. 2, *North America, Part 2*, edited by Bruce G. Trigger and Wilcomb E. Washburn, 329–99. Cambridge: Cambridge University Press, 1996.

Daniel, Richard. *A History of Native Claims Processes in Canada, 1867–1979.* Ottawa: Indian Affairs 1980.

– "The Spirit and Terms of Treaty Eight." In *The Spirit of the Alberta Indian Treaties*, 2nd ed., edited by Richard Price, 47–100. Edmonton: Pica Pica Press, 1987.

Daniels, John D. "The Indian Population of North America in 1492." *William and Mary Quarterly* 49, no. 2 (1992): 298–320.

Daschuk, James. *Clearing the Plains: Disease, Politics of Starvation, and the Loss of Aboriginal Life.* Regina: University of Regina Press, 2013.

Davies, Maureen. "Aboriginal Rights in International Law: Human Rights." In *Aboriginal Peoples and the Law: Indian, Metis and Inuit Rights in Canada*, edited by Bradford W. Morse, 745–94. Ottawa: Carleton University Press, 1985.

Dawson, Bruce W. "'Better than a few squirrels': The Greater Production Campaign on the First Nations Reserves of the Canadian Prairies." Master's thesis, University of Saskatchewan, 2001.

De Brou, Dave, and Bill Waiser, eds. *Documenting Canada: A History of Modern Canada in Documents*. Saskatoon: Fifth House, 1992.

de Charlevoix, Pierre-François-Xavier, S.J. *History and General Description of New France*. 6 vols. 1743. Translated by John Gilmary Shea. Chicago: Loyola University Press, 1870.

"Declaration of the People of Rupert's Land and the North West." Archives of Manitoba, MG3 A1–6. Accessed 14 November 2016. http://manitobia.ca/content/en/records/RRS/RRS_1869_1207.

Delâge, Denys. *Bitter Feast: Amerindians and Europeans in Northeastern North America, 1600–64*. 1985. Translated by Jane Brierley. Vancouver: UBC Press, 1993.

Dempsey, Hugh A. *Big Bear: The End of Freedom*. Vancouver: Douglas and McIntyre, 1984.

– *Charcoal's World*. Saskatoon: Western Producer Prairie Books, 1978.

– *Crowfoot: Chief of the Blackfeet*. Edmonton: Hurtig, 1972.

– "The Fearsome Fire Wagon." In *The CPR West: The Iron Road and The Making of a Nation*, edited by Hugh A. Dempsey, 55–69. Vancouver: Douglas and McIntyre, 1984.

– *The Gentle Persuader: James Gladstone, Indian Senator*. Saskatoon: Western Producer Prairie Books, 1986.

– "One Hundred Years of Treaty Seven." In *One Century Later: Western Canadian Reserve Indians since Treaty 7*, edited by Ian A.L. Getty and Donald B. Smith, 20–30. Vancouver: UBC Press, 1977.

– *Red Crow, Warrior Chief*. Saskatoon: Western Producer Prairie Books, 1980.

Dempsey, Hugh A., ed. "The Last Letters of Rev. George McDougall." *Alberta Historical Review* 6, no. 2 (1967): 20–30.

de Stecher, Annette. "Wendat Arts of Diplomacy: Negotiating Change in the Nineteenth Century." In *From Huronia to Wendakes: Adversity, Migrations, and Resilience 1650–1900*, edited by Thomas Peace and Kathryn Magee Labelle, 182–208. Norman: University of Oklahoma Press, 2016.

Devens. Carol. *Countering Colonization: Native American Women and Great Lakes Missions, 1630–1900*. Berkeley: University of California Press, 1992.

Dickason, Olive P. *Canada's First Nations: A History of Founding Peoples from Earliest Times*. Toronto: McClelland and Stewart, 1992.

Diubaldo, Richard J. "The Absurd Little Mouse: When Eskimos Became Indians." *Journal of Canadian Studies* 16, no. 2 (1981): 34–40.

Dosman, Edgar J. *Indians: The Urban Dilemma*. Toronto: McClelland and Stewart, 1972.

Driben, Paul, and Robert Sanderson Trudeau. *When Freedom Is Lost: The Dark Side of the Relationship between Government and the Fort Hope Band*. Toronto: University of Toronto Press, 1983.

Duff, Wilson. *The Indian History of British Columbia*. Vol. 1, *The Impact of the White Man*. 2nd ed. Victoria: Royal British Columbia Museum, 1969. First published 1966.

Duffy, R. Quinn. *The Road to Nunavut: The Progress of the Eastern Arctic Inuit since the Second World War*. Montreal: McGill-Queen's University Press, 1988.

Dyck, Noel. "The Administration of Federal Indian Aid in the North-West Territories 1879–1885." Master's thesis, University of Saskatchewan, 1970.

– *What is the "Indian Problem"?: Tutelage and Resistance in Canadian Indian Administration*. St. John's: Institute of Social and Economic Research, Memorial University, 1991.

Eber, Dorothy Harley. *When the Whalers Were Up North: Inuit Memories from the Eastern Arctic*. Montreal: McGill-Queen's University Press, 1989.

Eccles, William J. *Canada under Louis XIV, 1663–1701*. Toronto: McClelland and Stewart, 1964.

– *The Canadian Frontier, 1534–1760*. New York: Holt, Rinehart and Winston, 1969.

– *Canadian Society during the French Regime*. Montreal: Harvest House, 1968.

– *Essays on New France*. Toronto: Oxford University Press, 1987.

Edmunds, R. David. "Tecumseh's Native Allies: Warriors Who Fought for the Crown." In *War on the Great Lakes*, edited by William Jeffrey Welsh and David Curtis Skaggs, 56–67. Kent, OH: Kent State University Press, 1991.

Elbourne, Elizabeth. "Managing Alliance, Negotiating Christianity: Haudenosaunee Uses of Anglicanism in Northeastern North America, 1760s–1830s." In *Mixed Blessings: Indigenous Encounters with Christianity in Canada*, edited by Tolly Bradford and Chelsea Horton, 38–50. Vancouver: UBC Press, 2016.

Elias, Peter Douglas. *The Dakota of the Canadian Northwest: Lessons for Survival*. Winnipeg: University of Manitoba Press, 1988.

Elliott, D.W. "Aboriginal Title." In *Aboriginal Peoples and the Law: Indian, Metis and Inuit Rights in Canada*, edited by Bradford W. Morse, 48–121. Ottawa: Carleton University Press, 1985.

Ens, Gerhard J. *Homeland to Hinterland: The Changing Worlds of the Red River Metis in the Nineteenth Century*. Toronto: University of Toronto Press, 1996.

Erasmus, Peter. *Buffalo Days and Nights*. As told to Henry Thompson. Calgary: Glenbow-Alberta Institute, 1976.

Ewers, J.G. "Intertribal Warfare as the Precursor of Indian-White Warfare on the Northern Great Plains." *Western Historical Quarterly* 6 (October 1975): 397–410.

Fenge, Terry. "Negotiation and Implementation of Modern Treaties between Aboriginal Peoples and the Crown in Right of Canada." In *Keeping Promises: The Royal Proclamation of 1763, Aboriginal Rights, and Treaties in Canada*, edited by Terry Fenge and Jim Aldridge, 105–37. Montreal: McGill-Queen's University Press, 2015.

Fenge, Terry, and Aldridge, Jim, eds. *Keeping Promises: The Royal Proclamation of 1763, Aboriginal Rights, and Treaties in Canada*. Montreal: McGill-Queen's University Press, 2015.

Fenn, Elizabeth. "Biological Warfare in Eighteenth-Century North America: Beyond Jeffery Amherst." *Journal of American History* 86, no. 4 (March 2000): 1552–80.

Fingard, Judith. "The New England Company and the New Brunswick Indians, 1786–1826: A Comment on the Colonial Perversion of British Benevolence." *Acadiensis* 1, no. 2 (1972): 29–42.

Fischer, David Hackett. *Champlain's Dream*. New York: Simon and Schuster, 2008.

Fisher, Robin A. *Contact and Conflict: Indian-European Relations in British Columbia, 1774–1890*. Vancouver: UBC Press, 1977.

Fisher, Robin A., and Ken Coates, eds. *Out of the Background: Readings on Canadian Native History*. Toronto: Copp Clark Pitman, 1988.

Flanagan, Thomas. *Louis "David" Riel: Prophet of the New World*. Toronto: University of Toronto Press, 1979.

– *Metis Lands in Manitoba*. Calgary: University of Calgary Press, 1991.

– *Riel and the Rebellion: 1885 Reconsidered*. Saskatoon: Western Producer Prairie Books, 1983.

Flores, Dan. "Reviewing an Iconic Story: Environmental History and the Demise of the Bison." In *Bison and People on the North American Great Plains*, edited by Geoff Cunfer and Bill Waiser, 30–47. College Station: Texas A&M University Press, 2016.

Foster, Hamar. "We Are Not O'Meara's Children: Law, Lawyers, and the First Campaign for Aboriginal Title in British Columbia, 1908–28." In *Let Right Be Done: Aboriginal Title, the Calder Case, and the Future of Indigenous Rights*, edited by Hamar Foster, Heather Raven, and Jeremy Webber, 61–84. Vancouver: UBC Press, 2007.

Foster, Hamar, Heather Raven, and Jeremy Webber, eds. *Let Right Be Done: Aboriginal Title, the Calder Case, and the Future of Indigenous Rights.* Vancouver: UBC Press, 2007.

Foster, John E. "Program for the Red River Mission: The Anglican Clergy 1820–1826." *Histoire sociale/Social History* 2, no. 4 (1969): 49–75.

Francis, Daniel, and Toby Morantz. *Partners in Furs: A History of the Fur Trade in Eastern James Bay, 1600–1870.* Montreal: McGill-Queen's University Press, 1985.

Fraser, William B. "Big Bear, Indian Patriot." *Alberta Historical Review* 14, no. 2 (1966): 1–13.

Frégault, Guy. *Canada: The War of the Conquest.* Toronto: Oxford, 1969.

Friesen, Gerald. *The Canadian Prairies: A History.* Toronto: University of Toronto Press, 1984.

Friesen, Jean. "Magnificent Gifts: The Treaties of Canada with the Indians of the Northwest, 1869–1876." *Transactions* of the Royal Society of Canada, Series 5, Vol. 1 (1986): 41–51.

Fumoleau, René. *As Long as This Land Shall Last: A History of Treaty 8 and Treaty 11, 1870–1939.* Toronto: McClelland and Stewart, 1975.

Furniss, Elizabeth. *Victims of Benevolence: Discipline and Death at the Williams Lake Indian Residential School.* Montreal: McGill-Queen's University Press, 1992.

Giraud, Marcel. *The Métis in the Canadian West.* 2 vols. 1945. Translated by George Woodcock. Lincoln: University of Nebraska Press 1986.

Given, Brian J. *A Most Pernicious Thing: Gun Trading and Native Warfare in the Early Contact Period.* Ottawa: Carleton University Press, 1994.

Goddard, John. *Last Stand of the Lubicon Cree.* Vancouver: Douglas and McIntyre, 1991.

Godlewska, Christina, and Jeremy Webber. "The *Calder* Decision, Aboriginal Title, Treaties, and the Nisga'a." In *Let Right Be Done: Aboriginal Title, the Calder Case, and the Future of Indigenous Rights*, edited by Hamar Foster, Heather Raven, and Jeremy Webber, 1–33. Vancouver: UBC Press, 2007.

Goodwill, Jean, and Norma Sluman. *John Tootoosis*, 2nd ed. Winnipeg: Pemmican Publications, 1984.

Gough, Barry. *Gunboat Frontier: British Maritime Authority and Northwest Coast Indians, 1846–1890.* Vancouver: UBC Press, 1984.

Graham, Elizabeth. *Medicine Man to Missionary: Missionaries as Agents of Change among the Indians of Southern Ontario, 1784–1867.* Toronto: Peter Martin Associates, 1975.

Grant, John Webster. *Moon of Wintertime: Missionaries and the Indians of Canada in Encounter since 1534.* Toronto: University of Toronto Press, 1984.

Graymont, Barbara. *The Iroquois in the American Revolution.* Syracuse: Syracuse University Press, 1972.

Green, Joyce. "Sexual Equality and Indian Government: An Analysis of Bill C-31 Amendments to the *Indian Act*." *Native Studies Review* 1, no. 2 (1985): 81–95.

Gresko, Jacqueline. "Paul Durieu, O.M.I." *Dictionary of Canadian Biography.* Vol. 12, *1891 to 1900.* Toronto: University of Toronto Press, 1990.

– "White 'Rites' and Indian 'Rites': Indian Education and Native Responses in the West, 1870–1910." In *Western Canada Past and Present*, edited by Anthony W. Rasporich, 163–81. Calgary: McClelland and Stewart, 1975.

Gulig, Anthony. "In Whose Interest? Government-Indian Relations in Northern Saskatchewan and Wisconsin, 1900–1940." PhD diss., University of Saskatchewan, 1997.

Haig-Brown, Celia. *Resistance and Renewal: Surviving the Indian Residential School.* Vancouver: Tillacum Library, 1988.

Hall, David J. "Clifford Sifton and Canadian Indian Administration 1896–1905." In *As Long as the Sun Shines and Water Flows: A Reader in Canadian Native Studies*, edited by Ian A.L. Getty and Antoine S. Lussier, 120–44. Vancouver: Nakoda Insitute and UBC Press, 1983.

‒ *From Treaties to Reserves: The Federal Government and Native Peoples in Territorial Alberta, 1870–1905*. Montreal: McGill-Queen's University Press, 2015.

Handy, James Ralph. "The Ojibwa: 1640-1840: Two Centuries of Change from Sault Ste. Marie to Coldwater/Narrows." Master's thesis, University of Waterloo, 1978.

Hare, Jan, and Jean Barman. "Good Intentions Gone Awry: From Protection to Confinement in Emma Crosby's Home for Aboriginal Girls." In *With Good Intentions: Euro-Canadian and Aboriginal Relations in Colonial Canada*, edited by Celia Haig-Brown and David A. Nock, 179–98. Vancouver: UBC Press, 2006.

Harper, A.G. "Canada's Indian Administration: Basic Concepts and Objectives." *America Indigena* 5, no. 2 (1945): 119–32.

Harper, Joan. *He Moved a Mountain: The Life of Frank Calder and the Nisga'a Land Claims Accord*. Vancouver: Ronsdale Press, 2013.

Harring, Sidney L. "The Liberal Treatment of Indians: Native People in Nineteenth Century Ontario Law." *Saskatchewan Law Review* 56, no. 2 (1992): 297–371.

Harris, Cole. *Making Native Space: Colonialism, Resistance, and Reserves in British Columbia*. Vancouver: UBC Press, 2002.

Hauka, Donald. *McGowan's War*. Vancouver: New Star Books, 2003.

Havard, Gilles. *The Great Peace of Montreal of 1701: French-Native Diplomacy in the Seventeenth Century*. 1991. Translated by Phyllis Aronoff and Howard Scott. Montreal: McGill-Queen's University Press, 2001.

Hawthorn, Harry B., ed. *A Survey of the Contemporary Indians of Canada: Economic, Political, Educational Needs and Policies*. 2 vols. Ottawa: Indian Affairs, 1966–7.

Haycock, Ronald Graham. *The Image of the Indian*. Waterloo, ON: Waterloo Lutheran University, 1971.

Hearne, Samuel. *A Journey from Prince of Wales's Fort in Hudson's* [sic] *Bay to the Northern Ocean 1769, 1770, 1771, 1772*. Edited by Richard Glover. Toronto: Macmillan, 1958. First published 1795.

Henry, Alexander. *Travels and Adventures in Canada and the Indian Territories between the Years 1760 and 1776*. Edited by James Bain. 1901. Reprint, New York: Burt Franklin, 1969.

High, Steven. "Native Wage Labour and Independent Production during the 'Era of Irrelevance.'" *Labour/Le Travail* 37 (Spring 1996): 243–64.

Historical Atlas of Canada. Vol. 1, *From the Beginning to 1800*. Toronto: University of Toronto Press, 1987.

Hodgins, Bruce, and Jamie Benidickson. *The Temagami Experience: Recreation, Resources, and Aboriginal Rights in the Northern Ontario Wilderness*. Toronto: University of Toronto Press, 1989.

Ibbitson, John. *Stephen Harper*. Toronto: McClelland and Stewart, 2015.

Innis, Harold A. *The Fur Trade in Canada: An Introduction to Canadian Economic History*. Rev. ed. Toronto: University of Toronto Press, 1956. First published 1930.

Indian Association of Alberta. *Citizens Plus: A Presentation of the Indian Chiefs of Alberta to Right Honourable P.E. Trudeau*. Edmonton: Indian Association of Alberta, 1970.

Indian Claims Commission. "Inquiry into the 1907 Reserve Land Surrender of the Kahkewistahaw First Nation." Ottawa: Indian Claims Commission, 1997.

Jaenen, Cornelius J. "Amerindian Responses to French Missionary Intrusion, 1611–1760." In *Religion/Culture: Comparative Canadian Studies/Etudes canadiennes comparées*, edited by William Westfall and Louis Rousseau, 182–97. Ottawa: Association for Canadian Studies, 1985.

– "French Sovereignty and Native Nationhood during the French Régime." In *Sweet Promises: A Reader on Indian-White Relations in Canada*, edited by J.R. Miller, 19–42. Toronto: University of Toronto Press, 1991.

– *Friend and Foe: Aspects of French-Amerindian Cultural Contact in the Sixteenth and Seventeenth Centuries*. New York: Columbia University Press, 1976.

Jenness, Diamond. *The Indians of Canada*. 7th ed. Toronto: University of Toronto Press, 1977. First published 1932.

Jennings, Francis. *The Invasion of America: Indians, Colonialism, and the Cant of Conquest*. Chapel Hill: University of North Carolina Press, 1975.

Johnson, E. Pauline. *Flint and Feather: The Complete Poems of E. Pauline Johnson (Tekahionwake)*. 8th ed. Toronto: Musson, 1922.

Johnson, Ian V.B. *Helping Indians to Help Themselves – A Committee to Investigate Itself: The 1951 Indian Act Consultation Process*. Ottawa: Indian and Northern Affairs, 1984.

Johnston, Charles M., ed. *The Valley of the Six Nations*. Toronto: Champlain Society, 1964.

Judd, Carol M., and Arthur J. Ray, eds. *Old Trails and New Directions: Papers of the Third North American Fur Trade Conference*. Toronto: University of Toronto Press, 1980.

Jull, Peter. "Aboriginal Peoples and Political Change in the North Atlantic Area." *Journal of Canadian Studies* 16, no. 2 (1981): 41–52.

– "Building Nunavut: A Story of Inuit Self-Government." *The Northern Review* 1 (Summer 1988): 59–72.

– "Reflections on Regional Agreements: Yesterday, Today and Tomorrow." *Australian Indigenous Law Reporter* 2, no. 4 (1997): 476–93.

– "'Them Eskimo Mob': International Implications of Nunavut, Revised 2nd ed." In *Seven Generations: An Information Legacy of the Royal Commission on Aboriginal Peoples*. CD-ROM. Ottawa: Public Works and Government Services, 1997.

Kennedy, Dan (Ochankugahe). *Recollections of an Assiniboine Chief*. Edited by James R. Stevens. Toronto: McClelland and Stewart, 1972.

Kenney, Gerard I. *Arctic Smoke and Mirrors*. Prescott, ON: Voyageur Publishing, 1994.

Kina-nda-niimi Collective, ed. *The Winter We Danced: Voices from the Past, the Future, and the Idle No More Movement*. Winnipeg: ARP Books, 2014.

Klutschak, Heinrich. *Overland to Starvation Cove: With the Inuit in Search of Franklin 1878–1880*. 1881. Edited and translated by William Barr. Toronto: University of Toronto Press, 1987.

Knight, Rolf. *Indians at Work: An Informal History of Native Labour in British Columbia, 1848–1930*. Vancouver: New Star Books, 1996.

Knollenburg, Bernard. "General Amherst and Germ Warfare." *Mississippi Valley Historical Review* 41 (March 1955): 489–94.

Kroeber, Alfred L. *The Nature of Culture*. Chicago: University of Chicago Press, 1952.

Krech, Shepard, ed. *The Subarctic Fur Trade: Native Social and Economic Adaptations*. Vancouver: UBC Press, 1984.

Krotz, Larry. *Indian Country: Inside Another Canada*. Toronto: McClelland and Stewart, 1992.

Kulchyski, Peter. "'A Considerable Unrest:' F.O. Loft and the League of Indians." *Native Studies Review* 4, nos. 1 & 2 (1988): 95–117.

Labelle, Kathryn Magee. *Dispersed But Not Destroyed: A History of the Seventeenth-Century Wendat People*. Vancouver: UBC Press, 2013.

Lackenbauer, P. Whitney. *Battle Grounds: The Canadian Military and Aboriginal Lands*. Vancouver: UBC Press, 2007.

– *The Canadian Rangers: A Living History*. Vancouver: UBC Press, 2013.

Lainey, Jonathan. "Les colliers de wampum comme support mémoriel: le cas du *Two Dog Wampum.*" In *Les Autochtones et le Québec: Des Premiers Contacts au Plan Nord*, edited by Alain Beaulieu, Stéphan Gervais, and Martin Papillon, 93–111. Montreal: Les Presses de l'Université de Montréal, 2013.

LaViolette, Forrest E. *The Struggle for Survival: Indian Cultures and the Protestant Ethic in British Columbia.* Toronto: University of Toronto Press, 1961.

Le Clercq, Christian. *First Establishment of the Faith in New France*, 2 vols. Edited by John Gilmary Shea. New York: J.G. Shea, 1881.

Leslie, John, and Ron Maguire, eds. *The Historical Development of the Indian Act.* 2nd ed. Ottawa: Department of Indian and Northern Affairs, 1979. First published 1975.

Long, John S. *Treaty No. 9: Making the Agreement to Share the Land in Far Northern Ontario in 1905.* Montreal: McGill-Queen's University Press, 2010.

Loo, Tina. "Dan Cranmer's Potlatch: Law as Coercion, Symbol, and Rhetoric in British Columbia, 1884–1951." *Canadian Historical Review* 73, no. 2 (1992): 125–65.

– *Making Law, Order, and Authority in British Columbia, 1821–1871.* Toronto: University of Toronto Press, 1994.

Lower, Arthur R.M. *Canadians in the Making: A Social History of Canada.* Don Mills, ON: Longmans, 1958.

Lurie, Nancy Oestreich. "The World's Oldest On-Going Protest Demonstration: North American Indian Drinking Patterns." *Pacific Historical Review* 40, no. 3 (1971): 311–32.

Lutz, John. "After the Fur Trade: The Aboriginal Labouring Class of British Columbia, 1849–1890." *Journal of the Canadian Historical Association* 3, no. 1 (1992): 69–93.

– *Makúk: A New History of Aboriginal-White Relations.* Vancouver: UBC Press, 2008.

Lux, Maureen. *Medicine That Walks: Disease, Medicine, and Canadian Plains Native People, 1880–1940.* Toronto: University of Toronto Press, 2001.

MacGregor, Roy. *Chief: The Fearless Vision of Billy Diamond.* Markham, ON: Penguin, 1989.

– "The Feather: Elijah Harper and Meech Lake." *Windspeaker* 8, no. 8 (1990).

MacInnes, T.R.L. "History of Indian Administration in Canada." *Canadian Journal of Economics and Political Science* 12, no. 3 (1945): 387–94.

MacLean, Hope. "The Hidden Agenda: Methodist Attitudes to the Ojibwa and the Development of Indian Schooling in Upper Canada, 1821–1860." Master's thesis, University of Toronto, 1978.

MacLeod, D. Peter. *The Canadian Iroquois and the Seven Years' War.* Toronto: Dundurn, 1996.

Macleod, Roderick Charles. *The North West Mounted Police, 1873–1919.* Ottawa: Canadian Historical Association, 1978.

– *The North-West Mounted Police and Law Enforcement, 1873–1905.* Toronto: University of Toronto Press, 1976.

Macleod, Roderick Charles, and Heather Rollason. "'Restrain the Lawless Savages': Native Defendants in the Criminal Courts of the North West Territories, 1878–1885." *Journal of Historical Sociology* 10, no. 2 (1997): 157–83.

McMillan, Alan D., ed. *Native Peoples and Cultures of Canada: An Anthropological Overview.* 2nd ed. Vancouver: Douglas and McIntyre, 1995. First published 1988.

Magnuson, Magnus, and Hermann Pàlsson, trans. *The Vinland Sagas: The Norse Discovery of America.* London: Penguin, 1965.

Manitoba Métis Federation. "Position Paper on Child Care and Family Services (May 15, 1982)." *Native Studies Review* 2, no. 1 (1986): 125–39.

Manseü-Scanian. "The New Race." *The Missionary Outlook* 24, no. 5 (1905): 58.

Manuel, George. "Manifesto for Survival." *Macleans*, May 1973.

Manuel, George, and Michael Posluns. *The Fourth World: An Indian Reality*. Toronto: Collier-Macmillan, 1974.

Marcus, Alan R. *Relocating Eden: The Image and Politics of Inuit Exile in the Canadian Arctic*. Hanover, NH: University of New England Press, 1995.

Marshall, Daniel Patrick. "Claiming the Land: Indians, Goldseekers, and the Rush to British Columbia." PhD diss., University of British Columbia, 2000.

Marshall, Ingeborg. *A History and Ethnography of the Beothuk*. Montreal: McGill-Queen's University Press, 1996.

Martel, Gilles. *Le messianisme de Louis Riel*. Waterloo, ON: Wilfrid Laurier University Press, 1984.

Martin-McGuire, Peggy. *First Nation Land Surrenders on the Prairies, 1896–1911*. Ottawa: Indian Claims Commission, 1998.

McAdam, Sylvia. "Armed with Nothing More than a Drum and a Song: Idle No More." In *The Winter We Danced: Voices from the Past, the Future, and the Idle No More Movement*, ed. Kinonda-mimi Collective, 65–7. Winnipeg: ARP Books, 2014.

McGhee, Robert. "Thule Prehistory of Canada" In *Handbook of North American Indians*. Vol. 5, *Arctic*, edited by David Damas, 369–76. Washington: Smithsonian Institution, 1984.

Meijer Drees, Laurie. *The Indian Association of Alberta: A History of Political Action*. Vancouver: UBC Press, 2002.

Miller, J.R. *Big Bear (Mistahimusqua)*. Toronto: ECW Press, 1996.

– *Canada and the Aboriginal Peoples, 1867–1927*. Ottawa: Canadian Historical Association, 1997.

– *Compact, Contract, Covenant: Aboriginal Treaty-Making in Canada*. Toronto: University of Toronto Press, 2009.

– "Denominational Rivalry in Residential Schooling." *Western Oblate Studies* 2 (1991): 139–55.

– "From Riel to the Métis." *Canadian Historical Review* 69, no. 1 (1988): 1–20.

– "Great White Father Knows Best: Oka and the Land Claims Process." *Native Studies Review* 7, no. 1 (1991): 23–51.

– *Lethal Legacy: Current Native Controversies in Canada*. Toronto: McClelland and Stewart, 2004.

– "Macdonald as Minister of Indian Affairs: The Shaping of Canadian Indian Policy." In *Macdonald at 200: New Reflections and Legacies*, edited by Patrice Dutil and Roger Hall, 311–40. Toronto: Dundurn, 2014.

– *Residential Schools and Reconciliation: Canada Confronts Its History*. Toronto: University of Toronto Press, 2017.

– *Shingwauk's Vision: A History of Native Residential Schools*. Toronto: University of Toronto Press, 1996.

– ed. *Sweet Promises: A Reader on Indian-White Relations in Canada*. Toronto: University of Toronto Press, 1991.

Milloy, John S. "The Early Indian Acts: Developmental Strategy and Constitutional Change." In *Sweet Promises: A Reader on Indian-White Relations in Canada*, edited by J.R. Miller, 145–54. Toronto: University of Toronto Press, 1991.

– *A National Crime: The Canadian Government and the Residential School System, 1879 to 1986*. Winnipeg: University of Manitoba Press, 1999.

– *The Plains Cree: Trade, Diplomacy and War, 1790–1870*. Winnipeg: University of Manitoba Press, 1988.

Molloy, Tom, with Don Ward. *The World Is Our Witness: The Historic Journey of the Nisga'a into Canada*. Calgary: Fifth House, 2000.

Montgomery, Malcolm. "The Six Nations and the Macdonald Franchise." *Ontario History* 57, no. 1 (1965): 13–25.

Morrison, James. "The Robinson Treaties of 1850: A Case Study." Prepared for the Royal Commission on Aboriginal Peoples, 1993.

Morse, Bradford W., ed. *Aboriginal Peoples and the Law: Indian, Metis and Inuit Rights in Canada*. Ottawa: Carleton University Press, 1985.

Mosby, Ian. "Administering Colonial Science: Nutrition Research and Human Biomedical Experimentation in Aboriginal Communities and Residential Schools, 1942–1952." *Histoire sociale/Social History* 46, no. 91 (2013): 145–72.

Muise, Delphin Andrew, ed. *Approaches to Native History in Canada*. Ottawa: National Museum of Man, 1977.

Mulhall, David. *Will to Power: The Missionary Career of Father Morice*. Vancouver: UBC Press, 1986.

Munn, Henry Toke. *Prairie Trail and Arctic By-Ways*. London: Hurst and Blackett, 1932.

Murray, Laura J., ed. *To Do Good to My Indian Brethren: The Writings of Joseph Johnson, 1751–1775*. Amherst: University of Massachusetts Press, 1998.

Newman, Dwight G. *Revisiting the Duty to Consult Aboriginal Peoples*. Rev. ed. Saskatoon: Purich Publishing, 2014.

O'Malley, M. *The Past and Future Land: An Account of the Berger Inquiry into the Mackenzie Valley Pipeline*. Toronto: Peter Martin Associates, 1976.

Ormsby, Margaret A. "Douglas, Sir James." In *Dictionary of Canadian Biography*. Vol. 10, University of Toronto/Université Laval, 2003–. Accessed 2 August 2017. http://www.biographi.ca/en/bio/douglas_james_10E.html.

Owram, Doug. *Promise of Eden: The Canadian Expansionist Movement and the Idea of the West, 1856–1900*. Toronto: University of Toronto Press, 1980.

Pannakoek, Frits. *The Fur Trade and Western Canadian Society 1670–1870*. Ottawa: Canadian Historical Association, 1987.

– *A Snug Little Flock: The Social Origins of the Riel Resistance*. Winnipeg: Watson and Dwyer, 1991.

Paquin, Julien, S.J. "Modern Jesuit Missions in Ontario." Unpublished manuscript. Toronto: Regis College Archives, n.d.

Parker, Arthur C. "Iroquois Uses of Maize and Other Food Plants." In *Parker on the Iroquois*, edited by William N. Fenton, 5–119. Syracuse: Syracuse University Press, 1968.

Parks Canada. "The Franklin Expedition." Accessed 15 December 2016. https://www.pc.gc.ca/en/culture/franklin.

Parmenter, Jon. *The Edge of the Woods: Iroquoia, 1534–1701*. East Lansing: Michigan State University Press, 2010.

Patterson, E. Palmer. "Andrew Paull and the Early History of British Columbia Indian Organizations." In *One Century Later: Western Canadian Reserve Indians since Treaty 7*, edited by Ian A.L. Getty and Donald B. Smith, 43–54. Vancouver: UBC Press, 1978.

– *The Canadian Indian: A History since 1500*. Don Mills, ON: Collier-Macmillan, 1972.

– "A Decade of Change: The Origins of the Nishga and Tsimshian Land Protests in the 1880s." *Journal of Canadian Studies* 18, no. 3 (1983): 40–54.

Paul, Daniel N. *We Were Not the Savages: A Micmac Perspective on the Collision of European and Aboriginal Civilization*. Halifax: Nimbus, 1993.

Pennanen, Gary. "Sitting Bull: Indian without a Country." *Canadian Historical Review* 51, no. 2 (1970): 123–40.

Perry, Adele. *On the Edge of Empire: Gender, Race, and the Making of British Columbia, 1849–1871*. Toronto: University of Toronto Press, 2001.

Peters, Evelyn J. "Protecting the Land under Modern Land Claims Agreements: The Effectiveness of the Environmental Regime Negotiated by the James Bay Cree and Northern Quebec Agreement." *Applied Geography* 12, no. 2 (1992): 133–45.

Peterson, Jacqueline. "Many Roads to Red River: Métis Genesis in the Great Lakes Region, 1680–1815." In *The New Peoples: Being and Becoming Métis in North America*, edited by Jacqueline Peterson and Jennifer H.S. Brown, 38–64. Winnipeg: University of Manitoba Press, 1985.

Pettipas, K. *Severing the Ties That Bind: Government Repression of Indigenous Religious Ceremonies on the Prairies*. Winnipeg: University of Manitoba Press, 1994.

Pitsula, James M. "The CCF Government and the Formation of the Union of Saskatchewan Indians." *Prairie Forum* 19, no. 2 (1994): 131–51.

Plaice, Evelyn. *The Native Game: Settler Perceptions of Indian-Settler Relations in Central Labrador*. St. John's: Institute for Social and Economic Research, Memorial University, 1990.

Ponting, J. Rick, and Roger Gibbins. *Out of Irrelevance: A Socio-Political Introduction to Indian Affairs in Canada*. Toronto: Butterworths, 1980.

Price, Richard, ed. *The Spirit of the Alberta Indian Treaties*. 2nd ed. Edmonton: Pica Pica Press, 1987.

Purich, Donald. *The Metis*. Toronto: Lorimer, 1988.

– *Our Land: Native Rights in Canada*. Toronto: Lorimer, 1986.

Raby, S. "Indian Land Surrenders in Southern Saskatchewan." *Canadian Geographer* 17, no. 1 (1973): 36–52.

Ray, Arthur J. *The Canadian Fur Trade in the Industrial Age*. Toronto: University of Toronto Press, 1990.

– *I Have Lived Here Since the World Began: An Illustrated History of Canada's Native Peoples*. Toronto: Key Porter, 1996.

– "Indians as Consumers in the Eighteenth Century." In *Old Trails and New Directions: Papers of the Third North American Fur Trade Conference*, edited by Carol M. Judd and Arthur J. Ray, 255–71. Toronto: University of Toronto Press, 1980.

– *Indians in the Fur Trade: Their Role as Hunters, Trappers and Middlemen in the Lands Southwest of Hudson Bay, 1660–1870*. Toronto: University of Toronto Press, 1974.

– "Periodic Shortages, Native Welfare and the Hudson's Bay Company 1670–1930." In *The Subarctic Fur Trade: Native Social and Economic Adaptations*, edited by Shepard Krech, 2–20. Vancouver: UBC Press, 1984.

– *Telling It to the Judge: Taking Native History to Court*. Montreal: McGill-Queen's University Press, 2011.

Ray, Arthur J., and Donald Freeman. *"Give Us Good Measure": An Economic Analysis of Relations between the Indians and Hudson's Bay Company Before 1763*. Toronto: University of Toronto Press, 1978.

Ray, Arthur J., Jim Miller, and Frank Tough. *Bounty and Benevolence: A History of Saskatchewan Treaties*. Montreal: McGill-Queen's University Press, 2000.

Raynal, Abbé. *A Philosophical and Political History of the Settlements and Trade of the Europeans in the East and West Indies*. 8 vols. Translated by John Obadiah Justamond. London: A Strahan and T. Cadell, 1788.

Records of the Department of Indian Affairs. RG10. Library and Archives Canada, Ottawa.

Regular, W. Keith. *Neighbours and Networks: The Blood Tribe in the Southern Alberta Economy, 1884–1939*. Calgary: University of Calgary Press, 2009.

Reid, Gerald F. "'To Renew Our Fire': Political Activism, Nationalism, and Identity in Three Rotinonhsionni Communities." In *Tribal Worlds: Critical Studies in American Indian Nation Building*, edited by Brian Hosmer and Larry Hesper, 37–64. Albany: State University of New York Press, 2013.

"Report of the Special Commissioners Appointed on the 8th of September, 1856, to Investigate
    Indian Affairs in Canada." *Journals of the Legislative Assembly of the Province of Canada*. Vol. 16,
    Appendix 21. 1858.

Rettig, Andrew. "A Nativist Movement at Metlakatla Mission." *BC Studies* 46 (Summer 1980): 28–39.

Richardson, Boyce. *Strangers Devour the Land: A Chronicle of the Assault upon the Last Coherent
    Hunting Culture in North America, the Cree Indians of Quebec, and their Vast Primeval Homelands*.
    New York: Knopf, 1975.

Richter, Daniel K. *The Ordeal of the Longhouse: The Peoples of the Iroquois League in the Era of
    European Colonization*. Chapel Hill: University of North Carolina Press, 1992.

Robertson, Gordon. Foreword to *Arctic Smoke and Mirrors*, by Gerard I. Kenney, 11–14. Prescott,
    ON: Voyageur Publishing, 1994.

Ronda, James. "The Sillery Experiment: A Jesuit-Indian Village in New France, 1637–1663."
    American Indian Culture and Research Journal 3, no. 1 (1979): 1–18.

Ross, William Gillies, ed. *An Arctic Whaling Diary: The Journal of Captain George Comer in Hudson
    Bay 1903–1905*. Toronto: University of Toronto Press, 1984.

Rousseau, Jacques, and George W. Brown. "The Indians of Northeastern North America." In
    Dictionary of Canadian Biography. Vol. 1, *1000 to 1700*, 5–16. Toronto: University of Toronto
    Press, 1966.

Royal Commission on Aboriginal Peoples. *Final Report*. 5 vols. Ottawa: Indian and Northern Affairs
    Canada, 1996.

– *The High Arctic Relocation: Summary of Supporting Information*. 2 vols. Ottawa: Royal Commission
    on Aboriginal Peoples, 1994.

Ryan, Joan. *Wall of Words: The Betrayal of the Urban Indian*. Toronto: Peter Martin Associates, 1978.

Ryerson, Egerton. *Statistics Respecting Indian Schools with Dr. Ryerson's Report of 1847 Attached*.
    Ottawa: Government Printing Bureau, 1898.

Salisbury, Richard F. *A Homeland for the Cree: Regional Development in James Bay 1971–1981*.
    Montreal: McGill-Queen's University Press, 1986.

Samek, Hana. *The Blackfoot Confederacy, 1880–1920: A Comparative Study of Canadian and U.S.
    Indian Policy*. Albuquerque: University of New Mexico Press, 1987.

Sanderson, Sol. "Foreword." In *The First Nations: Indian Government and the Canadian Constitution*,
    edited by Delia Opekokew, v–vii. Saskatoon: Federation of Saskatchewan Indians, 1980.

Sawaya, Jean-Pierre. *La Fédération des Sept Feux de la vallée du Saint-Laurent: XVIIe au XIXe siècle*.
    Sillery, QC: Septentrion, 1998.

Scott, Duncan Campbell. "Indian Affairs, 1867–1912." In *Canada and Its Provinces*, vol. 7, edited by
    Adam Shortt and Arthur G. Doughty, 593–626. Toronto: Glasgow, Brook, 1914.

Sealey, D. Bruce, and Antoine S. Lussier. *The Métis: Canada's Forgotten People*. Winnipeg: Pemmican
    Publications, 1975.

Sheffield, R. Scott. *The Red Man's on the Warpath: The Image of the "Indian" and the Second World
    War*. Vancouver: UBC Press, 2004.

Sherwin, Allan. *Bridging Two Peoples: Chief Peter E. Jones, 1843–1909*. Waterloo, ON: Wilfrid Laurier
    University Press, 2012.

Shewell, Hugh. *"Enough to Keep Them Alive": Indian Welfare in Canada, 1873–1965*. Toronto:
    University of Toronto Press, 2004.

Shingwauk, Augustine. *Little Pine's Journal: The Appeal of a Christian Chippeway Chief on Behalf
    of His People*. 1872. Reprint, Sault Ste. Marie: Shingwauk Reunion Committee, 1991.

Shkilnyk, Anastasia M. *A Poison Stronger Than Love: The Destruction of an Ojibwa Community*.
    New Haven, CT: Yale University Press, 1985.

Shortt, Adam, and Arthur G. Doughty, eds. *Documents Relating to the Constitutional History of Canada 1759–1791*. Ottawa: King's Printer, 1907.

Sigurdson, Glenn. *Vikings on a Prairie Ocean: The Saga of a Lake, a People, a Family, and a Man*. Winnipeg: Great Plains Publications, 2014.

Silver, Arthur Isaac. *The French-Canadian Idea of Confederation 1864–1900*. Toronto: University of Toronto Press, 1982.

Simpson, Audra. *Mohawk Interruptus: Political Life across the Borders of Settler States*. Durham, NC: Duke University Press, 2014.

Sioui, Georges E. *For An Amerindian Autohistory: An Essay on the Foundations of a Social Ethic*. Montreal: McGill-Queen's University Press, 1992.

Smillie, Christine Mary. "The People Left Out of Treaty 8." Master's thesis, University of Saskatchewan, 2005.

Smith, Donald B. *Sacred Feathers: The Reverend Peter Jones (Kahkewaquonaby) and the Mississauga Indians*. Toronto: University of Toronto Press, 1987.

Snell, James G. "American Neutrality and the Red River Resistance, 1869–1870." *Prairie Forum* 4, no. 2 (1979): 183–96.

Snow, John. *These Mountains are Our Sacred Places: The Story of the Stoney People*. Toronto: Samuel Stevens, 1977.

Sosin, Jack M. "The Use of Indians in the War of the American Revolution: A Re-Assessment of Responsibility." *Canadian Historical Review* 46, no. 2 (1965): 101–21.

Sprague, Douglas N. *Canada and the Métis, 1869–1885*. Waterloo, ON: Wilfrid Laurier University Press, 1988.

Spry, Irene. "The Métis and Mixed-Bloods of Rupert's Land before 1870." In *The New Peoples: Being and Becoming Métis in North America*, edited by Jacqueline Peterson and Jennifer H.S. Brown, 95–118. Winnipeg: University of Manitoba Press, 1985.

Stanley, George F.G. *The Birth of Western Canada: A History of the Riel Rebellions*. 2nd ed. Toronto: University of Toronto Press, 1960. First published 1936.

– "The First Indian 'Reserves' in Canada." *Revue d'histoire de l'Amérique française* 4, no. 2 (1950): 178–210.

– "The Indians in the War of 1812." In *Sweet Promises: A Reader on Indian-White Relations in Canada*, edited by J.R. Miller, 105–24. Toronto: University of Toronto Press, 1991.

– *Louis Riel*. Toronto: Ryerson Press, 1963.

Statistics Canada. "Aboriginal Peoples in Canada: First Nations People, Métis and Inuit." Accessed 15 December 2016. http://www12.statcan.gc.ca/nhs-enm/2011/as-sa/99-011-x/99-011-x2011001 -eng.cfm.

Stevenson, Allyson. "The Metis Cultural Brokers and the Western Numbered Treaties. 1869–1877." Master's thesis, University of Saskatchewan, 2004.

Stevenson, Mark G. *Inuit, Whalers, and Cultural Persistence: Structure in Cumberland Sound and Central Inuit Social Organization*. Toronto: Oxford University Press, 1997.

Stone, Thomas. "Legal Mobilization and Legal Penetration: The Department of Indian Affairs and the Canadian Party at St. Regis, 1876–1918." *Ethnohistory* 22, no. 4 (1975): 375–407.

Stonechild, Blair, and Bill Waiser. *Loyal Till Death: Indians and the North-West Rebellion*. Calgary: Fifth House, 1997.

Sturtevant, Andrew. "'Over the Lake': The Western Wendake in the American Revolution." In *From Huronia to Wendakes: Adversity, Migrations, and Resilience, 1650–1900*, edited by Thomas Peace and Kathryn Magee Labelle, 35–73. Norman: University of Oklahoma Press, 2016.

Sugden, John. *Tecumseh: A Life*. New York: Henry Holt, 1998.

Surtees, Robert J. "The Development of an Indian Reserve Policy in Canada." *Ontario History* 61, no. 2 (1969): 87–98.

– "Indian Land Cessions in Upper Canada, 1815–1830." In *As Long As the Sun Shines and the Water Flows: A Reader in Canadian Native Studies*, edited by Ian A.L. Getty and Antoine S. Lussier, 65–84. Vancouver: Nakoda Institute and UBC Press, 1983.

Swain, Harry. *Oka: A Political Crisis and Its Legacy.* Vancouver: Douglas and McIntyre, 2010.

"Synopsis of the History of Wikwemikong." Typescript. Toronto: Regis College Archives, n.d.

Taylor, John L. "Canada's North-West Indian Policy in the 1870s: Traditional Premises and Necessary Innovations." In *Sweet Promises: A Reader on Indian-White Relations in Canada*, edited by J.R. Miller, 207–11. Toronto: University of Toronto Press, 1991.

– "Two Views on the Meaning of Treaties Six and Seven." In *The Spirit of the Alberta Indian Treaties*, 2nd ed., edited by Richard Price, 9–45. Edmonton: Pica Pica Press, 1987.

Tennant, Paul. *Aboriginal Peoples and Politics: The Indian Land Question in British Columbia, 1849–1989.* Vancouver: UBC Press, 1990.

Tennant, Paul, Sally M. Weaver, Roger Gibbins, and J. Rick Ponting. "The Report of the House of Commons Special Committee on Indian Self-Government: Three Comments." *Canadian Public Policy* 10, no. 2 (1984): 211–24.

Tester, Frank, and Peter Kulchyski. *Tammarniit (Mistakes): Inuit Relocation in the Eastern Arctic, 1939–63.* Vancouver: UBC Press, 1994.

Thistle, Paul Clifford. *Indian-European Trade Relations in the Lower Saskatchewan River Region to 1840.* Winnipeg: University of Manitoba Press, 1986.

Thomson, Duane. "The Response of Okanagan Indians to European Settlement." *BC Studies* 101 (Spring 1994): 96–117.

Thompson, Judy. "No Little Variety of Ornament: Northern Athapaskan Artistic Traditions." In *The Spirit Sings: Artistic Traditions of Canada's First Peoples*, edited by Julia Harrison, 133–68. Toronto: Glenbow Museum/McClelland and Stewart, 1987.

Thoms, J. Michael. "Ojibwa Fishing Grounds: A History of Ontario Fisheries Law, Science, and the Sportsmen's Challenge to Aboriginal Treaty Rights, 1650–1900." PhD diss., University of British Columbia, 2004.

Thrasher, Antony Apakark. *Thrasher … Skid Row Eskimo.* In collaboration with Gerard Deagle and Alan Mettrick. Toronto: Griffin House, 1976.

Titley, E. Brian. *A Narrow Vision: Duncan Campbell Scott and the Administration of Indian Affairs in Canada.* Vancouver: UBC Press, 1986.

Tobias, John L. "Canada and the Plains Indians." *NeWest Review* (February 1987): 12–13.

– "Canada's Subjugation of the Plains Cree, 1879–1885." In *Sweet Promises: A Reader on Indian-White Relations in Canada*, edited by J.R. Miller, 212–40. Toronto: University of Toronto Press, 1991.

– "Indian Reserves in Western Canada: Indian Homelands or Devices for Assimilation." In *Approaches to Native History in Canada*, edited by Delphin Andrew Muise, 89–103. Ottawa: National Museum of Man, 1977.

– "The Origin of the Treaty Rights Movement in Saskatchewan." In *1885 and After: Native Society in Transition*, edited by F. Laurie Barron and James B. Waldram, 241–52. Regina: Canadian Plains Research Center, 1986.

– "Protection, Civilization, Assimilation: An Outline History of Canada's Indian Policy." In *Sweet Promises: A Reader on Indian-White Relations in Canada*, edited by J.R. Miller, 127–44. Toronto: University of Toronto Press, 1991.

Tough, Frank. *As Their Natural Resources Fail: Native Peoples and the History of Northern Manitoba, 1870–1930.* Vancouver: UBC Press, 1996.

Tough, Frank, Jim Miller, and Arthur J. Ray. "Bounty and Benevolence: A Documentary History of Saskatchewan Treaties." Report for the Office of the Treaty Commissioner, Saskatoon, 1998.

Treaty 7 Tribal Elders with Walter Hildebrandt, Dorothy First Rider, and Sarah Carter. *The True Spirit and Original Intent of Treaty 7.* Montreal: McGill-Queen's University Press, 1997.

Trigger, Bruce G. *The Huron: Farmers of the North.* New York: Holt, Rinehart and Winston, 1969.

– *The Indians and the Heroic Age of New France.* Ottawa: Canadian Historical Association, 1977.

– *Natives and Newcomers: Canada's "Heroic Age" Reconsidered.* Montreal: McGill-Queen's University Press, 1985.

Trigger, Bruce G., and Wilcomb E. Washburn, eds. *The Cambridge History of the Native Peoples of the Americas.* Vol. 1, *North America.* Cambridge: Cambridge University Press, 1996.

Trudel, Marcel. *Introduction to New France.* Toronto: Holt, Rinehart and Winston, 1968.

Truth and Reconciliation Commission. *Final Report of the Truth and Reconciliation Commission of Canada.* 6 vols. Montreal: McGill-Queen's University Press, 2015.

– *Final Report of the Truth and Reconciliation Commission of Canada.* Vol. 1, *Summary: Honouring the Truth, Reconciling for the Future.* Toronto: Lorimer, 2015.

– *They Came for the Children: Canada, Aboriginal Peoples, and Residential Schools.* Winnipeg: Truth and Reconciliation Commission, 2012.

Upton, Leslie F.S. "The Extermination of the Beothucks of Newfoundland." In *Sweet Promises: A Reader on Indian-White Relations in Canada*, edited by J.R. Miller, 68–89. Toronto: University of Toronto Press, 1991.

– *Micmacs and Colonists: Indian-White Relations in the Maritimes 1713–1867.* Vancouver: UBC Press, 1979.

– "The Origins of Canadian Indian Policy." *Journal of Canadian Studies* 8, no. 4 (1973): 51–61.

Usher, Jean. "The Long-Slumbering Offspring of Adam: The Evangelical Approach to the Tsimshian." *Anthropologica* 13, no. 1–2 (1971): 37–61.

– *William Duncan of Metlakatla: A Victorian Missionary in British Columbia.* Ottawa: National Museum of Man, 1974.

Vachon, André. "L'Eau-de-Vie dans la société indienne." Canadian Historical Association, *Annual Report 1960*: 22–32.

– "Talon, Jean." *Dictionary of Canadian Biography* online. Accessed 13 May 2016. www.biographi.ca /en/bio/talon_jean._1E.html.

Van Kirk, Sylvia. *"Many Tender Ties": Women in Fur-Trade Society, 1670–1870.* Winnipeg: Watson and Dwyer, 1980.

Vaughan, Alden T. "From White Man to Redskin: Changing Anglo-American Perceptions of the American Indian." *American Historical Review* 87, no. 4 (1982): 917–53.

Venne, Sharon. "Understanding Treaty 6: An Indigenous Perspective." In *Aboriginal and Treaty Rights in Canada*, edited by Michael Asch, 173–207. Vancouver: UBC Press, 1997.

Waiser, William A. "The White Man Governs: The 1885 Indian Trials." In *Canadian State Trials.* Vol. 3, *Political Trials and Security Measures, 1840–1914*, edited by Barry Wright and Susan Binnie, 451–82. Toronto: Osgoode Society for Canadian Legal History, 2009.

– *A World We Have Lost: Saskatchewan before 1905.* Markham, ON: Fifth House, 2016.

Walker, James. "The Indian in Canadian Historical Writing." Canadian Historical Association, *Historical Papers 1971*: 21–51.

Walls, Martha Elizabeth. *No Need of a Chief for This Band: The Maritime Mi'kmaq and Federal Electoral Legislation, 1899–1951.* Vancouver: UBC Press, 2010.

Washburn, Wilcomb E., ed. *Handbook of North American Indians.* Vol. 4, *History of Indian-White Relations.* Washington: Smithsonian Institution, 1988.

Watkins, Mel. *Dene Nation: The Colony Within.* Toronto: University of Toronto Press, 1977.

Weaver, Sally M. "Indian Policy in the New Conservative Government, Part I: The Nielsen Task Force of 1985." *Native Studies Review* 2, no. 1 (1986): 1–43.

– *Making Canadian Indian Policy: The Hidden Agenda 1968–1970.* Toronto: University of Toronto Press, 1981.

Weaver, Sally M., et al. "The Report of the House of Commons Special Committee on Indian Self-Government: Three Comments." *Canadian Public Policy* 10, no. 2 (1984): 211–24.

Wherrett, George Jasper. *The Miracle of the Empty Beds: A History of Tuberculosis in Canada.* Toronto: University of Toronto Press, 1977.

White, Richard. *The Middle Ground: Indians, Empires, and Republics in the Great Lakes Region, 1650–1815.* Cambridge: Cambridge University Press, 1991.

Wicken, William C. *Mi'kmaq Treaties on Trial: History, Land, and Donald Marshall Junior.* Toronto: University of Toronto Press, 2002.

– "The Treaties of Atlantic Canada." In *Aboriginal History: A Reader*, 2nd ed., edited by Kristin Burnett and Geoff Read, 77–87. Don Mills, ON: Oxford University Press, 2016.

Wiebe, Rudy. *The Temptations of Big Bear.* Toronto: McClelland and Stewart, 1973.

Wise, Sydney F. "The American Revolution and Indian History." In *Character and Circumstance: Essays in Honour of Donald Grant Creighton*, edited by John S. Moir, 182–200. Toronto: Macmillan, 1970.

– "The Indian Diplomacy of John Graves Simcoe." Canadian Historical Association, *Annual Report 1953*: 33–46.

Woodcock, George. *Gabriel Dumont: The Métis Chief and His Lost World.* Edmonton: Hurtig, 1975.

Wroth, Lawrence C., ed. *The Voyages of Giovanni da Verrazzano, 1624–1628.* New Haven, CT: Yale University Press, 1970.

Yerbury, John Collin. *The Subarctic Indians and the Fur Trade, 1680–1860.* Vancouver: UBC Press, 1986.

York, Geoffrey, and Loreen Pindera. *People of the Pines: The Warriors and the Legacy of Oka.* Boston: Little, Brown, 1991.

Illustration Credits

Art Babych: Truth and Reconciliation Commissioners, 2009; Truth and Reconciliation Commissioners, 2015

Canadian Press: Stephen Harper apologizing, Image 5015802. Photographer Tom Henson

City of Vancouver Archives: Indian miners, J.S. Matthews Collection, P.25/ N.101; Oblate pennant, P.47/N.27

Cornwall Standard-Freeholder: Anti-gambling demonstration

David Garneau: Restless; Idle No More

General Synod Archives, MSCC photos: potlatch goods, P7538-53; Canon Edward Ahenakew, GS75-103-S6-83

Ian Getty: Harold Cardinal (right front); L–R: Lou Demerais, Georges Erasmus, Rob Robinson, and Harold Cardinal

Glenbow Archives: Big Bear and Poundmaker, NA 1315-18; Western pioneers, NA 1374-2; classroom, Sarcee, 1912, NA 1020-17

J.R. Miller: "Remember Oka"

Mary Miller: Chapel of the Mohawk

Library and Archives Canada: Jesuit map of Huronia, National Map Collection 6338–1657; (fanciful) beavers, C16758; Marie de l'Incarnation, C73422; Sarrazin receives pitcher plant, C69104; martyrdom of Fr Jogues, C1472; Iroquois on warpath, C3165; signature panel of 1764 Huron treaty, C135291; wampum belt, C38948; Meeting of Brock and Tecumseh by L.K. Smith, C11052; Shingwauk Home, PA182262; buffalo run by A.J. Miller, C403; Red River cart, PA138573; Cook at Nootka Sound, 1778, by M.B. Messer (after J. Webber), C11201; totem pole, PA60018; Metlakatla school boys, photographed by W.J. Topley, C15037; Big Bear trading, Fort Pitt, PA118768; treaty scene, Fort Carlton, C64741; Ahtakakoop, Mistawasis, and others, 1886, C19258; treaty medal, C70758; Mountie and Natives, C9570; Poundmaker, 1885, C1875; Lacombe and chiefs at Earnscliffe, 1886, PA45666; "Notice," 6 May 1885, C125263; Dewdney, Piapot, and troops, PA118775; Hayter Reed in costume, PA139841; Qu'Appelle school, PA182246; ploughing,

PA48475; Quewich and children, C37113; Christmas on the *Neptune*, 1903, photographed by J.D. Moodie, C1817; Inuit aboard the *Karluk*, 1913, PA74061; collecting Baby Bonus, 1950, photographed by S.J. Bailey, PA164744; Six Nations chiefs in council, C85137; Lt. F.O. Loft, PA7439; Canadian Patriotic Fund poster, C98670; Temporary Committee, NIC, PA164775

National Gallery of Canada: Joseph Brant by George Romney, no. 8005

National Library of Canada: Champlain in skirmish, NL 6643

New England Company: Symbol of N.E. Co.

Provincial Archives of Alberta: Sun Dance, E. Brown Collection, B 998

Provincial Archives of New Brunswick: Maliseet in canoes, George Taylor Collection P5/170

Ingrid Rice: Royal Commission on Aboriginal Peoples cartoon

Royal Ontario Museum: Jacques Cartier's Arrival in the New World, 949.150.1; death of Tecumseh, 948.120.1; Lake of Two Mountains by George Heriot (1807), 953.132.16

Scott Polar Research Institute, University of Cambridge: Female Inuk with frozen food, P72/16/9/280

Toronto Reference Library: Numbering the Indians T-1602

Whyte Museum of the Rockies: John Hunter preparing for Sun Dance, Byron Harman Photograph Collection, VZ63 NA 71-3147; Stoney on horseback, NA 66-1581

Lawrence Paul Yuxweluptun: *Red Man Watching White Man Trying to Fix Hole in Sky*, 1990 [detail]. Collection of National Gallery of Canada

Index

Lacombe, Albert, *198*
LaForme, Harry, 336
Laird, David, 224
Lamer, Antonio, 314–15
land claims: amendment outlawing raising
   money for, 228; BC government opens up
   to, 311; and extinguishment provision, 298,
   301; funding of research into, 275, 279–80;
   how they relate to self-government, 282;
   and Mohawk fight for at Kanesatake, 287–9;
   under Mulroney government, 292; and
   Office of Native Claims, 279–80, 286–7,
   289–90; Parliamentary committee on BC,
   258; progress on after 1985, 297–304;
   progress on in late 1990s, 317; as source of
   friction in NIC, 276
land settlement: acquiring land title through
   annuities, 98–9; in BC between 1880 and
   1920s, 227–8; change to payment of
   annuities, 111; and F. Bond Head idea, 110,
   111; government attempts to fashion First
   Nation ideas of land ownership, 208–10;
   government moves to buy back First Nations
   land, 224–5; and Gradual Civilization Act,
   117, 118; and Lord Selkirk Treaty of 1817,
   142; and Manitoba Act, 168–9; settler
   rationalization for taking land, 157; between
   settlers and First Nations in BC, 154–7
Langevin, Hector, 210
l'Anse aux Meadows, 21
Lavell case, 290
League of Indians of Canada, 259–60
League of Nations, 259
Lehrer, Tom, 247
Le Jeune, 9, 50
L'Heureux, Jean, *198*
Linden, Sidney, 324
Little Pine (Shinguakonce), 104, 109, 115, 186,
   187
Little Poplar, 191, 195
Littlechild, Wilton, 338, *339*, *340*
Loft, F.O., *259*, 259–60
longhouses, 8
Lorne, Lord, 187
Lougheed, Peter, 299
Louisbourg, 66, 71
Lovelace, Sandra, 290

Lower Canada, 96–7
Loyalists, 88–9, 93
Lubicon Lake Cree, 278, 299–300, 317
Lysyk, Ken, 297

Maa-nulth First Nations, 322
Macdonald, John A.: on assimilation of First
   Nations, 207; and cuts to Indian Affairs,
   189; on education, 215; and First Nations'
   land holding, 209–10; on Manitoba Act,
   169; and Métis, 192, 326; and Riel's trial,
   204–5; sends expedition to Red River, 168;
   and settling the West, 164
Mackenzie government, 172–3
Macpherson, David, 192
Maliseet, 6, *27*
Manitoba Act (1870), 167–9
Manitoba Indian Brotherhood, 262
Manitoba Métis Federation (MMF), 326
Manitoba Métis Federation case, 326
Manitoulin Island, 110
Manuel, George, 276, 354–5, 357
Maquinna, Chief, 147, 150
mariage à la façon du pays, 134–5
Marshall case, 317, 321–2
Martin, Paul, 324
Martin government, 321, 324
Mascarene's Treaty (1726), 73
Matonabbee (Dene leader), 232, 233
McDougall, George, 173, 174–5
McDougall, William, 164–5, 166, 167
McEachern, Alan, 303
McKenna, Frank, 305
McKenna-McBride Commission, 228, 257
medicine, 53
Meech Lake Accord, 286, 304–6
Membertou, Chief, 52
Methodists, 107, 110, 111, 113, 160–1
Métis: and Aboriginal title, 192, 194; attempts to
   resettle, 257; and bison hunt, 141, 142–3; and
   Constitution, 284; creation of reserves for in
   Alberta, 263; and federal government, 191–2,
   194, 316; hired as agriculture instructor, 221;
   origins of, 134–7; and Red River Resistance,
   164–9; relations with federal government,
   316; rift among, 140–1; role in North-West
   Rebellion, 191–3, 196–7; and Statement of

114; churches' part in assimilation in Upper
Canada, 106–7, 108–11; effect of firearms
on First Nations, 51–2; effect of French
evangelism on First Nations, 27, 32–4, 52–6,
68; First Nations' toleration of Europeans,
38, 39–40; and First Nations use of torture,
11–12; in fur trade, 129; importance to
Europeans, 16–17; Inuit, 232; in numbered
treaties, 226; spiritual element of treaty, 188.
See also missionaries; specific churches
reserves: accepted by First Nations during
hardship years, 187; and agricultural
production, 223; in BC, 154; government
attempts to end, 209–10; government
disappointment in, 253–4; and land
question in BC, 227–8; for Métis in Alberta,
263; as part of numbered treaties, 180–1,
182; as source of First Nations' political
organization, 257–8; Upper Canada
experiments of, 108–9
residential schools: abuse cases, 316, 334;
and administrative split, 338; and Bagot
Commission, 112–14; Christian churches
reconciliation for, 316, 332–3; First Nations
turn against, 121; Harper apology and
policy, 336–8; increasing negative opinion
of, 253–4; and IRSSA, 334–6, 338–42;
litigation of abuse cases, 321, 334; in
northern Canada, 226; as part of western
treaties, 215–20; phasing out of, 254–5, 277;
Province of Canada attempt at, 120, 121;
and RCAP, 313, 333–4; and Statement of
Reconciliation, 315, 316
Richardson, Hugh, 203
Riel, Louis: as bison hunter, 141; escapes to US,
169; as leader of North-West Rebellion, 184,
185, 192–4, 196; and Red River Resistance,
165–7; in Statement of Reconciliation, 315;
as symbol, 205; trial of, 200, 203–5
Riel Sr., Louis, 165
Robertson, Gordon, 246
Robinson, Rob, 285
Robinson, William, 120
Robinson Treaties (1850), 115–16, 172
Romanow, Roy, 299
Royal Canadian Mounted Police (RCMP), 244.
See also North-West Mounted Police

Royal Commission on Aboriginal Peoples
(RCAP), 246, 311–14, 315, 333–4, 354,
395n10
Royal Proclamation (1763), 72–6, 118, 172,
279, 289–90
Rush-Bagot Convention, 93, 103
Ryerson, Egerton, 114

Sagkeeng First Nation, 281–2
Sahtu Dene and Métis, 301
salt, 15, 23
Sarrazin, Michel, 46
Saskatchewan, government of, 299
Saskatchewan formula, 299
Saulteaux, 142, 171, 181
sauvages, 25–6
Sayer, Guillaume, 141
Sayer case, 141
scalping, 63
Schultz, J.C., 167
Schwatka expedition, 233
scientific racism, 102–3
Scollen, Constantine, 173
Scott, Duncan C., 229
Scott, Thomas, 167
Sechelt band, 293
Second World War, 244–5, 247, 264
self-government: advances on in 1980s, 293–4;
advice for First Nations leaders on, 356–7;
and Charlottetown Accord, 307; DIA
interference in, 258–9; and Enfranchisement
Act, 122–3, 163; First Nations' long claim to,
280–1; government attempts to foil, 208;
municipal-type, 293–4; in Nunavut, 302;
push for during Constitutional talks, 285–6;
questions and problems regarding, 281–2;
and Royal Proclamation, 75–6; and
Statement of Reconciliation, 315, 316
Selkirk, Lord, 136–7, 142
Semple, Robert, 137
Sergeant Preston of the Yukon (radio program),
247
settlers: in Atlantic Canada, 93–6; clashes with
First Nations in West, 170–1; first major
influx into British Canada, 87; and First
Nations farming schemes, 222; immigration
to Upper Canada, 97–8; and North-West